INTERDISCIPLINE

This book brings together two different discussions on the value of the humanities and a broader debate on interdisciplinary scholarship in order to propose a new way beyond current threats to the humanities. Petar Ramadanovic offers nothing short of a drastic overhaul of our approaches to literary scholarship, the humanities, and university systems.

Beginning with an analysis of what is often referred to as the "crises" in the humanities, the author looks at the specifics of literary studies, but also issues around working conditions for academics. From precarity and pay conditions to peer review, the book has practical as well as theoretical implications that will resonate throughout the humanities. While most books defending the humanities emphasize the uniqueness of the subject or area, Ramadanovic does the opposite, emphasizing the need for interdisciplinarity and combined knowledge. This proposal is then fully explored through literary studies, and its potential throughout the humanities and beyond, into the sciences.

Interdiscipline is not just a defense of literature and the humanities; it offers a clear and inspiring pathway forward, drawing on all disciplines to show their cultural and social significance. The book is important reading for all scholars of literary studies, and also throughout the humanities.

Petar Ramadanovic is Professor of English at the University of New Hampshire, USA.

INTERDISCIPLINE

A Future for Literary Studies and the Humanities

Petar Ramadanovic

LONDON AND NEW YORK

Cover image: © Getty Images

First published 2022
by Routledge
4 Park Square, Milton Park, Abingdon, Oxon OX14 4RN

and by Routledge
605 Third Avenue, New York, NY 10158

Routledge is an imprint of the Taylor & Francis Group, an informa business

© 2022 Petar Ramadanovic

The right of Petar Ramadanovic to be identified as author of this work has been asserted by him in accordance with sections 77 and 78 of the Copyright, Designs and Patents Act 1988.

All rights reserved. No part of this book may be reprinted or reproduced or utilised in any form or by any electronic, mechanical, or other means, now known or hereafter invented, including photocopying and recording, or in any information storage or retrieval system, without permission in writing from the publishers.

Trademark notice: Product or corporate names may be trademarks or registered trademarks, and are used only for identification and explanation without intent to infringe.

British Library Cataloguing-in-Publication Data
A catalogue record for this book is available from the British Library

Library of Congress Cataloging-in-Publication Data
A catalog record has been requested for this book

ISBN: 978-0-367-63548-0 (hbk)
ISBN: 978-0-367-63546-6 (pbk)
ISBN: 978-1-003-11961-6 (ebk)

DOI: 10.4324/9781003119616

Typeset in Bembo
by codeMantra

CONTENTS

Preface and acknowledgments   *vii*

Introduction: from crises discourses to interdisciplinary discipline   1

1   "We": crises responses and literary studies as a theory of interpretation   23

2   Mere reading: recasting hermeneutic epistemology in literary studies   62

3   Peer review: evaluation as a form of reading   101

4   What DH? return to formalism in the age of big data   135

5   Convergence: an interdisciplinary theory of interdisciplinarity   164

Conclusion: interdisciplinary curricular organization and the glue that holds it together   211

Bibliography   *219*
Index   *249*

PREFACE AND ACKNOWLEDGMENTS

Writing is marked by events. The first this book records is my wife's cancer: sudden onset leukemia, properly acute myeloid leukemia (AML), caught us by surprise after the first chapter was written, while we were preparing for a trip to my home town of Belgrade, now in Serbia, formerly in Yugoslavia, consistently in the Balkans. The second and third chapters were my hiding place during the summer and the fall of 2019 while Catherine was receiving therapy and my children, Georgina and Iliya, were, variously, falling apart, picking themselves up, behaving like adults. Catherine was brave. I distracted myself with this book. Just how that sublimation took place, I don't know. In this context, the covid pandemic caught us fully prepared, ahead of everyone, with masks, bottles of hand sanitizer, transitioned already.

The fourth and fifth chapters, and the rest came down during 2020 and early 2021.

Did we triumph? Yes, if by that, we mean that Catherine is still lingering around, happy that she can make plans, work.

It's a process.

The event put the writing of this book on entirely different tracks than what I expected when I thought that I would be writing it alone, in isolation, intervening from the left field of a public university in a small state. That is still true in one sense that a well-connected scholar would have, in my estimation, a harder time putting such a critique together.

For the most part, this writing was done in a community of people. First, there were neighbors and acquaintances who, just as acutely and suddenly as AML, turned into the most supportive friends. My Balkan small self could not believe what it was seeing.

Total strangers became neighbors, imposing themselves between this family and a disaster. Professional relations, my and Catherine's superiors at the university, colleagues across it, showed a face I did not know existed. I could tell my sister, who is still in the Balkans where friendship is the pillar of your daily life, "They are all here!" And she said in exasperation, "Here, they are gone when you need them. Afraid the misfortune is contagious."

I imagined us as Greek phalanx, tightening the lines in the face of the final onslaught.

Fascism comes from the same root idea, of course, but the support that carried us over is so distinct from it. Fascists relinquish membership in all other groups and seek shelter from fear with those they identify most closely. They then lash out to destroy those who are not like them as if it were the horror itself they were trying to exterminate—a different figure entirely from the selfless aid, support, and kindness we received.

Fascism, too, colors this book in the form of presidency of this awful, awful man who presided over the worst theater of cruelty a person (middle-class, white) could imagine for America. I could not understand why we did not continue the Women's march and, like the protesters in Hong Kong, stop everything through civil disobedience and show our will publicly and often. The book was written with the eye on the fledgling commonwealth that we were creating and failing to create for this country and ourselves (up until George Floyd was murdered when the pent up anger exploded), which we need to prepare for the threat larger by a few orders of magnitude called the effects of climate change.

I wish to thank Hsinya Huang and John Beusterien for the opportunity to publish in their special issue of *Comparative Literature Studies*, titled "Sustaining Ecocriticism: Comparative Perspectives." The publication meant an encouragement to proceed, making it possible for me to envision my scholarship beyond my first book and start contemplating this project.

My gratitude goes to the editors of *Cultural Critique*, Cesare Casarino, John Mowitt, and Simona Sawhney, and the journal's anonymous readers whose patience and advice helped me refine my argument concerning science and its institutional relation to poststructuralism, which was the first milestone on the way to *Interdiscipline*. I wish to thank the assistant editors, Andrea Gyenge, Marla Zubel, Sara Saljoughi, Dylan Mohr, and Vanessa Cambier. I take great comfort in acknowledging these people I never met in person and would not recognize on the street but on whose effort and labor I depended.

Publishing in *Memory Studies* was my first-hand experience of what it means to be read by colleagues from the sciences. My thanks go to Andrew Hoskins (general editor), Andrea Hajek (managing editor), and the reviewers for showing me, in most kindly ways, just how difficult and demanding it is to be interdisciplinary. You are where we all should be.

I experienced the best side of situationist interdisciplinarity with my buddy David Richman from the Theater Department at UNH. You always made our collaboration go smoothly, making me wish for more.

Part of the fuel to push through the two years of writing came from the Seminar in Dialectical Thinking (2018–2019), which met to read Heidegger's *Being and Time* at the Mahindra Humanities Center, Harvard University, and the two groups that discussed György Lukács and Susan Buck-Morss's works in late 2020. The enthusiasm and devotion of the seminar participants is an example of what Derrida means by professing. You all have my deep admiration.

Anonymous readers for *Poetics Today* of an early version of Chapter 5 helped me add specificity to my criticism of digital humanities. I am sorry they missed its chief point, which, I hope, they will find in the current version.

Polly Dodson's endorsement pushed the project to the finish line. I wish I could acknowledge the reviewers for Routledge by name. Your comments helped me add dimension and detail to the manuscript that would have been significantly weaker without them.

Samira Kawash and Roger Cooper were there. You are there! And, god, I hope you will be there for years to come. Many of our discussions have found their way into this book.

Andrew Ferris's advice, patience, help, willingness to listen and criticize were invaluable. I dedicate this book to him—a weak and awful substitute for an academic career in literary studies he cannot have since he decided to pursue his PhD too late. We all—not just English professors and academia but the entire society—lose when an individual talent like his is not adequately supported and realized.

Peripatetic conversations with Andrew showed me, again and again, that collaboration is the most natural form of research in literary studies. It is one of those immediate things that humanities scholars can learn from scientists and adopt for their institutional setups. This book would have been very different without you, Andrew.

I got financial assistance for various research and writing stages from the COLA Dean's Office, the Center for the Humanities, and the English Department, all at the University of New Hampshire where I work. I wish to thank Dean Michele Dillon, Chairs Rachel Trubowitz and James Krasner, and Katie Umans (assistant director of the center), who provided more than the financial support.

Most importantly, Catherine Peebles—she saw the whole thing through with me and more. Aren't we lucky!

INTRODUCTION

From crises discourses to interdisciplinary discipline

Crises

When I was hired in 1999 at the University of New Hampshire, we joked that my position was the penultimate theorist job in the United States. The true "last good job" (Aronowitz) went to my compatriot from the Balkans Branka Arsić at the University at Albany, where my spouse, another comparative literature graduate, was a finalist. The losses in this discipline's institutional prominence, together with the death or fall of theory (Davis; Eagleton; Nealon), were indicative of the reorganization that only accelerated in the new millennium. Rising were cultural studies, fragmentation, and pluralization, called posthumanities or postdiscipline, consisting of new area studies, specializations, and many forms of clustering. The change was so fast that already by 2009, Mario Biagioli could celebrate the presence of "modular cross-disciplinarity," constellations of fields, "clusters that may be too short-lived to be institutionalized into departments or programs or to be given lasting disciplinary labels," as well as forms like "clinical studies and trials" and double PhDs (Biagioli, "Postdisciplinary" 819).

At the same time, due to economic and political trends, university education was regarded more as a personal choice and less as the public good it was in the post-World War II years. The effect was most potent in the humanities, which were hit by the compounding of trends. The technocratic, neoliberal, consumer-oriented corporatization, emphasizing education as job training, came together with a reduction of faculty positions in literary studies and a rise in tuition costs from 25% to 30% of university revenue in the decade of the 1990s (Mitchell et al.). Bill Readings's groundbreaking *The University in Ruins* came out in 1996 and Michael Bérubé's landmark critique *The Employment of English* shortly after, in 1998. The trend only accelerated during George W. Bush's presidency, with tuition in public schools going from 30% to 40% of revenue by 2010 (Mitchell et al.). Then, the aftermath of the Great Recession saw even further and more drastic erosion of state budgets, further increases in tuition to half of the revenue (Mitchell et al.), and further destruction of faculty lines, with the humanities now commonly referred to as worthless degrees.[1] In total, in the last 20 years, tuition and fees at private universities jumped 144%, at public universities 165% out-of-state and 212% within state (Boyington and Kerr).

Politically, the anti-intellectual trends can be dated to the paranoid style in American politics (Hofstadter 1963, 2012) and further back to the politics associated with the rise of American industry (i.e., Taylorism, Fordism) in the early twentieth century (Donoghue). Ronald Reagan's two-term presidency mainstreamed on the federal level the anti-intellectualism and the defunding of public education he had perpetrated on California while being governor (Clabaugh).[2] Donald Trump's attempt to break the connection between knowledge and power came with definitiveness not seen beforehand.

In defense and alarm, many excellent works tried to halt senseless destruction, emphasizing what is unique about universities and the humanities, the vital social and democratic role higher education performs, and why we deserve better public support (Belfiore and Upchurch; Barnett; Collini; Eaglestone, *Doing English*; Gildea et al.; Hutner and Mohamed; P. Jay; McDonald; Sandel; Small). This book belongs to the same library but takes issue with the dominant argument and strategy. After we have made a case for the value of education and humanities' particularities, it is time to observe that every deep crisis presents a unique opportunity. The opportunity is for radical changes—to reinvent and rearticulate how we do what we do and how we see what we do. This book will be mostly about the literary studies—about, that is, a model of (poststructuralist) interdisciplinarity that has been integral to this discipline and which can be used for repositioning our understanding of the production of knowledge in general, including in sciences.[3]

The main task to be performed is the definition of this new model. I will assume that culture and science wars that began in the 1970s are, in fact, not yet finished, and that much work still needs to be done in defining what knowledge production (in poststructuralist terms) is, how this theory can serve as a basis for interdisciplinarity, and how it might help us understand and, then, reorganize institutional aspects that are integral to the creation of scholarship. By institutional aspects, I mean organizations like departments and their curricula, which are often the only stable representative of the discipline and the sole sources of scholars' agency and power—such as these are. The institutional aspects also include all the processes—peer and other forms of review and evaluation, most importantly—that help departments live and replicate, that make our careers, but are seldom understood to be what knowledge is made out of.[4] Literature scholars currently do not approach them as part of our scholarship or as a scholarly topic in their own right.

From the perspective of this book, the current state of literature departments is owed not just to the external crises but also to the transformation of poststructuralism that led from the early culture wars and the addition of viewpoints and approaches to the new, fragmented interpretative discourses and disciplines known under the catch-all term of cultural studies. If the situation is akin to balkanization, as many scholars have noted since Harold Bloom called us thus in 1994 (Bloom), there is a proviso. We are fragmented only in some aspects of our work, while other aspects remain shared. The primary example would be the belief that literary studies is categorically different from other disciplines. There are plenty more: use of the same interpretative model that sees literature as a view into a culture of a period (North), attitudes like favoring scholar's autonomy (Paulson), belief that the social relevance of work matters to its quality (Levin), reliance on a similar kind of close reading (Felski, *Limits*), and our complicity in the production of adjuncts (Donoghue). The balkanization coincides with the cessation of work on methodology and epistemology and, possibly—or likely as this book claims—is a *result* of it. Without epistemology, we do not know how balkanized and pluralized we are, and the diagnoses are, from the point of view of this book, obscuring more than they are revealing.

The fragmentation and pluralization have had a series of adverse effects that are seldom recognized as such. They have impacted our ability to organize politically and around the labor we do, cooperate with other similarly situated departments and disciplines like history and philosophy, and explain ourselves to scientists. They make it harder for generalist work to be published and to matter across the board. Fragmentation has thus weakened our ability to respond to the crises, while recent times have also seen drawing of new lines of demarcation, like those between well-off private institutions with large endowments that have benefited from the stock market rise, small liberal arts colleges that are dying, and public institutions, which themselves are impacted differently.

Works published in the new millennium that did try to respond to the crises by examining literary studies have done so by, as Paul Jay suggests in *The Humanities "Crisis" and the Future of Literary Studies*, proposing a return to some previous thing we do best, or a disciplinary core.[5] William Paulson offered reinvigorating "literary cultures" (Paulson); Stephen Best and Sharon Marcus tried to build on close reading to create a "surface" reading (Best and Marcus); James Williams saw poststructuralism as a solution (Williams); Rita Felski turned to critique and hermeneutics of suspicion (Felski, *Limits*); Caroline Levine, form (Levine); Franco Moretti, genre, period, and cultural tradition even as he was using digital technology to identify those (Moretti, *Graphs*). Joseph North recently went back to literary criticism (or aesthetics), which he opposes to literary scholarship in terms of left/right political orientation (North). These retrenchments and revisions have had many salutary effects. They expressed concern, made us pause, and take stock of what we have become as a discipline after the culture wars. However, the back-to-the-future arguments were not done with radical changes and reinvention of our discipline along the interdisciplinary model in mind, but to continue in a variant form. They engaged in what we can call a bargaining with the crises, where we give a bit to salvage the essential or non-negotiable values that make us who we are as a discipline. There was, however, no one to negotiate with and, for the most part, the efforts had little to no effect on the discipline, our teaching, and planning for the future.

Further pluralization—the work on posthumanities, postdiscipline, postcritique, including, for instance, Rosi Braidotti's, N. Katherine Hayles's, and aspects of Felski's *The Limits of Critique*—also bypassed institutional reform as well as epistemology. Braidotti, whose work on multimodal knowledge has received much attention, is frustratingly abstract and vague on details. From the perspective of this book, Braidotti offers proclamations in desperate need of support and explanations that never arrive. One can pick from her work at random:

> The point of convergence [interdisciplinarity] among different areas of posthuman knowledge production is recognizing the role of in/non/posthuman actors and objects of study, which acts against the pull of theory fatigue and endorses the calls for more conceptual creativity. It renews the mission of the conventional Humanities, lifting them out of anthropocentric habits of thought by offering more adequate concepts to deal with the ecological environment, media-nature-culture continuums, and non-human others. (Braidotti, *Posthuman* 59–60)

As we see, Braidotti is not addressing knowledge production that take place at actual universities, in buildings that need to be paid for. Knowledge that involves researchers who cooperate or fail to do so and everything in between; or that involves students at varying distance from research, and departments that house tenure. All of these are both practices and frameworks that shape how we think and do scholarship but are not named as such nor accounted for in the creation of what Braidotti calls "more adequate concepts." Without the institutional component, posthumanist knowledge is not poststructuralist in that, as I will explain below in more detail, the "apparatus" of knowledge production must include institutions.

The lines of thinking—back-to-the-future or posthumanities—make it hard to recognize the possibility that the crises are *not only* political, economic, and cultural—or caused from the outside knowledge production—but are epistemic and institutional, as well as general or total. As a result, what we need today is a thoroughgoing reinvention of what it means to *do* disciplinary work. We, too, need to start taking stock of exclusionary aspects of our work and what it, due to its current position and focus, leaves out or closes off.

The last time institutional reform and new epistemologies were on our main agenda was during the culture wars, when we criticized what we believed were unjust, insufficient, and untrue paradigms that hobbled the development of scholarship.[6] However, after that, literary scholars no longer saw epistemology's importance and abandoned the pursuit. Now, at least in part, it appears that the entrenchment of the current positions—the plural ones and the partially revisionist ones—established since the turn of the millennium stands in the way of a further and more thorough implementation of poststructuralism as a specific interdisciplinary theory (based on integration of disparate and diverging elements) used to define every aspect of scholarship and production of knowledge, starting with its institutions.

If it seems that *Interdiscipline*, too, argues for a return of sorts, to theory and poststructuralism, the relation, first, is better described as a revision—establishing a specific version of this theory that was never quite there in literature departments or in the form of institutional arrangement. Second, what distinguishes this variant is the scope of this theory's application beyond literary studies to general interdisciplinarity and institutional critique including epistemology, which we have not seen before—other than in the founding works of poststructuralism whose aim was precisely the kind of universal reform of knowledge production though without an actual institutional reform.

In another sense, *Interdiscipline* continues Karen Barad's *Meeting the Universe Halfway*. While their book provides a way to unify sciences and humanities around the practice of knowledge, I want to extend their notion of "apparatus" to include, beyond measuring instruments and cultural assumptions, forms of interactions between scholars and institutions like disciplines, area studies, and even current forms of interdisciplinarity that are based on additive logic. If for Barad, "boundary-making" is the primary function of knowledge production and is the role of the "apparatus" (Barad 148), for us, institutional practices—starting with the existence of departments—are the most obvious example of boundary-making. They, too, should count as the defining force of what knowledge is. Without acknowledging this grounding role that institutions play in establishing scholarly practices, Barad's general argument is not just incomplete; it is also without the specific material grounding that is implied in the definition of matter but not accounted for in the explanations since Barad does not focus on institutions, departmental division of scholarship, or other relevant elements of the setup that directly influence our epistemology.

As *Interdiscipline* argues, the so-called postdisciplinary practices do not appear post, after, or beyond a disciplinary regime or present openings with a staying power. They, instead, represent a current chaotic state that still relies on disciplines and departments as their reference point and is held together by the powers of the institution. For these reasons, the forms of multimodality or heteronomy can be seen as standing between the needs of research and scholarship on the one hand and disciplinary and institutional reforms on the other. Far from being a solution, plural formations prevent consolidation from taking place because we are fragmented. They give us the false sense that we are open and welcoming, while our form of multimodality often do not include sciences and are closed off to institutional critique. As we will see, in the same period that literary studies were becoming plural, the scientists gradually changed their opinion about poststructuralism and, by the end of the second decade of the third millennium, were producing new and innovative work with experimental confirmations of poststructuralist theory. One could go so far as to say that the science and social sciences are where poststructuralism is being developed today in most exciting forms, while its traditional strongholds of literary studies, philosophy, and humanities in general have little innovation to offer.

Stakes of epistemology

At stake in epistemology is not just or primarily the integrity of scholarship or its boundaries, but, more importantly, its ability to speak to itself and beyond of itself. By understanding how we know, we also learn who/what the *we* of this discourse is and what its others are.[7]

If this epistemology verges on politics, it is not, to be sure, an added value or a part of an either/or—either politics *or* scholarship—as critics from the right would have it, mostly based on the unscholarly notion of politics (Hanson). Politics, however, often stands in the way of building more comprehensive perspectives that cut through ideological lines, cross institutional boundaries (in new ways), and forge a general new view of what it means to *do* scholarship. Hence, this book claims that an act of interpretation is not equal to ideology and that this difference or distance provides a surplus from which we can rearticulate the production of knowledge and revise an ideology. I made a similar argument in "No Place Like Ideology (On Slavoj Žižek): Is There a Difference Between the Theory of Ideology and the Theory of Interpretation?"

Politics is a framework that outlives its usefulness at some point in time if it is not interrogated in a scholarly fashion and as integral to the apparatus of what we do.[8] We should not abandon politicization, but do politics by other means—first, through epistemology, since epistemology's role is to change the paradigm by introducing new methods, new ways of doing things, and new ways of being a *we*. To put this in terms of a study that is as close to a parallel to *Interdiscipline* as current scholarly production has gotten—Joseph North's *Literary Criticism: A Concise Political History*—on the other side of political discourse, there lies not neutrality, but another kind of politicization. I disagree with North on much, but agree with his central claim that what we are doing and how we are doing it in literary studies should be reconsidered and revised, and that revision should start with politics/institution (but also epistemology) as an element in our interpretative apparatus.

New term—Interdiscipline

One among the chief distinctions of *Interdiscipline* is its starting point. We begin by emphasizing beginnings, with poststructuralism as an interdisciplinary theory, and with literary studies as a field that focuses on interpretation. Bringing these together allows this project to be situated *in* a discipline (of literary studies) and *as* an interdisciplinary theory concerned with convergence. To explain this constellation, I use a new term, *interdiscipline*, signifying interdisciplinary discipline, that is supposed to capture a specific institutional standing, the structural specificity of our proposal, as well as its novelty.[9] The form denotes unity and plurality, specificity and universality at the same time. It, however, is not meant to be a unity of plural elements or plurality that is put together under a universal, but a way of thinking that is trying to be *at the same time* unifying and plural, local and global, systematic and open. The approach parallels—in an epistemological sense—what another new theory, transgender theory, has done with terms like sex and gender, feminism, and queer theory, offering a new way to organize and understand these categories—for instance, works like Julie L. Nagoshi et al.'s *Gender and Sexual Identity: Transcending Feminist and Queer Theory* and Heiko Motschenbacher's *Language, Gender, and Sexual Identity: Poststructuralist Perspectives*. Here "transcending," as I want to adopt it for my purposes, does not mean going beyond or erasing the categories like "man" and "woman," "homosexual" and "heterosexual" or in our context "specialization" and "discipline." It means offering a way to think these identity markers together, as relative, and on a continuum. Transgender theory also happens to be based on an emerging understanding of the complex biological coding of sex, which does not support the binary view of sex.[10] Philosophically, the case is for activating the in-between of the classical, exclusive, and opposing markers of identity and rethinking them from that kind of (institutional, epistemological) position without also abandoning the traditionally defined poles, at least at the current stage of reform.

The approach is anticipated in, for instance, Luce Irigaray's work from the early *Speculum* and *To be Two* to the more recent *Between East and West: From Singularity to Community* and *Sharing the World*. But in a significant reversal, transgender theory is a critique of Irigaray's hang-ups concerning homosexuality and her inability to follow through with the radical aspect of her theory. If Irigaray affirms the in-between, transgender theory and interdiscipline start understanding the identity of gender and disciplines from that position and do so without her reservations. *Interdiscipline* reimagines discipline and specialization as similar kind of duality of disciplinary and interdisciplinary traits.

This means, among other things, that we want to rely on the sense of continuity with disciplines and specializations to make our task easier and prevent the reform from disintegrating. Relying on discipline provides the continuity and what they do well (e.g., define methodology) and is a way to acknowledge the staying power of habits, history, and concrete institutional setups that are resistant to change. Disciplines, too, are in many ways already interdisciplinary and supply the material and the means for reform even as they do not allow it to happen.

At the same time, we want to recognize the importance of postdisciplinary and situationist arrangement and formulate a way for them to have lasting impact on the definition of knowledge organization and production. Thus, our goal is not to do away with either postdisciplinary formations or specialization or disciplines, but define a regime in which they can be done differently through common epistemology, paying attention to actual institutional limitations, and ad hoc nature of all cooperation.

The reason to relate to interdisciplinarity and not to the newer terms like multi- and transdiscipline is that the multimodality is not readily transferable to the institutional organization. At universities, knowledge production depends, among other things, on buildings and institutional setups, on funding over which universities often do not have direct control, on personalities working together. They are limited to multidisciplinarity that makes curricular sense, that does not jeopardize tenure, that supports the effective functioning of the institution as perceived by the administration, boards, state governments, and as defined by internal divisions onto colleges, schools, and departments, and so on. These bureaucratic and institutional factors set stark limits on how far the decentralization and multimodality of actual knowledge production and education can go and what boundaries it can and it cannot cross. The limitations are felt more down the economic institutional ladder.

The main question for reform is then not what kind of scholarship we prefer, but what kind of multidisciplinary form can our educational institutions accommodate and/or what kind of institutional reforms can most readily meet the situationist character of knowledge production and current focus on specializations. This is another reason to propose the model we are familiar with—discipline and specialization based—but as approached and practiced in radically different ways and in order to have some stability and continuity as we undertake thoroughgoing institutional reforms and as a means for those.

Interdiscipline will also define a set of steps for a curricular reform. An extant example compatible with our goals is Brown University's open, flexible, and rigorous curriculum. To be sure, their solution is not just interesting; it is also expensive, with close to 9,000 students, relatively small, and still based in disciplines and departments with many examples of (limited) clustering and convergence.[11] But it is a start. Another exciting model are the so-called humanities labs; research centers like the one at American University, which is based "on the understanding that the humanities offer modes of investigation that facilitate an active critical engagement with the world, an engagement with texts, contexts, and ideas that is lively, ongoing, experimental, and open-ended" (Humanities Lab). Building on such initiatives, we can define humanities and literary studies–based models for the investigation that can accommodate other disciplines and position themselves as forms of interdisciplinary inquiry because they foreground issues of framing and interpretation. These constitutes what can be called a new kind of infrastructure for the integration of knowledge production.[12]

Currently, a similar setup is the focus of, for instance, the Michigan Humanities Collaboratory.[13] We want to suggest that collaboratories—or co-laboratories—could become centers of cross-university collaborations of all kinds. The solution would compensate for the spatial and other limitations of university education and organization mentioned above and do so by consolidating multimodality, fitting it into physical and financial realities, while also providing the know-how for collaboration, which itself, like peer review, is not yet treated as a specific object of study or specialization in its own right (Priaulx and Weinel).

The relative lack of success among collaboratories and similar multidisciplinary setups can be ascribed to, in short, misapplication of poststructuralism which has resulted in the absence of a systematic approach, of emphasis on common epistemology, and not treating integration as deserving specific approach, trying to do too much with too little.

Role of philosophy

If it appears that *Interdiscipline* privileges philosophy in that philosophy or theory is used to define it (and therefore that it contradicts its interdisciplinarity proposal), this both is *and* is not the case. Western philosophy as the discourse of truth and epistemology can help us with its experience, depth, and variety of solutions. It may be banal to add, but philosophy does not own truth or epistemology, and the West does not own philosophy. Historically, works like Darwin's *On the Origin of Species* and Einstein's on relativity were not just specific theories, but also major new theoretical frameworks for organizing and institutionalizing scientific inquiry.

A thoroughgoing understanding of epistemology and institution critique should be prerequisites for being a scientist in the twenty-first century. By making epistemology—what this knowledge is and how it relates to that knowledge—fundamental to scholarship and education, we are also providing an opening to collaboration. The new organ would allow separate entities to connect to other entities and do so using an increasingly common language and set of routines. We will suggest development of yet another interdisciplinary area, namely, theory of interdisciplinarity, currently limited by both disciplinary approaches and disciplinary regimes with collaboration and convergence not yet having their widely accepted and established forms of evaluation.

Philosophy and theory stand to gain, too. Their scholars are in the position to learn how to communicate to different disciplines, since it is not sufficient for an argument to say that sciences are this or that. Instead, philosophy and theory have to find a language that would speak to scientists and explain to them, and from a point of view that is familiar to them, what a lack of neutrality implies and what we mean when we say that truth is relative and reality constructed or, following Karen Barad, that our knowledge does not represent the universe, nor does it create it, but meets it half-way. Working in our favor is that many scientists have already learned, as we will promptly show, fundamental poststructuralist lessons. In this sense, already neither philosophy nor literary studies define poststructuralism, its theory, and its interdisciplinarity.

To be a poststructuralist today implies that a scholar can occupy two positions—inside *and* outside the discipline. Such knowledge is predicated not on an internal agreement, but on the impossibility of closure and on understanding that the boundaries that define knowledge are imposed on it in the process of its institutionalization.

Poststructuralism

If poststructuralism is a theory of multiplicity, it does not follow that the theory does not also argue for forms of coherence and systematicity or that it, as a theory, is incoherent. Deconstruction, as Jacques Derrida insists in his early essay "Structure, Sign, and Play in the Discourse of the Human Sciences," is an alternative to destruction, not the means for it ("Structure"). A call for opening up of discourses and welcoming the other/Other at the end of that short early piece did not imply—let me use the well-worn metaphor—the burning of the house or dividing it into unsustainable morsels. Nor did it indicate partial pluralization, appropriate only in some domains (what can be investigated or who can be a scientist), but not in others (how we see and evaluate scholarly work).

The version of poststructuralism this book offers is also interdisciplinary. I understand poststructuralism in a broad historical perspective and as consisting of a set of core insights that have been the building blocks of much of contemporary knowledge. These insights or principles are grounds for contemporary mathematics, physics, and logic, and find their application in advanced forms of electronic technology like AI, not just in literature or selected philosophy departments—as one of my former compatriots, Vladimir Tasić, has shown in his extraordinary *Mathematics and the Roots of Postmodern Thought* (Tasić). Poststructuralism's insights concern the nature of knowledge creation that makes it such that it cannot be unified in the traditional Hegelian sense of that term—insights that find early formulation in Kurt Gödel's famous incompleteness theorems. His second theorem suggests that a system cannot demonstrate its consistency. (Another early example would be Niels Bohr's principle of indeterminacy that, too, defines an incompatibility. More on it in the last part of the last chapter of this book.) This theorem will serve us to suggest the distinction between, on the one hand, internal borders of a system that cannot be drawn and make the system coherent or whole and, on the other, external borders or those that are imposed on a system and hold it together (as a separate institutional field or department) through its delimitation from the outside.

For our purposes, we will take that this double understanding of demarcation is the characteristic of knowledge production such that there are also two kinds of unity. If the classical paradigm is based on unity of observed phenomena, in our understanding, the non-classical paradigm does not consist of adding a point of view (or changing scale) and multiplying systems of reference. Instead, we need to conceptualize unity in a new way, based on how knowledge functions and what rules it follows due to the lack of completeness. Non-classical paradigm is a new framework and it, too, deserves a proper name which for our purposes is poststructuralism.

Early in the twentieth century, there was Sigmund Freud's notion of contradictory coherence and the unconscious and Ferdinand de Saussure's understanding of language as a system of signs that derive meaning from their relations and not from their association with things or ideas. Here I will mention three more from the other end of the twentieth century that we will make use of in *Interdiscipline*. Pierre Bourdieu's notion of "habitus" suggests that behavior is not an expression of innate character, but a socially formed habit, skill, and disposition (Bourdieu). The more social groups or subject positions a person belongs to, the more beliefs they may hold, even if these are readily incompatible with one another. A practical implication is that as we surround ourselves with scientists, we will also begin to think and do like them and vice versa, forming new routines to replace the old ones. Gloria Anzaldúa's "borderlands/la Frontera" defines the identity compounds that are not representable in the accepted geopolitical or linguistic nomenclatures but can still serve to connect those (Anzaldúa). Intersectional theory (Crenshaw, "Mapping" and "Demarginalizing"; Collins, *Black Feminist Thought* and "Gender") offers a new compound tool to understand intragroup differences and uses these to figure out differences and commonalities between groups (Crenshaw, "Mapping"). These theories lend themselves readily to understanding interdisciplinary collaboration and the distinction between internal and externally imposed boundaries crucial for our approach. They, too, allow us to see the border (or borderlands) as an entity in its own right, not just a line of delimitation or compleation, a limit or enclosure, and to treat collaboration, convergence, and integration as fundamental forms of research. Boundaries are not only the sites of encounter and engagement but, as Roxanne Dunbar-Ortiz reminds in *An Indigenous Peoples' History of the United States*, also colonial formations, defined in the process of expansion (Dunbar-Ortiz 5). They cannot be either simply celebrated or transcended or negotiated but require us to acknowledge them and reformulate their significance in the light of the open systems.

Our notion of systematicity without a system will come out of Bruno Latour's recent lecture series published as *Facing Gaia: Eight Lectures on the New Climatic Regime* and out of a critique of both contemporary humanities and the sciences. He reproaches humanities for the lack of attention to the whole and scientists for hanging onto technological and teleological notions of systems, treating them as organized wholes made up of regulated parts. Our task will be to explain a structure that is neither whole nor the sum of parts, but derives coherence from its disequilibrium, which has endured over time. We will see disciplines in these terms *as* open wholes based on routines, habits, and institutional setups. With changing attitudes, foregrounding cooperation and convergence, the same practices should become sharable, ready for convergence. And so, we will see interdiscipline in the same terms, *as* open wholes based on integrative practices that foreground general compatibility of knowledge, placing convergence before specialization (supposing that specialization is here to stay and that it does not need special treatment to be maintained).

Our most immediate precursors are Karen Barad's notions of "mattering" and "apparatus" (*Meeting the Universe Halfway*), which they use to bring together relativist and positivist theories of knowledge. From the relativists, Barad accepts that the world is a construct and from the positivists, that the construction follows non-human rules. The result is an understanding that if social practices shape our views, the social practices are inseparable from the natural, material possibilities—matter as "an active agent participating in the very process of materialization" (Barad 151). While Barad calls their work posthumanist, from the perspective of our project, it is better described as a version of poststructuralism that offers realization for some of this theory's original promises and interdisciplinary ambitions. These can be summed up in their notion of a subject that is inter-active, co-constituted "through the material-discursive practices that they engage in" (Barad 168). In placing the accent on co-constitution, Barad allows us to focus on the incompleteness and process of boundary-making, which can now be approached within a new framework of materiality, including also the apparatuses of measurement. This means, for instance, that interpretation can bring together C.P. Snow's two cultures by providing an understanding in which interpretation is a part of the phenomena it interprets, as well as a material practice or apparatus. On this, sciences and humanities are different because there is a scholarly and institutional practice that separates them. The culture, in Snow's sense, is a result of what we do, not a condition of knowledge. Changing that practice/culture requires us to find notions, like the interactivity Barad offers, which reconceptualize the differences in frameworks and provide ways in which science and humanities produce the world together. Notions like "objectivity" are not lost in this translation, but are assigned a new meaning, dependent on the setup we call "science." The effects on the humanities should be just as radical in that the social construction can no longer be seen as the source, cause, and condition of the phenomena we analyze. Instead, material scholarly practices like knowing, teaching, reading, interpreting, and publishing are the foundation for the framework in which social determination appears as the origin of meaning.

In practical terms, this means that we will not be preoccupied with deconstructing texts, theories, or discourses, but will instead assume that all systems are non-totalities, exceeded by the very account we offer about them. A discipline is a system only in an institutional, routine, and historical sense, and through framing we impose on it through our reviews. It is not a system that can be methodologically or ontologically unified.

We take that deconstructing as undermining or decentering is no longer a priority. In some domains, that approach has worked perhaps too well. In the political sphere, for instance, it has routinely been used by the far right to disrupt the political system. In academia, disciplines and areas of concentration have become so porous that, as Silvio Waisbord notes (Waisbord), what holds them together is only the institution. In such a context, there is nothing to deconstruct any longer. What is possible is to rethink the framework within which we see scholarly production by understanding institutional boundaries as sites of common concern. So, we will propose that scholarship meets first around institutional practices like peer review that are customarily used to separate and maintain divisions and hierarchies but can be repurposed for creating shared procedures for evaluation of scholarship and then shared ways of knowledge production.

Changing poststructuralist landscape

The positive aspect of the general trends in the last two decades is that poststructuralism has been spreading across disciplines and has gradually assumed a very different institutional position from the one it occupied during the culture and science wars. "Narrative" and "storytelling" are employed widely and not only in business schools but also in biology (Hays), with, arguably, the most intriguing employment in neurology (Zimmerman). Columbia University already has a Division of Narrative Medicine, founded by Rita Charon, an MD with a PhD in English ("Division of Narrative Medicine"). Issues concerning interpretation, too, have found acceptance, for instance, under the heading of "bias," which is one of the hottest areas of research. Bias is included in the understanding of how programming and algorithms replicate the predispositions of their authors. Big data research has taken a turn in the direction of institutional critique and epistemology, offered by, among others, a prominent geographer, Robert Kitchin. In a "Big Data, New Epistemologies and Paradigm Shifts," Kitchin suggests a typical poststructuralist strategy:

> there is an urgent need for wider critical reflection within the academy on the epistemological implications of the unfolding data revolution, a task that has barely begun to be tackled despite the rapid changes in research practices presently taking place. (Kitchin 1)

Similarly, in *Sensemaking: The Power of the Humanities in the Age of the Algorithm*, Christian Madsbjerg, professor of applied humanities at the New School, uses poststructuralism to formulate a new approach to management philosophy.

Another key poststructuralist term, "construction," is now applied to identify how consciousness (Damasio) and emotions (Barrett) work and is, of course, the critical term of Barad's *Meeting the Universe Halfway*. Brian Nosek has made reproducibility a new direction in science development (Schooler et al.). The strategy rests on the poststructuralist mainstay of ideology critique. Reproducibility has recently been tested in cancer research with a failure rate of around 90% (Wen), which may lead to further reevaluations and reframing of the experimental method, giving this metacritical approach new prominence in scientific research.

Most surprisingly for us who lived through the science wars, Johns Hopkins University has a center that does experimental investigations of the constructed nature of reality called Perception and Mind Lab ("Perception and Mind Lab"). The even more important and promising new developments concern research integration on a large scale, like ones employed in cancer research. Scientists are beginning to accept that specific problems' complexity requires a systemic, integrative, or general approach that cannot rely on prior forms of universalization and needs to be met by entirely new kinds of convergence and epistemology. "When the amount of information and the complexity of the interaction in networks increases within any kind of dynamic process of knowledge," Marta

Bertolaso, a philosopher of science, writes in her "Epistemology in Life Sciences: An Integrative Approach to a Complex System Like Cancer," "a new level of regulation is necessary if the system is to function reliably" (Bertolaso, "Epistemology" 245).[14] The study of cancer already combines molecular (genetics) and cellular (biology) research and relies on cooperation between biomedicine and biophysics, which has made the epistemic difference between approaches and disciplines into one of the most pressing issues of the very research (Bertolaso, "Epistemology"). In Bertolaso's words, the "challenge is to confront concepts and vocabulary to make our discourse understandable and useful for different disciplines" (Bertolaso, "Epistemology" 246).

Behind the acceptance of the new philosophical views and multimodality are the exigencies scientists had encountered in their work. Empiricism and experience have put pressure on them to trade the understanding of a direct and unmediated experience or direct and unmediated access to general laws for an understanding common among poststructuralist scholars, "that the scientific theories are our own elaborations so that the procedures of experimental science are always interpretative" (Bertolaso, "Epistemology" 246). It is also accepted that the complex, systemic nature of phenomena like cancer dictates the complex approach, not the other way around, that disciplines or approaches should define what the problem is (Bertolaso, "Epistemology").

Interdiscipline disagrees with Bertolaso concerning the framework that the systemic complexity calls for. In her estimation as in much other recent work, this can be done in inter-, trans-, and multidisciplinary arrangements or pluralisms and multiversity of approaches—though she is vague on what those are. As far as I can tell, there are no extant forms of knowledge production, no epistemology, no how-to that can accomplish what cancer research requires. The best the existing frameworks—research, education, scholarship—can offer is, from our point of view, situationism. Among other impediments, fields revert to disciplinary peer review for evidence of quality. Scholars see, as we already suggested, collaboration in terms they are most familiar with. Their job prospects and career advancement remain, by and large, tied to their disciplines and departments. Getting grants depends on the specific readily recognizable specialist or disciplinary features of the proposal; and so on. Judging based on 2017 *The Oxford Handbook of Interdisciplinarity*, there are no commonly accepted principles of convergence, no commonly accepted habits of pluralization, few standard protocols on deciding what is common, and so on (Frodeman et al.). For these reasons, we do not see evidence of what scholars of interdisciplinarity call "integration" or "interaction" or "wholistic approach" (Choi and Pak). We are yet to organize a system of knowledge that would meet the needs of systemic phenomena and be interdisciplinary in the sense that it can be supported by a common institution and from a common perspective. This book suggests that poststructuralism was made to meet such goals, as a theory about a comprehensive approach to complex, multilevel phenomena—not as a theory that would disrupt systems.

In the same last two decades, literary scholars have begun to turn to sciences in more significant numbers. As a rule and from our perspective, however, literature scholars are not as sophisticated in their employment of interdisciplinarity as some scientists are because we still treat discourses as separate. For instance, recent work by Daniel Aureliano Newman's *Modernist Life Histories: Biological Theory and The Experimental Bildungsroman* relies on the author's training in biology and proposes that "experiment is the best way of resisting the force of habit which reduces complex realities to simple myths, experience into slogans, cultural constructs into immutable truths and curiosity into complacency" (Newman viii). The observation is the basis for a reading of modernist literature, an analysis Newman calls an "a substantial and systemic literary dialogue with biological models of development and evolution" (Newman ix). In our view, the work does not represent a dialogue with sciences, but is an example of borrowing, an additive form that follows the common formula like literature *and* psychology, literature *and* law. The same is also present in the once promising new field of cognitive studies of literature (Richardson and Spolsky, Zunshine 2015, 2010).[15] Newman confirms that this is his approach when he says that even though a literary study is "fundamentally congenial with the spirit of scientific enquiry [...] its objects and objectives are and should remain different" than those of science (Newman ix). We strongly disagree that science and the humanities cannot have shared object and objectives—for instance, issues of convergence and other organizational and institutional aspects of scholarly production. The approach, too, is consistent with poststructuralism, though this is a different poststructuralism from the one assumed in Newman's book.

Perhaps the shortest way from where we are now to universal convergence can be created through an epistemology, itself developed from the extra- and interdisciplinary perspectives. If a theory is open, and the university is without limits, as Derrida argues in "The University without Condition," scholarship, too, cannot be limited by the divide between the humanities and sciences, between interpretative and quantitative discourses. A further implication is that university cannot be organized around its many boundaries or limits (as Bérubé and many others proposed), between departments and disciplines, between its inside and its outside, with the "in" denoting scholarly or scientific protocols and the "out" calling for social justice, peace, or the utility of education. The question is also how universities can be integrated into cultures at large to educate their various audiences so that their various constituencies or stakeholders can be integrated into knowledge centers. This is my alternative to, among others, Slavoj Žižek's *In Defense of Lost Causes*, which, too, argues for a revised view on great narratives.

Construction

Knowledge has no limits, and our institutional arrangements need to strive to find ways to accommodate this feature in a manner integral to knowledge production. Our response to the common charge that construction and poststructuralism do not mean in humanities what they mean in sciences is the following. First, these cultures are going to be different if we continue seeing them from divergent points of view and assume the divide to be intrinsic to knowledge production, not a result of institutions and habits. Such setup makes it difficult, if not impossible, to approach the beyond of the divided horizon and recognize the continuity. An alternative is to see the already noted acceptance of poststructuralism in social and natural sciences as indicators that the boundary has been transcended through new material practices. Emerging notions of construction already merge cultural and physical aspects of organism's function. Experimental demonstrations in, for instance, cognitive science show how our brain creates the world using internal models and representations (Barrett, "Theory").[16] Work like Lisa Feldman Barrett's focuses on the functionality of the organism and denies the typological binary nature/nurture that is replicated and maintained in the Snow model and its cultural division, sciences/humanities. Physics, while on a track its own, is entangled in the same general trend. This we glean, for instance, from the recent article by Daniela Frauchiger and Renato Renner titled, to mimic Gödel's theorem, "Quantum Theory Cannot Consistently Describe the Use of Itself" (Frauchiger) and from the controversy that followed because the article calls for abandoning the essentialist principle that "objective data provide the platform on which scientific knowledge rests" (Healey).

Poststructuralism has also found acceptance on the level of discourse. Scientists readily recognize the construction of scientific setups (if not yet facts). For instance, a recent volume titled *Laboratory Lifestyles: The Construction of Scientific Fictions* examines how the architecture of laboratory buildings and spaces contributes to the development of science (Kaji-O'Grady et al.). But the question is not if scientists today accept the 1970s or 1980s poststructuralism and *Laboratory Life*, but instead if construction has become integral to scholarly work across disciplines, resulting in a new standard conceptual threshold that includes shared frameworks. The intersection could, in turn, enrich the original philosophical understanding of social construction with experiment-based models and neural construction of "emotion concepts … in the service of efficient physiological regulation" (Hoemann et al. 1831).

Following works like Barrett's, the theory of construction could account for the embodied making of affect, including a detailed description of mental and physiological processes. Barrett identifies her new approach as an "internal model" (Barrett, "Theory"), consisting of a representation that an organism—from single cell to human—has of itself and which it uses for self-regulation. These representations, Barrett suggests, are run through simulations—whole-brain scenarios "that anticipate (i) upcoming sensory events both inside the body and out as well as (ii) the best action to deal with the impending sensory events" (Barrett, "Theory" 7). Combining cultural with mental construction allows for a science-based link between external and internal representations—the link that the humanities usually assume but have no means of explaining fully or demonstrating. The result is a model of the mind and culture that determine one another: the mind that shapes perception (and bodily states) that shapes the culture that shapes the brain. The innovation bridges the traditional dichotomy between the nervous system and the mind, nature and culture, sciences and humanities, opening a different framework for inquiry where chemistry/biology and culture, sciences and humanities are elements of one open conceptual system. For our purposes, what is most interesting is the connection between cultural, theoretical, bodily, or emotional concepts that takes place through language (Hoemann et al. 1836).[17] If we recognize Freud in some of the links, the differences are crucial—the notion of construction emerging in psychology is empirically grounded, a result of thoroughgoing, precise explanations of neurological functions and processes. As such, it would help the humanities scholar understand how culture is determined and defined by chemistry, as in Barrett's work, which presents a de-essentialized and de-centralized model of the mind, with chemical life that is context-dependent and functional, with "large within-category variation as well as between-category similarity" (Hoemann et al. 1833). The link between social and chemical construction would help cultural studies acquire precision and new importance for interdisciplinary work.

Methodology

To put this interdisciplinary poststructuralist project forward, I use a methodology of metacriticism and an argumentative strategy that is not commonly employed in literary studies. There are book reviews, but those tend to be short and summary, informative rather than exploratory. They are not considered our primary scholarly genre. At my institution, they are not even counted toward promotion and tenure. Metacriticism, however, is a poststructuralist mainstay as evidenced by *diacritics*, the pioneering theory journal, whose chief genre is the review of secondary sources.[18] The reasons to approach knowledge development in this fashion are many. *Interdiscipline* does so under the assumption that the practice of knowledge, as embodied in scholarly publications, is the most reliable source for showing what we are as a discipline and how we *do* things.

Such engagements demonstrate not only what we argue but also the choices we make when we argue. Of our particular concern will be the lines of argument that are closed off due to how we position our inquiry—how we frame our investigations and what views and positions those frames make inaccessible. The result of such metareview of the scholarship will be a kind of negative picture that shows literary scholarship in a broader context, offset by vast possibilities that we did not choose to explore. The bringing of the left-out into the foreground displays work as a specific ideology, which then allows another author—me in this case—to interact with a limited, precisely defined set of practices; change some; accept others; and thus reformulate how we do things and how we understand what it is that we are doing.

18 Introduction

The second reason to follow this methodology is that all the discussions this book joins—about the crises, about what literary studies is, about poststructuralism, interdisciplinarity, and so on—have been going on for a while. At this point, most general positions have been taken, and the new contribution can consist in reframing those in entirely new terms and offering a different starting point (which is what we are doing), and/or paying attention to essential details and offering different interpretations of those while also creating new links between topics and issues (which is also what we are doing). One of the negative results of this approach is that my close readings will be limited and subordinated to the task of reframing and constructing a new argument, not to understanding nuance or ambiguities of extant scholarly works.

I will defend this position in the last chapter in detail when we get to Susan Buck-Morss's reading of Hegel and Haiti. Here I can say that from the position of *Interdiscipline*, the neglected nuances are not significant at this point in our academic life. In this respect, as in few others, *Interdiscipline* follows Bruno Latour. It is time to "bring the sword of criticism to criticism itself and do a bit of soul-searching" (Latour, "Why Has Critique" 227).

The last and most important reason for this methodology is that the epistemology that is the target of *Interdiscipline* consists not of the general rules that are then enacted by scholarship and policed by peer review. It is the other way around: actual examples of the scholarship make up an epistemology, showing what Paul Jay calls the "practice" of humanities (Jay, "Humanities" 83).

All choices outlined above amount to a specific scholarly agenda. I do not offer it as an imperative. It is an approach that, I believe, is most useful in the general discussion of literary studies and its interdisciplinary reorganization at a point in time when poststructuralism should be changing and when disciplines other than literary studies and philosophy have made significant contributions to it, and our goal is to create an actual example of convergence scholarship.

Future

As far as literature departments are concerned, I will end this introduction with a look at the current jobs that came to replace Stanley Aronowitz's "last good job" (Aronowitz):

> English department seeks a tenure-track assistant professor specializing in Shakespeare, Romanticism, Victorianism, modernism, post-modernism, post-colonialism, southern literature, Appalachian literature, African American literature, Caribbean literature, Irish literature before 1200, Croatian literature after 1853, Joyce, Chaucer, Hemingway, Morrison, Milton's lesser works, those damn Ayn Rand novels our male sophomores want to read, the non-sexy D.H. Lawrence books, and Soviet-era science fiction after Khrushchev. Candidates are expected to teach a 4/4 load of freshman composition. (Weber)

Well, at least, we can try to have some fun with it. Here are some actual job requirements from the 2016–2017 *JIL (Job Information List)*, the last job list before the cataclysm. Each ends where sentence ends. A department is looking for a new colleague to teach composition and literature. One candidate is sought with online course development and teaching experience to teach literary theory and criticism; undergraduate and graduate courses in gender studies; Victorian literature; seventeenth-century, modernist British, and/or commonwealth literature. Multimodal writing, feminist rhetorics, multicultural rhetorics, and/or distance education; writing program administration; combined with expertise in linguistics, literacy studies, and/or comparative research methodologies. Candidate, proficient in Middle English literature, who will contribute to college in a number of ways: engaging students in medievalism from the twelfth to the twenty-first century, developing courses on the Middle Eastern influences on medieval European culture, and/or participating in new programs such as Creative and Applied Computing; as well as create upper-level courses that emphasize the development of literary traditions over time. An emerging scholar is expected to complement internationally recognized faculty and high-profile visitors and demonstrate a rigorous research portfolio in the field of contemporary technology, culture, and society, with a focus on big data, social media networks, hacktivism, digital arts and post-internet practices, and so on.[19]

These actual job descriptions show the clash of two trends. The fragmentation dictates that each specialization, division, and set of combinations have to be mentioned. But, then, the piling is done as a mere addition, referencing elements of what once was a coherent curriculum, just as they do cultural trends (like DH) and fads like medievalism of all ages. Most such ads raise propriety issues as we continue to insist on what have become empty categories since the context in which they were formulated and thrived has radically changed or has altogether disappeared.

The covid pandemic has only accelerated the trend. *The New York Times* reports that the administration at Ohio Wesleyan intends to "merge religion and philosophy into one department and lump Black studies and women's studies into a single 'critical identity studies' program," starting what is, without a doubt, going to be a new trend (Hubler).

The above can also be read as evidence that the job market has already become interdisciplinary in ways we—associate and full professors in literature departments especially—are not. And it has become interdisciplinary in a manner and with results which we no longer can control. Unfortunately, these changes, too, do not allow us to say that we are now interdisciplinary. To be that, the discipline needs an updated epistemology and an understanding of how its institutions—including the new grotesque mergers—relate to and support such a definition.

Defining interdisciplinary institutional epistemology would give us new and prominent roles, perhaps some new good jobs for our future PhDs, and some control over the chaos that we have become. Teaching of writing may well be the territory that literary studies would have to call its own and use as an institutional

20 Introduction

ground to define their interdisciplinary configurations.[20] We take the notion of writing in a hermeneutic configuration—a part of the interpretation, construction, and relationship-making process to which we will devote this book—as the institutional and philosophical cornerstones of the future interdisciplinary literary studies.[21]

Notes

1 Information is not clear-cut on any aspect of humanities education. Publication by NCES (National Center for Education Statistics) supports the view that humanities degree holders are paid less (Hussar et al.). Citi Research Online notes some favorable trends for the humanities majors (Terras et al.). See also (Belfield et al.). Individual opinions define humanities not as useless but as worthless on the job market (Waechter). See also Bankrate ranking (Garcia). See, however, Hart Research for evidence that businesses prefer broad education and research experience. With the recently published Leonard Cassuto and Robert Weisbuch *The New PhD*, there is a new argument for a positive understanding of how literature and humanities degree holders can contribute to all fields and businesses.
2 Also see Newfield *Unmaking* and *Ivy and Industry*; Barrow; Geiger; Brint.
3 See Julie Thompson Klein's *Humanities, Culture, and Interdisciplinarity* for a recent account of interdisciplinarity in literary studies. See also Joe Moran's pioneering attempt in *Interdisciplinarity*.
4 Compare to James Chandler's "Introduction: Doctrines, Disciplines, Discourses, Departments," where institution is equated with a department and routines of reproduction that include curricula, peer and other forms of review are marginalized. Chandler, too, skirts the problems with methodology in recent literary studies and does not devote much attention to situationism as the prevailing disciplinary form. The result is that his notion of institution is rather hollow.
5 There were a few significant critiques of institution. I will comment on Michael Bérubé's *The Employment of English* briefly at the end of the introduction and will only name the significant others, Chris Baldick's *The Social Mission of English Criticism, 1848–1932*; Paul Bové's *Mastering Discourse: The Politics of Intellectual Culture*; Jonathan Culler's *Framing the Sign: Criticism and Its Institutions*; Anne Ruggles Gere's *Writing Groups: History, Theory, and Implications*; Gerald Graff's *Professing Literature: An Institutional History*; and Richard Ohmann, *Politics of Letters*; Bruce Robbins's *Secular Vocations: Intellectuals, Professionalism, Culture*.
6 See, for instance, Jonathan Culler, *Framing the Sign: Criticism and Its Institutions*. The culture wars were also the period that saw significant histories of our profession, like Gerald Graff's *Professing Literature*, initially published in 1987 (Graff), and Chris Baldick's *The Social Mission of English Criticism, 1848–1932*. It is a corollary of my point about epistemology to suggest that we no longer write histories either—until North's recent one (North).
7 There is a notable ongoing effort to define "moral epistemology" that does not include institution reform. See, for instance, Linda Alcoff's "Comparative Epistemology" (Alcoff).
8 Most recently, in the face of MLA's and the *PMLA*'s resistance to examine peer review, RaceB4Race, a group of premodern BIPOC scholars, has publicly raised the issues of publication criteria. We will see how *PMLA* will take the challenge (RaceB4Race Executive Board).
9 Term "interdiscipline" has been used before though not in the sense I am proposing. It has been applied to, for instance, translation studies (Snell-Hornby et al.) and humor studies (Zabalbeascoa). It has also appeared in the history of science as we will discuss in Chapter 5. Derrida uses a similar term, interscience (*Eyes*).

10 See, for instance, World Health Organization, "Gender," and Wu.
11 See, for instance, how the Brown University Africana Studies Department is organized ("Africana Studies," Brown University) and the general organization of departments/institutes ("Departments, Centers, Programs and Institutes," Brown University.)
12 Howes et al. note failed experiments in Japan with integrated rooms for thinking, saying that the "remarkable system-wide innovation failed due to lack of proper investment in development, support, and infrastructure that might have facilitated genuine enactment of curriculum innovation. Essentially such reform requires that teachers get plenty of thinking time too" (Howes et al. 9). We are trying to avoid the mistake by making the philosophical issues of framing and convergence a part of interdisciplinary scholarship. Put simply, the first and most important task of thinking rooms would be to find practical ways in which they can be integrated into the existing institutional divisions.
13 See Lane. See also Joselow and Breithaupt.
14 See also Bertolaso, *Cancer.*
15 Other significant attempts like sustainability studies or the use of the theory of evolution in literary studies fail for different reasons. Because of the focus on cultural studies approach or because of a poorly understood scientific theory. We will discuss these in passing in Chapter 1 and Chapter 5. See also Ramadanovic, "Between Post-Structuralism and Science."
16 See also "The Science of Subjectivity" podcast.
17 Hoeman et al. write, for instance, that "in running an internal model and generating predictions, the brain is continually constructing ad hoc, embodied concepts" that guide action and "meet the context-specific goals" (Hoeman 1837).
18 See also the journal *Intertexts.*
19 Elite universities have fared as Frank Donoghue predicted (Donoghue). Harvard still advertises positions with the traditional narrow focus like Medieval British Literature with teaching areas in "Old English, Middle English, Insular Multilingualism, and the History of the English Language." Harvard's interdisciplinarity needs are met by hiring more than one candidate/lecturer with different interdisciplinary backgrounds. But even these kinds of literature departments show the same tendency for combining larger and larger areas of knowledge. The effect is just achieved by other means. Yale wants "broad-ranging comparatists who work and teach in more than one literary tradition, in any genre (poetry, drama, narrative) and the period from antiquity up until 1900. Some welcome fields: non-European literatures; French literature; 18th-19th century European literature; literary theory;" as well as an additional hire in Old English, with expertise in "Medieval Latin language and literature and/or other early Germanic languages and literatures" noted as additional assets. Princeton wants a scholar "specializing in African American and diasporic literature and culture of the long 19th century (c.1789–1914); and another scholar specializing in Latino/a/x literature and culture" ("Job Information List"). More recent job lists are dominated by foreign and rich private university job positions. Even elite universities in the United States are not spared the trend since their graduate programs cannot survive tenure track job draught.
20 This will not exactly mean that *Interdiscipline* will be against composition and literacy studies. We will be critical of the tendencies in these disciplines to think of writing as independent of reading, hermeneutic theory, and discipline-defined contexts. While many scholars of composition and literacy deny that this is what they are doing, their scholarship and institutional behavior often show that they may not have an open enough understanding of what these imply about writing and its teaching. Often enough, scholars of composition do not see interpretation as the overarching category under which their scholarship and institutional life occur (Lamb and Parrott, Sullivan et al.). Similarly, despite the interest in technical and science writing, composition and literacy studies are not yet a field that has elaborated its interdisciplinary epistemology that would explain how it converges with the sciences and technology.

21 SUNY University at Albany has "The Program in Writing and Critical Inquiry" (WCI). As its web page describes it, it offers a focus on academic writing. Writing itself is described as "a discipline itself," as "an essential form of inquiry," a "vehicle for learning and a means of expression," as having "the essential role … in students' lives as citizens, workers, and productive members of their communities" (Writing and Critical Inquiry Program"). Among the reasons such a program can have limited success is because the traditional departments like English still exist, with the two bound to compete for the institutional space and weaken one another. The Program, too, does not have a strong enough role in the overall composition of the college and university education. It relies on a narrow notion of writing that does not include reading, literature, interpretative practices, disciplinarity, interdisciplinarity, and fails to represent a central node in a university.

1
"WE"
Crises responses and literary studies as a theory of interpretation

Introduction

English Studies: The State of the Discipline, Past, Present, and Future, a recent distinguished attempt to take stock of literary studies and help us out of our current crises, opens with the proposition that "[t]he challenge facing English scholars today is to position ourselves responsibly vis-à-vis this paradox [that our self-definition provides fodder for others to attack us], and at the same time to articulate what we value in English Studies" (Gildea et al. 1). This chapter will scrutinize the claim as a way to introduce several issues pertaining to and circling around what literary studies is as a discipline under the assumption that the response to the threat depends directly on who *we* are. Focusing on the *we*, we follow Bruno Latour's adage, which says, "[t]ell me how you comment on a scripture or an inscription, and I will tell you what sort of epistemology you hold on to" ("Enlightenment" 86). In our case, interpretative theory or hermeneutics is simultaneously a way toward a new epistemology and means by which we can acquire a new interdisciplinary identity for the discipline of literary studies.

I take *English Studies*—together with *The Values of Literary Studies* edited by Rónán McDonald—to be examples of the third generation of commentary that articulates a general argument explaining the value of the humanities to English and literature departments. I will address only in passing the immediate antecedents; for example, Helen Small's *The Value of the Humanities* (2013) and *Humanities in the Twenty-First Century* (2013), edited by Eleanora Belfiore and Anna Upchurch. And before those, we find similar texts, like Stefan Collini's *What Are Universities For?* (2012), Michael Sandel's *What Money Can't Buy* (2012) and Ronald Barnett's trilogy, *Being a University*, *Imagining the University*, and *Understanding the University*, which I will not engage at all.[1] A more substantive exegesis of these contributions is not called for because

DOI: 10.4324/9781003119616-2

of the uniformity of the arguments—centering on the value, alleging our uniqueness along the lines of non-instrumentalization, following the tradition of apologies, using persuasion as its method.[2] By and large, prior discussions of this issue have not considered that the humanities are the problem and insisted on employing that discourse to respond to the crises.[3] On the occasions when scholars saw literary studies was a problem, as Rita Felski did in her *The Limits of Critique* (2015), their critiques did not include institutional elements that make our discipline. As a rule, humanities/literary studies are reduced to the intellectual and scholarly realm with teaching and other practices—all the work we do in them as members of departments, colleges, universities, professional organizations, journal boards, hiring and other university committees, employees, and so on—disregarded as auxiliary and, apparently, unimportant for our self-definition.

In contrast, this chapter proposes that these organizational facets that appear marginal need to be brought center stage. This centering on the institutional has the advantage of addressing the fact that the humanities/literary studies can look very different at a public university—say, a community college in a rural part of a "red state"—then they might when our vantage point is the corner of Amsterdam Avenue and 114th Street (Hutner and Mohamed). Further, continuing to present the humanities/literary studies as unique and exceptional is at least a tactical mistake, as Karen Spierling suggested recently in "The Humanities Must Go on the Offensive". It is also, in my understanding, a political error. It segregates humanities/literature scholars from those who are most like us—our colleagues working in social and natural sciences—implying that we have different interests. In an age when one-third of the American military refuses covid vaccination, when science and expertise are regarded as a conspiracy theory, we have, if nothing else, a common antagonist (Baldor).

While I am proposing this displacement of our focus, I am not arguing that the humanities and literary scholarship do not hold the values the above mentioned works have ascribed to them. My point in this chapter is a different one. It concerns how we go about *disseminating* and *protecting* the values we generate and resources we depend on—and do that under the general heading of interdisciplinary integration. My point has specific philosophical weight, too, in that it suggests a different framework from those employed thus far. A point of view that begins to account for the institutional arrangement as determinative of scholarship and suggests a general epistemology on those bases. I take that everyday engagement—negotiating how we teach, what we teach, how we react to students, to each other, and colleagues from other colleges, schools, and departments—are both extensions of our scholarship as well as what grounds it and gives it staying power. We also draw salaries, participate in hierarchies, influence institutional decisions, construe "demand," "value," and other notions that define this profession. We teach in specific ways, make arguments that favor these but not those strategies, and, in general, move as cohorts with distinct habits, routines, and fashions of thinking and behaving.

Part I: the we we are

Totalitarianism

To get to the scholarly part of my proposal, we need first to distinguish arguments concerning the university (humanities, literary studies) that are at this point beyond academic negotiations and move them over into the social, legal, and political arenas where they belong. These include basic assumptions like the humanities being a public good, that affordable tertiary education is a right, that to be educated in the twenty-first-century one needs broad, deep, interdisciplinary, and multicultural education—values, in other words, that authors like Wendy Brown (*Undoing the Demos*) see as being under assault from "neoliberalism."[4]

The reason to suggest the bracketing of arguments is that it has become evident that the forces shaping university's increasingly precarious financial and social position are not limited to economy and demographics and are not just a matter of policies and different political or education philosophies. As Pew Research Center reports, in 2017, 58% of Republican and Republican-leaning independents believed that colleges and universities *hurt* the country, which is an increase of close to 20% since 2015 (Pew Research). In a similar ratio of two in three, conservative Republicans also suspect the results of the 2020 presidential election without any evidence. If the trends are related to one another and Trump's presidency as they appear to be, the polarization is no longer of a degree, a radicalized version of yearning for enlightenment vs. distrust of eggheads, as Andrew Delbanco put it in 2009 (Delbanco). It is, instead, a matter of two incompatible political and value systems, a difference of being for or against science, knowledge and expertise, evidence, post-Enlightenment norms such as equality between genders and races. The implications for tertiary education are as severe as they can be—it is at the brink of losing the mandate and the foundational role it has held since World War II, the GI Bill, and the Keynesian version of the redistribution of wealth.

From this perspective, the coalition behind Trump is most recognizable, not as neoliberalism but under the broader category of totalitarianism. Using Hannah Arendt's *The Origins of Totalitarianism* and its many updates by Anne Applebaum, we see the struggle between two opposite views of the world and two opposite social organizations. One of these is seeking to limit science and the pursuit of truth and impose itself as the arbiter and framework of reality. Scholarship cannot argue its point against totalitarianism since the former does not recognize common terms of a conversation or political and democratic deliberation and does not proceed by means we call rational. Totalitarianism simply and only seeks to impose itself over the totality of public space. A typical strategy is for its prominent proponents to create conflict, often by making outrageous and unfounded statements, sowing doubt that truth and facts can be determined, and propagating various kinds of conspiracy theories to replace obvious evidence. University and scholars cannot negotiate with such a coalition since it aims to change the terms of communication and the social contract on which the modern university is based—the social contract that has been in place since the last victory over a similar movement and ideology.

The contemporary context makes it relatively easy to explain precisely why knowledge production is not value neutral and why we should reframe the conversation to show just how instrumental humanities are for knowledge production of any kind. We are not value neutral because education and scholarship are grounded in the norms and value system that favor the pursuit of truth. Poststructuralism—the kind we get in Jacques Derrida's "The University Without Condition"—only confirms this view by insisting that truth is a construct and providing many precise tools for examining its productions. If the same theory also says that truth is relative, its relativity to a framework, not a "fake news"—itself not a kind of news or content or point of view, but a power move or discourse. When Kellyanne Conway states that the Trump administration relies on "alternative facts," these are not supposed to represent a well-defined point of view or apparatus. Instead, they are entirely defined by the goal of creating a new reality, independent of all other verifiable, documented, and testable or shared realities—a means of the assertion of Trump's power as absolute or total, capable of transporting its followers into a new universe.[5] The goal of "fake news" is the same as that of Trumpism in general, to subjugate and control or eliminate all who do not support it. As Applebaum suggests, the effect of lies is one of deeper interpellation, meant to strengthen the follower's conviction, the exclusivity of their views, their dependence on each other, and the level of their surrender to the cause (Applebaum, "History").[6] University discourses, even those coming from the elite schools that have not felt the crises as much, are powerless to challenge this form of reality production since they cannot speak to the cult's inductees. The most we can do is describe the regime the way Applebaum did, but our explanations are addressed to educated audiences—educated in this sense that they accept the post-Enlightenment norms of truth-seeking and conversation. To us, Applebaum speaks of the radical nature of the assault that education faces and reveal its true intent of absolute domination and control.

For these reasons, all the fine arguments defending the humanities and university and affirming its foundation and value do not reach the political constituency that is assaulting the post-Enlightenment values and the university's traditional social role. They, too, cannot challenge or change totalitarianism. The period in which many of the mentioned books were published saw the further and faster radicalization of the right despite the dissemination of those convincing explanations and the improving economy in the United States and across the developed world. These voters and the many neoliberal ideologues who profit from them are likely to remain unreachable by means scholars have available.

We say this after works like Lauren Kerby's *Saving History: How White Evangelicals Tour the Nation's Capital and Redeem a Christian America* have done much to explain one of the constituencies behind the totalitarian assault. *Saving History* shows how such ideology can be combated on individual level as Kerby accepts the evangelical terms of conversation which she then tries to complicate. Any challenge to the evangelical belief system, Kerby suggest, is likely to be met with a wholesale rejection.

There is an internal dynamic of totalitarianism that is pertinent for our discussion in this chapter. Its establishment and propagation require terrorizing of innocent victims. Arendt writes that originally the Jews became "an object of universal hatred because of its [their] *useless* wealth, and of contempt because of its lack of power" (Arendt 15, emphasis added). Union of Soviet Socialist Republics (USSR) used terror over their own, the Communist party members, their soldiers, peasants in Ukraine, even children, to the same end (Applebaum, *Red Famine*). Totalitarianism and terror in the United States have already had their victims from the Oklahoma bombing to Charleston and El Paso shootings, and the metaphoric ones, Mexicans and refugees, presented as murderers, rapists, and terrorists that siphon off the welfare. The police actions against unarmed black men and women and protesters carry aspects of the same cruelty meant to terrorize.

We should have these characteristics in mind as we position our response to the arguments and speak about the non-instrumental values of humanities education and the so-called soft skills we teach. These, too, happen to be not by chance the targets of totalitarian and neoliberal assaults, and by assenting to neoliberal terms of conversation, we are only weakening our position. The United States is also culturally and traditionally prone to anti-intellectualism and populism. Its norm is to scorn teaching as a profession. The resentment and envy are easily identifiable in, for instance, the traditional saying, "Those who can, do. Those who can't, teach." There are countless instances from publications like *Freefall of the American University* and *The Professors: The 101 Most Dangerous Academics in America* that use specific failures of the educational system for blanket attacks on the left, to cartoons—"Is that a real doctor, or just a PhD?" is a caption in a *New Yorker* cartoon and Homer Simpson's line to Rick Santorum calling Barack Obama a "snob" for wanting more people to attend college (Roller; Binder and Wood).[7]

That many faculty, scientists, and doctors are Jewish, foreign-born, and welcoming to African Americans, women, and sexual minorities, is a significant factor, of course, in these attacks on expertise. It is not by chance that conspiracy theories like QAnon include the same cast of characters which is yet another piece of evidence of how organized and self-consistent the current assault is. The general populist prejudices readily combine with the neoliberal politics and totalitarian ideology, profiting from the negative image of teaching as a profession, low regard for learning among certain groups, and a general disdain for displays of intellectual but not technological or physical (sports) brilliance. In the face of these hard attacks, it is a suicide to agree that humanities offer soft skills and no value and that they are not instrumental for knowledge, life in a democracy, postindustrial capitalism, and so on. Some of these issues were raised in Gordon Hutner and Faisal Mohamed's collection *A New Deal for the Humanities*, which rightly suggests that the changes required are nothing short of a New Deal in importance and size. The urgency for it should only intensify as stakes are as clear as they were in 1933.

What we do

Given the context, what we can argue in a book like this one is the question of what it means to *do* (in the many versions) humanities/literature scholarship in an institution of higher learning, and for this reason, we focus on it alone. This chapter will evaluate several common claims, ranging from the numbers of faculty lines and attitudes literary scholars hold to theoretical concepts of what the specific characteristics or methodologies, the object of study, and goals of literary studies are. The general proposition that will unite the critiques is that we are what we *do*—and what we do in literary studies is interpretation. We are also what we *do* in various contexts, and in respect to extra-academic knowledge production, which we can serve not by fostering soft-skills, as the common argument goes, but through theories of interpretation or metadiscourses that can bring knowledge production together and define what we should call "cross-cutting" skills that do not rely on the traditional divisions between disciplines and cultures of knowledge (Jay, *Humanities*).

The approach of defining literary scholarship in terms of practice has been tried in Michael Bérubé's *The Employment of English*. Bérubé focuses on blending "the intrinsic with the extrinsic, the literary with the nonliterary;" and suggests that "departments institutionalize a mode of reading that asks after the production, reception, and social effectivity of texts"—the famous *what* and *how* text means (4). However, Bérubé's *doings* have a limited scope. They include reading literature and other cultural materials. But in such readings, they produce new binaries between humanities and sciences, reinstating the nature/culture dichotomy. The frames limit poststructuralism to a humanities theory, barring us from trying to envision a common or shared scientific approach.

After establishing the terms for rearticulating specific aspects of what we do in literary studies, the theoretical basis for my intervention will follow in the second part of the chapter, through a reading of Jacques Derrida's essay "The University Without Condition." The reason to turn to Derrida's work lies in the title idea of limitlessness and the traits of his deconstruction, which can be defined as a strategy to identify, confront, and open up totalitarian tendencies. The opening is not just an intellectual move but a way to build broad new coalitions and allegiances and reorganize the existing hierarchies that define literary studies and turn them into intersectional convergence directed against totalitarian ideologies within and without.

Numbers

In his *The Humanities "Crisis" and the Future of Literary Studies*, Paul Jay has made a forceful case for reinterpreting the "crisis" and placing it in proper historical perspective. Jay's work was published in 2014, before the contours of the recovery from Great Recession very fully visible, before Donald Trump's presidency, and before the covid pandemic. Jay also makes the same mistake that Bérubé does in an essay published around the same time, "The Humanities, Declining? Not According to the Numbers." Both interpretations lack context. Both use numbers without sufficient precision, and their account is based on false equivalences among humanities departments. I will here offer a different picture, where the core humanities departments—literature and education together with philosophy and history—have a similar fate. Only communication and media studies are on the uptrend, closer to the general rise in the sciences.

The relevant situation is captured in Figure 1.1 from the "Preliminary Report on the *MLA Job Information List*, 2017–18," published by the MLA. Office of Programs. The graph shows the discipline's trajectory over the last 40 years in terms of institutional resources reflected in the number of jobs advertised in the *MLA Job Information List*.

The story is of the well-known, dispiriting, steady decline. In 1975–1976, there were a total of 2,965 jobs. In 1989–1990, we reached an all-time high with 3,948 posts. In 2017–2018, we were lower than we started, with only 1598 advertisements. In 40 years, we declined by a whopping 50%, while national trends saw a steady increase in faculty hires (Hinrichs). A different source, the National Center for Education Statistics, offers a complementary account with the number of conferred degrees. We went from 58,520 majors in 1975–1976 to 65,344 in 2014–2015 (English from 41,452 to 45,851, and Foreign languages and literatures from 17,068 to 19,493). While not as stark as the number of advertised positions, the statics supports the view that in the last 40 years, the profession could not grow.

This inability to grow is even more worrying when we consider that other disciplines fared very differently. In the same period, communication, journalism, and related programs rose from 20,045 to 90,658 majors. As did engineering, from 38,733 to 97,852, and health professions from 53,885 to 216,228. Psychology went from 50,278 to 117,573; social science and history from 126,396 to 166,971. Finally, business went from 143,171 to 363,741 and is the field with the highest number of conferred degrees. Education is the only other field besides literature without significant growth, decreasing from 154,437 to 91,596. Philosophy has gone from 8,447 to 10,157. Social science and history numbers are listed together, and they show a similar small increase from 126,396 to 161,230. All this while the overall number of students attending postsecondary institutions more than doubled from 9,037,000 in 1979 to 19,924,000 in 2018. The expenditure for the postsecondary degree-granting institution, in current dollars, also increased more than tenfold, from $38,903 million (or 2.3% of the G.D.P.) in 1975 to $583,000 million (or 3.1% of the G.D.P.) in 2016.[8] (The category that shows exponential growth is "Liberal arts and sciences, general studies, and humanities," which went from 18,885 to 43,661. The category is an outlier that concerns a relatively small number of students. Added to the number of literature, philosophy, and history majors, it does not change the downtrend.)

30 A theory of interpretation

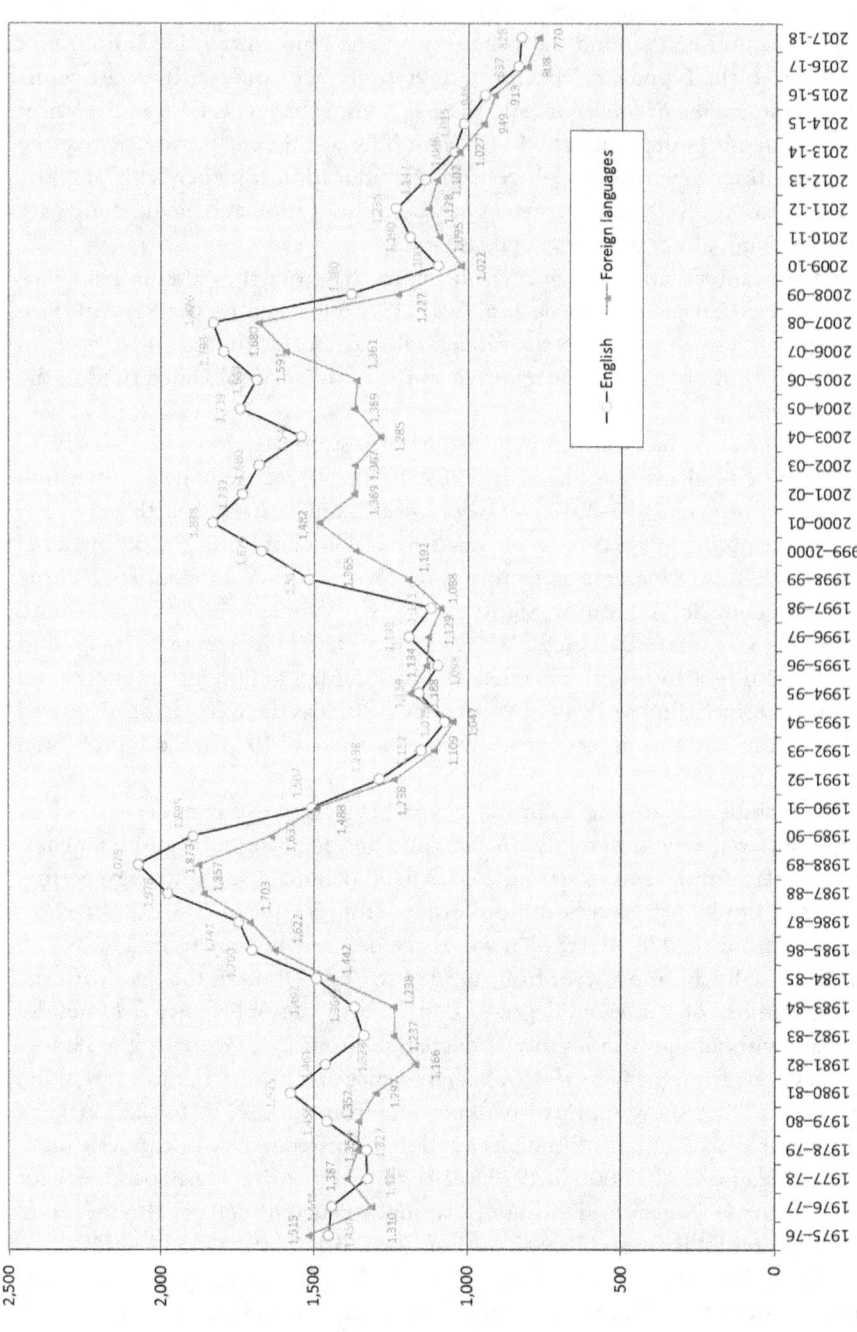

FIGURE 1.1 Number of positions advertised in the *MLA Job Information List*, 1975–1976 to 2017–2018.

The overall growth makes the stagnation and reduction in faculty positions in literary studies and humanities that much more alarming. We should note here the following, too: the MLA does not track data on teaching staff or literature majors. In decades that are supposedly defined by data analysis, MLA follows only the number of students enrolled in language classes.[9] Moreover, they do that with great effort—I was told in a private conversation. That language classes no longer define what the literary studies are about does not seem to be of much concern.

The above numbers are evidence of the stark rate of decline of literature departments, evidence for the staying trend of that decline that is made worse because of the context of the growth of other university disciplines, increase in funds for higher education, and growth of the population attending universities. The diagnosis should be obvious: the teaching of literature is disappearing fast, and the trend will continue unless there is a drastic change. The most recent report, on the number of majors, published in the *MLA Newsletter* from Summer 2021 seems to finally recognize that the downtrend is not reversible (Townsend).

Image

From the data on the number of conferred degrees by the National Center for Education Statistics, we can conclude that the part of literary studies that is most threatened is the one that resembles Education most closely. The American Association of Colleges for Teacher Education has no doubt what the problem with Education is. The number one reason for the enrollment drops in education schools is "the perception of teaching as an undesirable career"—which aligns close with the general understanding of the American political space we described above as dominated by the polarization between totalitarianism and expertise (Will).

Since the same is the case with English and literature majors, we face a different kind of crisis than the one we usually identify. It is not that we do not professionalize our students enough, or do not prepare them for specific careers (or that our work is not practical). Instead, the careers that we *do* prepare them for (or the careers they believe we prepare them for) are the problem. The same conclusion is supported by the increase in degrees conferred by communication, journalism, and related programs with steady growth from 20,045 to 90,658. Students associate these programs with exciting and rewarding prospects.

The image problem is not an ephemeral issue, but a key political one. It is also not ephemeral when specific constituencies are concerned, and it is not one that we can rectify by improved websites.[10] It is also not an ephemeral issue in terms of self-understanding. We are swimming in a sea of misunderstanding and misnomers in just about every aspect of our work. We call ourselves the "Modern Language Association," though most of us do not teach language. Our departments are called English thought that is no longer what we teach or study, and our students do not become "Englishers" (Eaglestone, "Future" 111) or comparatists when they graduate. We do literary criticism, but our students do not become literary critics. We help them become better speakers and writers, but they are not public orators or authors when they graduate. If they can understand their culture better, they are not culturologists, and so on. We call ourselves liberal arts though no one seems to know what "liberal" stands for—we just know that we should deny any connection to "liberal" politics.

Just to remind you, we are paying attention to the "we" under the presumption readily agreed on, that *who we are* is important because the assessment of the situation in which literary studies finds itself very much depends on the way we define the subject that is threatened. What scholarship on the university and literature scholarship has done thus far along these lines has focused only on the scholarly or intellectual aspect of literary studies and has not included the more mundane practices of discipline and institution creation—although that aspect is exactly what parents and students see first. I will identify several ways to separate ourselves from other professions, including attitudes like the care that we ascribe to ourselves but deny others; assumptions that literary studies are beyond criteria and beyond profit; and so on. These assumptions and beliefs directly shape how we imagine the crises as well as how we do scholarship. The implication here is that the threat (specific to our discipline) could look different if we were not the discipline presented in the studies. With the positive possibility, the new understanding might make it easier to organize, be more flexible, and respond to the many threats more effectively.

Beyond measure

The next misconception concerning our collective identity we are going to look at is the assumption that what literary studies does cannot be measured. The reason to go to it at this point of our analysis is that it is regularly offered as a part of the above argument concerning the crises. The discussion will help us transition from the common approach to the one we want to offer that reframes the general argument in terms of the new set of concerns.

Many different iterations of it are summed up well in Leigh Claire La Berge short article from 2019 published in the *Los Angeles Review of Books*, which is an online publication that "seeks to revive and reinvent the book review for the internet age, and remains committed to covering and representing today's diverse literary and cultural landscape (*LA Review of Books*). A venue, in other words, of the kind literary scholars should use more to explain themselves to the public at large, which is the reason for our choice of this essay.

La Berge positions her essay as a response to the crises, which she describes this way:

> [T]he humanities, particularly as offered in liberal arts schools, are not cost-effective at scale. Even worse, that scale itself is dwindling along with

the country's college-age population: a million fewer students were enrolled in U.S. higher education in 2018 than were in 2011. The Department of Education predicts that college closures will "triple" and mergers will "double" in the coming years, and Moody's notes that 25 percent of private colleges now run deficits. ("Market Correction")

La Berge then offers the reason humanities should be spared such destiny, saying,

> The humanities have offered colleges and universities a way to be perceived as genuinely distinct from corporations and banks, even as they become more influenced by and dependent on those bodies. A university and a corporation's scientific research organization are different but relatable entities, but no corporation has anything like the "priceless" form of value that a Comparative Literature department offers. ("Market Correction")

The conclusion is that the humanities "cannot be valued or priced by any consistent metric" because what we do is "a form of conceptual elaboration that has as their structure a refusal of a predetermined outcome. This open reflexivity contrasts quite sharply with the ends-oriented logic of profit" ("Market Correction"). La Berge writes this based on, among others, Christopher Newfield's argument that humanities "actually *make money* for the universities because they cost so little to administer" (Newfield, *Unmasking* referenced in La Berge, "Market Correction") and that humanities serve to give a non-profit identity to the universities, helping their financial status in that way as well. Newfield's argument is, however, misleading since humanities do not "make money" in the sense that they bring into universities new funds that are not already there. The argument also rests on the role humanities *still* play in the general set up of requirements but could quickly stop playing in a different setup. Moreover, while the humanities may be cheaper than disciplines that require lab space and special equipment, we still cost a lot to administer, especially given that our classes tend to be small when they are writing-intensive.

To my mind, La Berge understates the threat facing the university when she behaves as if there is still time for explanations, negotiations, and pleas. She does that also by accepting the terms of the conversation about the university as they are set in the neoliberal or populist contexts where the measure of success is expressed as "value," and "value" is explained in terms of numbers and dollars. La Berge also consents to the university's portrayal as divided by disciplines, into sciences and humanities, and not as united by what all departments and programs do, namely, educate students. A practical consequence of such a framework is that it does not operate using the category of students, say of biology and English, but compares a nurse or a lab technician to an artist, which are job market-dependent professional categories. To consent to such a setup and framework is to lose the argument even before it is fully formulated. We thus cede the ground to neoliberalism and the totalitarianism that is piggybacking on it, making it impossible for us to explain on the scientific basis what universities *do*, which is educate. In choosing to participate in conversations on such terms, we are further undermining the university and our political position.

Instead of criticizing the neoliberal argument that purports that tertiary education is a form of training, we have to reject its premise and assert a different, scientific framework that presents universities as institutions of education.[11] We do not make artists, and we do not create nurses or engineers. At universities, we do the education part of building modern individuals, preparing them to become professionals of various kinds. They are then shaped further in professional contexts. To expect the university to do both, offer education and training, and do that on a minimal budget means setting it up to perform both of these activities poorly.

The suggestion of the separation between education and training might sound strange at this point. We are accustomed to seeing distinctions like training/education as unstable, and schools (business, engineering, nursing) have already transitioned to a model where training is integral to education and are successful at it. What we are arguing here, however, is that the nomenclature is by and large nonsensical. To train, universities have to be able to meet the conditions that the actual jobs professionals perform which they cannot due to the inflexibility of the educational setup.

Instead, we want to see training as defined by its context and therefore understand that training in a hospital or an engineering firm is an activity that is categorically different from even the same skill set exercised at a university. We do this rearrangement of the argument because we want to acknowledge the difference between these contexts out of which all other characteristics of each institution—education, training—come. Between educational institutions and corporations there is a categorical distinction. One is constituted to be adaptable, have a unique product or service, and be responsive to changing market conditions. The other is created to be the opposite, a pillar of society, an institution that helps create individuals and advance knowledge. Once the building is built, lab equipment bought, scientists/teachers hired, parameters are set for education and training such facilities can provide. Hence, the common expectation that one is "going to university to get a job" should be replaced with "going to university to become open, flexible, and trainable." To goal for modern individuals should be to become versatile and have an adaptable wide and deep skill set that would serve them in various economies and at different stages in life.

Becoming a nurse depends on a significant number of variables specific to the job. Indeed, there is a tremendous variety of what being a nurse entails, depending on specialization, type of facility, area (rural or urban), kind of patients, and so on that no institution can represent. The same goes for engineers and managers, with each company having its own product, service, and profile. In such contexts, broad cross-cutting skills—like wanting to learn; having effective interpersonal, organizational, and analytic skills; broad and deep understanding of the world—are perhaps the best preparations for training and specialization that can happen only in a professional setting. Internships are a part-way solution because they tacitly acknowledge universities' limitations as they take place in actual companies. We should continue thinking of them as practices that bring the university and economy together or practices that connect two categorically different kinds of research and development and offer new interdisciplinary possibilities, based on a shared recognition of what a university can and cannot do well in producing a capable workforce and citizenry. On these bases, we should attempt to rethink also the role of community colleges and the certificate education like the one called Google Professional Certificates offered by Coursera.

Research does not detract from thus conceived shared educational setup but enhances it since investigation or seeking and creating are the tertiary-level forms of learning. In pitting humanities against sciences and universities against the industry, neoliberalism is weakening all stakeholders' positions and doing it on purpose since divided are easier to conquer. If anything, we should argue that to thrive, corporations should learn from universities. Companies like Google are already attempting to do that, giving more autonomy to workers, emphasizing the learning component of work, the inseparability of technology, science, humanities, and arts, and so on. With the pandemic, one hopes that the time of top-down, cubicle-bound culture is past, and that we can instead move toward the notion of a more independent, equal, and collaborative workforce.

For these reasons, we have to accustom ourselves to understanding that universities are not disinterested, and the worth of the humanities is not beyond measure, but instrumental to all forms of learning, creating, and living in a democracy. Our interestedness is our most crucial characteristic underlying all others. We have essential stakes in the post-Enlightenment values of education, the pursuit of truth; independence; and equality—essential interest in creating a system in which training and what is termed practical education are undertaken in corporations, which we can then see as a part of a greater educational system or what are well-termed cooperative extensions. We also have an interest in making a profit based on the product (education, research) we create. Insisting that our work is immeasurable or evades consistent metrics is absurd. It supports fascism, like saying that a kind doctor has the same value as a rude one; that a well-designed tool is just as useful as a poorly made one; that a commonwealth is the same as a society engulfed in fascist chaos. There are also, just as obviously, ways in which we are implicated in profit-making, capitalism (colonialism and racism, too), which universities have supported historically and continue to benefit from. We should embrace profit opportunities while recognizing how universities gained from discrimination, seeking not to repeat the same.

In what I do, I do not want to stand in the way of the logic of profit since there is nothing a priori incompatible between it and my teaching, research, or the theory I use. As Daniel Zamora put it recently, "Critiquing neoliberalism means not mirroring its own image of itself, but, on the contrary, deconstructing the mythology it's built for itself" (Boucaud-Victoire). While there are forms of profiteering—unfettered capitalism of Purdue Pharma's opioid campaign, racism that allots low-paying jobs to minorities, Trump University, and so on—that do not square with the values I propagate as an instructor or values I argue for as an author, there is nothing about the "ends-oriented logic of profit" as such that contradicts my way of being a scholar. Profit is a form of creation of value that we should recognize for the beneficial role it has in contributing to prosperous communities and societies. With language, markets are the most complex and fascinating of human creations. They bring the global community together and bring humanity out toward one another as they also shape who and what we are. Understood as a system, markets are as close as our species have gotten to creating a natural system's complexity. As the generator of qualities that can help further economic value production, the university has a fundamental and integral place in the economy. We should embrace that role and our interestedness even when our goal is to change the principles of distribution and make them more just. Based on my experience of the former Yugoslavia, I can say that if there is little to distribute, truth and justice mean little, too. I am also not disinterested in the many complex ways psychoanalysis can talk about concerning my plural investments and ties to the overall economy of meaning.

In place of the neutrality and lack of utility we will argue for the responsibility of professing below, in the part of this chapter on Jacques Derrida. Bringing the institutional position and its professional aspects into our discussion would readily ally us with other disciplines, which are similarly situated and consist, too, of professionals, researchers, professors, and scholars whose work is measured and evaluated, and so on. Moreover, beyond the confines of the university, such self-understanding would reveal alliances with other employees, workers, creators, union members, and so on, who, too, are not just laborers but engaged in forms of knowledge production in their own right. The most direct route to establishing relations with workers without university degrees would not be finding ways to "warehouse" them or include them in our classes, but to include them as they are by changing the limit between academic and non-academic knowledge production, this especially in the so-called rural counties that, by definition, are already decentered.

Coalition-building on such a basis would help us deal with the most insidious aspects of the crises. The fact that private and public, small and large, rich and poor state schools were all impacted differently (Brown and Hoxby). The Ivy Leagues and "Ivy Plus" colleges continue at the height of their power and prestige, with their literature departments and liberal arts colleges doing quite well (except for being able to place their graduate students in tenure track positions). Small private colleges are exposed more than any other kind of institution (Lamb and Mbekeani). Public universities are gasping for funds, but their schools live in two or three different financial cultures, with some prospering from government funding and student demand and others on life support. In the past 30 years, institutions with large endowments and stock market investments have significantly benefited from the trends.[12] Their success has set them apart from the rest of the group, aligning their interest, at least in part, with neoliberalism. When the financial crisis destroyed or damaged poorer, smaller, and some public institutions, it also weakened the whole system, making education, science, and expertise an easier prey for Trumpism.

A university coalition has to involve more general interests, like the social contract, but also the labor aspect of our profession, which itself can be combined with an even broader coalition and the confrontation with the totalitarian and neoliberal ideology that seeks to disempower experts and the impact of expertise on politics, culture, and economy. As we will explain in more detail in Chapter 5, this can be done by making collaboration into a separate area of study and an interdisciplinary specialization in its own right.

Interestedness of this kind does not predetermine political affiliation. If the university is in its foundation against totalitarianism, this does not translate into all scholars necessarily being leftist. After all, there is totalitarianism on the left, too. Party-based understanding of politics is limited and limiting, and it seems more advantageous for university constituencies to be for politics as coalition-building. If a professor is a Trumpist, as some are in business schools, the affiliation goes directly against their interests as professors, though it may have other benefits, psychological and economic, in the short run. Psychological benefits come from reinforcing a fantasy that one did it on his own, through sheer greet and tenacity, where the individual's material wealth is the proof of the success and character. The narrative is social Darwinism mixed with evangelical and Medieval stock scenarios, lone hero or a band of brothers against the world. It is no wonder that neoliberalism resonates so well with the populist, racist, nationalist, and military narratives that, too, harken back to knighthood and chivalry and hierarchies justified by social Darwinism. On realizing this, our response should not be, however, to discredit the belief as delusional and racist—such was Frederick Douglass's story, too—detrimental to the commonwealth and democracy as we commonly do, but to recognize the valor and the "self-reliance," its importance and contribution to the collective well-being while also seeking to reframe the conversation. We should celebrate individual responsibility and effort as a part of a different story about success in terms that avoid the binary public/private, individual/collective, competition/welfare which supports and sustain the neoliberal, totalitarian, and evangelical hierarchy of values.

University's lack of neutrality does not imply a kind of politics, only that modern universities requires specific conditions to operate, and when its freedoms are not protected in law and fact, its disfunction adds to existing social crises, making us all easier prey for totalitarianism.

Attitude

A corollary of the above critique is that we should also be critical toward attitudes that lead to further discord between institutions and professions. Unfortunately, literary studies has a history of defining itself against not only sciences but just about anyone who is not us.

To illustrate how literary studies does that, I will briefly compare two *PMLA* editorials from March issues published more than 20 years apart, one from 1998 and one from 2020. While the two differ on specifics, they stubbornly repeat the same strategy of defining who we are in opposition to another group. I am choosing my examples not to explain each but to give some concreteness to my analysis and to illustrate a trend.

The editorials are not representative of scholarship in literary studies—to that end, we will analyze scholarly work at the end of this chapter. Instead, they show an even more pertinent aspect when interdisciplinarity is concerned since it involves the creation of a self-image in relation with other constituencies. In what I will say, I will not comment on the content of Martha Banta's critique, which has merits, and want to accent what she says after it, and what, in my judgment, is an inaccurate and counterproductive portrayal of another profession.

The March issue of the 1998 *PMLA* editor's column written by Martha Banta is about the gap between "mental" and "metal" work. It is titled "Mental Work, Metal Work," and the author's goal is to "lessen the tensions that set" one "at odds" with the other (Banta 200). Banta does that by, first, analyzing two prior models of bridging the gap—W.E.B. Du Bois's argument concerning a new model of black intellectual manhood (203) and a woman in a "crisp white lab coat" (204), both transgressing traditional boundaries defining intellectual work. Banta's actual target, however, is the two-year study by the Council for Aid to Education (CAE), which is a part of RAND corporation.

About the study titled *Breaking the Social Contract: The Fiscal Crisis in Higher Education*, Banta says that Taylorism and Fordism pervade it, that the report takes the experience of the engineer and the manager as representative of the American work world, and that it sees education from that perspective alone. Supporting the criticism are phrases employed by the report that show the biased framing—phrases like "the kind of restructuring and streamlining that successful businesses have implemented," "improve productivity," "a systemwide process for reallocating resources among departments and other parts of the institution," "focus on their core competencies- the products and services they supply at a better quality and lower price than their competition," "a concerted effort to generate data on the costs and benefits of providing different services," "move toward systematic performance-based assessment," and "timely 'profit and loss' information" (Council for Aid to Educ. 3, 16, 17, 19) (Banta 205).

Banta then goes on to make another point that does not follow from this criticism, a point that concerns moral qualifications and categorical differences between, on the one hand, the subject of, and behind, *Breaking the Social Contract* and, on the other hand, us, professionals working in literary studies. These claims also go against her column's declared goal to "lessen the tensions" between mental and practical work (Banta 200). Banta says that while *MLA* members are guided by intellectual passion and care (207), the report is led by "cool rationality" (205). While we are devoted and selfless, they are the opposite. She writes, "it is possible to shake free from the fatalistic idea that mental work will always be at a disadvantage to the metal work privileged by the steely principles of scientifically managed administrations," and "[t]he scholarly community is what *PMLA* has to serve first, and the journal's primary task is not so much to alleviate the general public's misunderstanding of or uninterest in the scholar's life as to encourage the scholar to care, and to care deeply" (Banta 207).

To be clear, it is an important scholarly work to identify a bias in what is supposed to be a neutral assessment of education like *Breaking the Social Contract*. It is something else entirely to characterize the discourses according to the level of care and passion their authors display; do that using claims that are neither explained nor substantiated, and under the overarching assumption that the goal of a scholarly and professional forum is not to inform the public but to set moral imperatives for its members with the academic profession described as defined by "caring."

In comparison and fortunately, Wai Chee Dimock's recent column is muted and strategic.

Dimock addresses the opioid epidemic and explains the topic's concern as an example of humanities "raising" to the challenge (Dimock, "Opioid" 234). She offers several examples of how literature might do that, starting with the role of narrative in recovery, literature as a vehicle of making "their" stories become "our" concern, and ending with an analysis of the rhetoric (opiophobia/overprescribing but also of pain) accompanying the epidemic. But Dimock, too, ends with an unexplained and unsubstantiated opposition. On the one side are we, participants in an interdisciplinary approach, allies to patients in pain, and on the other, "the current state of health care in the United States," which makes it hard "that this new materialism [a form of working together defined by humanist scholars] would ever be implemented" (238). Perhaps by "the current state of health care in the United States," she does not mean doctors, nurses, and support staff that are tirelessly working on the epidemic and will die in numbers from the coming covid pandemic.[13] She may have in mind the Trumpian attempts to defund the Affordable Care. But the lack of precision shows the same mindset that produces ghosts and enemies to prop itself up. Indeed, the conspiratorial attitude represents the world as us/them, caring and not caring, allies and enemies—not far from Hilary Clinton's "deplorables" who, in a turn of events, happen to be also the class most impacted by the opioid epidemic and the constituency we are there to help.

The column also glosses over those substantive scholarly and political issues that would make scholarship interdisciplinary and collaboration easier. For instance, which shared epistemology does S. Scott Graham's "rhetorical-ontological inquiry" rests on? An omission is that much more obvious since Graham's work Dimock refers to as her primary example of literary studies scholarship centers on precisely the ways that discourses about pain can be integrated. Graham's book, *The Politics of Pain Medicine*, is exemplary in this regard, showing acute awareness that investigating "how to conduct" multidisciplinary analysis is integral to "an exploration of pain medicine" (Graham 7). I will return to it at the end of this chapter for a more concentrated look.

We often say that confrontation is a pedagogical model literary studies prefer—the position was argued recently in Natalie Melas's contribution to *The Values of Literary Studies*. In "Afterlives of Comparison: Literature, Equivalence, Value," Melas has one specific aspect of literature in mind, its outmodedness or its belonging to a different time and place, often also to a different culture. As Melas writes, "[o]utmoded objects, things 'that begin to be extinct,' remain as testaments to the unrealized aspirations and promises they once represented and as potential reservoirs of utopian impulses persisting in bygone forms" (187). The same goes for critical self-reflection, the so-called feminist "kill-joy" (Ahmed), or "culture of dissent" (Nussbaum). But trouble ensues when confrontation shifts from being one among critical and pedagogic tools to the default way we operate as a profession or the main prism through which we understand ourselves and others.

My politics

My goal here is to comment on certain tendencies and habits as they shape the profession. I will now briefly define my politics and will do that because it is integral to—though not crucial for—my argument.

As far as my political orientation is concerned, I agree with Greg Lukianoff and Jonathan Haidt's *The Coddling of the American Mind: How Good Intentions and Bad Ideas are Setting up a Generation for Failure*, which I find the most complete project of its kind in how it brings together teaching, goals of education, and a critique of those. In short, it recognizes the issues of cancel culture, microaggressions, and other contemporary phenomena as detrimental for the fundamental goals of education, free debate, and emancipation. The politics is not only in precepts but, more importantly, in the means by which we propagate and profess. I can accept the following recent leftist concern as my own: while there are racist cops, a likely more productive approach is to focus on racist behaviors, aspects of police training that lead to these, identify them and work on modifying them as specific behaviors. While there are racist students, historical facts and learning the complexity of historical records make views and positions broader and more open and may undermine mind blocks and entrenched habits. Black lives matter more when the slogan is used to lessen the division "us/them" through, for instance, community-building.

I see the strategy I follow in my politics as outlined in Ta-Nehisi Coates revolutionary "The Case for Reparation," which makes a case for a fuller historical record, reparation, reconciliation, and the nation's (not only African American) healing as part of linked processes (Coates). This is also what the Civil Rights Movement, specific feminisms, and some liberation movements teach under the heading of community- and coalition-building (Van Dyke and McCamon). Calling what Coates is doing patriotic and adopting the American flag as its symbol would be the next step in reframing current divisions and terms of conversation—though, of course, such a move would still have to account for the Native American experience.[14] White stars on the purple background started to signify for me at the time while I was living under a very different banner. I readily identify in them the kind of freedom Henry Louis Gates Jr. and Nellie Y. McKay speak of in their preface, "Talking Books," to *The Norton Anthology of African American Literature* where they link the specifically American yearning for freedom to the literary production of slaves and their descendants (Gates and McKay). I cannot agree more because I see what they say as a unitary or universalizing goal. If America is to become the land of the free, the meaning of "freedom" will be defined from its historical margins, internal, as well as external—more on this in Chapter 5 where we will read Susan Buck-Morss's *Hegel, Haiti, and Universal History*. Susan Neiman's timely *Learning from Germans: Race and the Memory of Evil* provides pointers for working through the totalitarian past, how a new patriotism (my term) may come to replace the old kind based in racism that should have been defeated with the Confederacy in 1865.

This politics are relevant for my argument because the practice of integration and universalization defines both. And vice versa, the goal of my politics is the same as my scholarship's, namely, creating community and shared culture where there was not enough of such practice before or where such practice was limited because focused on specific values. If shared or universal interests are foregrounded, we scholars have a better chance of not closing ourselves to what might reach even our fascist neighbors.

Empathy

The misconception that literary studies teach empathy comes together with the assumption we just identified that care distinguishes us from other disciplines and professors of literature from other professions. An influential opinion piece published in *The Washington Post* by Cathy N. Davidson offers a version of this argument focusing on how useful humanities can be for businesses. Google is the company of choice, and its preference for soft over hard skills the subject. Davidson writes,

> In 2013, Google decided to test its hiring hypothesis by crunching every bit and byte of hiring, firing, and promotion data accumulated since the company's incorporation in 1998. Project Oxygen shocked everyone by concluding that, among the eight most important qualities of Google's top employees, STEM expertise comes in dead last. The seven top characteristics of success at Google are all soft skills: being a good coach; communicating and listening well; possessing insights into others (including others different values and points of view); having empathy toward and being supportive of one's colleagues; being a good critical thinker and problem solver; and being able to make connections across complex ideas. (Davidson et al., "Surprising Thing")[15]

Here, the context is defined by STEM as well as by the Google employee cohort (who are a privileged group in every way) and cannot be generalized. If Google benefits from something, this does not automatically mean that other companies would or could, although it is understood in just such a way.

Further, Google's ostensibly surprising discovery that "empathy" and communication were among the most valuable skills could reflect their overall ethos, a preexisting lack of collegiality, that itself can have any number of causes. Indeed, it is a well-worn trope that technology workers lack social skills. This points to the even bigger problem with Davidson's piece: the assumption the soft skills are somehow related to the humanities but not to science or technology— as David Daming recently offered in his opinion article, suggesting that students would not have "valuable soft skills' like problem-solving, critical thinking and adaptability" without the humanities (Daming).

In no small measure, soft skills are cultural, as are most notions of interpersonal relations, decency, listening, and so on, which depend on family context more than they do on disciplinary regimes. We can claim that the atmosphere of the humanities departments is more inclusive, except that we do not have evidence. Some are, some are not—and some are because they feel threatened, not for reasons of genuine openness. It is equally inaccurate to say that by teaching technology, engineering departments are hotbeds of rootless individualism. Though humanities courses examine attitudes and cultural constructs about interpersonal relations, we cannot also claim to inculcate these no more than we can claim to possess these traits ourselves. The covid pandemic has shown us the face of professors we have not quite seen before (Hartocollis, Kellermann). While the situation is complicated, there is a lot of "me first" attitudes among the humanities faculty—perhaps less, if I can judge, among engineers and nurses.

The diagnosis Davidson offers is off mark for other reasons as well. While they believe in their exceptionality, there is nothing special about the Silicon Valley companies. Based on Anna Wiener's recent essay, all the cool startups are remarkably like older businesses (Wiener). Although they try to seem different, nonchalant, and egalitarian, they are top-down, exclusive, mostly male, and maintained by the belief in self-importance. They are, in other words, defined by institutional, corporate culture and structure more than by any other aspect of their work and need to be approached as such (even when they represent positive trends and are more like academia than older corporations).

If Davidson's essay was trying to speak to the industry in a language they could understand—empathy, soft versus hard skills—her strategy is still wrong. The best we can do is be true to what we are as a discipline. In this case, that would mean, as Paul Jay has shown, demonstrating how inaccurate, ineffective, and detrimental to business it is to continue understanding skills in terms of the binary soft/hard. Instead, as Jay has done, we can reframe the conversation and organize it around transferable, transitional, and cross-cutting skills— i.e., the skills that help us make connections and learn (Jay, "Humanities"). A different argument can be made of universities learning from corporations how to organize effectively and of corporations learning from universities how to increase their creativity, social responsibility, and happiness of their employees. The recent *The New PhD: How to Build a Better Graduate Education* by Leonard Cassuto and Robert Weisbuch offers some attractive proposition precisely because it tries to broach traditional divides with, for instance, the suggestion that humanities PhDs can do better what the MBAs are supposed to do.

Plurality of allegiance

The above-explained attitudes and expectations define us as a profession but are not usually a part of the conversation about humanities and literary scholarship. At this point, I will move away from those and toward my main topic relating to the theoretical issues that make literary studies.

Rónán McDonald puts it beautifully when, introducing his collection, he says that we are a discipline with a "plurality of allegiance":

> Of course, literary studies is not one thing, and neither are its values. A typical department of English or comparative literature might include one faculty member working on a research-funded project with colleagues from the sciences on neurological dimensions to narrative, another researching the philology of Icelandic quest narratives, another working on performativity and gender in relation to contemporary urban street theater, and another working on neglected social histories of Jacobean chapbooks. All these projects are informed by diverse agendas and methods and would provide widely different accounts of their *raison d'etre*. Each might have a different sense of the sort of knowledge acquisition, or "truth," it gives and what good that might bring to society. This plurality of allegiance is especially potent given the tendency of literary studies to ally itself to other disciplines such as history, politics, sociology, philosophy, and cultural studies. (McDonald 3)

The definition is offered in the context of realigning a response to the crises from a general humanities apology to a new track of what is specific to departments and disciplines. He comes to this conclusion by noticing, first, the contradiction between the qualities in humanities scholarship, which tends to be precise and specialist oriented, and the language that scholars would need to address the relevant audiences, like "the cold eye of policy makers, government officials, and prospective students" (McDonald 1) or saying that the case to be made should differ by discipline (McDonald 2). However, the two observations could have led McDonald to make a very different argument just as well. Not one based on specialization and the value *in* literary studies, but one defining the common good and doing that in terms humanists could readily communicate to sciences and lay audiences. Here, one can see again the presence of the "cold" trope as the quality we associate with those we perceive as our powerful other.

Choosing the value *in* literature, McDonald confirms the usual way of thinking. The value *in* literature is not just the value we find studying literature but also *internal to* literary studies. Whether this was or was not his intention, McDonald tacitly admits that what associates us with "history, politics, sociology, philosophy, and cultural studies" (McDonald 3), is not something of those disciplines but something *in* or about ours. On the flip side, the same "plurality of allegiances" is, then, a discipline that uses its manifold to distinguish itself from the lot. The plurality, this is to say, does not serve to connect us to others but to set us apart from them.

This tends to be the case in general. Literary studies are plural, but only in terms we are familiar with. The result is that our allegiances stretch only so far. While there are many thriving interdisciplinary journals—say the exemplary *Eighteenth-Century Studies*, which is housed at my institution, the University of New Hampshire—they operate based on a limited notion of interdisciplinarity restricted by periodization and a general historicist or cultural studies approach. Most interdisciplinary journals in which literary scholars regularly publish evince the same attitude and paradigm and do so without much deliberation about the criteria of what does and what does not constitute interdisciplinarity in general. We will continue this discussion of a period-based journal in Chapter 3 after we analyze peer review.

The conception of culture and multiplicity these publications are premised on, as *American Quarterly* announces, are "broad," and they are sources of distinguished scholarly reputation.[16] However, they are interdisciplinary and plural in the sense that they have moved beyond the rigid disciplinary distinction that, somewhat paradoxically, predates the culture wars and the dominance of the cultural studies/historicist paradigms. If topics we are interested in (neurology, philology, street theater) are considered interdisciplinary, this is the case because the model of disciplinarity we measure us against is an outdated New Critical monism that takes "literature" or "text" as its sole object—though New Criticism may or may not represent that paradigm (North).[17]

Even in journals devoted to explicitly interdisciplinary topics like climate, that by definition include the sciences and social science, we are rarely interdisciplinary on any bases besides that of cultural studies or historicism.[18] Much the same is the case with digital humanities that, too, tend to include science and technology as interpreted by a literary scholar. A case in point is the recent special issue of *PMLA* on DH that comes with many different approaches but not with an actual essay on the contemporary trends in big data studies or one arguing for a comprehensive approach to literary studies *and* digital technology. (We will return to DH in Chapter 4.)

We do not regularly publish outside areas of broadly conceived cultural history and our expertise tends to be limited to it. Hence, when our subject matter—take memory, for instance—is a subject of sciences—say, cognitive or social science—we don't have an adequate system of regulation in place that would tell us when our knowledge is merely inaccurate and cannot be supported by empirical evidence or expert approach.

As a rule, literary scholarship is evaluated by similarly situated scholars who share our narrowly defined interests and training. The "plurality of allegiance" is, then, a kind of scholarly constellation that mainly literary studies recognizes—one that sees itself in opposition to an entity we define sometimes as "a coherent, unified, academic discipline with clear-cut substantive topics, concepts and methods that differentiate it from other disciplines" (Barker 5). It centers around the undefinable notion of "culture" or "cultural production" (Melas 176). It, too, does not include what are, in the context of convergence, called "divergent" disciplines—disciplines with little methodological or institutional overlap.

It is, then, more accurate to say that we are interdisciplinary on the basis of an amorphous definition of culture or, in a newer addition, a turn to activism or engagement, which predetermines the kind of allegiance literary studies can build with other disciplines. This approach and the way we constitute ourselves as a discipline appears to be interdisciplinary only in comparison to the previous paradigm and its understanding of the object of study. As such—given the poststructuralist directions in sciences and the fact that amorphousness is not a poststructuralist quality—many traits of our present work we think of as exceptional are obsolete and present obstacles to interdisciplinary cooperation. These, for our purposes, come under the common terms of postdisciplinarity and posthumanism which, once again, are expressions of specific ideologies and attitudes that cannot be shared by other disciplines.

The limitations to our multidisciplinarity, of course, may not be just our shortcoming and may also involve attitudes and characteristics of other disciplines and institutions. But that remark changes noting about our responsibility for what we do and how we do it.

Part II: theories of interpretation

From Small

In Part II of this chapter, we change gears from we-discourses to affirming a new basis for the identity of literary studies. We will also change our style from describing and diagnosing the problem to offering a prescriptive explanation. The trait of literary studies we will emphasize is not new, of course. It is presented in, for instance, Helen Small's *The Value of the Humanities* but, significantly, not as her central point. The reason to address Small at this point in our argument is to provide a link with the work on crises but to do so selectively, to offer both continuity and point to considerable differences in views. And we are now trying to build our theoretical point to start working on literary studies as a theory of interpretation which itself will give a basis for discussions in the subsequent chapters about how we can relate to other disciplines, what we can do for them, and how poststructuralist literary studies can contribute to the general creation of interdisciplinarity as a common form of knowledge production.

The case Small makes for interpretation differs categorically from her other main arguments concerning value because it, as she recognizes, is "not a claim for value." Small explains that the humanities is the "study of meaning-making practices of the culture, focusing on interpretation and evaluation with an indispensable element of subjectivity" (Small 4). We understand this proposition in a specific way, not exactly as she meant it, but close enough to it that we can claim a continuity.

First, the object of study of literary studies is not texts or culture but rather meaning-making practices. We focus on the interpretation, which we understand as how things get to mean what they mean. We also focus on evaluation, or what things that mean mean for other things. We also account for the element of subjectivity, but not in contradistinction to objectivity, itself understood as the dimension of meaning-making that sciences deal with. Instead, subjectivity is an instance through which meaning appears—subjectivity, too, is the result of meaning-making practices. As Percy Bysshe Shelley said, poets "are the unacknowledged legislators of the World" ("Defence of Poetry"). The general is made out of specific utterances, specific word choice, and specific word order. Subjectivity, in this case, is the necessary or originary, or unique aspect of language, which then becomes transformed or shared when an utterance is written down by the poet, heard by their collocutor, read and cited, and travels around.

Meaning-making, as we want to describe it, is not a creation of a property that words carry with them. Instead, meaning-making is the activity that brings together meanings, words, people, activities, subjectivities, objectivities, and so on. (More on this in the next chapter and again at the end of our Chapter 5 where we will offer a general view concerning the practices that unite meaning and matter.) Small's definition is useful for our purposes because it discriminates among the humanistic disciplines and gives us, literary studies, primacy in so far as literary studies is closest to literature, which in Western cultures is historically the privileged form of art and the treasure house of historical subjectivities. On this, Small foregrounds not interpretation in general but those aspects that have their singular expression in literature, emphasizing the artistic, creative, interpretative, and subjective elements of cultural constructions over time. Hence, we understand the subjective also in a sense specific to literature and its study—unique and unrepeatable.

The general argument is that interpretation is instrumental for the conceptualization of how we exist as human beings. This is not an assessment of value, just as Small says, because we define thus a way of comporting and being-in-the-world or ontology. With this quality, the humanities allow our knowledge, too, to be in the world, to be a part of the created world and not some observational tool at a distance from phenomena that scholarship describes from a discrete vantage point.

We will now move to a source that is closer to our approach than Small. We choose "The University without Condition" not just because of how it defines the university but also because of the misreadings it was subjected to. The difference between the standard reception and our reading will allow us to, at the same time, speak critically about current institutional trends *and* posit our different vision for how universities, humanities, and literary studies should be understood.

Without condition

"The University without Condition" was immediately popular among humanities scholars. In *English Studies*, Derek Attridge shows why when he reads the essay as if Derrida meant to affirm that the liberal arts are free of any constraints, be they political, social, or economic. For reasons that remain unmentioned, Attridge stops short of including value among the conditions. If the university is really unconditional, it is without any foundation or basis, even those we like, like values. Attridge also fails to mention other free forms that can be readily given as an example, like the free market, of the unconditional condition.

I mean to suggest here that we tend to read Derrida in a way that is familiar and supports our views. This is in direct contrast to the spirit of Derrida's work, where the position he assumes is meant to challenge his way of thinking. Without condition cannot mean without only some conditions—concerning, for instance, the object of study; what assumption we can challenge; and how disruptive we can get. Without condition must also refer to other conditions that enable us to criticize and give us safety when we do that. Equally, we cannot condition the research by a specific author and maintaining their integrity. The challenge must include being deauthorized by the very work we do (for instance, by reframing disciplinary work as interdiscipline).

We, the authors, appear as a condition, for instance, when we divide knowledge into specialization areas, define those based on our expertise, and stake the intellectual space in terms of, say, being Derrida specialists, having a command of French which allows us to access his work in a proper way, and so on.

As in many other works, the proposition from the title, "the university without condition," is not what Derrida argues for. It is not a motto. It is also not a claim that implies that the university must be an institution without a condition. The proposition is instead a possibility Derrida examines. The result is that early on in the essay, we reach the understanding that "without condition" cannot be fulfilled since it is undermined in the attempt to describe, institute, and guard the non-condition. In simple terms, without a condition can only be a result of many conditions, intellectual, financial, political, and so on. These conditions are necessary to secure the "without condition" state. They so compromise it that it appears wise not to have a university without condition but the precise opposite, an institution whose condition is spelled out publicly and protected, not to say privileged.

To be sure, maintaining without condition is a laborious and expensive process.

After reaching and formulating this paradox that nothing can meet the "without condition" condition, Derrida shifts focus to the agency (we) and professors' responsibility. The "condition without condition" practically disappears from consideration, and the condition of professing responsibly takes its central place in the argument. I take that the condition of professing is the essay's actual topic, its description the essay's goal as an alternative practice that can help us get nearer and nearer to the "without condition" condition.

Reading closely

Now that we have this initial general understanding of Derrida's essay as being about professing, we can go back to the beginning to read it closely and to show by these means why we read the essay in this fashion. (More on the same again when we get to review in the next chapter.)

The essay starts with Derrida reaffirming the goals of the modern (post-Enlightenment) university, following the European model, with him saying,

> This university demands and ought to be granted in principle, besides what is called academic freedom, an *unconditional* freedom to question and to assert, or even, going still further, the right to say publicly all that is required by research, knowledge, and thought concerning the *truth*. ("University" 202)

He soon qualifies the notion of truth, "The horizon of truth or of what is proper to man is certainly not a very determinable limit. But neither is that of the university and of the Humanities" (204). That is to say, the truth we are after is without limit or open, not just without conditions. It is limitless in the same way that the university's pursuit of knowledge and human growth are without end. (Limits will come back into play in the second defining moment of our reading below.)

However, the university without condition is also "without any power of its own." Its destiny is to "capitulate without condition, to surrender unconditionally." We read the quotes as a warning that if the university is to be genuinely without condition, it cannot be sovereign since it is defenseless and various interests, internal and external, can and do overrun it. In Derrida's words,

> [t]he university cannot claim a sort of *sovereignty* without ever risking the worst, namely, by reason of the impossible abstraction of this sovereign independence, being forced to give up and capitulate without condition, to let itself be taken over and bought at any price. (206)

The way out of the predicament—which posits the university as unconditional but open to manipulation—is to arm the university by employing outside institutions to protect it—to, as we suggested above, protect higher education by law and policies that would be non-intrusive and ensure its economic stability and intellectual independence. This, however, leaves the university responsible to those outside agencies that guarantee its existence. It, too, leaves the university open to manipulation from the inside since nothing obligates the professors to profess in any specific way. The rest of the essay is, then, searching for ways to protect the university from both internal and external agencies, by making the professors responsible for what they do—addressing their "profession of faith, a commitment, a promise," based on an "assumed responsibility" (Derrida, "University" 209). The essay also turns from the quality—being unconditional—to the practice and process of professing or teaching, which Derrida uses as the general term for scholarship and all other activities professors do. The responsibility becomes central to our role, more important than "the authority, the supposed competence." It is "the guarantee of the profession or of the professor" (222). After all, the truth must be grounded somehow but not in a specialization since that would limit the truth.

The category under which professing responsibly is examined next, perhaps surprisingly to some readers, is work. Professing as work connects the university with its contexts, which, in the post-Enlightenment era, is defined as "the world." The most recent version is the product of globalization or, as Derrida calls it, *mondialisation*.[19] The reference for the discussion is the traditional dichotomy work/world presented in St. Augustine's *City of God*, where "the beginnings of the world originarily excluded work"—the world being a divine given. Work is introduced into the world through original sin with the effect that the "end of work" is also "the terminal phase of an expiation" (Derrida 223). After the fall, the general goal of professing is to correct the world by bringing work and the world into a new kind of relation, where work is a form of self-realization and a part of the force that creates human beings and separates them from the divine whom they, too, imitate in creating what was not there before. The secularizing task is uniquely suited for the humanists, and Derrida references Martin Heidegger and his "project" of freeing "being-in-the-world" from the Greek and Christian presuppositions (Derrida 224). Hence, the new task of professing is freeing the university from these religious and traditional (ethnocentric and so on) paradigms so it can assume its post-Enlightenment roles.

Also referenced is the *end of work* in the sense brought about by the so-called third revolution consisting of digitalization, automation, and artificial intelligence. Derrida follows Jeremy Rifkin (*The End of Work*) up to the point at which Rifkin refers back to the traditional solutions using the Christian vocabulary with Derrida commenting,

> the Christian language of "fraternity," of "qualities not easily reducible to or replaceable by machines," of "renewed meaning and purpose in life," of "renewal of community life," of "rebirth of the human spirit"; he even envisions new forms of charity, for example, "providing shadow wages for

> volunteering time, imposing a value-added tax on the products and services of the high-tech era to be used exclusively to guarantee a social wage for the poor in return for performing community service," and so forth. (Rifkin 291–293, Derrida, "University" 227–228)

That is, Rifkin, according to Derrida, harkens back to the tradition to describe the new global conditions of work in the technological era. This, then, serves Derrida to articulate his approach as openly leaning on the Christian vocabulary while reappropriating and redefining the system of values that it used to represent. In the place of the priest, Derrida argues for the humanists—the professors—who respond to the challenge with devotion. And their primary role is to secularize the world-work relation and wrestle it away from the Augustinian dogma but not from the truth as its goal. We will see a similar philosophical move again at the end of our discussions, in our last chapter, when we get to Bruno Latour's secular notion of systematicity. (In a parallel way, we can speak of work as labor and unionization as a form of both professing and coalition-building—provided they, too, have convergence and truth as their priorities.)

Derrida continues to present the figure of the professor in terms of faith and work, and singles professors out based on the particular dedication to what Derrida calls the "as if" or the "possible"—also termed messianic in other works like *Specters of Marx*—which takes the place of the god-figure while also preserving the context of devotion. Professing of faith in this context is not done concerning a deity or as a religion since that would be an intrinsic limitation.[20] It, however, takes place in the same direction, within a similar structure, facing the future, the possible, the yet to come, the "as if," with the similarity to priestly selfless surrender to the truth in its limitlessness. The truth is understood in the sense that whatever it is that will be found comes first.

It is only at this point in the transformation of the initial claim—after the selfless figure oriented toward the secular future enters the conversation—that we can return to the unconditional condition again, for reasons that should be obvious, since the church/university can be just as corrupt institution as any other. The unconditional condition is there to ward off the insularity of professing and its tendency to put institution ahead of knowledge.

The unconditional condition also undergoes a change. It now appears in a new way:

> It would be necessary to dissociate a certain *unconditional* independence of thought, of deconstruction, of justice, of the Humanities, of the university, and so forth from any phantasm of *indivisible sovereignty* and of sovereign mastery. (Derrida, "University" 235)

We take Derrida to mean that the sovereignty of university must be divisible or shared. Here again, we encounter the paradox that forced the discussion of the unconditional (university without limits) to focus on the act and process of professing. We read the ambiguity in a double way, referring to the mastery professors have over the material they teach and research, their so-called expertise, which is itself limiting the independence and limitlessness of thought. For as long as they put their interests (even their autonomy) ahead of their thought, they are not meeting their obligations. The sovereignty requires a political arrangement, an ivory tower separated from the rest of the society by the university's autonomy or an entity entirely under the political cap as it was, for instance, in the former Yugoslavia and other countries of the so-called Eastern bloc where the sovereignty belonged to the Communist party. Neoliberalism aims to create a similarly dependent university by evaluating it using criteria that do not come from education, teaching, and research but are imposed on it by "market" values which are taken to be the general values. If the university is genuinely and entirely autonomous (unconditional in that sense), its knowledge is limited, too, because it only answers to itself. And, vice versa, if the university is not truly independent, it does not perform its "cultural, ideological, political, economic, or other" role (Derrida, "University" 236) but acts on someone's bidding.

The discussion then focuses on the limit, as Derrida's often do, between the sovereign, separate university/professor, and the world of which it/they have to be a part. Here, however, he does not so much straddle the boundary, as his readers tend to see it. Instead, Derrida tries to open the structure of knowledge production, to get "exposed to reality, to the forces from without." This is done to "resist effectively" the isolationist tendency by "allying itself with extra-academic forces" that would help the university's goal—now defined as resisting "sovereignty" (Derrida, "University" 236). What needs to be resisted is not just the imposition and manipulation from the outside but also the same force originating from the inside, including professors calling for the university's autonomy.

If initially the unconditional was conditioned by sovereignty, now the new condition of the unconditional includes sharing by making allies outside the university and using these relations to counter the tendency toward autonomy and self-enclosure of each discipline. The reason this last statement is not a paradox (like the first one was) is that the relationships with the outside are not constant or consistent since the allies, due to the dynamic nature of the social, are continually changing, and we cannot fully know the effect these liaisons will have on the university. It is similar with the professor's relation to the beyond, which draws them to transcend what/who they are as professionals in their pursuit of truth. (In these terms, unionization can be a kind of freeing moment in so far as it provides an alternative form of gathering to scholarship and limiting in so far as unions tend to become absolutist.)

The stepping outside—and Derrida means it literally, too, "[t]he university without conditions is not situated necessarily or exclusively within the walls of what is today called the university" (Derrida 236)—also serves to realign the university's position in the world and constantly negotiate its relative independence.[21] The stepping out also leaves the university/professor open.

Following this discussion, we can address the frequently made claim that liberal arts education is central to a democratic society, which is also offered as an interpretation of "The University without Condition" in, for instance, the collection titled *Derrida and the Future of Liberal Arts* (Caputi and Del Casino Jr 2). When we argue such a claim, we also impose a specific political agenda on the humanities to maintain a deliberative democracy. As much as professors identify with this form of political organization as citizens, it, too, is a precept regulating and limiting the humanities; deciding for the inquiry what it should be, how it should unfold, and what results it should reach. Instead, Derrida suggests complex ways in which society and humanities would not limit but enhance one another, opening themselves to limitlessness. One thing that humanities need to be able to do—and the deliberative democracy model should not be forced to include total upheavals regardless of what Thomas Jefferson said—is to step outside themselves from time to time and radically disrupt their modus of operation.[22] And we should do this so that the society does not have to.

Academic?

In his essay's final act, Derrida asks if the exercise he presented was itself academic, failing to establish a relation to the outside. From our perspective, we can say that, of course, it was just such an example. Who else but academics could follow the meanderings of his thoughts? But, at the same time, the lecture did not quite follow academic rules. It did not offer support for its claims using the protocol that, for instance, Helen Small does in her work with extensive discipline-based commentary on other works on the same topic. Instead, Derrida offered, as I tried to show, a series of transformations of the initial claim, explaining parts of it and linking them to other subjects, that lead him to rephrase the original proposition. He thus preserved the core need for the unconditional while changing its realizations, looking for a way to bring the im/possible condition into his practice of writing and explaining and change what academic means.

In the following, we will understand this discussion of Derrida to have moved us from deconstructing specific conditions to looking for ways to keep sovereignty divided, and the system of knowledge production we are creating open to transformation and collaboration. If there is a way to not be academic and be scholarly, it, at this point in time, lies in that direction.

Bases

Following Derrida, on the one hand, literary studies cannot continue justifying what we do only on scholarly or intellectual bases and needs to formulate other criteria to evaluate our work in terms that are other to scholarship defined by disciplines. This is based on the pursuit of truth, which is the universal goal for both universities and democratic societies. On the other hand, because of this mandate to pursue the truth, professors do not have much choice but to support those anti-totalitarian political options that ensure universities can continue in their post-Enlightenment quest. And we must show our support publicly since that is a part of our social mandate and mission. Civil disobedience (Chenoweth and Stephan) could be our means toward that goal if nothing else works.

This does not mean that scholarship is a form of activism, however, or that just like that we can start identifying engagement as form of scholarship. Other than disciplinary concerns do not imply other than academic focus but require a different, interdisciplinary approach to education and scholarship that is open to extra-academic agencies, institutions, and concerns. Instead, at present, we can be scholars *and*, as private individuals, activists in a limited sense: fully submitting to the primacy of truth but also acting to overthrow the unbearable condition inconsistent with the post-Enlightenment values of equality and freedom, because these give support to our pursuit of truth. And doing so while also recognizing our limitations, the fact, one among others, that we cannot speak for everyone.

Europe and the United States faced challenges to the same system before and came out, after tremendous sacrifice, victorious. Third World countries were not as successful in their struggles, which also include colonialism and postcolonial dictatorships. The imbalance between results contributes to the current undermining of democracy and its guiding idea of the commonwealth. If globalization continues, it should be in these terms of the formulation of the new global social contract where what we can call a new Enlightenment would be undertaken as a universal and inclusive process.

Part III: literary studies

Principle

How this all translates into our understanding of literary studies we will begin to show by recalling the words of a reviewer of McDonald's *The Value of Literary Studies*, Andrew Bennett, published in 2016. We will first hear them as a useful summary of what literary studies are today.

> And yet, as Natalie Melas comments on the sub-discipline of comparative literature, although it is an 'amalgamated assemblage' that borrows from positivist and instrumentalist disciplines such as law, economics, political science, gender studies, and other fields, literary studies seems to be thriving even while it lacks a 'singular object' and a 'discernible set of methods.'

Bennett also adds,

> this lack of a clear disciplinary identity that energises the academic study of literature – an absence of definition and purpose that can indeed be seen to reflect the status of the literary object itself. (A. Bennett 1135)

I hope very much that we see why this account is not sufficient anymore and why we need to understand the study of literature in different terms.

Instead, we should argue that we have a clear disciplinary identity. We are the discipline that should have realigned literary object(s) around the same time that the literary subject—the author—died, in the early structuralist days when emphasis shifted away from the New Critical notion of "the text" as a sovereign source of meaning and instead "text" was understood to exists as a result of interpretative interactions. The creation of meaning is a complex process/practice that cannot be fully controlled or owned, and we are the discipline that understands that literary objects are like commodities, part of a general economy of meaning, ever in circulation and subject to change. Literary objects exist when animated by reading, when they become a part of reading practice, and enter into relation with the signifying beings to become objects of various activities. We are also that bold discipline among the first to claim that interpretative practices make objects, announcing what can be called the newest wave of construction theory (that started with Kant), according to which reality is dependent on the processes of interpretation. Today, we are entering a new phase of this theory and an attempt to see interpretation in its interaction with matter, indeed, as a form of matter.

And, no, the lack of clear disciplinary identity has not energized literary studies since at least the early years of the new millennium at which point it has become a symptom of a crisis: a disunited field at war with everyone and frequently itself. If at a point in time, right after the culture wars, we had a discipline that could successfully negotiate its own interdisciplinarity, even serve as a model, that, too, is no longer the case, not the least because other disciplines and the academic world in general have changed.

General relevance

Paul Jay has done a brave job distinguishing nonsensical and unsustainable definitions of what we do in literary studies. I will not go over his repertoire but will focus on the resulting point, which confirms what I just wrote above and adds a criterion we will call "general relevance." Jay says, "This kind of focus on reading practices is part of a larger movement in literary studies—and in the humanities in general—to foreground the practical value of training in close reading" (132). Using Jane Gallop and N. Katherine Hayles's work, Jay suggests that practice has to have a value that "lies in its applicability outside literature studies as a broadly social, cultural, and even political skill," informing a "general approach to our engagement with textuality across the discourses of the humanities—and the social sciences, as well" (*Humanities "Crises"* 136–137, Gallop 15), and includes "media literacy—and its analysis—broadly defined" (Hayles "How We Read," P. Jay 141).

If literature was the central cultural phenomenon, it definitively and irretrievably (barring a catastrophe) lost that status with the advent of digital culture. The result was the devastation of print media and professions defined by them like teaching literature, print journalism, and archival work. While the situation is changing and we do not quite know what the relation between the new and old media will end up being, it is certain that it no longer makes sense to insist on the literary, and to, instead, place the common practices of reading, writing, and interpretation at the heart of literary studies (which too can be renamed). Not only are these activities universally shared, but the approach based on them as objects of study is also philosophically more accurate. One can even go so far as to say that we never studied literature but always and only the meaning-making practices and forms of evaluation and classification.

We were always critical studies—deciding what things mean. Critical entails "involving or exercising careful judgment or observation." It forms words like "decide," "decisive," and "crucial." In math, it constitutes or relates "to a point at which some action, property or condition passes over into another; constituting an extreme or limiting case." In nuclear physics, it denotes "maintaining a self-sustaining chain reaction; esp. in *to go critical*, to reach the stage of maintaining such a reaction." Its etymology is "Greek κριτικός critical, < κριτός decerned, κριτός a judge; < κρίνειν to decide, judge" ("critical," *Oxford English Dictionary*).

The focus on reading practices is not without issues, starting with the basic ones of what constitutes them. We will face them in the next chapter. For the moment, suffice it to confirm the positive part of the solution, namely, that we can define literary studies in a coherent, simple, and unitary way that avoids unnecessary confusion and unfounded claims on multiplicity. It, too, avoids the outdated way of defining a discipline, around the object of study, and places, instead, a meaning-making or interpretative practice at the center, and does so in and for a context that transcends disciplinary concerns, allowing us to shift from print (and literature) because it/they no longer offer the organizing principle.

To clarify, the implication of the proposal is not that what we used to do is no longer significant. It is just that "asking literary questions: questions about the way something means, rather than what it means, or even why" (Garber 12 qtd. P. Jay 135) no longer means what it used to. But not because the method or the questions are out of date, but because the context has changed. When we defined these questions, their importance was self-evident because they were applied to an object—let us call it now an "aesthetic object"—that was a universal (Western) given. No one needed to prove the power of literacy, its dependence on the literary, since the national universe in which we read was defined in reference to the literary canon. Whether the nature of the universe has changed because of the end of the Cold War as Bill Readings has argued, whether neoliberalism has triumphed, whether the new technologies have altered the nature of meaning, whether we literature professors have something to do with the dismantling of the literary, we can no longer claim the same context, which is then to say that what we used to do, even if repeated verbatim, no longer has the same weight.

Then, the nature of the aesthetics has changed as well. The classical analytic of pleasant, beautiful, or sublime was broadened through the inclusion of the non-canonical works written by people who did not look like canonical writers or speak like them, through visual media, graphic novels, and then digital media, which introduced aesthetic specificities and the kind of objecthood alien to the Kantian vocabulary. Some attempts have been made to order the innovations and put together new aesthetics, for instance, by Sianne Ngai. I prefer the version of aesthetics that comes from trauma studies because it teaches us how to interpret in the absence of a coherent referential system. This is the approach to interpretation and interdisciplinary poststructuralism I prefer and will use throughout *Interdiscipline* as a model without acknowledging it beyond this point.

Here, briefly, is the description of that model, which provides the framework for how literary studies can be reconceptualized. I understand that trauma studies has gone furthest in revolutionizing literary studies because it offered a way to talk about exceptions, crises, and radical disruptions of frameworks. It did so as a version of poststructuralism, and in terms of establishing a new understanding of continuity, we can associate with open systems. Trauma studies also includes notable interdisciplinary examples that move beyond the additive form to present converging views—as in Cathy Caruth's collection *Trauma: Explorations in Memory* and Shoshana Felman and Dori Laub's *Testimony: Crises of Witnessing in Literature, Psychoanalysis, and History*. The same works were instrumental in disseminating poststructuralism, spreading storytelling, witnessing, and use of narrative beyond literary studies; in showing how to use theory and literature to comment on significant historical events in a new way (not without controversy, of course); in showing what a new discourse of politicization (in terms of witnessing) can be; and in showing how trauma can serve a new interpretive theoretical paradigm for determining what "text" is—namely, a practice—and how it means.[23]

The aesthetics of trauma studies is an approach that focuses on framing paradigms. It accounts for the materiality of meaning in different ways, considering what appears to be an object's mere aestheticism, the pleasure/pain it produces, the affect it contains, history it reflects, the vocabulary it makes available for talking about unclaimable or extraordinary experiences, and openings it creates for linking the extreme with the mundane (Ramadanovic, "Time of Trauma").

Interdisciplinarity without a discipline

I will end this chapter with a brief commentary on recent interdisciplinary works to specify the issues surrounding interdisciplinarity—what it is and what it is not or should not be. The first example is the already mentioned book by S. Scott Graham, *The Politics of Pain Medicine: A Rhetorical-Ontological Inquiry*. Graham's work is exciting but then also limited when it moves to actual interdisciplinary analysis, which displays a simplistic understanding of theory and offers stock insight regarding the issues of the medical system it analyzes.

Graham leans on philosophy more than on his discipline of rhetoric or composition studies and does that early on in the work as he has to clarify his methodology. His primary sources are philosopher Annemarie Mol and her *The Body Multiple: Ontology in Medical Practice*, and historian of science, Peter Galison and his essay, "Ten Problems in History and Philosophy of Science." The choice of sources is the first significant contribution this book makes concerning interdisciplinarity since philosophy and history of science are the two humanities disciplines with the most systematized insight into cross-disciplinarity. Second, Graham makes a bold suggestion that today's application of rhetoric to science requires first a thorough reorganization, even reinvention of the discipline of composition studies or rhetoric—his second book *Where is the Rhetoric? Imagining a Unified Field*, from 2020, pursues this direction. Graham's solution is a synthetic, or cross-disciplinary, discourse that he uses to reinvent and modernize composition studies. Third, Graham suggests that interdisciplinary work may need to go over the basics and build complexity gradually. Graham apologizes for the proposal—I see it as a necessity, a mainstay of creating interdisciplinary practices and will use it to develop *Interdiscipline*. Graham's work then falters when it has to demonstrate his suggestions in detail. Moving beyond the introduction, chapters are rehearsing superficial theoretical points, showing the author's lack of experience, expertise, and skill, which is, in part, understandable since *The Politics of Pain Medicine* was Graham's dissertation. The problem, however, is more profound and concerns the level of expertise in theory or philosophy, which has historically provided the standard language for cross-disciplinary conversations. Lacking it, it is hard to see how there can be any kind of disciplinarity beyond situationism, which is why *Interdiscipline* will try to create a common epistemology to compensate for the general lack of rigor and knowledge of philosophy in the United States institutions.

Here is also a brief commentary on a second example, this one of literary scholarship. I am choosing from October, 2020 issue of *PMLA* to record and qualify the present moment in the development of interdisciplinary. In the background of the essay we will comment on, we see a positive trend—scholarship that borrows skillfully from many disciplines to return to the study of literary texts—with the trend promoted, tacitly, as a new norm. The essay that opens the issue is titled "Flocking Together: Collective Animal Minds in Contemporary Fiction." It uses patterns like those made by birds and the associated metaphors to understand the bodily response. The author, Marco Caracciolo, offers this explanation:

> This article looks at how such embodied responses [Stephen Daedalus' attempt in James Joyce's *A Portrait of the Artist as a Young Man* to count a flock of birds "that readers are invited to trace in their imagination, kinesthetically"] to nonhuman assemblages are central to fictional narrative engaging with animals; how the social minds of herds, flocks, and packs can be expressed through verbal patterns that, like their visual counterparts, build on readers' embodied experience. (Caracciolo 239–240)

58   A theory of interpretation

For an essay to be interdisciplinary, the general rule is that the author has to explain either why the phenomenon is significant from another discipline's point of view or explain the middle or common terms, like pattern and metaphor. Usually connected are literary studies, philosophy, and a discipline like cognitive science that allows insight into how the human mind works. Caracciolo chooses all of the above, emphasizing rhetorical analysis of experience as it is presented in various literary works that bring together humans and animals as organisms and allow them to form a kind of collective.

The conclusion he reaches is, first, that the

> formal approach can be extended beyond the human domain, opening up an embodied route to appreciating human-nonhuman entanglements and questioning the very separation between human and animal life. (250–251)

Second, he suggests that "cultivating such embodied resonances for the natural world can deepen readers' sense of connection to the Earth's ecosystems." And third that "[t]hinking with nonhuman collectivities is [...] a central aspect of the answer" of how we rise to the challenge by Bruno Latour to tell a common "geostory" (Caracciolo 251).

The result is an integration of language, animal, and human and discourses from rhetoric to cognitive science to Latour's philosophy. The result is typical for a certain kind of contemporary literary studies that does not pause on the obstacles to integration and sees its success as creating a multiform. This pluralization is similar to our goal, and we are going to be careful here in explaining why we disagree with Caracciolo's way of making connections. In short, this is because he confuses suppositions with results and does not consider how the stories he has put together would look from the discrete points of view that he brings together. We can call it an interdisciplinarity without a discipline and without discipline.

In cognitive science, embodied resonance does not designate "inter" subjective relations but instead explain an *internal* or "intra" neurological mechanism underling the coincidence between performed and observed action. The process is described as "mirroring" (Gallese and Sinigaglia) because it happens *without* interaction between the observer and the observed. It involves doubling when the same brain area is activated during other behaviors with possibly some influence of the previous neural activity on the subsequent. For Caracciolo, the distance present in the cognitive models vanishes, internal becomes interspecies, and embodied resonance describes a situation that has no correlative in the sciences. Just like that, animals and humans, even the environment, are all in sync—thinking and feeling together.

The sciences do not support such understanding. Neither does Latour, whose work is one of Caracciolo's philosophical sources. For Latour, "geostory" is not built on symbiosis or any kind of harmony. Instead, it results from a new kind of narrative about the finitude of life on Earth and, perhaps surprisingly, on the supremacy of the whole over the elements. This version is more straightforward than the fusion Caracciolo describes because it is not predicated on crossing boundaries or doing things together, but on developing a point of view that recognizes how the whole is not the sum of parts. "Geostory" does not require us to think "with" nonhuman collectives, to share a body or experience, or to become many, only to understand that the system that sustains life is both immensely complex as well as precarious. In the wonderful lecture, "The Puzzling Face of a Secular Gaia," Latour explains James Lovelock's theory that ecosystem works without a design and that each of its elements, from viruses to trees and humans, functions autonomously as a distinct organism with what Lovelock called intentionality (Latour, *Facing Gaia*). Such system reaches homeostasis not because it is regulated by an external or some internal force or because there is some specific relation that develops between its elements—indeed, Latour is against the terms environment and harmony since they misrepresent how the Earth works. While we are used to seeing systems as organized, this is the dogma the secular view is supposed to shake us out of. Systems are systems because they persist—that is, there is something in their systematicity and form of endurance that has allowed them to function up to this point in time. Latour finishes the lecture by stating that the usual narrative of man in nature and the one he is proposing are different because in his version the background comes forward. The story, as Latour insist, is anthropomorphic, morphing or placing humans into a more realistic condition (chaos, cacophony come to mind as metaphors) as it is also a story that is decidedly told by humans to other humans. (More on it in the closing of this book.)

In Chapter 4 on DH, we will offer a similarly negative judgment of N. Katherine Hayles's work and much of DH for getting way ahead of what science can support. What follows from such line of criticism is a suggestion concerning what it is that literary scholars need to do to become interdisciplinary. Paul Jay's general suggestion was that our central discipline was critical theory and that we should become more critical (toward our own discourse among other things) and more theoretical. This is a good advice but suffers from an obvious lack of specificity and it, too, places too much faith in being critical. I still want to agree with Jay that literary scholars are in a unique position because of our proximity to language and meaning creation and philosophy, but we need to thoroughly rethink what it is that we do, what our place is in respect to other disciplines, and offer a new foundational narrative that addresses how our work can contribute to reinventing the classical scientific framework. Indeed, being critical when it means what it usually does—noticing elements that make up a point of view—is not sufficient.

Unfortunately, the same goes for what is called rhetorical analysis (by both Caracciolo and Graham) which figures as the main contribution of literary studies to analyzing scientific discourses. In many cases, rhetorical analysis simply means paying attention to terms used and does not include either a poststructuralist understanding of interpretation or analysis of frameworks. The deficiencies make the resulting criticism rather limited examples of what literary studies can do.

60 A theory of interpretation

In the next chapter, I will present several ways this transformation can take place, all of which are versions of and are built around interpretation. We will get to the literary scholar as translator or connector by understanding what close reading does when it is not limited by the New Critical "how" a text means or by our inadequate understanding of other disciplines. Our goal will not be to make the fusion possible by transcending particularities of discourses. On the contrary, we will draw on what is specific to literary studies and draw boundaries around discourses (for instance, in the form of peer review in Chapter 3) only to use those boundaries as channels of communication to bring disciplines together.

Notes

1 For views from other disciplines, see, for instance, Robinson et al. and Benneworth.
2 Collini's new *Speaking About Universities* is no exception in that it centers on the universities as a public good.
3 Few notable works disagree with the crises diagnosis, for instance, Braidotti, *Posthuman*; Donoghue; and Jay, *Humanities*. They, too, do not make a case for the reinvention of the humanities and continue to use the discourse to make their argument.
4 Brown defines neoliberalism as,

> a distinctive mode of reason, of the production of subjects, a 'conduct of conduct,' and a scheme of valuation. It names a historically specific economic and political reaction against Keynesianism and democratic socialism, as well as a more generalized practice of 'economizing' sphere and activities heretofore governed by other table of value. (W. Brown 21)

5 Karl Rove, one of the Republican party ideologues, actually said that this political system creates a reality:

> We're an empire now, and when we act, we create our own reality. And while you're studying that reality—judiciously, as you will—we'll act again, creating other new realities, which you can study too, and that's how things will sort out. We're history's actors … and you, all of you, will be left to just study what we do. (Suskind)

6 I prefer Applebaum's interpretation of Trumpism over alternatives that seem naïve and underdeveloped—like the view that conspiracy theories may be beneficial for democracies since "the same attitudes can work as a control mechanism, which is instrumental in preserving democratic institutions, as far as these attitudes keep the public vigilant and the élites under scrutiny" (Mancosu et al.); or the view that Trumpism was if not caused, then made possible "because established institutions—especially the mainstream media and political-party organizations—had already lost most of their power, both in the United States and around the world" (Persily); or the view that Trumpism is an example of populism (Brubaker).
7 See also The Simpsons episode "The Man Who Grew Too Much," Season 25.
8 Statistics sourced from the National Center for Education Statistics. "Bachelor's degrees conferred by postsecondary institutions," "Enrollment in elementary, secondary, and degree-granting postsecondary institutions, by level and control of institution: Selected years, 1869-70 through fall 2026," and "Expenditures of educational institutions related to the gross domestic product, by level of institution: Selected years, 1929-30 through 2016-17."
9 Looney and Lusin, "Enrollments in Languages Other Than English." See also "MLA Report to the Teagle Foundation."

10 In his recent opinion piece, "An examination of the strengths and weaknesses of the English major," Kent Cartwright offers the following:

> departments that have used their websites to showcase the major's attractiveness in catchy, even idealistic, ways have not lost as great a percentage of majors, it seemed to the committee, as have some comparable units. And the English department at Ball State University has completely rebuilt its number of majors, after substantial losses, by combining close attention to the undergraduate experience with innovative and systematic use of social media. (Cartwright)

I disagree with Cartwright's reasoning and think that his reading of evidence is selective. See also Ball State University's Department of English web page.
11 In her new book *Generous Thinking*, Kathleen Fitzpatrick proposes new forms of coalition-building to restore the lost trust.
12 See Mark Edmundson's critique of the trend in *Why Teach?*
13 Dimock should have referred to perhaps the legal system, not medical, or George W. Bush's DOJ or unfettered capitalism. See, for instance, Vivian.
14 Barack Obama used the term "patriotism" three times in his speech in Selma, Alabama, commemorating the 50th anniversary of the events of "Bloody Sunday." Among other things, he said, "What greater expression of faith in the American experiment than this; what greater form of patriotism is there; than the belief that America is not yet finished, that we are strong enough to be self-critical, that each successive generation can look upon our imperfections and decide that it is in our power to remake this nation to more closely align with our highest ideals?" (Obama). A not yet finished part would have to address the history of Native American genocides which opened the way for the American experiment.
15 See also McGurn. See also new article coauthored by Davidson and Katopodis.
16 See the description of *American Quarterly* on their web page ("American Quarterly").
17 One could argue that the measure which shows us as interdisciplinary is a comparison to other humanities disciplines like history or philosophy. Such explanation is based on poor understanding of these disciplines with history of science and philosophy being much closer to interdisciplinary epistemology than literary studies. We will discuss the two throughout *Interdiscipline*.
18 See Trexler and Johns-Putra; Alaimo, "Introduction."
19 "Unlike 'globalization' or *Globalisierung, mondialisation* marks a reference to this notion of world that is charged with a great deal of semantic history, notably a Christian history: the world, as we were saying a moment ago, is neither the universe, nor the earth, nor the terrestrial globe, nor the *cosmos*" (Derrida, "University" 224).
20 For more on Derrida and religion, see Coward and Foshay.
21 An example of universities outside universities would be plantations in the South, organized as tourist attractions. See Modlin Jr et al. A more usual example is responsible journalism. We can, too, envision cooperation with the industry through intermediaries like Makerspace.
22 "I hold it that a little rebellion now and then is a good thing, and as necessary in the political world as storms in the physical" (Thomas Jefferson).
23 I puzzled about how *Interdiscipline* should deal with Joseph North's *Literary Criticism*. In so many ways, it is a formidable project that could mark if not a turning point in literary studies, then the same in the context of recent efforts to reinvent, revise, and adjust. I have, however, fundamental issues with the book, starting with the division between aesthetic education and the cultural studies paradigm, which I find inaccurate. To use *Literary Criticism* as a landmark, I would have to wrestle with its too broad categorizations, generalizations, some too simplistic readings of primary materials, misunderstanding of Kant's aesthetics, and so on. Thus, my solution is the above paragraph which brings together aesthetic and cultural studies concerns under the heading of trauma and adds a dimension of theory and philosophy, showing the framing I prefer over what North offers.

2
MERE READING
Recasting hermeneutic epistemology in literary studies

Introduction

In Chapter 1, we saw how literary studies is not what it purports to be. Not that balkanized, multiple, interdisciplinary discipline, not that responsible discipline, or that cutting edge discipline or even that worm and caring discipline. We still maintain that literary studies hold unique promise for constructing an interdisciplinary epistemology due to its proximity to language and interpretation. This chapter investigates methodologies and processes by which we do literary studies and redefines those to show how we can put together a new interdisciplinary approach.

There are two main reasons this chapter will embark on a series of close readings. First, we consider epistemology to be what follows, not what comes before, what we do as scholars and teachers. Epistemology is not a set of general precepts or rules concerning knowledge construction but a result of choices we make at every step of our interpretative work. Such understanding of epistemology follows the general trends in both continental as well as analytic philosophy, which have abandoned the Kantian search for the universal condition of knowledge and the *a priori* divisions (Kitcher). Instead, as it is in for instance, Michel Foucault's work, epistemology is a part of the regime of truth or a framework that is constituted through scholarly engagements. In our case, the main kind of behavior is the one that takes reading and transforms it into scholarly, teaching, and institutional practices. How we read, in other words, is how we become what we are as literary scholars. In and of themselves, textual analyses are both the way into and the way out of epistemology. Throughout this book, we will not shy away from universalizing our conclusions—we have done a kind of generalization already in the previous chapter when addressing Derrida's notion of limitlessness or the condition without condition, which defines a framework for this inquiry into the practice of knowing. We, too, see universalization as compatible with poststructuralism, as already noted by scholars—for instance, Foucault's interest in Kant's notion of Enlightenment and, specifically, in the latter's "What is Enlightenment?" We will say more on universalization as an open system in the last chapter.

The second reason to start with close reading is to foreground it as a mainstay methodology in literary studies, make it an object of study, and create a standard for examining other notions like history and review, which we will address in this chapter. I take examples of literary scholarship—and not fiction or other cultural texts—as our primary source, this on an assumption consistent with our overall approach that, again, literary studies is the practice of scholarship, and by analyzing it as a practice, we determine what our epistemology is. For instance, when we claim, as Rita Felski does, that the current threat facing literary studies is "a legitimation crisis" (Felski, *Limits* 5), we do at least two things at the same time. On the one hand, applying literary scholars' skills, we say, for instance, that due to depleted social values, our current culture does not see much in "Beowulf or Baudelaire" (Felski, *Limits* 5). On the other hand, we constitute (perform, embody, and so on) a new framework. In the latter, literary studies is an institution that is self-defined through a critique of the crisis of legitimation which *itself* constitutes a new form of gathering, if not also a new kind of legitimation through exposure and criticism. We point to these meta-instances—Gilles Deleuze calls the approach "theory of practice" (22)—because in times of crises, this outer framework is threatened. It gives the sense of institution and overarching structure and holds (or does not hold) literary studies together to give it a specific value. It, too, is what needs to be scrutinized and, in the case we are making here, what needs to be changed.

We can say that there is a crisis of legitimation and a loss of specific cultural values but only from a specific point of view that sees these as defining traits of literary studies. In such a case, we suppose the cultural criteria where "literature" is the central national genre, where it is the norm for literacy, the source of cultural capital. The same does not hold in many marginalized Western cultures, or across the world, or, well, in the sciences. For this reason, the crisis of legitimation is indicative of the approach and of what we think literary studies ought to be, not of what it *can* be in a different, interdisciplinary framework.

When we change the narrative and focus on epistemology, or how we do things, our diagnosis will be different. When that is the case, we suggest another interpretative turn of no longer focusing on legitimation's values and narratives but on, instead, new framing possibilities. By new framing, we literally mean an entirely new way to conceive of and explain what literary studies does and is in respect to interpretation. Our diagnosis is that the current state is the consequence of an incomplete dismantling of framing narratives and of the lack of epistemology. We no longer know what we do even when we do just precisely the same thing New Critics did or exactly as other disciplines do—disciplines like philosophy from which we borrow our arguments, or disciplines like cognitive science from which we take the understanding of how mind functions or digital technology we hope offers a new way to analyze texts.

We will get to close reading after a brief contextual and historical background concerning methodology in the last 30 years. We will then encounter close reading through the "Theories and Methodologies" issue on Caroline Levine's *Forms* from the October 2017 issue of *PMLA*. Again, the reason to proceed this way by examining trends as they are present in particular works is because categories and notions are what they are as a part of textual/institutional practices, involving specific participants, specific dates, specific forums, in specific contexts.

Theories and methodologies

A welcome exception to the general lack of interest in literary studies methodology is the section of *PMLA* titled "Theories and Methodologies." The section has been among the liveliest parts of the *PMLA* journal since 2005 and Marianne Hirsch's editorship.[1] It also allowed editors to bypass blind submissions and offer the valuable space of this journal to invited authors. For our present purposes, I want to point to issues published since the one on Homi Bhabha's *The Location of Culture*, from January 2017. The discussions of literary studies from that date on seem motivated by a new kind of dissatisfaction with what we are as a discipline, together with a dawning realization that this time crisis might be different.

The Location of Culture was published in the mid-1990s and represents the point when the leading literary scholarship became definitively defined by a poststructuralist hybridization between approaches—postcoloniality and intersectionality. "Theories and Methodologies" treats the book, rightly, as a watershed example for the current attempts to "revamp, reconsider, and … refute" (Felski, *Limits* 2) arguments central to our discipline. In addition to Bhabha, "Theories and Methodologies," in this period covered three other major recent scholarly accomplishments—Felski's *The Limits of Critique*, Franco Moretti's *Distant Reading*, and the mentioned Caroline Levine's *Forms*. Felski focuses on "critique" to get a "clearer" answer to "how and why critics read" (Felski, *Limits* 2)—questions that should be unexpected given that the context in which she published this work is often defined as postcritique and post-truth times. Moretti's *Distant Reading* aims to go further back and reimagine the Enlightenment roots of literary studies, specifically comparative literature—that is, general, universal, or world literature—based on a new (Immanuel Wallerstein-inspired) notion of the "world." Levine also practices the return to the past to get to the future logic by focusing on the term "form," which, with content, forms our classic analytic pair. In doing so, she offers what she sees as a post-deconstructive, post-poststructuralist understanding of how our notion of "form" (as "network") can help other fields and social justice activism.

The first point here, then, is to acknowledge the accomplishment of "Theories and Methodologies" in what it has done in response to the crises and the threat to legitimation. It has noticed the crises, helped us reflect on ourselves, and take stock of where we have been and where we are headed as a discipline. Indeed, if there is a "we" of our discipline anywhere, most of it can be found in "Theories and Methodologies." But, second, there is a long list of what recent "Theories and Methodologies" did *not* do. Namely, it did not devote space to works like those we mentioned already at the beginning of the previous chapter that offer a general response to the crises (Gildea, McDonald, Small, Belfiore, North, Donoghue, Jay, and so on). It is hard to say exactly why this is the case, and we can only identify the obvious, that "Theories and Methodologies" shies away from the broad philosophical perspectives, framing issues, and the institutional aspects of knowledge production. Instead, it addresses topics of current scholarly interest with the representation of various viewpoints as a method for selecting contributions without interrogating validity of such approach.

It, too, is run by prominent scholars who do not teach at institutions most impacted by the crises. Their careers, jobs, and pay are not as threatened, and their discourses do not show the alarm that differently situated colleagues may have felt some time ago.

After the Levine issue, "Theories and Methodologies" included the following topics: how we write (133:1); Viet Thanh Nguyen's *The Sympathizer, The Refugees,* and *Nothing Ever Dies* (133:2); reencountering texts at different moments over the course of a life (133:3); new geographies of reading (134:1); Jennifer Egan's *Manhattan Beach* (134:2); Hillary Chute's *Why Comics?* (134:3); poetics and politics of fact (134:5); digital humanities (135:1); and aurality and literacy (135:2). Though *PMLA* is the organ of the Modern Language Association, which itself is a complex professional and scholarly institution, since the diagnosis of crises, there have been no topics related to our institutional life or to the interdisciplinarity that holds this unusual collective together. "Theories and Methodologies" also did not include works on methodology in the sense in which we understand that term here.

Other professional journals

Profession examines "the fields of modern languages and literatures as a profession" and covers "intellectual, curricular, and institutional trends and issues as well as relevant public policy debates" (Krebs). But it favors practical and particular issues over the sustained, collective, or general examination of frameworks. There are also, of course, *ADE Bulletin* and *ADFL Bulletin*. A recent joint issue of the latter two focused on literary curricula and canon in various teaching contexts (*ADE* 156 and *ADFL* Vol. 45. No.1, 2018). It included articles by Domna Stanton and John Guillory, who were among the key protagonists of the culture wars. There was also an issue on close reading (*ADE* 149 from 2010). But the inclusion of such topics did not result in a directional change or lead to more debates and spread of the concern with framing narratives. Instead, the efforts remained isolated indications that something might be wrong with the way we do things, and the culture wars' protagonist might have something to say again.

The same issues also offered short articles and a cursory, not sustained look at close reading. In general, the mentioned journals do not consistently engage fundamental theoretical, institutional issues, nor do they see their purpose in taking stock of where we as a discipline are.

Culture wars

The last time we were preoccupied with framing narratives, literary scholarship was led by questioning precisely what is in common (Badiou 9), asking, as Eleanor Goodwin and Geraldine Finn put it, *Who is This We?* But, post culture wars, there was a new trend. By and large, we stopped following epistemological issues and turned toward developing *kinds* of readings. The turn toward "ethics" in a sense indicated by, for instance, J. Hillis Miller ("The Ethics of Reading") was all too often also the turn *away* from epistemology as an outdated discourse about truth. The ethics of reading meant attention to language and meaning that is ethical precisely because it goes beyond a defined epistemology. The principle devaluated epistemology even further, making it an outright obstacle to reading. The emphasis on the diverse range of arguments and attitudes came together with a belief that the multiverse of readings makes a shared or common epistemology impossible or irrelevant.

Just after the culture wars was also the last time we could say that we are interdisciplinary and know what we mean.

This same period saw slight increases in the number of majors, the first since the late 1980s, which might have served as indirect proof that we were on the right track toward recovery. The first signs of crisis, which appeared in the mid-1990s, seemed to reverse between 1995 and 2007, with a bump from 49,928 to 55,122 degrees conferred in English (as per the National Center for Education Statistics) with similar increases in foreign languages and literatures as well. At the very least, it appeared that the worst devaluation was behind us. That, of course, was not the case with the bump possibly a reaction to two contradictory trends. On the one hand, there was a booming stock market, and, on the other hand, there was its bust, which English major numbers registered with a delay.

Forms

From recent "Theories and Methodologies" topics, we choose Caroline Levine's *Forms* issue because the book is more representative of literary scholarship than our other options. *Forms* is based on a historicist approach, addresses different genres and social justice, applies what seem like fashionable theories but itself is not a work of theory, and so on. The essays on *Forms* also happen to be polemical, making our differences and similarities that much easier to observe.

When approaching our kind of close reading, we are guided by a goal of capturing institutional history, just as we have already done above. To that end, we will pay attention to peripherals: the frameworks and basic assumptions literary scholars take for granted, the procedures we follow because these define literary scholarship as we know it. These institutional issues should capture our attention because our negative choices—what we leave out and do not do, consciously, automatically, semiconsciously, unconsciously—make a pattern. Identifying that design, what in a different context Rosi Braidotti called "recurrence of patterns of exclusion" ("Theoretical" 15), can help us understand how much and what we share as well as what we actually are as a discipline.

We will choose our examples to provide access to the scaffolding that is both unacknowledged and assumed. This method contrasts with the usual approach that would, in the case of close reading, start with the most complex, sophisticated, and thorough definition. We are not abandoning that path fully, and consider all works we analyze as belonging to that category of the best literary studies has to offer. But we also treat our sources based on the additional criterion as representative of a way of thinking. They define a paradigm and capture a moment in the institution's life, exemplifying general professional conduct.

If our choice of these examples is wrong and they do not represent a trend but are outliers due to, for instance, my flawed primary research, the resulting discussion should still be of interest. Again, this is because we are analyzing a tendency present in our sources by definition—article published in leading journals and books by leading scholarly presses, written by authors teaching at leading institutions.

Review

One drawback of this attempt to look at the marginalia is evident as we start our interpretation. As it has already, our analysis will have to go on detours. Before we can get to the moments of close reading or employ the common procedures of paying attention to the meaning of the text as it is present in the text, we have to unpack and do a close reading in another sense. This other close reading consists of inquiry about the setup and the procedures that enter the text's construction but are not subject to scholarly interpretation by those same works. For instance, a question—how scholars should respond to scholarly work—is not presented in any of the contributions on the *Forms* even though their goal is just that, to review a book.

Before we can read a text, another sort of close reading should occur concerning the conditions that make it into a text. The fact that we do not regularly ask such a question (like what a review is) as a part of doing a review tells us, in and of itself, a lot about the profession in general and, in this case, about the genre of review as well. The absence implies that the "review" is a common procedure and that its practice is settled. We do it on all levels and almost daily. From students' papers, theses, and dissertations, to articles before and, as is the case with *Forms,* monographs after publication. And we review following the established rules. One seems to be that the higher the source is in the hierarchy, the more the reviewer has to repeat and the more the reviewer has to be suspicious of the source. In the case of a book review, the review's task is to determine what is missing from the argument and what is not represented in the interpretation. Following these (for the most part) unwritten but well-established rules, when the resulting effort is to appear in a prestigious journal like *PMLA,* the review is defined by the book author's area of expertise as well as by the reviewer's area of expertise. The review's importance seems to lie in and to be measured by polite one-upmanship. (We will analyze a variant of the review, namely, peer review, in the next Chapter 3. We will also finish this argument about the review as a genre below, where we will offer reconstruction as a model that reviews of scholarly work could follow.)

And so it goes for the articles on *Forms.* A scholar of Russian and East European literature, Marijeta Bozovic, as the author herself acknowledges, is inevitably driven to Russian formalism and "its immediate intellectual heirs" (Bozovic 1182), which is not addressed in Levine's book. A scholar from the University of Birmingham, in Great Britain, Angus Connell Brown, distinguishes between "an American tradition of formalist criticism" and "British intellectual heritage," and situates "*Forms* in relation to" his neck of woods, "Cambridge English, British Marxism, and cultural studies" (A. C. Brown 1188). Doing what is familiar, the next contributor, Michael W. Clune, a literary theorist, suggests that Levine's forms are, actually, ideas. And so on, and so on, of course. Other contributors follow the same path and logic of the review that brings what is analyzed into their specializations and issue their judgments from their perspectives.

Almost all reviews mention the same key passages. They start with the statement of Levine's goal: "it is time to export ... to take our traditional skills to new objects – the social structures and the institutions that are among the most crucial sites of political efficacy" (Levine, *Forms* 23). There is a note about Levine's father—"a liberal humanist and a historian of ideas"—and the choices he made as a scholar "to understand the intentions of authors" (IX). The reading of *The Wire* is a model for the open form, "far from an ideologically coherent society with power lodged in the hands of a few ... *The Wire* gives us a social world constantly unsettled by the bewildering and unexpected effects of clashes among wholes, rhythms, hierarchies, and networks" (2015: 149). There is also the explanation that the term *affordance,* borrowed from design theory, captures the clash of forms and becomes an example of how disparate forms can be fitted together.

Only Anahid Nersessian's review explicitly mentions a "perspective exterior" to *Forms* (Nersessian 1224). Nersessian is also the only reviewer who focuses on the limits of the basic approach—she challenges Levine's competence in understanding a fundamental theory like dialectical materialism. Most importantly, Nersessian is also the only author who prominently notes that Levine's argument excises and cuts off vast possibilities or paths of interpretation concerning form. (To be clear: other contributions focus on what *Forms* lack and what the project should or could have included, stopping short of regarding blocked paths.) Nersessian's contribution ends with a question with which I want to suggest we should begin more often than we do, "What happens [...] to the thought [*Forms*] makes impossible, that it expels in order to prevail?" (Nersessian 1225).[2]

We could also say that Nersessian is the only contributor that takes review seriously, except that she does not do it with the directness and intention needed for reform of literary studies as an institution. For Nersessian, the framing pertains to the argument and not to the institutional practices and policies, which she, too, wants to leave as she found them.

This issue of "Theories and Methodologies" thus suggests a few things about the profession, and this, to repeat before we have started reading the essays. Already, we find that so much of what makes Levine's book is left unread. Thus, it appears already that when we look at the procedures, choices in the setup, the way we make decisions, MLA scholarship is not all that balkanized or multiple but rather uniform. We do not usually ask about the paths our investigations close off. Or, put differently, we do not regularly ask about the discursive practices our scholarship follows, only about discursive practices that are the target of our analyses.

If reviews follow the established logic centered in the author's competence area, intending to point out ways an argument can be made more complete or thorough, our discipline is defined by these qualities. The sense of scope, mastery, interdisciplinarity—in a word, its many boundaries—are all established in this repetition of the routine.

I should not be understood as claiming that there is something inherently wrong with the genre—after all, I have just offered a variant of the detective work on what is missing, albeit in terms of what is cut off. I want only to point out that we have specific, common forms of seeing—forms in which we reproduce knowledge. They constitute our dominant practices through which we build the institution of literary studies as well as its methodology. The effects and consequences of these practices agglomerate, shaping our disciplines in ways that have remained beyond our sustained consideration. This, too, is done not just by our most skillful readers but by everyone who publishes in the many venues and forums we have available. The implication is that we have also created methods and ways of doing things we do not know in addition to the discipline that we know—one, say, that is undergoing a crisis of legitimation.

On that, as far as I can tell, no reviews showed any kind of "crisis of legitimation" in their analyses—to the contrary. Like most other *PMLA* authors, they seem confident in their use of discourse, its importance, their expertise, and processes that authorize them to speak as experts. They, too, seem so confident that one might well ask, what crisis?

In the next two discussions, I will assess "close reading" and "historicism" in a similar way, looking into what cannot be said because of what is claimed. I will get back to the review to wrap our argument in this chapter with an interdisciplinary comment on the construction of emotions. Taken together, these discussions of fundamental practices should amount to several building blocks of a new basic epistemology of literary studies, and to, also, a new path of interpretation

70 Recasting hermeneutic epistemology

that should start with the institutional framework interrogating established procedures. Altogether, to repeat, the readings are geared toward defining an open system or what we call a systematicity without a system or an epistemology without a system which is the goal of our book.

Part I: close reading and mere reading

Close reading

Close reading is our first topic because, as scholars usually note, it makes us distinct from other disciplines. (We will see shortly why this is not a correct assumption.) We are on the opening page of Levine's *Forms*, where the author claims that there is form, that that form is related to close reading, and that close reading can be exported to other disciplines and, further, to the activities outside academia. The sentence, the first of the "Introduction," says,

> If a literary critic today set out to do a formalist reading of Charlotte Brontë's *Jane Eyre*, she would know just where to begin: with literary techniques both large and small, including the marriage plot, first-person narration, description, free indirect speech, suspense, metaphor, and syntax. (Levine, *Form* 1)

Is this all there is to close reading? Does close reading have to focus on the formal aspects of the genre, "literary techniques" like plot, type of narration, descriptive language, and so on? And, we can go a step further to ask if such "formal" analysis actually reads the text closely? Or at all?

Since Levine and her *PMLA* reviewers all take the fundamental notion for granted, we again have to look elsewhere—Levine does offer commentary on some aspects of New Criticism that are close to close reading, but she does it in the context of the analysis of form, mainly in the first and second chapters, without directly commenting on close reading. I will take the 2016 "What Was 'Close Reading'?" by Barbara Herrnstein Smith as a recent and representative account on close reading pertinent for the present discussion. I will discuss below a few more sources—by Jane Gallop and Jonathan Culler. The available bibliography is not all that long. Briefly, Frank Lentricchia and Andrew DuBois's reader, *Close Reading*, brings together selected historical essays on close reading but does not itself interrogate, analyze, or interpret the tradition, approaches, or methods they represent. It, too, operates, for instance in the Introduction, with a category of "formalism" derived from and dependent on the meaning of close reading but not interrogated as such. Annette Federico's *Engagement with Close Reading* is exhaustive on how we can teach close reading but has many features like positioning close reading against historicism and cultural studies, making it not relevant for *Interdiscipline*. Close reading is often mentioned in the works critical of current methodologies—of which Smith's is a representative—usually in the context of challenges presented by DH that rely on a different sort of reading, as in, for instance, Martin Paul Eve's *Close Reading with Computers* and Moretti's *Distant Reading*. There are, however, no conferences on close reading, and no ongoing general conversations; PhD students are not encouraged to write dissertations on it; and it is hard to imagine that a monograph on close reading would be regarded as a landmark in the sense that, for instance, Lauren Berlant's *Cruel Optimism* or Sianne Ngai's *Theory of the Gimmick* are held as exemplary literary scholarship.[3]

One explanation of this low interest would be that close reading, being a basic methodology, is supposed to be discussed when the paradigm is in crisis and change is in the offing. The claim is a common one. I disagree with it for two reasons. A crisis can't be more profound or broad, and close reading is not the subject of urgent conversations. Even those who seek new forms of reading, like surface or distant reading, propose methods that are not meant to replace close reading fully but to complement what we commonly do. Second, and more importantly, there is no significant disagreement on what close reading is, why it is the core methodology, or why it provides continuity with New Criticism *because* we do not discuss it. Were we to commonly take it up, better understanding and more and broader disagreements would follow.

Barbara Herrnstein Smith's first significant contribution to understanding close reading is that she identifies our discipline as "Anglo-American literary studies" ("What was" 57)—we will explain shortly why this is the case. Smith's primary source for "close reading" is the New Critical cohort of I.A. Richards, William Empson, T.S. Eliot, Cleanth Brooks, and Robert Penn Warren. However, her most representative source—in many ways, her only source—is a short programmatic essay by John Crowe Ransom, published as "Criticism, Inc." Smith cites from it at length and uses it as the defining source for what close reading is.[4] In one of the key passages, she writes,

> Though close reading is often described as a method of interpretation, the New Critics—certainly the first generation of them—were concerned less with establishing the meaning of a text than with understanding its operative machinery. Indeed, a New Critical "reading" was something like an exercise in reverse engineering: the examination of an artifact to see how it was made and how it worked. (Smith, "What was" 60)

The definition intends to capture the specific differences that constitute literary texts—their operative machinery and how their elements work together. Ransom, perhaps unexpectedly, calls his approach "scientific" by which he means "precise and systematic [...] developed by the collective and sustained effort of learned persons." One that has or should have a "proper seat ... in the universities" (Ransom 587, Smith 62).

Smith makes much of only some of the features of Ransom's understanding, but not of others like the designation of our work as scientific and Ransom's explicit identification of location and context where the definition of close reading is to take root. One of them is in the title of Ransom's article in the form of the "Inc.," which refers to an incorporation of the business of criticism into an autonomous entity called a department and, of course, has a rather glorious history thanks to Derrida-Searle debate. On this, Smith follows the main line of thinking we already identified in the previous chapter. She acts on the common assumptions that specific frameworks like departments are auxiliary to the definition, to self-understanding in general, and to the understanding of close reading in particular. Jane Gallop does the same in her hilarious pronouncement, "[w]e became a discipline ... when we stopped being armchair historians and became instead painstaking close readers" (Gallop, "Close Reading" 183), which overlooks the obvious. This seat could not have been seated in a library or a private "room of her own" or any other extra-academic place but required finding a space in a building, in an institution, a department at a college or school, delimited from other departments by walls—precisely that thing that may soon disappear in many public universities and small liberal arts colleges.

The point that is missed is the main point of Ransom's essay. His argument is something like the following: poets—anyone else for that matter—can read closely, looking in private into the engine of poems for their ends such as aesthetic education. However, when literary scholars do so in a scientific fashion, focusing on literature as their object of study, following common critical criteria, and, of course, in a specific department, it can give rise to a new discipline and a new profession. This is not to say that some English departments did not already exist but that they were profoundly transformed by shifting their focus away from the history of literature toward literature. Ransom is clear on this when he says, following Ronald S. Crane's "History Versus Criticism in the University Study of Literature," that "the students of the future must be permitted to study literature, and not merely about literature" (Ransom, "Criticism" 588). If, in other words, there is to be a department of literature, there should also be an object and methodology proper to it just as it is the case in departments across the university.

What we understand from this discussion is that a definition of close reading cannot be limited to "the examination of an artifact to see how it was made and how it worked." The understanding should also come with at least two additional clauses. First, the affirmation that this influential definition is offered within and applies to an Anglo-American institutional framework but perhaps not to others. Second, there should be an understanding that this emphasis on the poetic aspects of written language (and the deemphasis of interpretation) has been, principally, our institutional or organizational common ground which allowed us to notice literature and organize its study around the terms and methods that are proper to it, which then define our kind of professionalization and separate it from, most importantly, what they do in history and philosophy departments. The emphasis on poetics distinguishes literary scholarship from the rest of knowledge production and is meant as the exact opposite of what we usually assume about the usefulness of close reading across disciplines.

It is evident that literary studies is not a branch of analytic philosophy. However, still, there is something about its designation as an Anglo-American institution that rings true and needs to be addressed since some traits of this discipline are easier to explain using analytic tradition. In the first generation of New Critics like Ransom, such characteristics include the mentioned link to sciences that came along with the insistence on a separate department and precision. There is also the focus on the text's poetic qualities, which just happens to coincide with those aspects of language that analytic—aka language, aka Anglo-American—philosophy does not interpret. Beyond New Critics, the culture wars generation continues to value the traditional boundaries like periods and genres and to insist on the separateness of approaches with rigidity and demarcations that are alien to continental philosophy. They, too, still value "poetic" qualities and/or ideological underpinnings and do not notice writing and interpretation enough. "Teaching the conflict" (Graff, *Beyond*) that embodies the spirit of culture wars rests on the boundaries that the chief poststructuralist authors like Derrida would not draw and attitudes that he would (on most occasions) disagree with. There is a positivism in the post culture wars generations, in emphasis on history, utility, and application of literary studies, with the discipline finding its justification outside academia. These are not just some disciplinary characteristics, but reasons that it is not poststructuralist yet or enough.

Something similar can be said about the first part of Smith's definition of close reading that says that it is "the examination of an artifact to see how it was made and how it worked." When by "how," we mean poetics, we create a problem for the discipline that pretends to be interdisciplinary. Focusing on the artiness of a work of art may also not be reading closely since the approach rests on the definition of what are and what are not artistic elements or techniques and is often limited by such cultural or technical demarcations. As in the recent book by Barry Brummett (*Techniques of Close Reading*), the approach often foregrounds the "techniques of close reading" but does not consider the discourse that defines those techniques should itself be subjected to analysis and understanding and a kind of close reading. We "see" and "hear" without asking, as a part of the very same line of inquiry, what makes "seeing" and "hearing" possible. Without the latter question, close reading cannot translate into a universal skill, and neither can the discipline that practices it be poststructuralist.

A form of close reading (that does not focus on the poetic qualities or techniques) is regularly done in theology, philosophy, history, law, and in parts of other disciplines that define themselves using texts. In the crowded field, paying attention "to how meaning is produced or conveyed" (Culler 22) may not be sufficient or precise enough as a tool or relevant.

Mere reading

I am offering this criticism only to point to an alternative that does meet poststructuralist standards and has a different starting point. Not New Criticism, not

Ransom's essay, not the moment of the institution of Anglo-American literature departments, Paul de Man begins, in a text titled "The Return to Philology," with an encounter between poststructuralism and the practice of New Criticism. He calls what he finds there "mere reading" and offers its explanation as the main point of an article that explains to American audiences what theory is. According to de Man, mere reading is,

> able to transform critical discourse in a manner that would appear deeply subversive to those who think of the teaching of literature as a substitute for the teaching of theology, ethics, psychology, or intellectual history. Close reading accomplishes this often in spite of itself because it cannot fail to respond to structures of language which it is the more or less secret aim of literary teaching to keep hidden. (24)

This close reading is not about literary techniques. First, it is about the "structures of language" that are used by, shaped through, and hidden in literary techniques and discursive practices. By "structures of language," de Man means the way that language imposes itself onto the reader: the meaning and experience of it are not covered by genre and other constructs employed in the process of understanding. The reading can be called de-construction in a literal sense, denoting an undoing or interruption of the internalized models the human mind applied to make sense of the internal and external worlds. A part of this process would be to realize the constructed nature of these two realities we can identify as "internal" and "external," following Lisa Feldman Barrett's work.

Mere reading reveals a moment when a text becomes something else, a language practice or a practice of language and results in a moment of epiphany like the one de Man had in Reuben Brower's class entitled "The Interpretation of Literature," "better known on the Harvard campus and in the profession at large as HUM 6." De Man describes the experience in the following way. Brower, he says,

> believed in and effectively conveyed what appears to be an entirely innocuous and pragmatic precept, founded on Richards's "practical criticism." Students, as they began to write on the writings of others, were not to say anything that was not derived from the text they were considering. They were not to make any statements that they could not support by a specific use of language that actually occurred in the text. They were asked, in other words, to begin by reading texts closely as texts and not to move at once into the general context of human experience or history. Much more humbly or modestly, they were to start out from the bafflement that such singular turns of tone, phrase, and figure were bound to produce in readers attentive enough to notice them and honest enough not to hide their non-understanding behind the screen of received ideas that often passes, in literary instruction, for humanistic knowledge.

> This very simple rule, surprisingly enough, had far-reaching didactic consequences. (23)

While we can read the quote in the conventional way, emphasizing not reading into the text, identifying techniques ("turns of tone, phrase, and figure"), the passage allows us to make a very different claim. Namely, what we do to and with the text should start with "the bafflement" that the "singular" use of language produces in a reader. We know that this is de Man's main point since it is identified in the title, "The Return to Philology," a branch of knowledge that deals with language, structure, and development but not meaning.[5] Explaining the novelty of this theoretical approach that returns to language, he writes that, "in practice, the turn to theory occurred as a return to philology, to an examination of the structure of language prior to the meaning it produces," which he also calls a pragmatic orientation (24). In short, this mere reading is a part of a comprehensive poststructuralist strategy that is also meant to bring practice and theory of reading together. Its aim, as de Man says, is to "transform critical discourse" (24).

Again, the turn to language that brackets meaning could be understood as a poetic turn like Ransom's that focuses on "how" the text is made. For de Man, however, the turn to language is not defined by theories of signification or language as a system of signs or language as meaning, but, precisely, against such overinterpretations and as a practice. Following Martin Heidegger, for de Man, language is understood in a primordial way, as defining the human way of being (Powell), which is an approach that de Man brings to the study of literature. There is an important difference from Heidegger as well. For the latter, language is *logos*, discourse, speech, and silence (Heidegger). For de Man, language is writing and reading, which makes for two different understandings of interpretation. If for Heidegger, language always means *as* something, de Man moves the attention to the reading as performance and the effect it produces which can be simple and immediate or mere.

The subversion in mere reading is not only the disruption of a paradigm we are using to identify it or of our prejudices. What is being subverted or destroyed (in part) is the agency (the "self") that does the reading. This turning-on-self of mere reading is lost on many scholars who insist, like Annette Federico, that close reading is a kind of critical reading that helps us understand the text and the author. She says, for instance,

> What I am calling *close reading* is essentially … the cultivation of self-consciousness about the reading experience, a desire for more awareness of what's going on—the kind of reading that opens the door to a deeper, more critical understanding of the *particular* work being read, and of the *experience* of reading as a whole.… Close reading is technique we use to shrink the distance between ourselves and a writer or a text. (Federico 9)

In response, we say, to the contrary, close reading should start as an interruption of the order connoted by "self-consciousness." In place of mastering and empowering strategies of meaning creation, mere reading should help us overcome the initial need for those. To be sure, our students should learn the reading skills Federico identifies but do so on an encounter with the limitations of one's self-imposition on the world around us and the text we read. Building self-consciousness, more critical awareness, and so on are shields preventing a reader from reading. They, too, are forms of colonization or imposition. In the age of mindfulness, the proposition should not be all that strange that our way of reading is our way of comportment, our way of being, not only our way of understanding and relating. Reader who has what Du Bois called "double consciousness" (*The Souls of Black Folk*) should find this methodology easier to practice.

The usual kind of instruction in close reading along the lines Federico suggests, even when we ask students to go beyond their presupposition, expects them to behave in predictable ways and be critical in the specific sense. Trigger warnings, microaggressions, and courses with long reading lists speak to this eloquently.[6] And so do other common practices and assumptions. Curricula are organized so that close reading is a means and a specific skill, not an experience and a way of being. We, too, often teach writing with great tolerance for the facile use of language, which fosters attitudes antithetical to mere reading. If words can be used in any which way, language matters less and less, and so does the information texts convey.

The precept de Man describes is nothing like Richards's "practical criticism" even though he cites the influence on Brower and some of the procedures seem similar. The result is also not in line with "practical criticism" in the sense that a student who can merely read is not necessarily also a better critic. This is how de Man describes the effect, "Perhaps the most difficult thing for students and teachers of literature to realize is that their appreciation is measured by the analytical rigor of their own discourse about literature, a criterion that is not primarily or exclusively aesthetic" (de Man, "Return" 24). For us, the effect, strictly speaking, does not belong to any discipline and that is exactly the point of the experience and the approach to language that turns against one's own way of reading and understanding. We take analytic rigor to describe the restraint as well as the willingness to undergo a de-authorizing experience which is why the experience can be described as close to "double consciousness."

A simple method I can suggest for literature classes is lingering over the text and spending the semester on a few complex readings considered in depth. The same would go for student writing, which is given extended attention and multiple opportunities for rewrites. Coverage is important, but perhaps it could be effectively achieved through high expectations, peer pressure, and independent projects that require students to read widely.

The implication of this argument for our interdisciplinary role is the following. Literature departments can define themselves based on what is unique in the human relation to language, meaning production, and a way of comportment that places the experience of language at the heart of what it means to be human and what it means to do basic activities of interpretation, reading, and writing. The same can help us construct a new understanding of the world in which humans are not the referential measure—an experience that should start with mere reading.

For de Man, we as literary scholars do not deliver content the way theology might, teaching about specific historical (religious, legal, philosophical) material, traditions, or experience. We, instead, engage in creating a unique experience of language, meaning, thinking, and being. We also engage in understanding how interpretation takes place. And we do that by interrupting habitual ways of thinking, reading, and writing to set up new terms for understanding language, for being in language, developing it and culture that comes out of this immersive experience.

Culler and Gallop have addressed similar instances of loss of control to those I just mentioned. There is, however, a crucial difference between their notions and de Man's mere reading. Coming from this Heideggerian background, the bafflement de Man describes is like estrangement from what is familiar described by Culler (Culler, "Closeness" 24). But mere reading, once again, is also attempting to get beyond even such a decentered state and just be an experience. The experience includes a bird's eye view of the self and a feeling of immersion in the language. One has to be tempted to call them mystical or oceanic, except that they are ubiquitous. Bewilderment may come more easily to those like de Man who live and write in a foreign tongue and often get to the place of being overwhelmed with language—words, sound and pronunciation, many meanings, and orthography. Gallop makes a similar point about her experience of French, except that it is not central to her understanding of reading (Gallop, "Close" 17). I can attest to the difficulty and hardship of using language as someone who stopped speaking his native tongue with regularity 30 years ago and relies almost entirely on a learned, professional, so-called second language. Otherwise, bewilderment is the basic characteristic of language. Words are not private, but they can be used in unique and creative ways. They can reflect intention but just as quickly resist our use. Their meaning is obvious yet hard to understand. There are specific rules that follow from their use, but it is still language even if those rules are not followed. Language, too, is a unique kind of system unlike anything else we have created and can be used to understand it. Then, there is that question of who speaks when I speak or who understands when I understand which opens another avenue of inquiry into mere reading.

Literature is about language (and representation on which more in the next section), and only secondarily about the plot, characters, context, technique, form, style, ideology, and so on. This assumption that literary studies is concerned with language and its use in literature positions our discipline in such a way that it has a much more comprehensive purview and object of study, a different kind of methodology (not about the text but meaning, reading, and other symbolic practices), and a fundamental reach—a discipline that is very different from the one we have in mind when we say, "Anglo-American literary studies" or "print" and "book." In homage to Ransom, we could call it a discipline that notices language and meaning-making practices. In this context, we can also redefine what we mean by "poetic." Not the techniques or the way meaning is constructed, but, first, an encounter with language as language.[7]

We, of course, do not have to follow de Man and should be bold enough to construct for ourselves the experience of mere reading and a course of study that it supports.

Construction

Above we suggested that mere reading as we understand it agrees with contemporary cognitive science that claims that mind is a construct. Our chief reference is Lisa Feldman Barrett's work which offers a novel approach to emotions. In short, Barrett proposes that even our emotions are constructed. At first glance, such a theory goes against our supposition that we can clear up our mind of constructs through mere reading. However, the judgment is based on a superficial understanding of what constructs are and how they work. The misunderstanding is a common one. In literary studies, it is ubiquitous in what we mean when we say that identity is a social and historical creation.

Feldman's understanding can be applied to the received knowledge of cultural construction in the following way. First, historically, the cultural construction theory was meant to replace the nature-based concept of sciences, which suggested that the root of identity and behavior were in physical characteristics (genes, hormones, neurons, innate personality characteristics, and so on) with a more sophisticated version that the environment or context plays a role in how meaning or behavior were manifested, shaped, and understood. Second, in not relying on science, cultural construction theories could explain the "how," but only in a limited sense. Materialist theories, including psychoanalysis, added some of the determining factors and specificity, like production system, division of labor, the unconscious, how a thing becomes a sign, and so on. Cognitive theory helps us make a new addition regarding which specific role representation plays in constructing human behavior, its understanding, and what those representations are made of. According to Barrett, the mind has internal (nonconscious) representations of itself and the organism. These representations help the mind coordinate among the elements and processes that make its complex neural network. The mind's position as a shield or barrier between the inside and the outside simplifies its tasks and functioning since it has to deal not with the infinitely variable reality but with a reduced version created through predictive projections.

One of the consequences of this model is that terms like construction, representation, and reality are reaching a new kind of limit of usefulness, and their relationships need to be redefined again. If cultural construction theory replaced the notion of what is "real" with "representation" or "construction," we now need a step further to separate them and free each term for the use outside of a relationship with the other. Now, reality and representation are the same, and they can be also different, for instance, when an external point of view assesses the same situation. The internal reality is a representation because it expresses our history and is representative of it. It is also a reality in the same sense because it expresses this specificity of a singular mind functioning and serves it as a basis for prediction.

Representations are a physical expression of the chemical processes that depend on culture, environment, personal history, etc. And they are also cognitive events that allow the mind to organize emotional as well as physical behavior so that it can respond quickly and efficiently though not with nuance. They are—in the sense of hormonal level, neural activity, and so on—objective and measurable. They are created about a reality characterized by sheer multiplicity of which we and others around us get reduced but different versions that can nevertheless be negotiated and reconciled.

The consequence for close reading is that it can confront the reader with the way the mind works. It can help us understand our prejudices and biases and how minds filter what we read and create meaning out of the noise. According to this theory, the experience of the unarticulated and unorganized clamor is entirely possible. It only takes work and perhaps paradoxically education. Since this process of "figuring out how your mind works" is scientific and personal, mere reading requires work on the self and a certain level of knowledge and understanding. Started early enough, it can readily become second nature, preparing us for a more thoroughgoing engagement with the world. The early instruction in writing and reading should spend more time showing nuances in the meaning of words, their polysemy, relations, and etymology, and stop regarding words as objects or tools.

In short, we can go beyond construction, not because of its opposition to reality but because of this process's sheer complexity, its dependence of chemistry, on the unconscious process, the fact that it is singular and shared, that it can be changed through the use of language, that it is measurable, negotiable, and so on.

Five kinds of close reading

Smith's "What Was 'Close Reading'?" Culler's "The Closeness of Close Reading," and Gallop's "Close Reading in 2009" allow us to see how we came to be specific Anglo-American departments at universities in the United States, through a reduced and simplified adoption of poststructuralism. They do not address the process's key components, either language or the hermeneutic and cognitive practices or the level of engagement that take place in mere reading. How meaning is made and conveyed depends not only on literary techniques, or on prejudices we confront, but, more importantly, on the complex notions of language and signification—including notions of sub-structures like Freud's unconscious or Foucault's ideology or de Man's interruption or Barrett's construction—we discover in the process. These are incomprehensible from the New Critical perspective but also from many other perspectives literary scholars rely on. Besides the New Critics and the many structuralist and poststructuralists we already mentioned in the previous chapter and the introduction, we should also regularly teach and acknowledge as a part of our epistemology Russians formalists, as indicated by Bozovic, as well as German philosophers who defined the hermeneutic circle (Friedrich Schleiermacher, Wilhelm Dilthey, Martin Heidegger); later phenomenologists like Roman Ingarden; and semioticians like Louis Hjelmslev, who help us understand why we want to study literary works of art, what methodology we can use, how we can organize our discipline, and so on.

It may appear as a contradiction that mere reading requires and is supported by theories that explain how meaning and signification work. As mere reading, reading is supposed to go beyond received knowledge but also habits, routines, and the frameworks of our experience. This confrontation with the noise—because it is so challenging to become uncultured—is a part of the cleansing, redeeming, rejuvenating aspects that mere reading activity engages us in. At the same time, this disbarring is among the more sophisticated processes readers can perform. It requires not only discipline but also knowledge of theories of interpretation that explain the process of deinterpretation and decolonization. Mere reading, then, is a reading that takes place on two tracks (at the same time or not); as a most rudimentary activity, and as a scholarly spectacle of sorts. How would we know that we are doing a mere reading and not just a critical reading or symptomatic reading if not for the metadiscourse? In the classroom, these roles can be divided between students and teachers, who would gradually exchange them.

With this remark, we have identified a third kind of close reading, the metadiscourse that follows from what de Man says about mere reading and is there to guide and evaluate mere reading and does so in a parallel sort of way without interfering with the mere aspect of mere reading. Thus, we have already several kinds of close reading: (1) the usual examination of facts and details of writing; (2) de Man's mere reading and experience of language; (3) and a metadiscourse, or a guide for the close and mere readings. We can also offer one more, fourth kind, that follows from the previous: (4) close reading of frameworks. This is the strategy we already employed in *Interdiscipline*. While the barred paths may appear to be many, this is regularly not the case. When, for instance, we present close reading as critical reading, we are making only one approach—mere reading—impossible. For instance, when Joseph North opposes practical criticism, aesthetics, and close reading to what he calls "Theory" at the beginning of the second chapter of his book, he is obscuring the genealogy presented in works like de Man's "The Return to Philology" and the plain historical fact that poststructuralism, as presented in that essay (and de Man casts a wide net), is creating a version of practical criticism, aesthetic education, and close reading. De Man is merely skeptical of specific notions and uses of aestheticism common in teaching literature before the culture wars, not of aestheticism in general.

In another typical move, *Close Reading with Computers* excludes discussion of reading as a hermeneutic practice and attends to theories of interpretation as data gathering or detail/pattern identification. Martin Paul Eve uses the term hermeneutics as he suggests that "there is no such thing as 'raw data,' and hermeneutics remain core" to literary investigation (2), but he never actually discusses hermeneutics of any kind. A word search of his book in pdf format shows that Eve's use of the term is limited to the introduction, which surveys the field of literary interpretations. Most of his uses are part of quotations and most of those refer to the "hermeneutics of suspicion." Thus, to suggest that there is no raw data means to be against mere reading and poststructuralist hermeneutic theory like the one developed in de Man's "The Return to Philology." More on why data is not raw or, rather, why all data is just that, raw, in our Chapter 4.

Views that our approach closes off are relative to our theory, and for that reason, they are limited in kind. When he says that the opposite of close is a sloppy reading, Culler sets literary studies on a path that takes us further and further away from mere reading, as I will explain in more detail in a moment (Culler, "Closeness"). Gallop's insistence that close reading is attention to detail is an antidote to projections, as she says, but it is also a strategy that leads away from a language, whose function is the opposite, namely, generalization and gathering (Gallop, "Close").

Next to close reading of argument frames is our next (or fifth) kind of close reading; (5) a close reading of the flow or organization. All too often, close readings focus on segments or fragments of a text without including also a bigger picture or indication of their place in the poem or story. In this case, closeness is an expression of the shortness of the excerpt not just of detail. While there is an important characteristic to be found in particulars, there is also a salient point in identifying what general organization the selection is a part of. I take that Culler's and Gallop's commentary—his on de Man's discipline, hers on theory and French that depart from what appears to be their focus on close reading—are integral to understanding what they have to say about close reading. In these cases, a departure from the closeness is an extension of their main point and so a category in their theory which is a strategy to avoid mere reading. We find the same in works of other readers who are usually seen as close to de Man, like Barbara Johnson. She describes close reading thus:

> How to notice things in a text that a speed-reading culture is trained to disregard, overcome, edit out, or explain away; how to read what the language is doing, not guess what the author was thinking; how to take in evidence from a page, not seek a reality to substitute for it. (Johnson, "Teaching" 140 qtd. in Culler, "Closeness" 23)

Again, in this account there is a gesture toward mere reading in "how to read what the language is doing." There is, then, a shift to extraneous issues that have no direct relation to mere reading. In what we see as a *non sequitur*, Johnson warns the reader against guessing what the author was thinking, about evidence gathering, all being of a completely different order from the mere encounter with language.

We could justify Johnson's not noticing language by saying that in the above quotation her goal is to present a general point about close reading. But that exactly is our criticism. In Johnson's quotation, we see the tendency to talk about close reading by focusing on everything but language and to do so in the context of scholarship whose own tendency is not to offer extended consideration of close reading unless it is presented as a tool or in relation to poetic techniques.

Culler does the similar evasion in the following passage:

> I would stress that close reading need not involve detailed interpretation of literary passages (though there is plenty of that around in close reading, especially when the texts in question are difficult to understand), but especially attention to how meaning is produced or conveyed, to what sorts of literary and rhetorical strategies and techniques are deployed to achieve what the reader takes to be the effects of the work or passage. Thus it involves poetics as much as hermeneutics. (Culler, "Closeness" 22)

Right. But to figure out how meaning is produced or conveyed, one first has to be experientially aware of reading. Just to pay attention, a reader has to be there, constituted as a reader, conscious of the process we call mere reading.

Close readings are necessarily meandering, varying in closeness, but the closeness cannot be understood—as de Man's work on rhetorical figures shows—in terms of the distance from the literal meaning. Because meaning is always a construct, staying close may mean any number of things. Sometimes, we need to go far just for a mere reading to occur, depending on how dense the received knowledge is. As suggested already in the title of Alison Booth's "Mid-Range Reading," the closeness of close reading should not be understood as a spatial metaphor or as a metaphor at all. Closeness is a hermeneutic category. Its significance is discernable using theory alone, which underscores the necessity of a metadiscourse or a hermeneutic theory. In the absence of a carefully developed and used metadiscourse, our habits take its place—which again is countered by processes of mere reading.

Moretti claims that we can closely read only a few works and that the method is limited to canonical literature and is a teleological exercise (Moretti, *Distant* 48). From our perspective, closeness is not only or primarily a methodology but an attitude, comportment, and framework within which meaning is to be constituted. Moretti has no trouble recognizing that quality in his distant reading, which he calls *"a condition of knowledge"* just after he disparages close reading (Moretti, *Distant* 48).

By asserting the importance of theory as a metadiscourse, reading of close reading's closeness should not lead us to assume that close reading follows specific steps or rules. It might and they might be helpful, but best practice is not to accept them as precepts. Readers can agree on rules others have put together but should not do it in terms of imperatives like those that, in Federico's versions, say that we must read works whole. No, we need not do any such thing. We, too, need not be critical. Or read attentively, more than once. I include these suggestions on my syllabus, of course, but expect that my most productive students will arrive there following the path they set for themselves, not because they are expected to do it. Other students would follow by immersion and imitation.

In Chapter 4, where we will discuss digital humanities, we will offer another look at Russian formalism and pattern analysis and present it as a kind of close reading. This list of close readings I am putting together is not meant to be exhaustive, but instructive in a different way of thinking about close reading, since, paradoxically, we use close reading as if it were not a type of engagement, but, indeed, a tool for dishing out meaning, reverse reproduction, or personal growth.

Literalism

Because it is a type of engagement, close reading has the opposite, Culler suggests, "something like sloppy reading, or casual reading, an assessment of 'life and works,' or even thematic interpretation or literary history" (Culler, "Closeness" 20). But these are just the degrees and kinds of close reading that accompany even the most engaged and influential interpretations. For instance, de Man's readings have been found to contain inaccuracies (Ellrich). The opposite of close reading, we would like to propose instead, is a discourse like Socrates's speech (*Phaedrus*), a non-interpretative reading which takes the meaning to be literal and transparent, a dictation of sorts, speaking without an intermediary or midwife, with the authority of its creator.

There are two significant examples of this for our purposes. One is the so-called biblicism or the way some American evangelicals read the Bible—biblicism being, as Christian Smith argues, an impossible to fulfill "theory about the Bible that emphasizes together its exclusive authority, infallibility, perspicuity, self-sufficiency, internal consistency, self-evident meaning, and universal applicability" (viii).[8] The other is the totalitarianism we referred to in the first chapter.

No symbolic or poorly done *practice* is antithetical to close reading. There is instead a step, a political act, an imposition of an authority, an assault we identified at the beginning of the previous chapter that limits reading and replaces the process of interpretation with authorization. It usurps the text's independence and installs a figure, an agency with extratextual power. Such appropriation of meaning is, no doubt, empowering as it is also reassuring to their authors. But it, too, divides and displaces in order to prevent and limit the development of meaning. When fundamentalists use it, it has the same effect as "fake news." It asserts the author over and against any form of interpretation, ending the process of reading and replacing meaning with control. The same happens, of course, in the discourses of microaggressions, cancel culture, and so on, which, too, assign intention with authority that is itself not subjected to interpretation. We must also mention that the KGB, who were masters of interpretation, have perfected the agitprop and disinformation and laid the foundation for the current digital manipulation, under some influence by the same source poststructuralists found fascinating, namely, the Russian formalism.

Thus, on the one hand, close reading is the practice that inaugurates literary studies. On the other hand, it can either be the methodology that limits literary studies or enables it to participate in creating an interdisciplinary discourse. The latter can happen by including all theories, not just text-based, like biology, neurology, and cognitive science which, too, are beginning to see themselves as theories of signs (and therefore interpretation) of some sort. The general relevance of the described discipline hinges on its unique relation to language, what it does with it, how it brings it into our experience, and how it allows us to be enriched by it.

I am tempted by a lapidary formula—it is either reading or literalism. The claim should be understood in a broad sense: if a reader does not nurture the experience of exposure afforded by mere reading, eventually they stop reading.

Why literature

We are staying close to literature because it, more readily than other forms of writing, allows our discipline to notice language. It allows language to be language—not meaning, not communication, not a means, but a system of signs that somehow hangs together. In short, we are interested in literature not because of what it is as a genre, but because of how it treats and presents language.

If the reader is going to see this reasoning about interdisciplinarity as still privileging literature, that, indeed, is our goal. We want to use what has traditionally been called literature—the discourse where fiction/truth, inside/outside are not the organizing principles—and define an approach to language that this discourse makes possible due to its specific characteristics.

The usual understanding that genre distinctions are porous is not helpful to this thinking and understanding, because some boundaries are, some are not; some are sometimes and sometimes they are not—it depends. Porousness, too, is not a quality that allows us to rethink boundaries but another way to extend their significance without precise insight into what they are doing, how they are imposed, and why they are useful. As we have been thus far, we understand the boundaries like the one that separate fiction from other genres as helpful because they are provisional, relative, posited for a specific reason, and dependent on the framework. Because these boundaries do not form an enclosure but are open, they do not require us, interpreters and readers, to open them up. Instead, the relative contours they delimit can serve to establish connections between discourses—between, in this chapter, mere and close reading, close reading and history, history and review, and so on.

When we devote attention to the existing institutional boundaries, this is because they are not defined with intention or used provisionally and deliberately but are, instead, results of routines, expectations, and automatic actions. Such boundaries limit scholarship because they are not intentionally set up. They do not enable our work but direct its development in ways challenging to account for.

In short, we remain scholars of literature because it has a specific way of dealing with borders that afford readers kinds of freedom, insight, and experience that are not readily available through other discourses.

If our concept of literature is Western, we see no issue with it as long as the fact is acknowledged, and its implication held in the open. However, we also think that this notion of literature represents only a starting point for a conversation about convergence that is open to adjustments and takes the same quality of openness of interpretation (not literature) as its chief topic. As it figures here, literature is not just a historical entity but a form with specific characteristics described above—a fiction just as every lie is, which should ensure its universal relevance.

Then, again, we should keep in mind that scholars cannot speak for everyone even when we are invested in including and developing all possible voices.

Part II: history

While the library on close reading is short given its importance, it is quite different with history. It has been the object of constant debate since the culture wars and the inauguration of new historicism in works like Harold Aram Veeser's 1989 anthology, *The New Historicism,* with essays by Stephen Greenblatt, Catherine Gallagher, and other prominent scholars. To make matters more complicated, another topic—namely, formalism or aestheticism—is regularly about history and historicism. Under the heading of fighting unacceptable "anti-aestheticism" (Armstrong), the discussion is understood to be about defining what literary studies is.

Our take on history will be limited to what is consistent with our approach. It will also rely on several claims that cut across the formalism/historicism division that we find detrimental to literary studies. Our first assertion is that literary studies, being a study of literary form or literature as a form, cannot be antiformalist. No matter how far it moves from a literary text or form, our approach is informed by, or about, the native or original formalism which is constitutive of any form of reading.

Our second claim is that structuralist and poststructuralist theories are formalist theories. This follows from the basic understanding that a theory is structuralist—because it focuses on repeated, basic patterns like kinship structure and family connections as in Claude Lévi-Strauss's work. Ideology critique is formalist in a similar sense, because ideology is a form of thinking, behaving, and a belief system. Ideology critique, too, follows in the footsteps of aestheticism as in work on the aestheticization of politics (M. Jay). So does phenomenology in its focus on body and perception (Merleau-Ponty). If aestheticization was subjected to critique (Eagleton, *Ideology*), it does not follow that the critique is antiformalist.

In short, pleasure and affect are significant for poststructuralist scholarship because they are mutually informed with history, reading, and other practices (Hardt and Negri).

Aestheticism and historicism

In literary studies, it is evident that aestheticism and historicism cannot be separated from one another even though they are regularly presented as opposed to one another, which scholars do for institutional reasons. The side we agree with depends not on the approach or type of interpretation, but on how the authors see themselves as scholars.

Formalism as a critique of the institution is perhaps most obviously presented in Jonathan Loesberg's 1999 article "Cultural Studies, Victorian Studies, and Formalism," which he published on the way to writing his 2005 *A Return to the Aesthetic*. In the article, the author is clear about his antibureaucratic agenda, which he presents this way:

> I will argue, a return to a consideration of aesthetic form may, in its recognition of its own limits, return a genuine interdisciplinarity to Victorian studies, if one intends by interdisciplinary studies not the work of literary scholars treating non-literary texts, but the participation of scholars from different disciplines with different and possibly conflicting grounding questions, concerns and modes of analysis in the study of the same subject matter. Moreover, cultural studies has little to fear from this turn, since its founding gestures are deeply dependent upon the aesthetic formalism to which I propose a return. (537)

Loesberg also recognizes that his proposal does not undercut cultural studies, which depends "upon the aesthetic formalism." Loesberg means that cultural studies and new historicism are informed by "literariness" and use formalist procedures (544), as he also recognizes that formalism can only have "artificial boundary" (540). That is to say that the staying boundary that defines formalism can be drawn from the outside, usually by institutional practices.

Marjorie Levinson makes the same point under the opposite heading of critique of new formalism. She arrives to it by charging that formalism does not amount to a theory or method but to a movement (Levinson 560). Not being a theory, formalism cannot be exclusive or independent, which she proves by making an argument similar to Loesberg's that historicism does not do away with formalism but relies on it. Regularly, Levinson writes, the accusation "that contextual reading sets its face against the pleasure of the text falls flat when tested against the likes of Stephen Greenblatt and Jerome McGann" (561). She means that the complex readings inevitably show the inseparability of historicism and formalism.

Here is another example from Paul Jay's *The Humanities "Crisis" and the Future of Literary Studies*. Jay follows the norm of literary studies when he presents new formalism from George Levine's anthology *Aesthetics and Ideology* as an example of the challenge to historicism. Jay introduces the formalist charge this way:

> ideological criticism shifts attention from the artistic elements of the text itself and how it operates to "questions about the systems that contain them, about material conditions," about "mediation, discourse" (2). This has lead, in his view, to a "resistance to the idea of literary value" and of "literary greatness" altogether (2). (P Jay, *Humanities* 118)

The point, of course, is that "artistic" elements and "ideology" are but two names for the same thing. And so Jay proposes a more useful view on the aestheticism/historicism debate. He suggests that "any serious study of both the aesthetic qualities *of* literature, and aesthetic experience *in* it, requires that we reconceptualize our inherited notion of the aesthetic" (P. Jay 127) and offers to pare inquiry into aesthetics with critical theory as in works of Isobel Armstrong and Sianne Ngai.[9]

When the aestheticism/historicism debate is looked at this way, there is no anti-aestheticism or pro-aestheticism argument. There is, instead, overwhelming evidence of ontological inseparability between form, content, and context. And this unity or dependence is there regardless of the approach we choose, Loesberg's, Levine's, or Armstrong's, Jay's, Levinson's, or de Man's. The conclusion is so insistent that we see no reason to spend more time on it and will continue by assuming that historicism and aestheticism are intertwined. If they are separated, this is usually done in terms of an institutional argument, along the lines of what literary scholarship is supposed to do or what discourse has primacy—a turf war, in other words.

Reading history

Our choice of mere reading determines the role history can play in literary scholarship. Given that mere reading entails forms of deauthorization and the fact that authorization is a historical process, we can say that de-historicizing and interrupting our theoretical paradigm rather than historicizing must be the goal of literary studies. We must formulate such a demand clearly to start to understand the role history can play in literary studies. That role is different from the one suggested by Frances Ferguson in the following, "the writing of literary history and the reading of individual texts as projects that strain against one another—and that have done so at least since the expansion of literary critical and historical discourse in the eighteenth century" (658).

Ferguson goes on to offer the history of "a gap between the things of our experience and the names by which they are called" (660). The goal of her 2008 essay is to reassert literary history as a discourse that negotiates the gap between categories and experience and defines literary scholarship. It does that when it "sets a limit to generalizations, or makes them proceed haltingly" (662). In respect to the system of meaning (comparative literature, literature in general, nation-building, globalization), Ferguson explains, individual instances, often those most disadvantaged, define it as a universal category, thus, again, closing the gap as they also open a new one. Close reading, she concludes, "involves not just the demonstration of what we call literary evidence but also a deductive process that underpins such evidence even as it isn't contained in it" (Ferguson 682).

Here then is another way to explain the importance of mere reading and its role in reorganizing literary studies as we create an alternative to how Ferguson understands the relation between reading and history. Mere reading works by offering an alternative to the recursive reading and writing practices whereby individual instances serve to upend and reconstitute general rules. The latter, employed by Ferguson, has a Kantian imperative model where the action does not merely follow a general principle but instantiates it as a principle. The explicit purpose of mere reading is to reorganize the relation between naming and experience, general and particular, such that no principle can explain an activity. On it, we act the way we act; we name the way that we name; and we read the way we read. That is, as Hegel showed, Kantian aporias break down every time we act.

Or again, if there is a dialectic between history and reading, there is a point in fully stopping the exchange and stepping outside of the cycle. There is a point, too, in then regarding this moment when a text does not belong to either history or reading as the critical moment that defines interpretation and literary studies with it.

De Man's essay "Literary History and Literary Modernity" can be understood along the same lines as Ferguson's, whereby we notice history best from a naïve and fresh—modern in de Man's terms—perspective and vice versa, uniqueness of the literary is sharpest from the opposite, historicist view. However, de Man's goal is to move through and beyond the opposition and open up other interpretations.

De Man writes,

> literary language cannot be treated within the limits of this paper. We are more concerned, at this point, with the question of whether a history of an entity as self-contradictory as literature is conceivable. In the present state of literary studies this possibility is far from being clearly established. It is generally admitted that a positivistic history of literature, treating it as if it were a collection of empirical data, can only be a history of what literature is not. At best, it would be a preliminary classification opening the way for actual literary study and, at worst, an obstacle in the way of literary understanding. On the other hand, the intrinsic interpretation of literature claims to be anti- or a-historical, but often presupposes a notion of history of which the critic is not himself aware. (de Man, "Literary" 401)

And his solution follows the question he asks:

> Could we conceive of a literary history that would not truncate literature by putting us misleadingly into or outside it, that would be able to maintain the literary aporia throughout, account at the same time for the

truth and the falsehood of the knowledge literature conveys about itself, distinguish rigorously between metaphorical and historical language, and account for literary modernity as well as for its historicity?

The answer he gives is,

> The task may well be less sizable, however, than it seems at first. All the directives we have formulated as guidelines for a literary history are more or less taken for granted when we are engaged in the much more humble task of reading and understanding a literary text. To become good literary historians, we must remember that what we usually call literary history has little or nothing to do with literature and that what we call literary interpretation—provided only it is good interpretation—is in fact literary history. (de Man, "Literary" 403)

That is, reading is a practice or making of history. The requirement that it is a "good" interpretation, we understand, not as meeting a specific standard but whether it, as a practice, accomplishes what the mere reading is supposed to do. The reading is an experience with language in literature such that it does not support inside/outside or truth/falsehood distinctions and lacks referentiality. The separation between metaphorical and historical language takes place when we understand history as practice and metaphor as produced by the metadiscourse of naming or describing that practice. Reading is good if it demonstrates not the possibility of generalization but the opposite, resistance to it. Such reading, again, has a direct relation to history because it is attempting to de-historicize itself and to free itself or depart from the past and the present as well.

When scholarship presents history and reading experience as informing one another, it does so because it has found a mediating element related to the two. The notion of the text provides such common ground as in, for instance, Jean Howard's famous 1986 essay, "The New Historicism in Renaissance Studies." Howard's chief proposal is that literary studies should see history as a kind of text and that, therefore, there can be no "text *and* context," only text *in* context (24). But this is the case only because history has become accessible as a text. As Howard admits, unless literature is taken to be a simple representation of history, literature's history is a matter of interpretation and reconstruction. She says, "to see how a text functions in the construal of reality means seeing it in an intertextual network of considerable historical specificity" (Howard 27). Or, as Frederic Jameson puts it in *Political Unconscious*, while "history is *not* a text, not a narrative, master or otherwise," it is "inaccessible to us except in textual form" (35). This, of course, we cannot agree with since history is accessible through acts (of, among others, interpterion). Now, we want to suggest a change in emphasis concerning explanations like Howard's. If we read her claim—usually as describing the historical specificity in the works of literature—we should also read it as being about an act of seeing or interpretation. Paramount for identifying history as an unconscious text is, as Jameson indicates, Althusser and Lacan's works, whose merging has resulted in political unconscious appearing through works of art. Once we understand that this process of choosing a viewpoint or theory inaugurates our ability to "see" or register history in a work of art, there is also a new framework that itself needs to be subjected to scrutiny (and mere reading provides a shortcut by, to repeat, interrupting this symbolic ordering). This is to suggest that historicization is, then, not really a form of generalization, but a form of framing a text, choosing a context, which are interpretative moves that close off other readings. Scholars of literature have a foundational interest in making mere reading possible to understand how their apparatuses of interpretation work, how a relation between a text and context is established, how an interpretation is an act, and so on.

Besides, after 30 years of dominance of this approach, historicism does not present what it did in the mid-1980s when it provided what seemed a fresh new look at literature. Today historicism comes together with a score of positions, including knee-jerk rejection of corporate America, capitalism, and colonialism, while the proponents, in their professional and private lives, enjoy the fruits of corporate capitalism and discrimination as members in the middle class and intellectual elite.[10] Critique often stands in the way of being thoughtful, and so on. The last 30 years of tensions between literature and history is likely the source of the post-culture wars fragmentation in our profession. As we can see in Marjorie Garber's 2003 *A Manifesto for Literary Studies*, already by the turn of the millennium, literary scholars felt they were forced to choose sides, whether or not, in Paul Jay's terms, "theoretical and methodological approaches to literature" are put "ahead of literature itself" (45).

Today our challenge is different from the one historicism responded to initially: to figure how to interpret processes and create assumptions that are disciplinary and interdisciplinary, unique and shared, representational in the new sense. Interpretations that are manifold and mere, and for that reason, have a specific relation to an ideology that they exceed.

We do not regard this opening of context as just another abstract philosophical characteristic. Keeping the opening open and making the mere reading possible requires work, scholarly and institutional—this not the least because the prevalence of historicism has sidelined other priorities. This maintenance also has to account for new insights into the thus far not considered dimensions of reading that can be introduced through cognitive science and neurology. We will briefly look into the neurology of reading and then with more detail at accepted history-making practices as they are presented in Levine's *Forms*.

To be clear, this is not an argument to do away with history but to understand and do it differently in accordance with mere reading.

Neurology

There are aspects of reading and writing that depend on neurology and evolution. Because reading was acquired late in human development, it is a learned activity our brains have a hard time adjusting to. But what is hard for the brain also tends to be good for it. The Blavatnik Institute for neurobiology website sums up what happens in the brain when we read this way:

> A number of brain regions are involved in reading and comprehension. Among them are the temporal lobe, which is responsible for phonological awareness and for decoding and discriminating sounds; Broca's area in the frontal lobe, which governs speech production and language comprehension; and the angular and supramarginal gyrus, which link different parts of the brain so that letter shapes can be put together to form words.
>
> In addition, there are several important white-matter pathways involved in reading ... White matter is a collection of nerve fibers in the brain—so called for the white color of myelin, the fatty substance that insulates the fibers—that help the brain learn and function. (Harvard, "Reading and the Brain")

This is to say that reading requires the simultaneous engagement of multiple specialized parts of the brain, sound, and visual centers. Because these are located in different lobes, there is an additional level of complexity of coordination between two halves, which the brain is not all that good at. The participation of myelin, the insulating sheet of neurons (that goes bad in Alzheimer's), means that the brain's overall health, immune, and perhaps other systems play a role as well.

Recent studies have indicated that the cerebellum (aka "little brain") might play a role, too (Alvarez and Fiez), as well as the possibility that different languages are processed by the brain differently (Tayeb et al.), which opens up additional levels of differentiation and complexity. Neurological research, however, focuses on reading impairments since that is the area of gross general differences detectable by current imaging technology. If, indeed, fMRI imaging can distinguish between more and less proficient readers (Cullum et al.), perhaps it would be possible also to distinguish a range of readings from mere to close to critical and support literary theory through it, too.

History in Levine's forms

Again, Levine's employment of history is instructive for our purposes because it shows routine practices that make up our actual epistemology. We will also learn how understanding history's presence through a "text" gets developed.

Levine voices a general view when she states that our work "situate[s] literary objects in thickly described, local contexts." The situation provides specificity and even an ethical dimension to her readings (*Forms* ix). The positioning is done out of interest in particulars of the past that give the authentic color to material and because details we discover constitute opportunities that we can use as models for our behavior. In Levine's words, "[t]he past shows us what is possible—and we return, again and again, to its arrangements: the ordering of bodies and spaces, hierarchies and narratives, containments and exclusions" *(Forms* xii). The past is like a theater in which we can learn how to act and what role or stories are available to take on. It is ethical because something other than ourselves emerges as a model or so the thinking goes.

But the approach works in *Forms* as Levine uses the TV serial, *The Wire* as a model to measure and assess, and then give meaning to, her other examples. She says, for instance,

> By shifting its focus from the power of individuals or elite groups to the intricate "political ecology" of a whole world of contending forms, *The Wire* allows us to see networks as linking other forms, but also derailing them and being derailed by them.... Far from an ideologically coherent society with power lodged in the hands of a few, *The Wire* gives us a social world constantly unsettled by the bewildering and unexpected effects of clashes among wholes, rhythms, hierarchies, and networks. (149)

She means that a present example allows us to see not only this one text in these terms but many other texts as if there were something in those texts that participates in the "intricate 'political ecology.'" Despite all of its diverse contexts and their specificities, the entire history of form becomes legible as a sequence of networks that continue and interrupt one another—which happens only when we start with the example that gives us the optics.

As is the case in many other historicists' works, Levine's chapters have a chronological order, with the one on *The Wire* being last though, in the epistemic sense, it is the first. *The Wire* gets the place of a conclusion, despite *Forms* meaning to show just the opposite of what that order suggests. The past, hence, emerges *after* we establish the perspective informed through a reading of *The Wire* and Bruno Latour's network theory, but is laid out as if the past comes *before* the present. Furthermore, historicist works are evaluated by the optics they employ and are expected to use the latest theoretical issues to be considered relevant. This suggests that the past is not like some other land we encounter for the first time but what we reveal or discover using specific tools of our design, where the generalization of that tool, not discovering the past, is the primary goal of the interpretation. And so the context in which we read is simply the theory we employ, not a specific historical moment other than our own—the historicists also usually deny that they are theorist and therefore do not feel responsible to explain the deployment or the framework that they rely on.

We can, however, also agree with Levine's intentions to show that historicism and formalism cannot be separated. Given that goal, I think she should have presented her argument differently, not by focusing on "form" but on the network theory as a formalist or structuralist theory that constitutes her analytic tool. The explanation could have been followed by demonstrating *The Wire*'s structure and how its political, formal, and ideological choices are intertwined. Then, she would have faced the problem of relevance, which is, in the published configuration, hidden by the assumption that this book accounts for the past in a new way.

Theoretical concerns

Philosophically speaking, literary scholarship does not have to solve the problem of history or the past and its representation. Instead, its most historical question is how we understand the present. As Hans-Georg Gadamer put it in *Truth and Method*, "historical consciousness is itself situated in the web of historical effects" (300). Again, the claim is usually interpreted as the assertion that history is not about dates and deeds but the network of relations as these are presented in the works we read or watch. Our understanding is different. First, the claim is about my historical consciousness as a researcher. It is the author of interpretation who is themselves a historical effect. When they write, they are not the bystander who chooses the window through which to see history. Instead, we are immersed in the web that is acting on us in ways we cannot understand, or when we can understand them, our understanding is bound to lag our position in history. We, then, necessarily have only partial access to our place in history, our so-called present, which needs to be reflected in our scholarship, its vocabulary, and claims. The main point here is that this "partiality" of our view, position, and the possibility to interpret *is* historical and that we can have only a limited understanding of it, which itself is an expression of historicity.

When I inhabit this subject position and behave as a scholar, I am already a product, not a source. When I put together my interpretation, I am already acting historically. Not accounting for this positioning results in an interpretation that "resembles statistics, which are such excellent means of propaganda because they let the 'facts' speak and hence simulate an objectivity that in reality depends on the legitimacy of the questions asked" (Gadamer 300). We understand Gadamer to mean that unless we disclose the necessarily partial position from which we speak as integral to the production of our interpretation, we are presenting what we say as a "fact." By legitimacy of the questions asked, Gadamer means to point to the theories we employ as what frames and forms our interpretations and legitimates or grounds them. The commentary does not so much as complicate our historical work but reroutes it to an understanding that "history is not … fundamentally different from understanding language…[and] [t]he infiniteness of the past, and above all the openness of the historical future, is incompatible with the idea of a historical universe" (Gadamer 209, 248). Gadamer likens history to language to show the relative relationship to humans, indicate the limits of their mastery of it, and try and describe its vastness and layered structure.

Usual historicity often equates past and history and assumes that the backward point of view is somehow proper to scholarly discourse. History, in other words, is presented as necessarily about the past. One has to go to the first half of the twentieth century USSR to find the alternative where history regularly connotes what is to come. There, literature and other arts are a vehicle by which the future can be made present. This is done in a manner dissimilar to science fiction by presenting what is far as near. (Science fiction often does the opposite, projecting the present onto the future to make it available for retrospection.) I do not mean to recommend that aesthetic but to remind that historically history is not necessarily defined by the past and that literary representation is not a repeated presence of a past event but a projection.

The openness of perspectives is a matter of reading—mere reading has this as its goal, to produce this not-wholeness, the impossibility of totalization as an empirical fact of interpretation. Levine seems to make a similar suggestion when she speaks of unboundedness, claiming that the relation between unbounded networks and bounded wholes "allows us to grasp culture as an object of study." And so she poses what she identifies as a fundamental challenge to poststructuralism: "Are networks containable or uncontainable by bounded shapes?" (*Forms* 117). In our view, such suggestion is based on a misunderstanding of how poststructuralists see networks and forms, which Levine finds to be still theorized in reference to a "bounded whole." The answer is readily available: for poststructuralism, they are neither bound nor unbounded. As we can conclude from, for instance, Derrida's reading of the *khôra* (a formless container) published in *On the Name* or from Latour's understanding offered in *Reassembling the Social*, where he says that form is "one of the most important types of translation" (223). The form is not an entity and to the extent that poststructuralists use it, it is what brings things, shapes, or signifying entities into relation—a bottle and liquid, a poem and its meaning, and so on. Both mentioned theorists and other prominent poststructuralists maintain that no language-related, interpretation-dependent structure can be a totality or bounded form. Using Lovelock, Latour claims the same approach for life on Earth. Structures are neither contained nor uncontainable in Levine's sense. Totality and wholes are, instead, impossibilities that, when they do appear, are projections, results of desires for the whole, or fantasies. Making "patriarchy," "supremacy," and other forms of oppression into such wholes does not, in my understanding, decisively contribute to solving the social justice problems historicism addresses. It only imposes a view on the structure that gives us the illusion of comprehension and control which then justify our interventions.

We can start the work on history and literature with the assumption that the world exists in constant "movement of relative validity" (Gadamer 248), in which "being is time" (Gadamer 257). This dynamic, poststructuralist notion of history favors possibilities, relations, and transience and what we can call future aspects of meaning. Futurity—delay, not-yetness, and so on—unfortunately is not among the common categories of our historicism. This, even though "difference" is and it, in poststructuralist theory, cannot be separated from the term "deferral," which defines time as the mode in which difference exists. Derrida, famously, coined a new word—*différance* (*Writing and Difference*)—bringing together difference and deferral to capture a temporal duality.

Networks are formed as systems of differences that first impact the speaking—writing, thinking, interpreting—subject. This subject is constituted in the spatiotemporal network through the process of interpreting a work like *The Wire*. Thus, the network is not, to repeat, a way to understand a TV series and history behind it, but to understand how "self" (including the self of the author like Levine) relates to language, how it relates to representation, how text (our writing) captures a moment in time by being an event in language, and how we make sense of the world around us using language.

The condition is explored and performed to a great effect in a recent biography of Jacques Derrida by Peter Salmon, titled *An Event, Perhaps*. Salmon's work offers a way to make a person's history consistent with Derrida's philosophy.

To sum up

Based on this discussion, when we hear "history," we should not think, as we usually do, about the bygone or the relationship between what happened and a now; or about identities and roles that are available to us; or about the limitations of our perspective. When reading, we should instead suppose that the past is not finished, that the present does not provide a vantage point, and that we live in an animated, symbolically charged world of continuously lurking and changing possibilities that define us.[11] This emphasis on presentness is also an argument to see representational aspects of literature as performance (not as mimesis in Plato's sense).

In short, literary studies is not about the past (first), but about the framework that is established or assumed in the process of setting up or positioning an interpretation.

History produced by literary studies is an exercise in the possibilities of interpretation, making unusual connections, and creating new meanings. History *about* literary studies can be a significant discourse in constructing literary scholarship because it helps us account for different frameworks and the institutional life of our arguments, which are indispensable at this point of our evolution as a discipline. I used this approach in this chapter to present, first, definitions of close reading, then definitions of historicity, which we consider to be the facts of the history of literary scholarship *as well as* products of our interpretation. Our history is propositional, as in, for instance, our general claim that poststructuralism is not incompatible with universalization, which we offer not as a summary of what we find in poststructuralist works but as a framework that we, then, support with textual evidence we understand in a specific way. I used the same method to show why reading in context is inadequate (because the author's theory defines the "historical" context but is not understood as a part of what needs to be analyzed) and why we want to understand the relation between interpretation and historicity in terms of the present and future, not the past (because we set up the framework in the present). With mere reading, our task is to open relationships that we establish as scholars and use the mere reading not as a critical tool but a tool that interrupts our discourse and shows our framework for what it is, namely, an arbitrary viewpoint and a set of assumptions.

This demonstration of the partiality of our point of view is what allows us to claim the universality of our approach. Poststructuralism is not a universal theory because it is valid for all but because it shows the conditions under which we can universalize, based on frameworks and the openness of the systems we identify as we create our scholarship. After the particularization of the point of view and the disappearance of the classical paradigm, what is left are not the elements, because fragments and multiforms are still defined in reference to the presumed whole. Instead, what is left is a question if theory can account for a different totality and do so by means other than one/all.

In the next section of this chapter on review, we will focus directly on defining an understanding of what review can be. We will return to history in the last chapter and Susan Buck-Morss's *Hegel, Haiti, and Universal History* where we will also offer an account of what a universal poststructuralist theory might become.

To end this section on history, we will again borrow from Paul Jay. His recommendation for future scholars of literature lays out what seem like reasonable criteria. He writes,

> The best candidate for most jobs will be the young man or woman who was required to think conceptually, critically, analytically, and theoretically not only about the texts they were required to read but also about the historical construction of their value and the competing critical methodologies that have been used to interpret them.
>
> A humanities education that takes an aesthetic education seriously in the kinds of ways I have been discussing has the potential to make the whole question of aesthetic experience interesting and engaging to twenty-first-century students by linking it to their own cultural and social experiences. (131)

Much had changed since 2014 when Jay's work was published. From our point of view, the best candidate for a job in literary studies is a student who can think beyond the parameters that defined literary scholarship since the culture wars. Of course, such expectations may seem absurd since we do not offer much to create such scholars. Still, the demand is quite clear—the demand is the reason I decided to adopt sometimes a didactic laying out of the argument and develop *Interdiscipline* by going over the basics. The tone is necessary when the goal is a thoroughgoing revision.

Part III: reconstruction/translation

The emphasis on the futural character of interpretation makes the wholeness of a scholarly work and holes in its content appear less pertinent and less determinative of the work's values. It also foregrounds the issues of the epistemological frameworks that literary studies is operating with and within. The futural also suggests an alternative to the review genre as we typically practice it—namely, a reconstruction.

Put another way, if we give primacy to mere reading, the quality of presentness of the novel, and its ability to set and change frameworks, there are specific implications for the scholarly genres we use. In the next chapter, we will talk about peer review; here we can conclude the above analysis with a note on form (scholarly review) that links interpretation and evaluation and thus fashions a scholarly product (which is itself subject to peer review).

For our purposes, reconstruction is to be understood as showing the unrealized possibilities and future of what could be made out of the same sets of data. Reconstruction does that by first noting the critical epistemological issues, namely, the interpretation framework. It, then, assumes the original work's point of view, asking how it might be put together again, at a different point in time, at a different place, in a different context or framework. The questions are raised in, for instance, *Not Saved: Essays after Heidegger* (2017) as a part of Peter Sloterdijk's interpretation of Heidegger.

Reconstruction asks not the usual questions—what is missing from this argument? Or what the past was? Rather, how might these suppositions be put together or refashioned in a new context, and what are other possibilities for interactions with data and interpretations?

In the *PMLA* accounts, following Latour's understanding of form as a type of translation (*Reassembling* 223), Levine's critics could have understood their task as translating between the reader and the general issue of form in literary interpretation. Their heading could have been something like "After Form" or "With Form/Against Form." Levine's book's shortcomings make this direction of scholarly engagement that much more suitable as an opportunity to reposition and radically refashion, not to say correct, her approach to "form." I believe this chapter performs this function of repositioning *Forms* in the sense that I have interrogated its "frameworks" (because this is the hallmark of my theoretical approach) as the starting point of thinking about form and have then offered an analysis of discourses on form, like close reading and historicity that define it. The general claim in this argument is that framework should be regarded as the most formal of issues in a study of interpretation since it positions what we say and relates it to everything else, its insides and outsides.

One way to understand reconstruction is to negotiate positions, choosing a nodal point from which we can begin to formulate the network that our interpretations stand for. Indeed, interpreter or middleman or negotiator is a traditional role of every literate person—a synonym for it, as it follows from Stephen Greenblatt's "What is the History of Literature?" Literary studies is intimately familiar with this role and its many iterations like the one noted in Bhabha's *The Location of Culture*. As Robert J. C. Young emphasizes, translation is an alternative form of critique that produces "not a resolution or negation in the mode of an *Aufhebung* that preserves and cancels" as the usual reviews try to do, "but something 'new, *neither the one nor the Other*'" (Young 189), which resonates with the sense of interpretation as a meeting point between horizons, and with the reconstruction as a genre of literary scholarship.

A literary scholar can be an archivist, activist, historian, theorist, *and* cultural mediator, all at the same time, because they are readers and because symbolic forms cannot be bound. I would venture to say that being-in-between/reader (being interdisciplinary and disciplinary at the same time) is perhaps the most effective way to perform all of our other appropriate roles. The role can extend to functioning as mediators/readers between the disciplines within the humanities and, even to mediating between the sciences, on the one hand, and humanities, on the other hand. Because of its proximity to language and interpretation, literary studies is the discipline that can most readily accept other disciplines into itself, adopt and employ their methods and theories, and remain itself. It is, in short, the most open, most malleable form of scholarship created. And the reason literary studies is the most open discipline lies, to repeat, in the approach to its object of study. The specificity is usually presented as coming from literature's access to an alterity which is itself explained in the representational sense that works of art present other times, places, peoples, and points of view or contexts. That is the case, to be sure, but such alterity does not go beyond information and identification, and the approach says little about why the information can be accessed and understood from a different point of view. Instead, we presented the specificity of literary studies in employing methods/experiences like mere reading, which open access to language and the understanding of how interpretation works that other disciplines are not equipped to create.

The translator's role exemplifies this as it requires fluency in many languages and familiarity with many cultural and disciplinary contexts, including different periods, and supposes, in an organic way, multiculturalism, open-ended structure, endless exchange, wide and widening perspectives, intersectionality, and so on. That is to say, we do not need design theory or *The Wire* to serve us as a model when we have the age-old stock figure of middleman that embodies what a literary scholar can be as a cultural, economic, and political figure (Pym).

Construction of emotions

To the notions of text we usually hold, we have to add the new forms of textuality and materiality based on how cognitive science and neurology see certain brain functions. As Steven Pinker explains in *How the Mind Works*, the brain does not merely internalize reality, it, instead, "*supplies the missing information*" (28). "We don't just passively perceive the world, we actively generate it. The world we experience comes as much, if not more, from the inside out as from the outside in," as Anil Seth explains in his TED talk, which argues that our conscious reality is a hallucination created by our brain (Seth). This is to say that our brain does not decode but encodes or translates between concepts and surroundings, building a reality on its suppositions about what we will see, and adjusting its "predictions" based on experience.

The brain shapes perceptions using "modules" or "built-in assumptions" (Pinker 32). It is skilled and efficient at this activity of predicting, recognizing what something is by applying what it has learned previously—the matrixes, the formulas, the narratives, the figures of speech—and by understanding the stimuli under specific headings or formulations. It is more adept at creating this kind of bigger picture that fits our prejudgments than at anything else it has to do, especially identifying idiosyncratic details.

Emotions are constructed in this fashion as well, as Lisa Feldman Barrett argues in her *How Emotions Are Made*. According to Barrett, our brain creates our "experience of emotion" (xiii). The way we understand the internal stimuli depends—in part—on our social surroundings, upbringing but also on the overall state of our organism. She says, for instance, "If you didn't have concepts that represent your past experience, all your sensory inputs would be just noise … With concepts, your brain makes meaning of sensation, and … [that] meaning is an emotion" (31). She adds that "construction extends all the way down to the cellular level," as new synapses are formed based on novel experiences (34). If the "reality" and brain modules differ, "new information" shapes future predictions. This foreknowledge is a "fundamental activity of the human brain" that "not only anticipate[s] sensory input" but also "*explain[s]* it" (59).

When, for instance, poets invent new linguistic forms, they are creating new ways of seeing, representing, and understanding experience. They are also changing our predictive powers and creating new pathways in the brain. Literary studies has a privileged insight into these pathbreaking activities and can, in its way, detail what they are, again, because we are readers, present when meanings are created, recreated, and codified. There is also a point in understanding constructions of emotions where we should try for the experience of "noise" or mere reading to take place. This is a way of integrating knowledge about the construction that takes place on cellular, linguistic, and textual levels. We can liken this to witnessing of our own experience and how it is put together.

For the end of this chapter, let me take a note from Audre Lorde. These all are reasons why poetry is not a luxury: "It is a vital necessity of our existence. It forms the quality of the light within which we predicate our hopes and dreams toward survival and change, first made into language, then into idea, then into more tangible action" (37). Lorde's words can pretty much be the motto of the new literary studies because they put together existence, language, and action, we see as inaugurating or positioning an interpretation. Lord also speaks about the future and sees literature not as a representation but as a projection and extension.

Notes

1 "Theories and Methodologies" appeared first in the May issue of 2005. It was the "memorial and tributary" section devoted to Susan Sontag's work, as Hirsch explains in her "Editor's Column." See also Hirsch, "Editor's Column: What Can a Journal Essay Do?" as a companion manifesto.

2 Stephanie Sandler's review unfolds as a challenge to Levine's form, asking what would happen if Levine "privileged not narrative but [...] poetry?" (Sandler 1227). Sandler, then, offers an answer to that question with references to Levine's *Forms* which explains the usefulness of what Sandler believes is the most significant contribution of the book, namely, identifying four forms, *whole*, *rhythm*, *hierarchy*, and *network*. As Sandler presents it, poetry does not represent a new framework, only a different genre within the same.
3 Once again, Joseph North's *Literary Criticism* is an exception to the rules I just defined. I am not engaging his work because it offers a review of similar material in theoretical and political terms that this project does not agree with. The reader should, however, see North's take on the history of New Criticism for an in-depth look at its diversity.
4 In his introduction to *Close Reading*, Andrew DuBois also claims Ransom as the chief—and, at times, it seems the only—proponent of the version of reading we know today as New Criticism.
5 See also Sheldon Pollock's "Future Philology? The Fate of a Soft Science in a Hard World" which analyzes the discipline in the context of interdisciplinarity.
6 My work is on trauma, and I am not dismissing trigger warnings or microaggressions. Instead, I am critical of them when they take the form of interpretation, are used to define the limits of reading, relations in the classroom, and otherwise stand in the way of the bewilderment with a text and the mere experience.
7 In this definition, the reader should hear an echo of Roman Jakobson definition of the poetic function of language (Jakobson).
8 Biblicism is a "theory about the Bible that emphasizes together its exclusive authority, infallibility, perspicuity, self-sufficiency, internal consistency, self-evident meaning, and universal applicability" (C. Smith viii).
9 See also affect studies, Hogan.
10 To be clear, I am commenting on the double standard, not on individual choices.
11 Deferral has been presented as a part of literary interpretation, to my mind, most precisely by Shoshana Felman in her *Testimony* on which I have written elsewhere. The reader should bear in mind that what appears as trauma in the context Felman interprets is, for the present discussion, an imperfect, unfinished, and open character of temporal modalities.

3
PEER REVIEW
Evaluation as a form of reading

After our close investigation of literary studies in the previous two chapters, we move to a related concern. Peer evaluation is an example of the review genre we practice at every level of the profession, and it is also the most peculiar institution that frames our discipline and defines it as a modern discipline. But though integral to everything we do—research and career advancement, how fields and new discipline are divided and formed as autonomous units, even our personal happiness—in the humanities and literary studies, peer review is not an object of specific or continuous scholarly scrutiny. To make matters worse, we undertake the review, for the most part, in secrecy and believe that despite problems, the practice is fundamentally sound.

The discussion that follows is about the ways we can elevate scholarly and collegial standards for peer review and bring it closer to how we read literary works. The path for examining peer review we propose rests on the assumption of mutual dependence between peer review, interpretation, and methodology, all of which come together to define us as a discipline, department, and institution.

We will also show that our discipline is not fragmented because of the inherent qualities that make it so but because it is shaped by a fragmented peer review process that divides the discipline into small autonomous areas of expertise and keeps those boundaries in place. To remedy the problem, the chapter will suggest specific changes to peer review criteria—a preference for a general and interdisciplinary approach as well as understanding peer review as integral to scholarship—as the quickest and most effective way to alter literary studies.

As in previous chapters, we start again from the decades of the culture wars and the reforms we want to continue. The fact that we are returning again and again to this moment in history should suggest as well that culture wars are, in fact, not over. They are no longer fought primarily in the academic departments

DOI: 10.4324/9781003119616-4

but define the general political context in the United States and influence our discipline by those means as well.

Part I: peer review: current and history

1970s

In 1978, Douglas Peters and Stephen Ceci were young assistant professors at the University of North Dakota facing the prospect of tenure decisions. At lunch one day, someone suggested that "a recent publication in a prestigious psychology journal would never have been published if the author had not been an eminent researcher from Harvard" (Peters and Ceci, "Study of Journal Publication"). Peters and Ceci were intrigued by this claim. They put together a study that ultimately made their careers. They resubmitted 12 articles to the journals that originally published them, having changed only the wording of the opening paragraphs and the author's affiliation (to fictitious institutions like Tri-valley Center for Human Potential). The results were devastating. Out of twelve essays, only three were recognized for what they were, and the remaining nine went on through the peer review process. Of the nine, eight were rejected, some because of serious methodological flaws (Peters and Ceci, "Naturalistic"). The study pointed to systemic faults and marked a beginning point of a thorough peer review reassessment.[1]

At around the same time, 1978, William Schaefer, then the MLA Executive Director, published "Anonymous Review: A Report from the Executive Director", a summary of the MLA Executive Council's debates about peer review—debates that were in many ways ahead of the trend. The report's goal was "to ensure that in making their evaluations, readers are not influenced by factors other than the intrinsic merits of the article" (4). As a result of the report, two main changes were instituted in 1980: the MLA resolved "to require that articles be outstanding of their kind but not necessarily of interest to everyone" and to adopt "the practice of anonymous submission" (Showalter 851), which Schaefer himself opposed. The main reason offered were the biases inherent in the non-blind process (Schaefer 4). Among the arguments cited in favor of this change were the preferences expressed by female and young scholars to remain anonymous (Schaefer 5).

In 1995, a *PMLA* editorial by Domna Stanton offered an assessment that confirmed the positive effects of the changes instituted in the early 1980s. She surveyed the honorable mentions and the winners of *PMLA*'s prestigious William Riley Parker Prize for their opinions on the journal's review process. Stanton recognized that her sample was not representative (983) but nonetheless presented the conclusions as if they held general significance. Summarizing the responses, she wrote that the *PMLA*

> peer-review system elicits good marks, ranging from 'reasonably adequate to the needs of a discipline stretched to its limits in the attempt to capture

... the very world of words' (Morris Eaves) to 'well tailored and well managed' (Ong) and 'on balance, admirable' (A. Kent Hieatt). (986)

Only E. D. Hirsch complained (about the length of the process), but even he was happy in the end (990). The image of *PMLA* was then what it remains to this day: an exemplary journal of the highest standard where even rejections can be seen in a positive light since authors get useful reviews and advice on how to improve their articles (990).[2] However, no concrete or precise or detailed examination of the process of evaluation was offered; only general, self-congratulatory marks like "good," "well tailored," "admirable," and so on.

Literary scholars' views on peer review have not changed much since 1995. The search "SU: peer review" in the MLA Database leads to only one article published since 2016, an essay by Michael Bérubé from the January 2018 issue of the *PMLA*, titled "The Way We Review Now." The first ten hits—research was done in May 2019—also include: two dissertations, both on student to student reviews (Byrne, Saenpoch); two articles on the student to student review (Keating, Grant); two articles from the *Cinema Journal* that are short notes, barely over three journal pages each (Mittell, Denson); and four full-length articles from the *Journal of Scholarly Publishing*, which covers general issues in academic publishing and is not regularly cited or otherwise engaged with by literary scholars (Segado-Boj et al., Edington, Lipscombe, Sabaj Meruane, et al.).

This quick look at the MLA Database should illustrate a central point of this chapter: after Peters and Ceci's study, the primary reform instituted by literary studies was responding to identity bias and took the form of making peer review double-blind. Other disciplinary or epistemological concerns have not been addressed. And when there was another opportunity to do that in 2004, on the occasion of the MLA Task Force on Evaluating Scholarship for Tenure and Promotion, the authors showed no concern with any element of peer review, focusing on genres, monograph versus article, and digital versus paper publications (Stanton et al.). The lack of interest correlates closely with the status of methodology which is also absent and which makes our field ill prepared to communicate with other disciplines.

The chapter will start with a formulation of the problem as we look at the institutional status of peer review and a few expert views. We will then move to the history of peer review to identify the model we prefer because of its interdisciplinary potential. The chapter will then turn to methodology to align how we interpret a text with how we review, which is the core of our argument. The chapter will end with a look at newer, so-called open peer review from the point of view of the interdisciplinary model of this practice as we defined it.

The reason to devote attention to peer review is that it directly responds to our methodology; examining it, we are actually creating methodology and assumptions that enter into its construction.

Why peer review

The reasons to pursue an interdisciplinary peer review and not other models are both extrinsic and intrinsic. This is the direction sciences are following since at least 1989, which is the date of the first multidisciplinary, international Peer Review Congress (Rennie and Flanagin), which itself was among the responses to Peters and Ceci's study. This interdisciplinary turn already reached a major landmark in 2010 with the publication of *The Oxford Handbook of Interdisciplinarity*, leaving little doubt where the most interesting research into peer review lies.

And the intrinsic reason is that we want to acknowledge that history of literary studies—beyond the New Critical close reading, beyond Arnoldian nationalism—in which this hermeneutic discipline appears as an interdisciplinary discipline with the capacity to accommodate other disciplines and methods while remaining coherent (Fish 1989). From this angle, we are late to the interdisciplinary party by some 20 years but still in the position to make a substantial contribution. But only if literary scholars are, as we said already, willing to again become enthusiastic about areas of scholarship like methodology and epistemology that have received little attention in recent times and now need to be rearticulated to address interdisciplinarity.

We are still using the term interdisciplinary loosely to identify the general tendency of collaboration and openness to other disciplines' methodology. Chapter 5 will deal with the shortcoming.

And my final introductory note: the reader should be conscious of a specific attitude prevalent in peer review discussions. As Drummond Rennie, one of Peer Review Congress organizers, noted, the attitude can be likened to Churchill's view on democracy: dysfunctional, but better than the alternatives ("Editorial" 10). We note this perennial status only to emphasize the new trend that comes with interdisciplinary peer review. When, as in the Oxford volume, peer review is treated as a scholarly topic on par with others, the dissatisfaction seems to give way to an excitement about opportunities. As peer review moves from an auxiliary method to a process integral to creating knowledge, the whole scope of knowledge production changes along with it. The closer we are to the problem, once again, the more exciting it gets.

This switch occurred in the sciences, where there was a shift from seeing peer review as mere quality control to recognizing it as an essential developmental step in knowledge production. This is perhaps the most critical change that happened since the 1989 congress and one that we should emulate in literary studies.

Journals, a cursory look

A cursory look at scholarly journals in literary studies demonstrates what might well be the main circumstantial reason for the dearth of articles directly addressing the epistemological or scholarly dimension of peer review. It shows no home in literary studies for inquiries into what form of peer review is most suitable for literary studies, what peer review is as a form of interpretation, and so on. I will cite here just three journals I consider exemplary. First, *Comparative Literature Studies* describes what it publishes as

> comparative critical essays that range across the rich traditions of Africa, Asia, Europe, and North and South America, examining the literary relations between East and West, North and South. Articles may also explore movements, themes, forms, the history of ideas, relations between authors, the foundations of criticism and theory, and language and translation issues. (*Comparative Literature Studies*)

A list of requirements for submission adds the following criteria:
 A comparative article for *CLS* should contain most if not all of the following:

- demonstrated polylingual competence;
- an approach that illuminates the various authors explored, or that treats in breadth and pluriexemplarity national traditions, literary forms, literary theory, or world literature;
- a unique contribution that is clearly articulated and demonstrated through coherent argument;
- situation of the author's contribution within relevant existing criticism of the work(s) under investigation;
- one or more close readings of the text(s) under discussion, that bring to light aspects not immediately discernible on a cursory or uninformed perusal of the passages; and
- at minimum, reference to, and most likely active deployment of the most

> prominent theoretical elaborations of the topic(s) being explored. (*Comparative Literature Studies,* Submissions)

This is to say that an article like this chapter, though it treats matter relevant to comparative literature scholarship and is inspired by this field's interdisciplinarity, would not be appropriate submission to *CLS*.

This is also the case with journals with a more general ambit, which have a declared stake in epistemological issues. For example, *New Literary History*'s website suggests that it is "the first English language journal devoted to literary theory and general questions of method and interpretation" (*New Literary History: About NLH*). The general questions of method about which the journal is concerned, needless to say, have yet to include peer review.[3]

And my final journal example—since my point is already clear—is *diacritics*. The paradigmatic journal of literary theory, this publication again offers nothing on the topic, as if peer review is not among key framing issues. There is "The Essay, in Theory" by Brian Lennon from 2008, which makes a case for expanding our scholarly genres but does not spend time on peer review or the question of how peer review shapes the environment of genres.

The obvious conclusion is that peer review is not an essential part of our scholarship or a fundamental theoretical issue on the same level as various kinds of thematic content like more commonly regarded topoi such as authors, cultural and political issues, forms of expression, periods, genres, theoretical questions that are pertinent to specific areas, other framing issues, and so on.

The same conclusion holds even if early readers of this chapter are correct when they suggested that area studies, MLA suborganizations, and journals discuss peer review. Even if that is correct, such treatment does not meet the four points of this critique. First, peer review is treated as a scholarly topic integral to the production of scholarship. Second, it is treated as a general issue that concerns literary studies in its entirety. Third, it is deliberately developed as an interdisciplinary tool based on our understanding of interpretation that accommodates our discipline and humanities and sciences. Fourth, it is not used as an authorizing instrument for a narrow body of knowledge but as a critical instrument that is a part of general and interdisciplinary orientation of scholarship. The four characteristics are not just what a poststructuralist reform of knowledge production would require. They, too, lift the scholarly standard of peer review, develop it into an instrument based on comprehensive insights into theory and practice of interpretation and evaluation for which literary studies is uniquely equipped and positioned.

To say that we discuss peer review but do not do it with systematicity afforded to scholarly topics is but to state the problem that this chapter is reacting to. It is like suggesting that we do not need to focus on cars and traffic but can think of transportation in terms of destinations like houses and buildings, homes and offices. Throughout this chapter, a different picture will gradually emerge of peer review—not the method to sift between poor and acceptable scholarship, but as an practice of creating connections or a substructure or an infrastructure on which institutions and production of knowledge are built.

The above cursory look at the prominent journals in literary studies confirms that we construct our fields based on scholarly content and with little regard for other aspects of knowledge production (except pedagogy, which is, however, never central to how we think of any field of literary studies). We also see that the journals accept that they are shaped by themes or periods but not by forms or methodologies we use to evaluate scholarship. The characteristic should remind Bruno Latour's readers of exactly those reasons that prompted his and Steve Woolgar's, *Laboratory Life*, namely, that practices, not just suppositions or intellectual content, make science. If we use Latour's networks but do so without accounting for the institutional context, we are borrowing only a part of the theory and in isolation, with a result that what we take is not a poststructuralist interpretative tool and such networks share but a name with Latour's.

Bérubé

When peer review has received scholarly treatment, it has mostly been occasioned by issues that have nothing to do with the process as such. That occasion can be the emergence of a new area of specialization like "film studies" and the need for it to be legitimated as a field. In such cases, the matter discussed tends to be narrow and conservative, about the specificities of the genre (or activity like translation) in question, showing how these fit the existing concepts of what a field and scholarship are. Cinema studies has led in this respect and has recently also generated reflection on the new forms of peer review such as open versus closed (Dovey, Denson, and Mittell). As important as these efforts have been, they did not include a thorough reassessment of what peer review specific to literary or cultural studies is or should be. As such, they are not directly relevant for our discussion at this stage primarily because they repeat, rather than interrogate, the authorizing force of peer review. At the ending part of this chapter, we will address open review borrowing from a different context.

Besides new fields, the technological challenge was the second general occasion for some reflections on peer review. The emergence of digital publication and the likelihood that it will replace paper-based publishing was the topic of Kathleen Fitzpatrick's *Planned Obsolescence: Publishing, Technology, and the Future of the Academy*.[4] An incident in social media occasioned Michael Bérubé's "The Way We Review Now," which we will examine shortly.

Generalist works like David Shatz's 2004 book *Peer Review*, whose goal is very similar to ours in this chapter—to "examine critical ethical and epistemological issues" (4)—are rare. This work is also the only one that is acutely aware of the controversy started by Peters and Ceci's study of the history of peer review in the *PMLA* and is speaking from that position to offer an exhaustive philosophical analysis of the peer review.[5] It, however, suffers a predicament of being outdated. Because of those technological and political changes that happened since 2004, Shatz's work cannot respond to the most pressing concerns we have today about interdisciplinarity or to the changing role of the humanities in academia.

We will take only a quick look at the three mentioned examples and will read them with an eye for, first, the habit, attitude, and the trend they represent; and, second, for elements, we can use to create an interdisciplinary model.

Michael Bérubé's article "The Way We Review Now" starts with the controversy that followed the investigation of transracialism by Rebecca Tuvel published in 2017 and the subsequent demand (which reached over 800 signatures) that *Hypatia* retracts the article (Winnubst). The angry petition appeared on Facebook, as did the reply—an "apology" by the "self-described majority of associate editors of *Hypatia*" (Bérubé, "Way We Review" 132).

Bérubé's main issue is that the "apology" "repudiated not only the article but also the review process that approved the article for publication" (132). Bérubé defends the process against a danger that looks very much like mob rule (and reminds of the Trumpian uses of Facebook during the last elections). He ends with this dire warning about the fragility of our discipline:

> the very possibility that they [traditional forms of peer review] can be challenged if not undermined by Internet campaigns should serve as a warning and a reminder: in academe, professional, peer-reviewed forms of disagreement are worth preserving, all the more so when they involve protocols of scholarly communication that, like so many artifacts of literate civilization, are far more valuable—and fragile—than most people realize. (137)

He identifies the agency he disproves of as "people outside an area of disciplinary expertise," who offer "extrascholarly review" (134). He contrasts what they do with the process of peer review, which "gave scholars autonomous intellectual authority over the means of production in their fields." By *autonomy* here, he means autonomy from "a system of scholarly communication overseen by the administrators of one's university" (135).

But when he seeks to show the intrusion of power, the only other example Bérubé points to is a 100-year-old controversial firing of Edward Ross from Stanford University, which may or may not have happened because of Ross's toxic, racist newspaper article against Asian emigration published in *The Independent* from New York City. From our perspective, "How We Review Today" presents a relatively straightforward case where certain democratic aspects of peer review are used to represent the whole and are opposed to an extreme erosion of freedom and autonomy. The picture it paints is a simple one: we either choose a dictatorship of all that can have power over us (and there are many of those, god knows) or a peer review process understood in vague terms as an expression of our autonomy, which is policed and guaranteed by "experts." The conception of the discipline that the article represents is equally simple in how it figures who is an "expert," with the lines of expertise coinciding with the boundaries of narrow fields, where the inside is identified with knowledge and the outside with the lack of the same. The logic seems to be that local policemen are better than the mob.

We think of peer review as irreplaceable and fundamental and would go to some lengths not to change it. In this essay, Bérubé uses peer review—and we say this agreeing with his defense of Tuvel's fine essay—to protect the current configuration of literary studies and the sense of expertise resting on the fragmented fields, and not to interrogate such boundaries. So, what emerges above all is a conservative message that in the face of changes and challenges, we must preserve what is ours already.

Fitzpatrick

Kathleen Fitzpatrick's 2011 book *Planned Obsolescence: Publishing, Technology, and the Future of the Academy* is prompted by the transformation in the materiality of texts and what Fitzpatrick sees as the end of the epoch of paper texts. Fitzpatrick positions peer review in the most useful way when she says it is "at the heart of everything we do – writing, applying for grants, seeking jobs, obtaining promotions." Peer review, she adds, is "arguably, what makes the academy the academy" (10). And we can appreciate this summary judgment as well:

> [P]eer review as we currently know it has a different history than we might assume. Very little investigation of the historical development of peer review has been done, and the few explorations that do attempt to present some sense of the system's history largely cite the same handful of brief texts. Moreover, nearly all of the texts exploring the history of peer review focus on the natural and social sciences, and almost none mention peer review in scholarly book publishing. (20)

Fitzpatrick goes on to offer a history of peer review in the usual terms of firsts and earliest, drawing on Mario Biagioli's article "From Book Censorship to Academic Peer Review."[6] However, for our purposes, a different genealogy—one about the editorial function of peer review—is more pertinent, and we will get to it shortly.

The rest of *Planned Obsolescence* is devoted to larger issues outside of the question of peer review, like the changing status of authorship and text in the digital era, Fitzpatrick's main topics. For our purposes, Fitzpatrick's situating of peer review at the heart of our writing is significant as well as symptomatic. She continues to treat it like we usually do—as a process, we submit to when we are done with research and want to do something with it. But then she also repeats the general assumption that academic knowledge is distinguished from non-academic based on this institution of quality control.[7] This is, however, an unhelpful mystification, since scholarship on peer review again and again shows how unreliable and biased it is. Further, it should be obvious that we can no longer position our conversations in respect to the distinction between academia and its outsides, especially as a part of any kind of interdisciplinary inquiry.

Shatz

David Shatz's 2004 book *Peer Review* aims to "examine critical ethical and epistemological issues" and, in order to do so, "utilizes methods and resources of contemporary philosophy" (4). This characterization leads him to speak about peer review regarding a version of C. P. Snow's two cultures thesis. Shatz introduces his research with reference to the critical differences between sciences and humanities that concern the different status of "the truth."

> While philosophical trends and views change, in today's climate many philosophers and professors of literature would not view their conclusions as "the truth." Those in the humanities are likely to be influenced, even if

only subtly, by relativism, historicism, skepticism, and pluralism, and thus to have more inhibitions about conceiving their own views as "the truth." (Shatz 6)

The same distinction between modes of truth makes *Peer Review* also outdated for our purposes. If we are to progress beyond the present crisis of the humanities and move in an interdisciplinary direction, we can no longer uphold such distinction—the truth as mimesis or correspondence in sciences and truth as a revelation in humanities (Eaglestone, "Framing Theory" 164).

The two-cultures division is an expedient way to cut through complex issues and give a view of the humanities we wanted: as distinct from but equal to in importance with the sciences. Since the theory of relativity, the sciences have been moving (perhaps slowly) toward more and more philosophically complex notions of truth, understandings how conditions of experiments determine their outcomes and how socially constructed the scientific method can be. And, the inverse, in the humanities relativism was understood poorly, as meaning that truth is relative to a subject position, whereas most important poststructuralist sources argued something entirely different, as we are reminded in Bruno Latour's "Why Has Critique Run out of Steam?" published in English in the same year, 2004, as Shatz's book.[8]

Today, most exciting about the two "cultures" is that many scholars readily recognize the importance of interpretation and framing for any kind of inquiry. This is done across the board as confirmed by the spectrum of research into bias across disciplines, or, in a different way, in the reassessments of groundbreaking experiments like the work in psychology led by Brian Nosek ("Prospective Replication Project" Munafo et al.).[9]

A suggestion we can draw from this criticism of Shatz is that there should be a new reference point for an inquiry into peer review. Not two cultures, but instead an inquiry into what sciences and humanities have in common, despite their noticeable methodological, theoretical, historical, and, yes, cultural differences—where by culture we mean, in the main, how a discipline customarily imagines itself which itself is different from what it can be demonstrated to be. Despite our categorial disagreements with Shatz on the two cultures model, *Peer Review* remains an invaluable source regarding the details of what peer review is and how it is conducted.

Burnham

In her genealogy, Fitzpatrick ties peer review to the royal power and discipline, suggesting that these are the main originary components of peer review as an institution. An alternative to that view is the more nuanced account that considers the emergence of editorial review and offers a different, less organized, and more open-to-chance history. Such genealogy is presented by John C. Burnham in his article, "The Evolution of Editorial Peer Review," and we are going to spend a moment with him to offer that history since we find it the most fruitful source for discussing interdisciplinary peer review.

As a historian of medicine, Burnham is especially interested in the difference between scientific and medical journals and uses that angle in his investigation. The two disciplines—science and medicine—have a different past. In the nineteenth century, medical journals were developing in close association with personal journalism, as a variant of the diary. These "personal mouthpieces" were editor-centered, with editors writing "much or all of the content" (Burnham 1324). In addition to this journalistic medical journal model, a second model developed as "the official publication of a continental research institute." These scientific journals did not need outside referees because the editor-professor-administrator was the expert in the area, and most reviewing was done in-house. Peer review, Burnham continues, developed by necessity, "in situations in which an editor or editors lacked the specialized knowledge that would have permitted them to make decisions about highly technical articles" (1324).

After World War II, this need for more specialized review was exacerbated by the fragmentation of knowledge,

> Expertise ... was limited in many cases to just a few research sites, and even experts outside those communities were no longer peers as such; instead, expertise came to be based solely on membership in a very limited community indeed, again raising the question of the extent to which any given referee who might have general rather than very specific expertise would be doing "peer" review any more than was done by the old generalist editors. (Burnham 1325)

The peer review model with two reviews that we follow today developed in the *Journal of Clinical Investigation*, where the editorial board consisted of a committee of experts. There, each "manuscript went to the board member best qualified by scientific credentials to judge it" and, then, as new fields proliferated, the "journal switched to what the officers called the 'wide open' refereeing process, using not only members of the sponsoring society but any outsiders needed in addition" (Burnham 1327).

In contrast, grant reviewing had a more centralized history because national agencies and the government—like the National Cancer Institute (NCI) for which formal procedures were established by law in 1937 (Burnham 1328)[10]— were involved and could use laws to dictate what peer review is. Journals were relatively slow to adapt to peer review and the same expert-based model because of their top-down hierarchical structure, relative autonomy, and the fact that their editors and boards could have considered themselves self-sufficient in all areas because of their expertise. For example, the *Lancet* did in house reviews as late as the 1970s (Burnham 1328). Burnham ends his article by reemphasizing the "untidiness of the historical record," uneven progress of various models, and the "complexities" of the peer review as an institution (Burnham 1328).

The article is beneficial for our purposes because it allows us to identify two forces that shaped peer review, which are not acknowledged as much as they should be. First is that the form and content of peer reviews has a complex reciprocal relation to the knowledge it evaluates; that the relation between them is not of dominant and subordinate practice; and that each can influence the other as they can also be shaped by the outside forces like popular genres or government policies. Second and more important is that government agencies played the deciding role in defining both the shape of knowledge and how peer review is supposed to be conducted. This tells us that peer review followed the specialist direction because that was the trajectory of knowledge that accelerated after World War II because government agencies in the United States put their money behind that paradigm.

The proliferation of fields of expertise is no longer the dominant tendency. The new trend in the United States for the last 30 years involves creating larger units, cooperation between disciplines, fields, and areas, and other forms of interdisciplinarity (Casadevall and Fang). This is so particularly since 1993 when the Government Performance and Results Act (GPRA) defined the new criterion for funding as "societally relevant outcomes," dictating the direction of the National Science Foundation sponsored basic research (Holbrook 329), which itself contributed greatly to the ongoing "transdisciplinarization" (Holbrook 330) or cooperation between different experts.

This history provides us with the chief reason to understand peer review as not merely a quality control measure or a means to separate good scholarship from junk. Peer review is, instead, an institutional practice run by institutional and individual scholarly interests, dictating and reflecting trends in the development of knowledge, in sync with the goals set up by agencies that fund primary research, and in interdependent relation, too, with the broader social, cultural, and political trends.

There are two other significant consequences of such standardization to be noted here since they bring peer review into relation with our other concerns. The first is that the standardized and well-organized peer review opens the space for other contenders to enter the field, like the private publishing industry, that can now employ it and then monetize it (Larivière et al.). Second, and more consequential for our purposes, is that the standardization of peer review also leads to further commodification of the academic knowledge market and further neoliberalization of the university context (Raaper), which itself, as we noted already, makes universities more and more vulnerable to other attempts at unfair competition. While the elite universities can adopt the role of a business more easily (while maintaining the education model), most universities are undermined in this process that treats them as equivalent to corporations.

This then means that we inherit peer review lodged in a double-bind we need to be mindful of. On the one hand, improving peer review leads to more autonomous functioning scholarship and institutions, but, on the other, baring additional safeguards, the same can lead to further weakening of what is specific to university production of knowledge, undermining the conditions that support peer review.

Symbolic effects of peer review

Peer review is also a symbolic practice, because it confers status, authority, and prestige. Fitzpatrick reckons with this symbolic significance in her work by borrowing from Mario Biagioli's reading of Michel Foucault's *Discipline and Punish*. She says, peer review is "not simply ... a system that produces disciplinarity in an intellectual sense, but ... a mode of disciplining knowledge itself, a mode that is 'simultaneously repressive, productive, and constitutive' of academic ways of knowing" (Fitzpatrick 21; Biagioli, "From Book" 11). Fitzpatrick's view is widely shared, once again. According to it, peer review makes us submit to a specific mold, relinquish some autonomy, and, in return, rewards us with status, career, and livelihood, and autonomy from other holders of authority like university administration. For universities, peer review is a warranty of the quality of its tenure track professors demanded across the board. The non–peer-reviewed scholarship is most often assigned second class status *if it is acknowledged at all*.

Fitzpatrick and Biagioli's understanding can also explain rather neatly the connection of the term "disciplines" with disciplining as a form of punishment—namely, peer review helps create a scholarly discipline by disciplining its members. There is, however, a major issue with the explanation.[11] The discipline and disciplining can work in the described way only if there is a general belief in, and consensus about, that discipline—what makes it, how it should be propagated, and, not the least, if there is an agreement on the peer review process itself. If there is discord, as in Tuvel's case, or a crisis of fragmentation like the one we have in literary studies, then the peer review process is merely repressive, hardly the type of general institution Foucault can be applied to. This is among other reasons because fragmentation makes "peers" harder and harder to identify.

If Foucault must be our choice, the *Power/Knowledge* is a much more suitable source since it can capture power differentials and the consequences of fragmentation and does so in terms of an epistemology (Alcoff, *Real Knowing*). Using that aspect of Foucault, we understand that the current kind of peer review produces an imbalance between the power/knowledge pair. While knowledge confers status (power), and knowledge is also an instrument of power, the two cannot be equated, as "knowledge is not reducible to power, even though it cannot be properly understood as dissociated from power" (Alcoff, "Mignolo's Epistemology" 79–80).

The conceptual dyad power/knowledge can help explain what is currently going on in literary studies and how fragmentation negatively impacts our prospects as a discipline. When peer review is used to reify fields that remain separated from and may be irrelevant to, other literary fields, and this is its principal application, we are facing "the delimitation of the 'regime' (or sphere) of the truth, or what passes for truth" (Alcoff "Mignolo's Epistemology" 80). We can continue to adopt from Alcoff's critique of colonialism (as methods for establishing what legitimacy/power looks like and for doling out that legitimacy and power) verbatim because our field fragmentation follows in the image of our scholarship:

> epistemology needs to work with this better and more truthful description of how actually existing knowledges (as opposed to idealized reconstructions) emerge, and needs to incorporate not only an analysis of power in its analysis of knowledge but also a set of normative criteria for judging various relationships between power and knowledge. Foucault provided such criteria in his epistemic assessments of hegemony-seeking versus subjugated knowledges: subjugated or local knowledges always tend to do less violence to the local particulars and are also less likely to impose hierarchical structures of credibility based on universal claims about the proper procedures of justification that foreclose the contributions of many unconventional or lower-status knowers. (Alcoff, "Mignolo's Epistemology" 80)

When the local functions in a system without a hegemonic center—as there is no one anymore to represent it in literary studies since the New Critics—the local becomes the new site of power. The decentralization takes place in the form of slow disassociation between the produced knowledge and gained status. There are fewer and fewer scholars whose work shows an affinity for, or interest in, general literary studies. Perhaps only lecturers are left with some stakes in the umbrella term as both a labor and a scholarly issue because their jobs are defined by teaching demands that tend to favor a generalist approach. Thus, a paradox that the least privileged may be the most interested in the integrity of literary studies as a whole.

The imbalance can also be phrased in terms of the sway particularized fields hold over the discipline. On the one hand, as far as knowledge is concerned, any single field's influence over others and general studies is minimal. On the other hand, the fragmentation holds the discipline hostage to particular interests, making any collective, institutional response difficult as we lack even the established ways of reaching consensus. In such a constellation, fields that are most particularized have also the most impact, just as in a gerrymandered electoral map, the most radical options have the advantage.

When the field is fragmented, and there is no longer a representative disciplinary center, wealthy institutions can concentrate power/knowledge with their imprimatur becoming the sole guarantors of quality—which was one of the effects that the anonymous peer review defined in 1980 in *PMLA* was supposed to counter.[12]

In this setup—when status (power) takes precedence over knowledge, when subfields dominate the discipline—the demand of discipline becomes impossible to fulfill. Thus, what is repressive about peer review is simply repressive and not productive of disciplinary norms or unity. Peer review, in other words, does not serve to evaluate scholarship but to draw boundaries between narrowly defined scholarly areas, to police these, and to make them hard to transcend, with the general result that elite institutions are better and better off and the humanities scholarship is losing its relevance.

Transition

At this point in our argument, after this discussion about the current fragmentation in literary studies, we need to ask how we can address the reality of where literary studies is today and, at the same time, work toward the goal of interdisciplinary peer review. The above discussion makes our answer obvious, and I will offer two different arguments to support it.

The advice that would come from the sciences would be that we work on a common methodology. What peer reviews actually review is, or follows from, a methodology—and any attempt at interdisciplinary peer review must take into account not only "a novel conceptual framework" but such a framework as it relates to "distinctive methodological tools" (Huutoniemi 313). Put another way, the road to interdisciplinarity leads through an understanding of how methodologically distinct disciplines differ from each other and what a possible common methodology could be—which may well be the first step toward interdisciplinarity. The argument would allow literary studies to rethink our fragmentation, express the differences between various areas in interdisciplinary terms, consolidate as an interdisciplinary discipline, and offer a way to bring other disciplines together based on a similar blueprint.

The same advice can also be reconstructed out of Linda Alcoff's use of Foucault. When fields behave like postcolonial power centers, we need to see the multiplicity not just as a reflection of our scholarship but as a specific belief system that needs to be interrogated as a regime of truth and epistemology. The last time we assumed epistemology was critical was in the 1980s. "We" were, to repeat, the winners-to-be of the culture wars who defined ourselves in opposition to the old, patriarchal, New Critical curmudgeon, who was the common enemy.

Now our common enemy is us.

Feminisms

Before we get to our main and only source on methodology in this chapter, a brief note on the sources we are not going to cover. The then-emerging fields like literary feminism considered methodology among chief features, as we can conclude from Judith Kegan Gardiner's "In the Name of the Mother"—a review of various feminist methodologies. Gardiner starts with Sandra Harding (*Feminism and Methodology*), who defines "methods" as "technique[s] for gathering evidence." For Catherine MacKinnon, the method "organizes what is taken as verification." Ellen Messer-Davidow lists "methods of reasoning such as differentiating, integrating, using principles, seeking causes, inferring between parts and whole, and making analogies" (Gardiner 239). Gardiner also mentions trying to connect the biographical with the professional (240); reading from a women's or mother's perspective; reconceptualizing the figure of the mother in psychoanalysis (241); gendering relationships between a writer, her text, and her reader, known as "empathetic engagement" (242). Gardiner, lastly, defines principles that feminist methodology follows: de- and re-authorization; triangulation/juxtaposition; familial analogy and identification; and recontextualization (243).

My reasons to prefer Stanley Fish's *Is There a Text in This Class?* include that it offers more general as well as more basic analysis of literary interpretation, focuses on what we do with language, and pertains to all reading. Fish's take presents a typical, theoretically rigorous view representative of the poststructuralist paradigm as it was accepted and shared by literary scholars (including feminists) of this period—especially his understanding "that the meaning of a text is mediated by the interpretive community in which the reading of the text is situated" (Flynn and Schweickart 50), which was among the primary new assumptions of that period. Additionally, engaging Fish would allow us to show again the main line of disagreement with New Criticism. Fish will also help us build on the mere reading practice we defined in the second chapter as we discuss peer review, interpretation, and methodology together. In this respect, our question will be: how can interpretation take place after a mere reading?

Part II: Fish, interpretation, and new peer review

Method

In the essay "Literature and the Reader," originally published in *New Literary History* and later as the first chapter of *Is There a Text in this Class?* "method" appears as part of a critique of William Wimsatt and Monroe Beardsley's "The Affective Fallacy." Wimsatt and Beardsley argued that we should not confuse *what* a poem is with what affects and responses are produced through reading it (21). Fish's goal is to show that text's meaning is related to practice or, in his lapidary formulation, that text means only what it does. He mentions the concept of "method" to explain two examples of close reading he performs. "Method," he says, underlies textual analysis and consists in "the rigorous and disinterested asking of the question, what does this word, phrase, sentence, paragraph, chapter, novel, play, poem, *do*?" (Fish, *Is There a Text* 26–27). Such reading understands meaning as a practice or performance, not, as it is usually the case, meaning as content or referent. And text is not a container of meaning, but instead text is what is constructed through the acts of reading and interpretation. When this is the case, as we will show promptly, text, too, cannot be limited to any one context since there is always a reading of a reading (for as long as literary studies is there).

Fish goes on to explain that the above question of what a text does and approach accomplish two things. First, it slows the reading down "so that 'events' one does not notice in normal time ... are brought before our analytical attentions."

Slowing down, in turn, helps us identify the process by which meaning is created through the interaction between the reader and the text—with the interaction replacing the consumption or decoding model. And here we have two critical elements of Fish's method: one pertains to making text into an event or happening; and the other shifts the understanding of meaning from being "in" the text to being a result, or product, of a slow and prolonged interactive experience (Fish, *Is There a Text* 41).

In the title essay of the collection, Fish adds another, third step that accompanies the two described above. To do any kind of interpretation, we first "recognize" a text as a poem (Fish 322). The act of recognition or framing is an expression of the discipline's protocols and the definitions concerning what a "poem" is (323). Only after the "poem" is identified in this institutional and ideological fashion, after it is given proper frame and genre, does it become an object we can analyze as a text. Fish can then conclude that "[i]t is not that the presence of poetic qualities compels a certain kind of attention but that the paying of a certain kind of attention results in the emergence of poetic qualities" (326). And these three steps are what our basic methodology is made out of: slowing down the reading, understanding it as interactive, and recognizing that it takes place within a specific framework or context that reading both establishes and exemplifies.

The phrase "the reader's experience of it" (Fish, *Is There a Text* 41) can be misleading since it might imply agreement with Anatole Frances's infamous motto, "The good critic is he who relates the adventures of his soul among masterpieces" (France 1). What Fish means is to reiterate the phenomenological assumption that signifying and aesthetic phenomena (texts we analyze) are what they are not in and of themselves, but as they are represented and reworked by our mind in the process we call reading. Texts are made significant through the interaction with the signifying being of the reader who, too, becomes that signifying being in the process. Such reader, again, is not an individual. It is a role, an occupation, and a practice we learn as a part of our socialization—a role we inhabit and perform *as* particular individuals. This reader is, then, also a kind of text; a product of the interpretative processes, and a kind of performance resulting from engaging and interacting with written (cinematic, cultural, digital) texts on multiple occasions and over time.

Our methodology is that process that makes it possible to identify the text/meaning in terms of interpretative practices. It is also that process through which a "text" is made to mean, and a person becomes a reader. From this position, Wimsatt and Beardsley's argument looks philosophically naïve because they suppose that signifying objects can exist on their own and do not require discourses and practices to enable them—which is a cultural view that some in the sciences still share.

To become an informed reader, we need to become a "number" of various kinds of readers, "each of whom will be identified by a matrix of political, cultural, and literary determinants" (Fish, *Is There a Text* 49). Hence, an informed reader is a reader who knows several divergent subject positions, themselves built up through readings, and can somewhat authentically speak from those perspectives (without at the same time pretending to speak for someone else). We, this is to say, can engage and occupy multiversal positions by becoming more proficient, more generous, and more general readers who have their eye on the common good.

Fish explains the goals of his textual strategies in opposition to the kind of literary criticism exemplified by Wayne Booth's *Rhetoric of Fiction*, whose goals are to evaluate works of fiction and define the difference between poetic and ordinary language, between literature and everyday expression. In turn, the new textual strategy "allows for no ... aesthetic and no ... fixings of value. In fact, it is oriented *away* from evaluation and toward description" (Fish, *Is There a Text* 50-51). For Fish, as for phenomenology in general, the goal is to collect information about the processes of reading, meaning creation, and how signifying entities are constructed. The practice becomes a way to resist goal-oriented readings (52) because they, in many ways, misconstrue the text/meaning they are supposed to evaluate. They, too, close down the many possibilities for what can be done with and through reading and interpretation as acts of bringing divergent and disparate entities together.

From this perspective, we can see the importance of mere reading perhaps more clearly and how it can help us understand the process of the reader becoming a part of global and diversified meaning production. With mere reading, we are supposed not to resist the meaning-making but develop an ability to monitor how we engage with text, language, and interpretation, and how we *occupy* specific positions. Holding frames and context creation in abeyance is perhaps the simplest way to describe what the mere reading does. And we identify these, to repeat, not because we want to do away with the frameworks, but because we want to use the strategy to create more and different kinds of connections between them, different attitudes toward cooperation, convergence, and coalition-building.

No method

In conclusion to the essay, Fish goes on to claim that what he has described "is not a method at all" (66), although up to that point, he consistently identified it as a method. The injunction can be interpreted along the lines of the reception of Paul Feyerabend's *Against Method*, published originally in 1975, which was received as a proof that poststructuralism rejects methodology. This, however, is not what Fish means and not what Feyerabend meant either. Feyerabend corrected this misreading in the "Introduction to the Chinese Edition." As he explains there, *Against Method*'s main goal was to "support people, not to 'advance knowledge,' " adding, "[m]y main motive... was humanitarian, not intellectual":

> The 'progress of knowledge and civilization' – as the process of pushing Western ways and values into all corners of the globe is being

called – destroyed these wonderful products of human ingenuity and compassion without a single glance in their direction. (3)

Against method means, for Feyerabend, being against haphazard, violent Westernization that destroys local knowledge through the introduction of alien ways of doing things; against, also, equating science with what the West sees it as. Feyerabend makes his views on this clear as he concludes this introduction by saying,

> I have tried to show, by an analysis of the apparently hardest parts of science, the natural sciences, that science, properly understood, has no argument against such a procedure [learning from traditional, local, non-Western sources]. There are many scientists who act accordingly. Physicians, anthropologists and environmentalists are starting to adapt their procedures to the values of the people they are supposed to advise. I am not against a science [or method] so understood. Such a science is one of the most wonderful inventions of the human mind. But I am against ideologies that use the name of science for cultural murder. (4)

It was unfortunate that this explanation was added only to the third edition of *Against Method* in 1993, too late for many of Feyerabend's readers to see the author's understanding of methodology in a more positive and useful light.

A similar misreading clouds Fish's assertion that "this is not a method at all," but for different reasons. There is no method in literary studies in the sense that interaction with the text is always new and unique, dependent on place and time, and subject(s) involved. There is also no method as an independent, accurate tool that can tell the truth from falsehood, knowledge from junk, the literary from the non-literary. Fish writes,

> [S]trictly speaking, it is not a method at all, because neither its results nor its skills are transferrable. Its results are not transferrable because there is no fixed relationship between formal features and response (reading has to be done every time), and its skills are not transferrable because you can't hand it over to someone and expect them at once to be able to use it. (It is not portable.) It is, in essence, a language-sensitizing device, and as the "ing" in sensitizing implies, its operation is long term and never ending (never coming to the point). Moreover, its operations are interior. It has no mechanisms, except for the pressuring mechanism of the assumption that more is going on in language than we consciously know; and of course the pressure of this assumption must come from the individual whose untrained sensitivity it is challenging. Becoming good at the method means asking the question "what does that ⎯⎯⎯⎯⎯⎯⎯ do?" with more and more awareness of the probable (and hidden) complexity of the answer, that is, with a mind more and more sensitized to the working of language. (Fish, *Is There a Text* 66)

This is to say that there is no method in those other senses we have detailed above—regarding *how* we interact with the text, based on what assumptions—all of which are demonstrable and teachable practices. These, too, are experiences (mere readings) we can stage, which offers yet another way to understand no-method method. Since performance in the context of reading depends on the actual participants involved, there is no universally prescribed way in which it should be done. There is no Kantian imperative, no proper context that historicism identifies. There is also no predetermined aesthetic form whose existence has to be detected and affirmed. There is only—Hegel (*The Philosophy of Right*) and Marx (*The 18th Brumaire of Louis Bonaparte*) make this vocabulary available—here and now. We do not teach the world what it ought to be but *do* the teaching and reading through which we construct the world and ourselves.

In yet different registrar of performance art, the work is an event (not a thing) with performers (not actors) executing acts (not pretending).

The establishment of a non-method method follows on a performance of mere reading. The way that it can help us distinguish between scholarship and junk like "fake news" also pertains to frameworks. One of these is verifiable from divergent point of view and the other one isn't. The explanation gives us yet another reason for developing convergence since it serves to test and negotiate differences between individual or fragmented perspectives.

Fish on peer review

Fish has also published a landmark critique of the double-blind peer review process, titled "No Bias, No Merit," that stems from the same understanding of reading, interpretation, and methodology. The conceptual unity is evident in, for instance, identical turns of phrase. If in "Is There a Text in this Class?" he writes, "[i]t is not that the presence of poetic qualities compels a certain kind of attention but that the paying of a certain kind of attention results in the emergence of poetic qualities" (Fish, *Is There a Text* 326), in "No Bias, No Merit," he says that "merit, rather than being a quality that can be identified independently of professional or institutional conditions, is a product of those conditions" (740). The essay's main idea is that institutional performance—an actual peer reviews—defines merit. While we can prescribe what we want peer review to do, make a checklist, and ensure that our reviewers follow the process, the "merit" will still be the product of actual reviews, because reviews will depart from the requirements in the very process of following them as each author does it in their own way. The agglomeration of these acts form the "professional or institutional conditions" which collectively define what merit is and do so in specific terms that reflect the setup more than the checklist or the values we prescribe.

This way of doing things can be liberating because it tells us that "merit" is not one quality or mold to which an article has to conform, defined independently from the process of scholarly engagement. But, on the other hand, because this form of scholarly engagement called peer review is not itself sanctioned, the process must necessarily be open to interpretation and therefore misuses. Fish's point is not to state the ambiguity but, as I will show here, to get us through it and help make the process more productive.

The essay, "No Bias, No Merit," was originally written to respond to a debate that followed William Schaefer's report, "Anonymous Review," mentioned at the beginning of our chapter. It was written in 1979 but had to wait for over ten years to be published in 1988 when it appeared in the *PMLA* as a "Guest Column." The delay made it possible for Fish to include the trends represented in Peters and Ceci's study and use those to support his critique further. We should underscore this point that Fish encountered the problem of peer review sooner than most. It was close to his understanding of interpretation and reading for the same reason that it is close to ours in this work, namely, because of the fundamental assumption that methodology, the institution of evaluation, and frameworks are integral to reading and interpretation. They, as Fish says, *make* the interpretation.

In the text, Fish takes issue with the notions of "true merit" and "extraneous considerations" as they appeared in Schaefer's original report—Schaefer had defined the goal of double-blind review: "to prevent 'extraneous considerations' from interfering with the identification of true merit" (Fish, "No Bias" 739).[13] Fish opposes that claim with his thesis, "that there is no such standard (which is not the same thing as saying there is no standard) and, second, that while we may, as a point of piety, invoke it as an ideal, in fact we violate it all the time by practices that are at once routine and obligatory" (739). As with many of Fish's other claims, this one was poorly understood, which we can judge based on the outcry that followed.

Fish received a deluge of criticisms, each harder to square with his text than the next. One claimed that his argument was incoherent (Harpham) and another that he was weakening the weak (Skoblow). Yet others saw him championing the capitalist marketplace (Holstun, Lug), attacking fundamental values (Hyman), and, later, that he claimed that all editing is personal (L. Smith), and that he denied the importance of intentionality (di Leo). The general sense was that Fish was a nihilist intent on destroying all values and standards just because he said that "true merit" is not a neutral category.

Fish's main point is a relatively simple one, and in a time when "implicit bias" is an everyday phrase, we may be better primed to hear what he meant. He says only that the notion of "true merit" is the contingent result of institutional practices and individual biases. In a somewhat looser formulation, we can say that literary scholars are expected to think, write, and argue in a specific way. And only if they do it just so can they earn the "true merit" badge. We are loath to admit this—that we are driven by interests—because we do not like to think of literary studies as anything but a meritocracy (Fish, "No Bias" 745). Merit is the quality conferred on submission when an individual reviewer recognizes it in just such a way that they are willing to put their name behind the project.

There is also another corollary. Fish is not just saying that standards necessarily include our expectations that may not all be scholarly. There is also a point that scholarship itself is built out of standards that are not, strictly speaking, the result of scholarly activity. The institutional standards may seem added and are often unacknowledged, but they are—as we suggested—integral to knowledge production. Once we realize that, a possibility opens up that a field would set up different procedures to wet and evaluate. That can be done most efficiently when peer review and the evaluation process begin to be seen as essential to scholarship; when they stop being mere evaluation and become a part of the process of definition of what literary interpretation is all about.

If a reader asks but isn't peer review sometimes helpful? Our position is that such question is only tangentially related to this discussion since its meaning hinges on what we mean by helpful. This discussion, again, is about ways in which we can elevate scholarly standards of peer review and articulate its procedures from the point of view of the hermeneutic theory of literary studies as an aspect of scholarship. We cannot do away with institutional bias completely, but we can lessen it and account for it through a more transparent process of review. Thus, yes, peer review is always helpful to our carriers when we get the go-ahead to be published, but it is not necessarily helpful for the development of knowledge. To the extent that it confirms a field, peer review is building the scaffolding that, again, may or may not be in the best interest of future knowledge creation.

Fish opens his article with the most glaring contradiction, the one between what we expect from an academic essay and how we evaluate it. In this profession, Fish says, "you earn the right to say something because it has not been said by anyone else, or because it is a reversal of what is usually said, or because while it has been said, its implications have not yet been spelled out" (Fish, "No Bias" 739). But, in contradiction, the peer review process consists of a series of tests that judge how an essay conforms to the preconceived notions of what a good article should look like. The notions are left for the expert reviewer to define which they do consistent with their expertise. While the process may seem rational, since it leaves it up to experts to define the norms, it is also set up to prefer the conservative arguments, individualism, and specialization over other qualities.

To use the most recent example from the MLA Database available at the time of my writing, an essay published in 2015 by Brian Singleton, the editor of *Theater Research International* and co-editor the Palgrave Macmillan series "Studies in International Performance." In the essay, entitled "Peer Review," Singleton describes his role: "[a]s Editor, I was the first line of quality control" (27) and ends his essay repeating the standard, "[m]ost peer reviewers take the job seriously, situating the submission within a wider field, ensuring the research is at the cutting edge, and offering constructive feedback, particularly important to new scholars" (29). Seen from Fish's perspective, such review is focused around the institutional mechanisms of reproduction and not at all on the "habitus" (to employ Bourdieu's term) of the reviewed article. When we take our job "seriously," the reviewer submits themselves to a specific set of recognized rules and assumes the specific point of view of an expert which they honed over a long period. They, then, having transformed themselves into an "expert," subject the reviewed essay to the same process: they measure it against a set of constructed expectations. Only a rare reviewer pauses to ask what the procedure has to do with the article being reviewed, how much their own interests and expertise stand in the way of their reading the article, and so on. The rational process then appears not to be all that rational since it is biased against works that do not share the same framework, the same understanding of profession and professionalization, the same sense of specialization, and so on.

To repeat, the main issue Fish has is with us thinking of peer review as a neutral form of quality control, denying that it is an application and exercise of an "industry," "machinery," and "mechanisms" that make our institutions (Fish, "No Bias" 742, 743). This claim should make it obvious why Fish disagrees with both sides of the argument—the one for anonymous or double-blind review as well as the one against it—regarding what needs to be discussed when we discuss peer review. The "work to be done is not [on] what the institution responds to," for instance Edmund Spenser's work, but on the "industry" that Spenser studies "*creates*" and becomes (742). Fish's advice is, then, that because the review cannot be blind or unbiased, we need to make the analysis of the *mechanisms* by which we reproduce scholarship a part of our standard procedures. He hence argues that we should review the way we read, with an eye for the framing and demarcations between discourses, making the entire process (not just the norm against which we measure a submission) as transparent and scholarly as it can be made.

In this case, to de-industrialize something would mean showing how we get from "reading" Spenser to standardizing and professionalizing readings of Spenser. If for New Critics, the goal was to define Spenser-the-text, with culture wars, the scholarly goal shifted to a creation of a whole ecosystem we call "Spenser studies" including texts, contexts, as well as various approaches which constitute the framework all of which are necessary for even a mere reading of Spenser. To put it simply, Spenser studies come with their own values, being about Spenser studies first. In such a setup, the primary task of a scholarly interpretation is to show itself as a legitimate work in the area that meets all the standards of Spenser studies. And if it aims to contest the whole setup, it can do so *only* if it first accepts the Spenser studies' terms of scholarship, which ensures that the specialization would continue regardless of the criticism it receives and for as long as there are funds to publish its journals.

Spenser studies are not made just out of professional standards. On each occasion when the industry is confirmed, there is a specialist who also has personal interests in the mechanisms of its reproduction; whose career depends on it; and who may therefore have strong psychological reasons to protect it. Thus, it is not just that Spenser-the-industry needs to be conserved as an industry, but scholar's identity comes into play, too. Perhaps now we can understand more readily why we do not discuss peer review as a scholarly topic. The solution appears to be just as obvious, namely, that peer review and specialization need to be at odds if any reform and especially interdisciplinary efforts are to succeed. Changing peer review by adding an interdisciplinary or generalist expectation—a version of general relevance we mentioned in the first chapter—would be the quickest, surest, and most direct way to set the profession on a different track.

Here, we can also understand why the common strategy for improving peer review by adding more numerous and precise instructions for reviewers is counterproductive and goes in the wrong direction. The more detailed demand limits the reader's engagement with the text. They thus support the notion that is incompatible with the reading that we hold as a discipline. One reads to understand, the other to evaluate. One is meant to be responsive and creative, the other limited and strict. One prefers showing how much the reader is involved in creating meaning, the other shows adherence to the accepted knowledge. One is led by keeping experience wholistic, the other by detecting wholes and what is not presented.

Suggestion for immediate changes

Based on our discussion, the following changes in the peer review process can be made right away.

First, that reviewers should start by reading the submission as expert readers, not as specialist scholars. They can also read as specialists but with an eye to interdisciplinarity and position of the work in the general context.

Second, reviewers should then evaluate the submission on general terms, and only after they do so should they measure it against specialist standards they deem appropriate. The standards applied and a detailed rationale for their application should be included in the review. These because standards are an expression of bias.

Third, non-blind reader reviews should be preferred, and at least those who are already tenured should be expected to sign our names when we review.[14]

Fourth, the review process should also include an opportunity for a brief rebuttal from the author. (Separately, we should work on making the review process closer to both scholarship and learning. Some possibilities for that will be noted below when we address new opportunities made possible by digital technology.)

Fifth, to shorten the period of review to weeks instead of months, we should value peer review labor as central to profession and count it as both service and scholarship. For example, three reviews can equate to one published article and/or one committee assignment.

Sixth, editors should have sole power and freedom to shape journals. This should go some distance toward establishing "public accountability" (Shatz 70–71) for what is published. The editors should be able to reject submissions (even most of them) without a review process, with a brief explanation of their reasons.

Seventh, each journal should offer its readers an exhaustive annual report on reviews, identifying and justifying its practices in scholarly terms.

PMLA, as our main common forum, should return to the 1975 policy of publishing articles of general interest and institutional concern to assist us in consolidating the discipline. The shift would go a long way to providing a forum for the kind of critique that needs to happen at the most visible stage we share as a profession. The journal should also become a leader of reform, showing what needs to be done and why, just as it has been the leader in setting our standards thus far.

These recommendations should help the profession become less fragmented. It could indirectly help with the cliquish nature of many journals that rely on the cohort of "good" authors and rarely publish submissions. The multiple criteria that include a rigorous theoretical foundation would raise the quality of writing and scholarship.

I am advocating general criteria in specialized journals, too, since there is no other kind anymore. If these are not focused by topic, they are by approach, authors they publish, and other editorial choices that support current divisions. The tasks that need to be accomplished include: raising standards and relevance of writing and scholarship as we focus on developing interdisciplinary paradigm which includes sciences, epistemology, and institution critique, while also shifting organization and focus of the discipline from literature to language (as it appears in literature), from history to interpretation, from text to frames (that define our approach).

In practical terms, Spenser studies would have the option of minimal reform with inclusion of consideration of analytic frameworks or maximal where the scholars would devote attention to how focused and centered studies can be brought to bear on topics of general, interdisciplinary, and intersectional concerns. The latter can be misconstrued to mean interdisciplinary or international uses of Spenser, a kind of Spenser multiverse. That is the current practice and not what we have in mind.[15] The difference is in the focus of attention on Spenser or the notion of studies we use to define what Spenser means for us with a leading question if there is a way to organize research without starting from either Spenser's work or its many contexts? What is left are the terms of interpretation and conversation.

Again, I am not advocating the abandonment of history or Spenser as an object of study, but a change in priorities, addressing history as coming out of an interpretation and no longer using history as a justification for readings or as a horizon for our scholarship since it, philosophically speaking, does not perform that function well. The suggestion is given with awareness that we have an excellent library of historicist works and that history can be done differently, not in tension to reading closely, but as an integral to the theoretical framework we create. It also comes with full support for work on thus far unacknowledged histories that should be a privileged area of research for as long as fundamental discoveries can be made. Similarly, I am not arguing against cultural studies, only for a different version that would be theoretically rigorous, include experience with language, and be in sync with sciences. Literary scholars have produced some marvelous works like Svetlana Boym's *The Future of Nostalgia* or Paul Gilroy's *The Black Atlantic* that help us explain ourselves to ourselves more effectively than other discourses can because we rely on all sorts of cultural texts and have methodological freedom other disciplines do not. The future of cultural studies, to my mind, lies closer to the sciences, truth, and creation of a universal perspective.

Part III: bias and open review

Bias and discrimination

Requiring general or interdisciplinary criteria is the most efficient way to change the nature of literary scholarship. For a discipline that studies interpretation, general and interdisciplinary qualities can help it gain a new status among other disciplines. In this case, interpretation should include peer review as a general practice of framing literary studies, defining the discipline in the epistemological and institutional sense. Our practices of doing scholarship, reading scholarship, and evaluating should be understood as one and the same. Peer review, in this context, is the process of creating and confirming what is scholarly.

From this perspective, we can understand and evaluate the studies like the recent "Reviewer Bias in Single-Versus Double-Blind Peer Review" (Tomkins et al.).[16] The study set out to measure single and double-blind peer review formats and decide which one is more democratic. On that question, its results were inconclusive. What it did find conclusively concerned single-blind review, that reviewers were biased in predictable ways. First, they prefer to read fewer papers, and second, they assume that evaluating papers by authors from elite universities and top companies would be more rewarding. Tomkins et al. write,

> In conclusion, the heart of our findings is that single-blind reviewers make use of information about authors and institutions. Specifically, single-blind reviewers are more likely to bid on papers from top institutions and more likely to recommend for acceptance papers from famous authors or top institutions, compared with their double-blind counterparts.
>
> The primary ethical question is whether this behavior is acceptable. In one interpretation, single-blind reviewers make use of prior information that may allow them to make better overall judgments. As a consequence, however, it may be that other work is disadvantaged, in the sense that two contributions of roughly equal merit might be scored differently by single-blind reviewers, in favor of the one from a top school, while double-blind reviewers may not show this bias as strongly.
>
> Clearly, our understanding of the implications of reviewing methodologies remains nascent. Nonetheless, we feel that program and general chairs of conferences should seriously consider the advantages of using double-blind reviewing (12712).

For us, this study exemplifies the typical, biased setup of peer review analysis. First is the assumption that this process can and should be used to democratize the profession or, at least, to prevent us from becoming less democratic. Placing such a burden on peer review and having such expectations are among the reasons this evaluation method does not work. As Fish shows, peer review does not prove merit; it only proves/reflects what we are as a discipline. If we separate the two goals, one of treating scholars more democratically and the other of evaluating scholarship, we are more likely to make progress in both. At the very least, we would be able to measure the relative effect of each. Discrimination—gender, race, class, and sexuality—is an intractable and omnipresent problem in American society. It should not be approached at an endpoint, after all education, research, and writing are done. At that point, it is too late. As Drummond Rennie writes,

> In 1998, my colleagues and I conducted a five-journal trial of double-blind peer review (neither author nor reviewer knows the identity of the other). We found no difference in the quality of reviews. What's more, attempts to mask authors' identities were often ineffective and imposed a considerable bureaucratic burden. We concluded that the only potential benefit to a (largely unsuccessful) policy of masking is the appearance, not the reality, of fairness. (Rennie, "Let's Make" 32)

Institutions and individuals whose identities stand for prestige do not only have the obvious advantage afforded by their names, which then disappears in the double-blind review setup. They have the advantage of the support apparatus, networks of friends and colleagues, their education, and material wealth, and can rely on the fact that their background is compatible with the formation of the context, discipline, and value system in which they compete. To, then, suppose that the withholding of the names is *the* characteristic on which we should focus attention is not itself just neutral or inadequate. It directly contributes to discrimination by deflecting inequality through its partial measures and concerns.

The article "Reviewer Bias in Single- Versus Double-Blind Peer Review" garnered a response from Katherine Egan Bennett, Reshma Jagsi, and Anthony Zietman, editors of the *International Journal of Radiation Oncology, Biology, and Physics* (IJROBP). This medical journal specializes in the use of ionizing radiation to treat cancer and other conditions, which will help us add more detail to our criticism. The journal represents a small field consisting of around 4,000 researchers in total. Its editors are writing because they just made the journal peer review double-blind and want to share their experience. As justification, they offer that they did a poll of about 10% of their membership, of whom a large majority was in favor of double-blinding. The authors reason that the preference for double-blinding is the authors' relative youth and their lower academic rank, which aligns with the interest in the double-blind format. The authors conclude by asserting that, "We have even been told that this [double-blind review] is now viewed as an attractive aspect of our journal's editorial process for some authors who are considering where to submit their research" (E1940).

The case displays several stock features of how review of peer review is conducted, similar to how MLA made its decision during Domna Stanton's tenure as *PMLA* editor we discussed at the beginning of this chapter (Stanton, "Editor's Column"). First, a decision is made based on polling. The results are treated as if they were a will of the majority, though they represent only a small segment of scholars, and partial evidence about prestige bias or h-index is taken as support for the change. The procedure is then related to as if it were scientific, democratic, and fair mainly because the authors believe that it conforms to such standards and reflects the general opinion.

If we ask what conditions are conducive to discrimination, it is precisely the kind that results from this attitude where substantive problems with research evaluation are brushed aside, using the simplest of solutions like polling and then removing the problems of both evaluation and discrimination from notice. The consequence is an entrenched opinion that "validation offered through peer review remains one of the essential pillars of trust in scholarly communication, irrespective of any potential flaws" (Tennant et al. 8 citing Haider and Åström) while peer review continues to support an institutional setup that is neither neutral nor fair.

Were these same scholars to behave like this in their scientific work, relying on practices that can readily be shown not to perform that function, they would soon stop being scientists. As Fish has shown, there are no neutral terms under which researchers can compete. To present a double-blind review as such is to present incorrect assumptions and treat them as true. The same imperative toward the truth that drives science requires us to try and level the field as well, which itself necessitates that we start by acknowledging the problem with our evaluative apparatuses and the institutions they define. As many studies have shown, peer review is not only a biased instrument, it is also enmeshed in a biased organization and way of thinking (for instance, Bruce et al., Lee et al.).

From this argument, our inference is the precise opposite of the accepted views on double-blind peer review. Double-blind peer review is problematic and ultimately undemocratic *because* of its lack of transparency. If it provides benefit for newcomers and underrepresented categories of scholars, the benefits studies have been able to find evidence for is so small (Darling) that it cannot counterbalance the weight of the negative impact on the integrity of research and evaluation processes.

The kind of discrimination we are talking about here is not a result of individual moral failing that can be improved by the improving the honesty and character of the reviewers or by better information about lives of the disadvantaged or by more just review formats. Discrimination, instead, is an issue of the truth of American history which is a history of discrimination that was obscured by the story of equality and opportunity, which has wide use and purchase even among the scientists who should know better. This is an issue related to the truth also because inequality requires secrecy to be maintained. A strange kind of secrecy to be sure since the effects of discrimination are obvious, only that they are regarded as natural, right, or acceptable costs of freedom.

Discrimination is also an issue of truth in a more general sense that observing how a system functions is integral to that system (just as peer review is integral to the scholarship we produce). When regulation and control mechanisms fail or fail some groups, they fail not by chance but by design that reflects the given setup and helps perpetuate its build-in hierarchy. In general, transparency is the best friend of equality, and the lack of it, regardless how well-intentioned, leads to more bias, either directly or indirectly, as it also leads to fragmentation and scholarship that cannot support truth and justice in all of its dimensions.

Put another way, control mechanisms like peer review are not auxiliary processes. They are processes through which we support hegemony and a given setup. It requires effort to repurpose them and use them in more open ways. But the effort does not concern peer review itself first. Instead, it concerns the change of attitude and mindset, and, then, the setup of evaluation practices such that they are regarded as scholarship.

Another corollary of our argument is that we should present issues of discrimination not in terms of social justice, as it is usually the case, but in terms of truth. I believe in social justice as a goal, the horizon toward which our activity, to use Martin Luther King's verb, "bends." However, the means toward that goal should be a category that scientists and scholars, in general, can readily recognize; one that pertains to their research and has direct consequences on it and its quality.

We speak of discrimination at this point in the study since it is directly related to evaluation and the kind of framing that is revealed when we start the inquiry into blindness and lack of transparency that accompany quality control processes. This is because the evaluation's goal is a delimitation and identification accomplished through drawing boundaries, which is but another name for discrimination. For us, the question is how we undertake such processes. With or without: transparency, focus on framing devices, and quality control as integral to identity production.

To be clear, I am not calling for abandoning the strictness in peer review; to the contrary. Rigorous evaluation and rigorous scholarship are the same. The notion of "rigor" should no longer be based on the narrow definition that stems out of and supports specialist knowledge but should also include understanding why transparency in the process of evaluation contributes to an improved science. Education about the system of oppressions—history and how reality is created—is integral to becoming and then being a scientist. Again, this is because hegemony defines the institution of science, how it is done, and how individual works are evaluated. It also defines the reality in which we live and work as scholars.

Sciences must recognize what it is that their discourse *does* as an integral part of what science is and means. For instance, how sciences have contributed to the suspicion toward vaccines and expertise in general by being insensitive to actual wrongs scientists committed in the past—from those readily recognized, like eugenics and polygenesis, to those like the impact of scientific work and way of thinking on maintaining dominant ideologies like white supremacy.

Evidence-based medicine is great for as long as it is practiced with care and we understand that scientific institutions are not neutral, that they operate within specific frameworks, with limited apparatuses that privilege unambiguous results, that the access to science and scientific way of thinking is limited, and so on. All of these are forms of evidence as well. They should enter into the construction of what it means to *do* evidence-based scholarship across the board. As sciences are today, they cannot do such self-scrutiny and self-evaluation or pursuit of truth without humanities though with STEM education, they are attempting to create just one such setup where humanities would play either no role or be included as a parallel approach. We will return to this point of why poststructuralism does not support such arrangement in the last chapter.

Peer review at the heart

Once peer review is based on the theoretical and historical understanding of how frameworks support scientific work, we have also defined a role for the humanities in scientific education. In an institutional sense, this would be a central role because it allows disciplines to meet around a shared concern and the practices that make them into disciplines and scholarship. Thus, peer review provides a crucial knot for our interdisciplinary project, a heart where all the lines of inquiry meet and out of which they spread.

Using peer review as this kind of interdisciplinary meeting or merging point makes it possible for us to claim interdisciplinarity and disciplinarity at the same time, because the focus on the commonalities in the evaluation process offers a new sense of boundary that makes up each discipline and relates them to the mutual concern of interpretation, evaluation, boundary-making, and intersectionality.

In simple terms, peer review is already a general and a common specialization. The fact that scholar across disciplines can readily understand the work that has been done on peer review proves the point. Defining it, we employ the work we have done in the first two chapters bringing it to a kind of summary, which itself provides a practical pivot for the reform. Change the peer review, a reform of how we *do* knowledge will follow.

Open review

We can now present possible shortcuts and opportunities that new digital publication technologies provides for improving peer review. We could not have done so without the above discussion of epistemology and processes that make peer review since modifications should be in concert with the analytic development. Books, too, lag behind shorter forms in becoming digital-only, and for that reason, digital platforms provide a partial solution at least for the humanities. Additionally, due to downsizing, literary studies is among the older and more conservative disciplines whose adoption of digital forms of publication is perhaps slower than in more vigorous disciplines.[17] It is not only that we have a relatively small number of online only journals but that literature and humanities scholars do not participate in many new media that are available, like *arXiv* (an open access archive), *Open Journal Systems* (open-source application for publishing journals), and *ScienceOpen* (which offers post-publication reviews).

Hypothes.is provides annotations to help with the de-fragmentation of science; *Paperhive* makes reading of scientific material a collaborative process; *Pubpeer* allows for shared commentary on articles, and so on. Humanities scholars do not commonly partake in any of these and do not have comparable general networks or services. We might even have digital problems of an entirely different order, like a lack of a comprehensive database, reliable search engine for the same, and so on. On the positive side, many archives have been digitalized.[18]

New technology makes one of the cornerstones of peer review obsolete, or at least partially obsolete, as "A Multi-Disciplinary Perspective on Emergent and Future Innovations in Peer Review" suggests (Tennant et al.). If peer review is a way to manage scarce resources like the space on a page, or a space on a page in a prestigious journal, digital technology makes such space theoretically limitless. The same article posits the problems with peer review with the following set of questions:

> who are the gatekeepers and how are the gates constructed; what is the balance between author-reviewer-editor tensions and how are these power relations and conflicts resolved; what are the inherent biases associated with this; does this enable a fair or structurally inclined system of peer review to exist; and what are the repercussions for this on our knowledge generation and communication systems? (Tennant et al. 9–10)

The innovations considered include forms of open review. *PLOS ONE* asks reviewers not to assess novelty and focus instead on how the research was conducted and if conclusions follow the presented information. Currently, *Publons* offers comprehensive tracking of research impact and "verified" peer review and journal editing history. *F1000 Research* publishes articles not after but before formal peer review, which is then conducted continuously as the article is updated. A version of this is a new kind of collaborative research that makes the different status of referees possible, from simply acknowledging their names to them becoming coauthors. Another open review novelty, portable recommendations, allows authors to use previous reviews in a new venue. Greater participation and acknowledgment of the reviewer's work opens other avenues. The most exciting possibility seem to be that reviewing could become a specialty in its own right, and being a reviewer could become a second scholarly specialization, an option at a later career stage for example.

The integration of evaluation into research and its recognition as a form of research provide much-needed incentives for reviewers and increase the quality of reviews. But the same article ends on this sobering note, which we cite here as evidence that the new environment and technology would not in and of themselves solve any of the problems with peer review. This, as we already suggested, because the inadequacies of evaluation do not stem from peer review itself but from an inadequate epistemology. Tennant et al. write,

> Rigorous, evidence-based research on peer review itself is surprisingly lacking across many research domains, and would help to build our collective understanding of the process and guide the design of ad-hoc solutions (Bornmann & Daniel, 2010b; Bruce et al., 2016; Rennie, 2016; Jefferson et al., 2007). Such evidence is needed to form the basis for implementing guidelines and standards at different journals and research communities, and making sure that editors, authors, and reviewers hold each other reciprocally accountable to them. (Tennant et al. 35)

"A Multi-Disciplinary Perspective on Emergent and Future Innovations in Peer Review" is significant in our context for another reason, too. It exemplifies the kinds of authorship and collaboration that are becoming possible due to changes brought about by digital technology. The article has 33 coauthors, representing 37 institutions and various humanities, social sciences, and sciences. With authors working together, the article offers an unparalleled example—an enormous amount of material, historical, interdisciplinary, as well as philosophical. As it might be expected, the same organization also accounts for its shortcomings, with the chief one being the lack of a unifying explanation.

The jarring repetitive structure of "A Multi-Disciplinary Perspective on Emergent and Future Innovations in Peer Review" would deserve less attention were it not doubling the critical issue with digital media and technology in general. The result is that issues like bias repeatedly appear but without reference to previous mentions or graduated and organized development. Most significant is the lack of direct address of the overarching structure that makes this into one article, which is the perennial problem with digital technology. There are elements but no instance, discourse, or agency that can gather and unify them. We already addressed those with respect to literary studies and are now going to a broader perspective in the Chapter 4, to digital humanities, and Chapter 5, to forms of interdisciplinarity. Our inquiry will be looking for ways to make further connections between pieces of knowledge as we build new more general frameworks for our interdisciplinary approach. Here we can already suggest the next step regarding what Tennant et al. say concerning the advantage of digital technology. They write, "The major benefit of such a system [a hybrid, integrated peer review and publishing platform] is that peer review becomes an inherently social and community-led activity, decoupled from any journal-based system" (Tennant et al. 35). If the system is inherently social, this is just to say that an understanding of social systems becomes a part of the necessary knowledge for anyone who wants to be involved in knowledge production or its evaluation. As we will claim in the last chapter, given the nature of evaluation, interdisciplinary work on explaining how knowledge is made and how it works also provides an epistemology that can be shared among divergent disciplines. The claim, too, defines rather precisely and clearly what basic role humanities can play in knowledge production, namely, one of negotiating, explaining, and monitoring the social and cultural aspects of research both within and outside of academia.

In respect to the digital technology, it can readily improve peer review process in the humanities by, for instance, allowing for more transparent process (including open review); exchanges between reviewer and author; and concurrent publications of different digital and print journal editions which is already the case in creative writing world.

Notes

1. See Sabaj Meruane et al. for the latest review of scholarship on peer review.
2. See Showalter's editorial report from 1984, which says, "[a] large majority even of those whose articles were turned down replied that they found the review process beneficial; the specialist readers' critiques represent free consulting of excellent quality" (Showalter 852).
3. See, however, McGann. Though McGann argues that the central problems our discipline is facing "are institutional and political, not technical" (McGann 78), his discussion addresses peer review only in the latter, technical context as if peer review were not an ideological form.
4. See also Davidson.
5. See, however, Fitzpatrick *Planned* 27–28.
6. For the history of peer review, see also Lipscombe.
7. Similar views persist. See recent example in Edington.
8. See also *Science Wars*, edited by Andrew Ross, that predates *Peer Review* by almost a decade and positions science/humanities in a more useful fashion.
9. See Schooler et al. See also many works that are now trying to understand the upheaval that Nosek's reproducibility tests caused like Devezer et al.; and the report on reproducibility by the National Academies of Sciences, Engineering, and Medicine. 2019.
10. See National Cancer Act of 1937.
11. In his "Postdisciplinary liaisons: Science studies and the humanities," Biagioli expresses some reservations toward the use of Foucault's notion of discipline (819).
12. See Wellmon and Piper for quantitative analysis which suggests "that publication patterns largely reproduce significant power imbalances within the system of academic publishing. Systems of academic patronage as well as those of cultural and social capital seem not only to have survived but flourished in the modern bureaucratic university, even if in different form" (Wellmon and Piper).
13. In his text, Schaefer does not use the phrase Fish identifies under the quotation marks.
14. Compare to Rennie, "I believe that … open review is the most ethical variety, and its practicability is established" (Rennie, "Let's Make" 33).

15 See, for instance, The International Spenser Society and the latest issue of *Spenser Studies* on race (Britton and Coles).
16 See, however, database-based research that does show different, negative effect for single-blind reviews on newcomer scholars, Seeber and Bacchelli. See also Darling for review of reviews.
17 Some exceptions are *Digital Medievalist* and *PhilaPapers*.
18 See Clement and Gueguen.

4
WHAT DH?
Return to formalism in the age of big data

Part I: statistics is not an interpretation

Discussion of digital humanities is forced on this project because literary scholars often assume that DH does what this book purports to do. It updates literary studies; it brings sciences, technology, and humanities together; and it presents a new paradigm for knowledge understanding and production. We will show that none of this holds. From our perspective, DH has a future but not in the currently prevalent version that emphasizes distant reading and pattern analysis, also called Computational Literary Analysis (CLS). More promising are teaching practices—like those at the University of California, Los Angeles, among other institutions (Booth and Posner; Koh) and work like J. Nathan Matias's on Citizens and Technology—that offer insights and skills scientists and engineers need to understand evaluation, systems of oppression, and other framing practices. As it is currently set up, DH makes an effort in the opposite direction of importing technological know-how into the humanities—it is not known for exporting the humanities and shaping or influencing the use of digital technology according to our standards.

The discussion of DH will also be an opportunity for us to begin to address the consequence of there being too much knowledge, which we will develop further in the following chapter on interdisciplinary forms. This chapter will show close reading in a new, formalist sense, which is our version of distant reading. It will offer a critique of attitude behind DH which is as an obstacle for interdisciplinarity among divergent disciplines. Its uncritical celebration siphons off the already scarce resources without at the same time advancing our understanding of technology and big data or improving the chances for the survival of literary studies.

Objection

Our objection to DH—as it is presented in a recent issue of the *PMLA*, "Varieties of Digital Humanities," that is supposed to represent the field; Stanford Literary Lab; TXTLAB; *Digital Humanities Quarterly*; in the series from Minnesota University Press titled, Debates in the Digital Humanities, and so on—follows from Rob Kitchin's recent observation in "Big Data, New Epistemologies and Paradigm Shifts," that

> (1) Big Data and new data analytics are disruptive innovations which are reconfiguring in many instances how research is conducted; and (2) there is an urgent need for wider critical reflection within the academy on the epistemological implications of the unfolding data revolution, a task that has barely begun to be tackled despite the rapid changes in research practices presently taking place. (1)

Much of DH does not draw on the critical potentials of literary studies, and epistemology has not been on its agenda. Consequently, the new field has developed without a call similar to Kitchin's for "critical reflection" that would lead to an examination of its "epistemological implications." Instead, proponents of DH tend to answer criticism by repeating their belief that quantitative analysis can have qualitative effects, as we can see, most recently, in the debate that followed the publication of Nan Z. Da's "The Computational Case Against Computational Literary Studies," in *Critical Inquiry*.[1]

Even scholars who recognize the importance of Da's critique—as does, for instance, Leif Weatherby—do not acknowledge the full implications of what she has demonstrated. On the one hand, Weatherby says that DH "will have to confront this problem of the relationship between data and domain in far more direct and theoretical terms than it has to date" (892), but, on the other, he believes that more and bigger DH can substitute for hermeneutics and that DH can provide the "bridge between quality and quantity" (895). This itself represents divergence from what Kitchin and social sciences have done at the same stage of digital technology development, when Kitchin proposed a more consistent look at epistemology of big data. We will repeat some of Da's critique from her landmark "The Computational Case Against Computational Literary Studies," including her general points like her claim that many arguments in DH or CLS are based on "logical fallacies," that DH "has very little explanatory power" (601, 604); that it does not use big data; that it requires a disproportionate amount of resources; that it confuses data interpretation with text interpretation, and so on. Our critique will be, however, presented in a different order, starting with general philosophical issues; with a different choice of terms (those pertaining not to DH exclusively but to literary interpretation in general); with a different context in mind (among others, the context of narrative studies from the 1960s and 1970s which practiced a form of distant reading); and with goals consistent with

Interdiscipline. Our analysis will also add a concern and solution lacking in Da's essay that is compatible with it, which is epistemology. The chapter will diverge with Da's essay on several details, like the use of structuralism in DH. While she is right that models like "Claude Lévi-Strauss's attempt to define the structure of myths using the formula $^f x(a): {^f y(b)} \cong {^f x(b)}: {^f (a-1)(y)}$, are not operationalizable" (607), there are other ways in which structuralism can contribute to setting up of DH research and to its use of pattern analysis. This chapter will emphasize two of those, with one being the example of Vladimir Propp's *Morphology of Folk Tale*, which is about the relation between pattern analysis and the background theory. And another, based on a critique of the same Propp based model from a poststructuralist perspective, can position pattern analysis/framework issues in a less centered manner. We will also claim a distinct critical role for the humanities (providing insight into framing devices) regarding the use of digital technology consistent with the existing curricular organization in most humanities departments and one that can be easily employed following the UCLA example.[2] This is our preferred scenario for the future. In such context, critical theory and close reading are our most readily available resources that can be used to build interdisciplinary humanities and thus contribute to the trends represented in what we can now call early DH.

I will approach this critique as a non-specialist. My justification for it is closely related to the overall argument of this book concerning interdisciplinarity. It also happens to be the opposite of what DH scholars, including Da, seem to think; namely, DH, like every other field or discipline in literary studies, has its own rules and that only the specialists who understand those are in the position to formulate a relevant critique. On this thinking, criticism requires, as an anonymous reviewer of my manuscript put it, "engaging with the complex and nuanced epistemological arguments that undergird statistics such as EDA vs CDA, modeling such as Bayesian approaches, and the role of data viz as a way of knowing."[3] On this thinking, disciplines are autonomous fields made out of norms that scholars in each area agree on over time. Published articles, conference papers, and other forums set up a field and define it through peer review, indirect conversations, as well as debates like the one that followed Da's article.

From our perspective, such an organization is like a branch of a tree that has no trunk. There are many fields and disciplines, and if truth or the approach in one field is not consistent with truth in another, it is hard to see why it should be accepted at all. Why should we agree with the notion of unity on the scale of DH but not on the level of the compliance between DH and literary studies, literary studies agreement with philosophy, and their agreement with sciences? What reasons are there to privilege the small scale and specialization over the general view and do that for a discipline that purports to have a new way of analyzing and interpreting information that is generally applicable?

If we are going to build an interdisciplinary edifice and rely on it to develop knowledge further, scholars cannot pay attention only to what similarly situated, and educated peers do. For an enduring, relevant body of knowledge, the consensus is required from many, if not most of these interpretative communities. This goes especially for similar approaches, like DH and big data that are practiced in traditionally different disciplines like literary studies and sociology. The same goes also for the subdisciplines, DH, in respect to literary studies. If its branch is not going to be supported just by the number of DH initiates but by general and verifiable practices, they need to adhere to rules and regulations resulting from DH and literary studies' convergences. In other words, it is DH scholars who have to explain themselves to the general audience which they have not done in a way that would bring DH and hermeneutics together.

We will insist that literary studies already has a general criterion and that if DH or CLS wants to be what their names suggest, DH scholars have to define their findings in terms of hermeneutics in general and literary interpretation in particular. A way to put this charge most simply is that literature involves the reader and reading, which have been—as our previous chapters show—the main elements in the critique of the New Critical approach and pillars of the poststructuralist theory of literature. A word search of Da, Ted Underwood, and Weatherby's response published in the *Critical Inquiry* illustrates the point with the glaring absence of the term "reader" from the discussion.[4] Without a theory of reading, DH cannot be a theory of signs or hermeneutics, and cannot represent a discourse in literary studies. If DH scholars limit themselves to the current supposition that algorithms are doing the reading and that quantity turns into interpretation, DH will never have a theory of reading.

To repurpose Lisa Feldman Barrett's explanation: the pattern that shows in graphs is not a depiction of the content in a work of art "but merely a statistical summary of a highly variable set of instances" (*How Emotions Are Made* 15). Statistics no matter how situated is not a reading.[5] There are many just published books for general audiences—among others, Brian Christian's *The Alignment Problem*, Tim Harford's *The Data Detective,* Melanie Mitchell's *Artificial Intelligence,* Deborah Stone's *Counting*—arguing this point on their way to rearticulating what computers and AI can do for us.

General issues with DH

Our first content issue with DH is based on a conflation of human and artificial intelligence, reducing both ways of sorting information—computing *and* thinking. As we will argue here, beyond fiction, strictly speaking, there are no cyborgs, and there is no artificial intelligence. There is technology's increasing capacity for computation, independent work, and prediction, *and* there is human intelligence as a part of complex embodied systems whose general interconnectedness and functioning are still poorly understood. When we assume a continuity as in the usual phrases like neural networks and machine cognition, we take a small part of human intelligence for the whole and equate it to the particular ways in which machines task independently, which we then call "learning," though it is evident that machines and humans learn in very different ways, that their problem solving is vastly different, and so on. By extension, the same symbiosis is assumed for the digital humanities in terms of quantity to quality transformation, with the quantity of data leading to a new interpretive approach and a new discipline. We cannot say this one loud enough: "processing and visualization of data *are not* interpretations and readings in their own right" (Da, "Computation Case" 606).

We have three additional principle issues with DH. As N. Katherine Hayles put it in her influential book, *How We Think: Digital Media and Contemporary Technogenesis*, "we think through, with, and alongside media" (1). The general suggestion behind this claim is that media shape our thinking and that when a new medium like digital technology is emerging, then thinking and even being must be different. This could be correct in the case of writing, which, as we already explained, was acquired late in the evolution and requires various parts of the brain and the two hemispheres to coordinate each with others. In this sense, because it challenges and changes the way the mind works, writing could be described as the medium of thought that has radically altered thought. Its function as a depository and easily portable registrar offer new cultural possibilities and a new notion of authorship/authority, as Socrates was quick to note in *Phaedrus*. In the case of digital technology, there are no new tasks that the brain has to perform. If we get depressed or our social attitudes change, that concerns the *effects* of technology use and not the *prerequisite* function that enables us to do it (Giedd). The digital universe only makes the adoption simpler and easier to accomplish but does not alter the death of the author paradigm in any way. Digital technology, too, depends on writing in ways that are so essential that whatever the technology seems to offer can be, by and large, explained in terms of improvements to the fundamental discovery of the printing press. Improvements allow letters and images to circulate in larger volumes and with incredible speed, but, again, quantity does not translate into quality as of yet.

The assertion that the medium changes the paradigm is a version of Karl Marx's proposition (*Capital*) that relations of production or production itself determine our consciousness, which is taken to mean that every technological age has an appropriate and distinct culture if not also behavior and psychology. Hence, the popular terms that take events in science and economy and use them to name the period like industrialization or automation or electrification or digitalization or capitalism, socialism, and so on. These are seen as delimiting a distinct cultural epoch from another. Labels are helpful since technology and the economy do change our lives by, for instance, accelerating them. These labels are deceptive in so far as they suggest that technology/economy is a source or force that compels an *ontological* change. The same can be said about any similar deterministic view that claims an age to be an age of something or supposes that there is one dominant paradigm that defines all other entities belonging to the same system, as is the case in popular books like Jared Diamond's *Guns, Germs and Steel: A Short History of Everybody for the Last 13,000 Years*. This way of thinking is common to structuralism, which attributes the determination to a central source (or a limited number of these) like media or technology, which dictates the nature of other entities in its constellation. When proposed today, it is also a way of thinking meant to counteract poststructuralism and its understanding that relations in general, not just those of production, including chance, make things into what they are. Such critique returns the certainties of a top-down, center-periphery organization to the world that poststructuralist theory has disrupted.

As with other forms, media are dependent on framing provided by the user. The medium can be the message only in a restricted sense that does not account for how media are constructed and maintained.

Perhaps because of that denial of the constructed nature of media and as a way of hiding it, DH is supported by the theory of evolution with striking regularity. A case in point is Hayles' most recent essay, "Can Computers Create Meanings? A Cyber/Bio/Semiotic Perspective," published in *Critical Inquiry*. The article extends Hayles's notion of "assemblage" from her *Unthought* to include a symbiotic relationship between humans and technology. The essay starts with this:

> Biological evolution, having proceeded for a few million years and produced humans, has now entered a new stage …. The result is biotechnoevolution, a hybrid process in which information, interpretations, and meanings circulate through flexible interactive human-computational collectivities or, in my terminology, cognitive assemblages. (32)

It appears that machines and humans are connected not just through use but also in more fundamental ways that allow for biology and technology to form one common "cognitive" or informational system through what Hayles calls intermediation and heterarchies. The effect is that "such moves [the dynamic transition that enabled humans to become cognitive during their evolution] … are useful because they locate the central question of computer cognition within the larger and older context of biological evolution" (33).

The theory itself is based on the assumption that a pattern "repeats at multiple scale levels," starting with atoms going to molecules, then proteins, to species, called "evolutionary emergence" by an evolutionary biologist Terrence Deacon (Hayles, "Can Computers" 33). Deacon, according to Hayles, "shows how meaning-making practices develop" from simpler to complex organisms, and Hayles expects that machines would follow the same pattern of emergence to become intelligent (33). However, neither neurology, genetics, nor theory of evolution can offer a detailed understanding of where cognition comes from, how and why human cognition differs from the cognition of higher mammals and apes in particular, or how and why human cognition developed in the specific ways it did (Laland). While we can think of evolution in terms of information processing as Richard Dawkins (*The Selfish Gene*) indicated, there are too many steps that separate Dawkins's suggestions from Hayles's application of it to explain how machines develop intelligence and make meaning. Deacon is careful not to make the same leap Hayles does between the processing power of machines and human intelligence, emphasizing that the former has no "sentience" or self-awareness that characterizes the human mind (Deacon 491). Deacon's work is well respected among anthropologists as a rigorous thought experiment (Doyle; Logan). In Hayles's essay, the caution and probabilistic nature of that project are treated as an accepted theory, which then serves her to build on Deacon's notion of evolution as the backbone of the relationship between humans, signification, and machines. *Incomplete Nature* thus provides "Can Computers Create Meaning?" with the grounding that the book itself, being a thought experiment, does not pretend to possess.

As science stands now, machines and humans have coevolved only in a pop-culture sense, not based on shared biological, genetic, or evolutionary processes. There is no evidence of any new stage in evolution that would directly result from the interface with machines. We have gotten only as far as suppositions, like Deacon's, of what we might learn from machines about thinking (Deacon 494) and are in a position to offer probing theories of what seeing biological processes as information exchange might provide.

Similarly, Hayles supports her use of "biotechnoevolution" not with the latest in biology but with cultural and linguistic theories and the notion of biosemiotics and embodied signification developed in Wendy Wheeler's *The Whole Creature: Complexity, Biosemiotics and the Evolution of Culture,* and *Expecting the Earth: Life/Culture/Biosemiotics* and Jesper Hoffmeyer's *Biosemiotics: An Examination into the Signs of Life and the Life of Signs*, and *Signs of Meaning in the Universe*, neither of which addresses technology. Biosemiotics, in general, has developed not to define the "bio" part of its name but to offer a new context for an understanding of the sign. As Donald Favareau puts it, biosemiotics is devoted to explaining "the use of sign processes and sign relations both between and within organisms" (Favareau 2). Such biosemiotics is not a branch of biology, and it does not make assertions about unifying biological and semiotic systems or explaining evolution in Darwin's sense of the term. Which is to say that the same theory does not offer an element for a unified theory of artificial and human intelligences, only an expansive understanding of sign and signification that can be applied to biological entities.

As Bernard Dionysius Geoghegan reminds in an article titled, "From Information Theory to French Theory," world "organized into a discrete series of signals and messages that invite our recognition and interpretation" is the common structuralist assumption present in works like Claude Lévi-Strauss's *The Savage Mind* (96). But syncretism is limited by the common denominator it suggests. If all signals are reducible to information, they, too, cease to be signals and become information. This is but another way to phrase the issues with the structuralist approach to which Derrida reacts in "Structure, Sign, and Play." Derrida's article, once again, offers a new starting point for thinking about signifying structures under the assumption that they cannot be centered or closed. Seen from that perspective, various systems can productively relate to one another, but only if scholars respect the relative autonomy of each. We can know using computers not because human and digital cognition are one and the same but because an interface (for instance, a human hand) was created through evolution that allows humans to develop and use technology. It, therefore, makes sense to say that machines can enhance ways of thinking. It is, however, counterproductive to then go on and abolish the boundaries and regard the openness of a system as if it were the same as limitlessness. When we say that a tool or labor has changed the human in the sense that Marx and Heidegger do, the point is about forming the specificity of human organs, and the hand in particular. As Jacques Derrida shows in "Geschlecht II: Heidegger's Hand," through evolution, the hand acquires characteristics of the tool it handles while also maintaining traits of an ape-like extremity. The hand ends up somewhere between an instrument and an organ, having characteristics of all three, an animal, tool, and human. The transformation that takes place in this process is of the human body through practice. Strictly speaking, it is not the effect that the stick has on the hand, but that work, practice, or usage have.

In other words, it is not the stick that makes the hand but an interaction of the hand with it and then the changing attitude toward the use of the stick (technology) that arises out of this interaction and becomes integral to the construction of what it means to be human. For Heidegger, as Derrida insists, the hand is the organ that both connects us to and separates us from animals and, in particular, apes ("Heidegger's Hand" 173). For Derrida, in turn, reading of Heidegger's understanding of the hand becomes a way to bring back the bodily and the animal aspects into thinking/handling in general. Technology is in this handling, the extension of the human, neither the source nor the product, but an element in the bodily/cognitive arrangement. It is the organ-tool of intermediation. To use a hybrid like cyborg the way Donna Haraway has done would be to emphasize one resulting point (Haraway). For Derrida, animal-human-machine is a form of encounter and a process of integration, an exchange that exceeds each. It is not a cyborg for the simple reason that it is not one or two things but a practice. The process consists of, on the one hand, an autonomous entity called human being and, on the other hand, technology, which lends itself to use following specific rules. When machines can develop these rules further, there is no qualitative change in the setup, only a new distribution of labor with human delegating part of the work that can be automated to the technological apparatus. Intermediation still remains on the side of the human, a characteristic of their kind of sociality and physicality.

The fear of machines and the hope we invest in technology, as Steven Pinker has shown in *Enlightenment Now*, are much like Frankenstein's monster: a projection of our insecurities, misunderstandings, and desires. There is no doubt that we need a better understanding of the complex relationship between biology, signification, and technology. As we will claim later in this chapter, we have such a theory already in the theory of ideology, which has been one of the most critical contributions that poststructuralism has made. Given poststructuralism's relation to ideology, it should be easy to understand why this criticism is not done out of a belief in human exceptionalism or autonomy, nor is our critique of

Hayles based on some human-centered theory. The difference is one of the basic assumptions that we would again characterize as a difference between structuralism and poststructuralism. One assumes that identities need to be decentered and the other that they are always open. One assumes that decentering leads to a hybrid unification of what was heretofore understood as the opposites. The other that boundaries serve useful functions and that they can also be employed to delimit/bring-in-contact and help us think the relation.

The difference between human and artificial intelligence matters for each. If there is common signification, it is achieved through ideology, not through biotechnical symbiosis. Furthermore, if technology influences mind, cultural, and social norms, these are accounted for by the theory of ideology created for such understanding. This is the case even when we regard technology as bringing in a new kind of sociality, mediating human-to-human contact, and creating societies of people who are alone. In such instances, the tendencies of late capitalism—shrinking distances, mediating closeness—are only exaggerated further.

Spectacular results

The third prominent characteristic of DH is a promise of spectacular results that are regularly not delivered. Consider the following: "the underlying *social psychological processes* that drive a story have never been directly observed using scientific tools. Until now, that is" (Arc of Narrative). And the big revelation that follows—for Emily Bronte's *Wuthering Heights*—is, well, anti-cathartic (see Figure 4.1).

And for the movie *Raiders of the Lost Ark*, see Figure 4.2.

Since the authors do not accompany their graphs with explanations of how the lines respond to the *"social psychological processes"* they are supposed to represent, we, too, will leave them without interpretation. Instead, we note the change that happens when the same authors present their graphs in a scholarly article published in *Science Advances*. There they say only that "this is the first set of studies that have provided empirical support for classical theories of the underlying dimensions, and structure, of traditional narratives" (Ryan et al.). Indeed, the graphs are just illustrations of the oldest narrative theories.

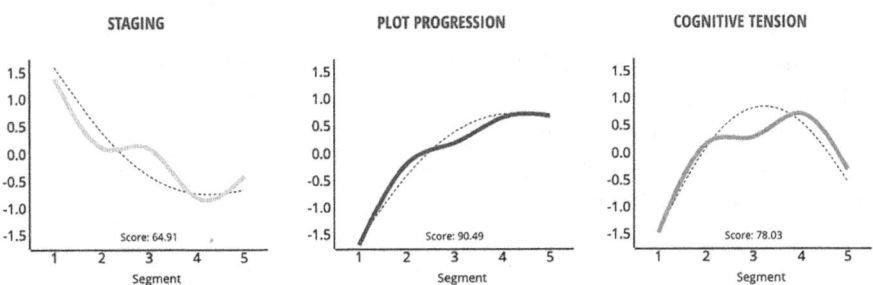

FIGURE 4.1 *Wuthering Heights* (Arc of Narrative).

144 Return to formalism

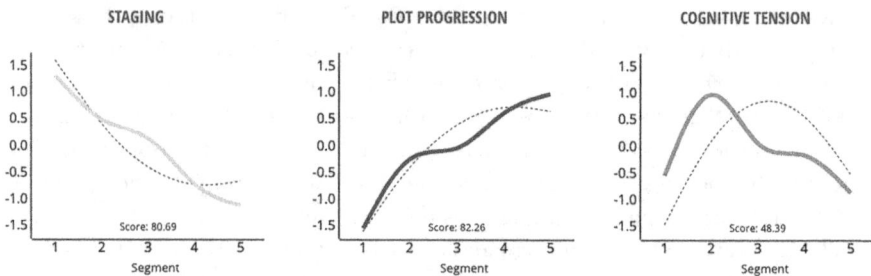

FIGURE 4.2 *Raiders of the Lost Ark* (Arc of Narrative).

But even that claim is not precise enough. What the graphs exhibit is nothing like "deeper story structure of a text" ("How it works") but a realization of the chosen mapping system. To define their search, the authors divide the text into five different segments, priming it to express the traditional concept of the narrative arc. Then, they chose their search terms following the same traditional theory, making the approach conform further to the expectations. The result is then not discovering some new element of narrative unfolding, but a graphing or visualizing the framework applied to the story's analysis. What is added is perhaps a specificity that can distinguish between *Wuthering Heights* from the *Raiders of the Lost Ark*. But what kind of specificity is this? What is the importance of the minute differences between the two squiggly lines? Such questions are left unaddressed and variants unexplained. We can say that this absence is a necessary result because algorithms only conform to the terms that define and organize the data set and do not supply a theory of signs but illustrations.[6]

As this chapter will show, many of the DH findings are similarly drawings or representations of the suppositions. They are not qualitatively new findings made available due to the employment of new technology and its new ways of understanding the world, but renderings of arguments that have been made using traditional methodology. We will turn to big data below since it differs from DH in precisely this respect: what models could accomplish.

Following such expectations, digital humanities are not just humanities using algorithms but also a new discipline with an aura of relevance, correctness, and overall importance, more real and up-to-date than the old, non-digital humanities. Walter Benjamin ("The Work of Art in the Age of Mechanical Reproduction") can be amended for the digital age which brought about a new halo, gained when our work is hip—or merely claims to be hip.

The exaggeration is in concert with the overall pop culture, Hollywood, and general Internet age pumping up of technology. Here is the latest (at the time of writing) about Elon Musk:

> Musk has hinted at some of the health-focused capabilities Neuralink's technology could develop, specifically in individuals who are neurologically compromised. Installation of a chip replacing a small portion of the

human skull, for instance, could restore limb function, improve human movement, resolve issues with eyesight and hearing, and help with diseases like Parkinson's. (Ferris)

In reality, the description is fictitious, meant to enhance Musk's image and reach. This is simple propaganda, manipulating expectations and needs. The prediction hides the vast amount of time required to make numerous technological discoveries that would lead to a successful brain-machine interface and presents it as if a restored limb and digital cure for Parkinson's were just around the corner. As things stand, we do not even know a reliable method for the first step—how to insert electrodes into the brain and not get an immune reaction that would prevent electrodes from receiving signals.[7] And when that issue is mitigated, the bandwidth or the amount of information that electrodes can transmit will present the next plateau, and so on. This same criticism accurately describes where we are today regarding human-machine interface; at the very beginning facing uncertain prospects, on this side of a major breakthrough which itself may never come.

Much of DH functions by association with possible hyper accomplishments, with, that is, the promise of control either on our behalf or over us. When a scholar says, "cognition extends through the entire biological spectrum, including animals and plants; technical devices cognize, and in doing so profoundly influence human complex systems" (Hayles, *Unthought* 5), they are not merely describing a posthuman condition in which humans are no longer the center; they are also asserting a new kind of omnipotence. In this reality, machines define and serve as connections that can unify the world since they are the only ones with enough "cognitive" power (Vinge). In such a world, machines are the only ones that can "profoundly influence" what learning, cognition, analysis, and even what science is—Chris Anderson, the editor in chief of *Wired*, was blunt in 2009, "the data deluge makes the scientific method obsolete," also adding that correlation is an explanation (Anderson).[8] AI has thus ushered in a new age of knowledge that does not rest on understanding but on the belief in computational power. Digital era, too, has created a new economy with few companies like Google, Amazon, Microsoft, and Facebook in the United States and Tencent, Baidu, Alibaba, and JD.com in China, as the pools of wealth and power (Morozov).

The switch is evident in the often-repeated phrase "it is only a matter of time" until machines achieve this or that result or acquire this or that skill. Counting on such continuity is nothing but an expression of faith in the dominance of technology. We do not know if AI—tools like auto-encoders—will be able to "generate sense in grammatically correct and even aesthetically pleasing, information-saturated sentences and images" (Da, "Computational Case" 918). Making sense could be a layered and recursive activity so complex that what appears easy and automatic for the mind may be impossible for a machine.

Part II: no epistemology, no hermeneutics, no reading

Underwood

We will extend the above criticism of DH with a close look at a representative essay, Ted Underwood's "Machine Learning and Human Perspectives," which is the leading article of the mentioned special issue of the *PMLA* on DH. The article also represents a digest version of Underwood's well-received *Distant Horizons* published by the University of Chicago Press. It, too, is more theoretical than the norm. The analysis of Underwood's work will allow us to spell out our concerns with how scholars go from the general hermeneutic issues to those specific to DH which exclude interpretation.

Both Underwood's article and the book start the same way, warning that data does not come with an interpretative methodology. Invoking Stanley Fish, Underwood adds that "it's one thing to prove that Swift uses a lot of connective words and another to give that isolated fact a literary interpretation" (Underwood *Distant* xi; see also Underwood "Machine Learning" 92). In the book, Underwood goes on to solve the problem between quantity and interpretation in terms of "scale." The "expansion of digital libraries" has "made it easier to pose broad historical questions, and historical breadth has given quantitative inquiry a better social foundation," with the "sheer scale [being] only part of the story" (xi). He then explains that the inflection is possible because,

> we [DH] have recently graduated from measuring variables to framing models of literary concepts. Since a model defines a relationship between variables, a mode of inquiry founded on models can study relationships rather than isolated facts. (xi–xii)

In the article, the transition to the new paradigm happens even more quickly. He declares that "the boundary between quantitative and interpretive methods was always permeable, and recent intellectual advances have made it easy to traverse," to add, "[s]ince learning algorithms rely on examples rather than fixed definitions, they can be used to model the tacit assumptions shared by particular communities of production or reception" (Underwood, "Machine Learning" 93). He means that the quantitative method becomes a new kind of interpretation when it is fed not just a text of a primary source (like a literary work) but models that consist of interpretative supposition or relations between concepts. This is to say, DH no longer feeds the "raw" data but instead relies on sets that have been ordered through interpretation and could meet Katherine Bode's requirement that they are historically situated date sets (Bode, "Why You").

Here then lies the confusion. DH scholars think they are using interpretative models because their algorithms use "examples rather than fixed definitions." They also believe that because they analyze interpretations or because their algorithms include complex relations, the results can account for reading practices.

We who rely on poststructuralist definition of metadiscourse have a different view. Just as counting connective words cannot become an interpretation of Swift, neither can the approach of paying attention to connective words (or the historical situation of libraries and data sets) become an interpretation by its mere inclusion. It may be confusing, but data, data sets, and models are interpretation only in the researchers' hands. As a part of a model, data is just data—raw, dead/alive like that poor Schrodinger's cat. If no prior technology allows us to make this distinction, with DH we can claim the precise opposite of what Underwood and other DH scholars assert, namely, that data require interpretation at every step and that what algorithms do with data is not interpretation but classification, following the lines of distinction between interpreting and computing or the older distinction between a book and a reading.

As Fish has taught us, interpretation is a product of an act of *recognition* with which the process of interpretation begins. Machines cannot recognize even when they can classify kinds according to complex criteria or come up with the predictive result. This is because algorithms do not know what they are doing, or, put another way, because algorithms cannot simultaneously classify and recognize or do metadiscourse.

While data/interpretation boundary was always permeable, as Underwood suggests, that was the case only in the scholar's hands because "scholar" (not data) is a porous concept without a stable boundary definition. In this thinking, all data is raw—up until the point human being reads the results of computer models whence data is just like other texts, a product of a framing practice.

When we say that algorithms do not interpret, we mean that even for demonstrably biased situations. In such a case, and strictly speaking, it is not the algorithm that discriminates. The source of discrimination lies in the processes, routines, and institutions the authors used to define the sets and algorithms, whose bias, henceforth, gets built into the system. This is then to say that facial recognition is the product of the history of recognitions (and of the setup used to make the product), not of computing, which is but a means for the former's repetition and dissemination. This is yet another way for us to draw a sharp distinction between human and artificial intelligence. One of them discriminates, the other mirrors. To say that artificial intelligence discriminates is, for this reason, both inaccurate and deceptive, giving the machine more power and status than it has and, of course, diminishing the responsibility of the creators. As Underwood himself admits (we will return to this below), scholars judge computer models based on their prior knowledge and the scholarly framework they subscribe to, not based on a new framework the digital technology has created.

The first example of DH that follows is about the gendering of words used in character portrayal. The data set consists of 87,000 works published from 1780 to 2007 in the English language. The algorithm employed is called BookBPL. Underwood spends no time explaining how it works, except to say that it is a program that clusters the "words grammatically associated with each" character (Underwood, "Machine Learning" 93–94) even though the algorithm constitutes the interpretative heart of the research process. Data analysis is given in the form of a graph (95), which is surrounded by a lengthy description of what it is supposed to represent. Patterns are predictable in that there is a clear correlation between gender and terms associated with it—men with beard and swords; women with dress and hair. There are a few "unclear" details like "why writers claim the stomach and feet for their own gender" (95).

Underwood does not attempt to reflect on the outliers as one may expect, given the discourse's popularity (Gladwell). Nor does he mention why he does not pursue that line of thinking. There is a surprising number of such dead-end asides where Underwood notes that certain data is not "something we fully understand even now" (Underwood, "Machine Learning" 95; see also Underwood, *Distant* 9) and leaves it at that. The neglect of outliers is not unique to Underwood. One significant difference between him and other authors writing on DH is that he readily admits their presence. Underwood also notes other shortcomings of the approach—he does it in a major way in the chapter titled "The Risks of Distant Reading" from his *Distant Horizons*. We will get back to it below.

The first research example is then followed by a second where inputs are not as clear-cut and familiar as traditional gender characteristics. The purpose is to show that DH does not require us to have a definition of terms we want to research and can operate based on hybrid figures. We can, instead, use genre as a fluid category and change the goal of computation to tracing "gradual mutations" (Underwood, "Machine Learning" 97). Computers, Underwood notices, can be especially helpful for this research when we do not have a stable definition, and categorization can be "inferred only from examples" (97), as in the case of female authors and science fiction or fantasy labels. Underwood says that the goal of such research is to "represent real practices of selection so that we can trace degrees of similarity among the perspectives of different places and times" (97).

The advantage of such research is that we do not need to know how to define, for instance, "fantasy" in order to do research and reach meaningful results (Underwood, "Machine Learning" 97–98). Preparing the machine to do its analytic work means training it to make the same choices as past readers and apply the reading method or pattern to other data. (The approach breaks down in the next step, when this "reading" needs to be codified in a way that the machine can understand it.) Based solely on punctuation and word choice, computers can distinguish mystery from other genres with 93% accuracy (Allison et al.; Underwood, *Distant* 34–67; Underwood, "Machine Learning" 98).

What we learn from such scholarship, according to Underwood, is "fascinating" (Underwood, "Machine Learning" 99). Fascinating as this: fantasy "can often be recognized by the words *tale, sunlight,* and *seven*" (99). Another captivating conclusion comes a few pages later, after an extended commentary on genre research. It says "that genre theory needs a more flexible framework than our present habits of argument can give" (102). The issue with the above claims is that either the results are trivial and meaningless or do not need DH to formulate them or support them.

The same goes for much of what appears in DH. Either the mapping is narrow—novels in the twentieth century tend to use more colors than those of the eighteenth (Underwood, *Distant* 10)—and/or we could have come to the same conclusions by other means—for instance, that postwar science fiction is invested in social as much as in physical experiments.[9] And here again, Underwood agrees, emphasizing that DH results are not exclusive or more authoritative than other kinds of evidence. Tacitly admitting that DH does not come with its interpretation or framework, he writes,

> I have not been arguing that numbers give these conclusions any special authority. Statistical models are just one more form of evidence, to be weighed along with all the others. This article recommends numbers to literary scholars not as a uniquely reliable form of evidence but as a flexible descriptive language especially suited to historicist questions of perspective and of degree. (Underwood, "Machine Learning" 105)

Significantly, in the quotation, when he says that numbers do not "give these conclusions any special authority," Underwood acknowledges the limit of DH that he glossed over at the beginning of his projects, where he claimed that quantitative method could just like that become interpretative method. He also says that data and algorithm searches are "just one more form of evidence" (105).

I must digress at this point to clarify. With my criticism, I do not mean to disparage Underwood's work. It is my target because the author is doing carefully and precisely what he sets out to do, namely, promote new discourse. Underwood's version is, in short, as effective as DH in literary studies has gotten. His book and the essay are opportunistic scholarship (when opportunities are few and far between) whose premise I am trying to prove is limited and deceptive despite his frank admissions, like the one above, that DH cannot deliver what it promises. Because they are asides, his admissions serve to strengthen the overall case for DH since they show Underwood as a thorough scholar.

At this point in our institutional life, what we expect DH to accomplish, namely, bringing us closer to sciences and technology, to generations Z (1995–2012) and Alpha (2012—2025), updating and rearticulating literary studies, is not going to be accomplished by it. I do not see the relevance of the DH findings, and I do not expect students to *recognize* them either. Especially in a world defined by the increasing number of totalitarian regimes, with white supremacy contending for the White House, they will not be coming to the English department in droves to hear which three words characterize tragedy. I also do not see how such discourse can attract scholars from other disciplines. What exactly would they find in the "fascinating" results? Or how could they use them in their research? Underwood speaks of DH registering social processes and change over time and helping us present conflicting perspectives. But that is a most deceptive way to put it. All analytic work for these questions about social practices precedes the deployment of the quantitative method. The only authentic result of the computation is a graphic image of the change, while the other evidence is also readily available, and the picture can be approximated with freehand drawing. And there is no point of inflection, no "could" that transforms quantitative into the interpretative methodology.

Most importantly, DH results come at great expense and effort, requiring us to either hire a specialist or embark on learning hard new skills on our own. All that so that we can offer not proof but a visual illustration of the correlations.

Terms of research in DH studies are dominated by the traditional categories like genre and gender with a reason. We see this already in Moretti's *Distant Reading*, which purported methodological novelty while recycling just about the oldest question modern literary scholar could ask, concerning the length of the novel, its structure, geographical and historical distribution. Not to mention that nations and national language define the notion of unity on which this research is based or that periods are taken to be starting positions for investigation. In *Distant Horizons*, Underwood is caught in this web of unifying, traditional categories, affirming their importance even as he tries to reframe some questions and perspectives around the so-called fluid concepts.

With taxonomy being offered as a form of knowledge, this scholar was concerned that the intent of DH is to turn away from close reading just so that it could return to the past of earlier distant (structuralist) kind of reading while making us believe that we are moving into the future at lightning speed. Especially worrying is that the behavior fits a pattern. When a group feels a threat from the outside (like the one we described in the first chapter), it retrenches what appears to be its core or fundamental values. In the case of *Distant Horizons*, the center stage is devoted to the terms of stylistic analysis with authors like Wayne Booth—whose *The Rhetoric of Fiction* was published in 1961 and was reissued with significant additions 20 years later, in 1983—raising again to occupy the referential place the way he did in the decades before the culture wars.

The issue here is that there is a recreation of the past and what version of the past is put out. Why *The Rhetoric of Fiction* and not the more theoretically sophisticated form of distant reading from the *Morphology of the Folktale*? Or from the actantial model of one Algirdas Julien Greimas? Why, in short, promote this rhetoric over semiotics? This especially because, in the meantime, the latter had a future that connected to computational linguistics, providing what is perhaps a more logical route that runs from literary studies to computer-assisted analysis of language. I will return to this below after I contrast DH with the use of digital technology in social sciences, which offers additional perspectives on the inadequacies of DH.

Distant

Early readers of this manuscript have complained that it did not engage Moretti's work. I am supplying my criticism of it here because Moretti's *Distant Reading* is a blueprint for *Distant Horizons* and much other work in DH. More importantly,

I will use the opportunity to define the model on which distant reading rests with more precision. In my understanding, the work represents another attempt to reinvigorate literary studies by moving away from close reading and toward what is presented as a new approach. However, it harkens back to structuralism and does so without an epistemology or thoroughgoing explanation of the connection between it and the narrative theory or the rhetoric of fiction popular in the 1960s and the 1970s that, again, exemplify earlier emanations of distant reading.

The popularity of *Distant Reading* is likely owed to the apparent simplicity of its solutions coupled with the use of technology and exact and practical results. As we just mentioned, the book also happens to give currency to the traditional vocabulary of literary studies that appeals to many scholars who might be politically on the left but who still understand their scholarship in conservative terms like periods, geographic areas, national languages/cultures, and genres. With roots in technology, traditional versions of literary studies, and new historicism, *Distant Reading*, too, offered stability for the times of crises, more so than just about any work published in the new millennium. Contrast it, for instance, with the 2010 Frank Donoghue's *The Last Professors: The Corporate University and the Fate of the Humanities*, where technology is, by and large, a villain, and the tone of doom and gloom, and we can understand why *Distant Reading* was the hit in 2013 when it first appeared.

A cherry on top is the many neat explanations for obscure scholarly questions, such as why are novels long. They receive precise replies, like they tell of adventures (165). Moretti means only that novels, like Homer's epics, have additive structure. In comparison, most competing ideas for reinventing literary studies sound too convoluted. In the second decade of the new millennium, there was, apparently, something utterly seductive about displaying our scholarship about the novel along the axes of distribution or graphing them—perhaps a new form of legitimation.

In the special issue of the *PMLA* on his book, Moretti explained that this project "arose from my fascination with (nonliterary) conceptual models—evolutionary theory, and the Braudel-Wallerstein view of world history—and with their explanatory potential for literary Study" (Moretti, "A Response" 687). We see Moretti's model in action in the middle chapter of the book, titled "Evolution, World-Systems, *Weltliteratur*," where the author applies World Systems and evolutionary models together to conclude that two incompatible principles—diversification and sameness—govern literary production at the same time (Moretti, *Distant* 128–129). And the claim also comes with nuance or warning that diversification and sameness, though they appear incompatible as principles, can combine. Moretti's conclusion here is that not all diversification leads away from the sameness as when one culture appropriate from another, say the wheel or a sonnet form, the borrowing can change the adoptive culture fundamentally and forever (130) as it can also revolutionize the usage of the wheel, if, say, it adds the internal combustion engine to it. That, in turn, leads Moretti to conclude that divergence and convergence are the simultaneous forces governing the histories of literature. The same structuralist views are at work when Moretti moves from the cultural and historical scenes to literary genres. About the novel, Moretti says that it is a "*composite* form" because it combines "story" and "discourse," or "plot" and "style." The plot being the sequence of events and style "their verbal presentation" (132). The plot is the more easily borrowed element, whereas the style, being a linguistic entity, is tied to a time and place and depends on the language. For these reasons, it does not survive diffusion and translation (133). This built scheme allows Moretti to put together better tools of assessment, and he ends "Evolution, World-Systems, *Weltliteratur*," saying that World Literature canons are based on "great" or "relevant" works have two aspects.

On the one hand, after culture wars, we seem to be using an entirely different paradigm. But, on the other hand, "both [pre and post culture wars] positions are profoundly *normative* ones," and both are concerned "much more with value judgments than with actual knowledge" (135). This leads Moretti to propose a future work on the thoroughgoing reconceptualization of literary studies (135) where canonical and non-canonical approaches are thoroughly revised.

What model would that be we see in the next chapter, "The Novel: History and Theory," that also unfolds on a general scale. It tackles a change in the rise of the novel in eighteen century Europe and how it reflects the emergence of a new, bourgeois class, which itself has more idle time on its disposal and new habits of mildly distracting entertainment (174–178). In China, where novels had different aesthetic characteristics (much longer, with the group, not individual, as the protagonist), there was no similar change in the eighteenth century. Reading novels remained what it was for centuries, a kind of scholarly, intensive, interactive activity.

In her "Why Distant Reading Isn't" published in the *PMLA* special issue on *Distant Reading,* Johanna Drucker criticized Moretti by saying that he has no interpretative model. As she explains, digitalization requires "tokenization," setting up the terms for the creation of meaning that "an automatic process can recognize" (Drucker 629). She writes,

> For texts or collections of texts to be read computationally, they have to be divided into meaningful units that an automatic process can recognize. This process is known as tokenization, the decision about how to break a string (or set) of elements (or phenomena) into meaningful units. What is considered meaningful will vary depending on the model of research. (629)

Our claim is the opposite. On the contrary, Moretti offers a coherent interpretative model. It is just that his "reading" either goes unexplained or is superficial. Moretti's reliance on evolution is a case in point. He treats the evolution of organisms as if it happened in historical or measurable time—one that can be readily grasped and graphed into a picture that looks like a tree. Science tells a very different story: evolution has a wholly unique kind of duration, unlike any other.

At present, this duration cannot be scaled down. Even the fundamental genetic mechanisms like the difference between genetic and epigenetic changes, or evolution's shifts between extremely slow and abrupt, are still beyond grasp. Lacking this understanding, we do not yet know if evolution is to be represented as a tree or not or what scale and proportions this tree and its branches would take.

The issue does not just skew Moretti's understanding of history. It also shows us where his theoretical interests are coming from. If we are intent on using the term "evolution" in literary studies, it would require critical engagement with the generation of scholars that already claimed it and employed it in the same sense that Moretti does—the work of scholars like Robert Scholes, James Phelan, and Robert Kellogg, who are the authors of *The Nature of Narrative* (published in 1966, with a revised edition in 2006).[10] These works should be seen as the primary support for distant reading, not World Systems theory, as Moretti claims. As represented in Scholes' *Structuralism in Literature*, the trend is a version of structuralism—meant to take the place of the more radical poststructuralism of Derrida, Lacan, and Foucault—as a science about literature. It applies to narrative the general structuralist approach originally addressing language.

Scholes's main point is that structuralism is interdisciplinary and revolutionary because it focuses on relations. He, however, also assumes, in a typical move, that the goal of structuralism is to explain the whole of literature; that its approach is scientific by which he means a specific self-consistent framework (Scholes, *Structuralism* 10). For the Scholes generation, that unity is the property of each system, be it language or narrative, and the goal of the scholarship is to explicate it together with wholeness.

Countable elements (*Graphs, Maps, Trees* is the title of Moretti's book from 2005) go only so far without an epistemology which Moretti explicitly refuses (Moretti, *Distant* 139, 158). Without it, the only reference point the elements can have is the already existing systems of classification and classes, precisely those entities (concentration, area, discipline) that new trends of inter-and cross-disciplinarity seek to displace and reorganize. Only in this perspective can Moretti's questions—say, whether the novel could have developed in verse rather than prose—be significant. We consider such questions contingent on a premise that should not be used as the framework for inquiries that pretend to any kind of novelty. Instead, the question should be what is that framework that compels us to classify disparate and different works as novels, why continue to organize investigation using that category, and what do we think that the genre-based research has left to tell us.

And then also: Did this kind of interpretation based on genres contribute to literary scholarship losing significance and general importance, including the appeal to young people? Alternatively, what is the future and the size of the discipline that Moretti imagines? Can it have a general purchase? How many scholars should go out in the field to measure lengths of literary production in various cultures across time only to come up with a response that relates to the most prominent aspect of their structure (like additive adventures)?

Moretti's questions like "why are novels long?" properly speaking, always have only one reply. Novels are long because such a view maintains the novel (and genre) as a valid object of study. We have to construe a superstructure that validates such objects, proving that elements we are treating belong to the same kind, that they have diverse parts, that these elements are both unified and different, that they have specific characteristics that can be measured and compared. The reason novels are long is because scholars see them as meeting the necessary standard called length that makes our scholarship appear organized and scholarly and pays bills.

Novels are long because we are scholars of literature who see length as a defining characteristic. In contrast, in *Morphology of Folktale,* showing how folktales are put together was a by-product of a more important goal. It demonstrated theoretical principles of analysis that moved the focus from the content to form and treated the latter as the former, following the then-new Marxist insights into how signification works. Propp's book was a demonstration of a theory of interpretation, not just counting of traits. More below.

Social sciences

Compare what DH does with the much-maligned (in literary studies) social scientific use of big data, and the version of DH described in *PMLA* special issue gets stranger. My primary source is a work published in 2019, entitled *Big Data and Social Science* (Foster et al.), a primer teaching how social scientists can employ data.

The first significant difference is in terminology. What we call digital humanities, social scientists call "big data" and "data science." Their question is not how scholars can use computational methods in general, but, specifically, how "big data" and "data science" can create more complex research models. Data is not mined but serves as a theater of sorts to test new theories.

Social sciences approach "big data" and "data science" as an applied issue, not as a framing device. This, again, is a categorically different approach. DH is expected to change the parameters of analytic inquiry in literary studies—"rethink our work in the archives" (Lee and Beckelhimer 111) or alter "aspects of our reflection about" humanities (Ortega 159) or "reframe" patterns of storytelling to cover more extended periods (Underwood, *Distant* 9). In social sciences, the new tool may help change the nature of the scholarship over time but is not itself a new paradigm.

Composing a dataset is often also integral to research and one of the chief goals. Such data are not only immensely complex and big. Most importantly, they contain a wide *variety* of sources. In literary studies, we use a database of selected novels written in English between two dates (Underwood, "Machine Learning"); or English language materials, although the context of research is Anthropocene (Lee and Beckelhimer 112); or materials from one newspaper (Klein L.). In such an instance, there is no big data. There is just some data that, due to its composition, cannot serve the representational or modeling requirements that big data can.

There is also a major difference in objectives. Social science research aims not to get to know the data in the database but to use it to create models with predictive powers, which does not translate readily into literary studies' research since prediction does not carry the same importance. We tend to look back more than forward, which may well be a mistake as we already indicated.

Lastly, in contemporary social sciences, problems with big data are among the central issues. As Ramón Spaaij and Ansgar Thiel write,

> big data are neither neutral and objective nor necessarily valid and reliable, although they are widely believed to be so. Big data sets often turn out to be less robust than they seem. Essentially, we are faced with similar methodological issues as we were before in the small data environment, for example, about the need to understand and be reflexive about the sample of a data set and the forms of interpretation involved in the data process (boyd & Crawford 2012). (Spaaij and Thiel 1)

Big data is plagued with further problems, including reliability and significance of findings, and it may not have the scientific validity expected initially from it (Jagadish; Kitchin). As with other digital technology uses, it is hard to figure out how to control for and evaluate results (Calude and Longo). These present new avenues of inquiry that now dominate the academic part of the general conversation concerning the widely used computational and statistical models.

The same cannot be said about DH in literary studies. Although authors regularly warn about some of the same issues, they, like Underwood, do it in what seem asides. Buried in the text is, for instance, Underwood's admission that he expects only a few scholars to be interested in the DH. At a late point in his book, he calls the discourse not DH, but the sociology of literature which gives the project an entirely different appeal (Underwood, *Distant* 165). From our perspective, the unusability and unreliability of big data and its incompatibility with interpretation should be the central questions of DH. They should be addressed in the first, not in the last chapter as in Underwood's book. And they should not be issues under the rubric of risks, but under the headline of the approach's viability and validity.

In literary studies, we may also have more immediate and mundane issues with data. Issues like: how can we make MLA database comprehensive? Does the MLA database have a reliable search engine? And if not, what are we doing to improve it? What would "improvement" mean exactly? And so on.

Simultaneously, there are already viable ways to use digital technology in literary studies and continue humanities scholarship. Only they are not like the DH described above.

Interdisciplinary humanities or DH that is not DH

As Miriam Posner reports in the introduction to the same issue of the *PMLA*, digital humanities can also function as an interdisciplinary "window" for scientists to simply take more humanities courses (Booth and Posner 13; see also Burdick et al.). This—Booth and Posner call it informatics—is an effective way for us to become more acceptable to the techies and engineers generally and to forge cooperation with them.

Posner speaks excitedly about her experience at the University of California, Los Angeles, with graduate students eager to become well-rounded (Booth and Posner 13). At UCLA, there is a Program in Digital Humanities (of which Johanna Drucker is also a member; Hayles, too, was at UCLA) which offers courses that are most accurately described as humanities courses graduate and undergraduate, that use digital technology.[11] There are no required technical skills for the undergraduate classes listed on the website (research was done in February 2020, before the Coronavirus pandemic). And the reasons to include digital technology, like 3D photography, are specific, not general, with digital technology being either the only or the most appropriate tool. This is to say that computers are not central to learning, that they do not provide a new framing or interpretative paradigm, and that the curriculum is of contemporary humanities that relies on the tools of its age.

There is a theory that suggests that successful forms of interdisciplinarity are small group creations. Interdisciplinary humanities can follow that situationist model encouraging actual collaborations, person-to-person contact, creating lasting bonds, and a culture in which humanities/engineering/science work will be normalized. The role of humanities in such endeavors would be, as Posner and Booth indicate, more or less traditional, helping scientists identify and confront their biases; improve their ability to recognize otherness and its importance; build a more complex world view and greater critical distance toward their work. In short, all those skills would ready the twenty-first-century scientists to understand the complexities of the world around them and prepare them for the interdisciplinary work, which is the new dominant paradigm in sciences. Imagine us doing for technology and science what we have done with gender, sexual orientation, race, class, and so on.

This kind of DH (which is not DH) is worthy of our attention and not only because of the "threat" in which humanities find themselves today but, more importantly, because it is based on an existing practice that can readily lead to more cooperation and reliable and lasting forms of interdisciplinarity.

Part III: another DH

Structuralism

Since there are some striking similarities between data mining and early examples of structuralism or—as it is often referred to—formalism, I will spend a moment to outline these and introduce what is perhaps a more viable model for modeling. This structuralism directly relates to computer modeling via linguistics, which was equally influenced by semiotics and has a respectable record of employing mathematics for language analysis.

In general, math, logic, and literature are not far apart, as Underwood rightly emphasizes. Syncretism of this kind was in the air when Vladimir Propp started his work on folktales' morphology—the book was published in Leningrad in 1928. By morphology, he meant form or structure of stories, those elements that are common to a group of works or genre. The proposition is simple: there is a basic pattern that distinguishes folktales from other narrative forms, and even those that are also folk creations like myths and legends. The results were revolutionary, allowing for a creative activity to be mapped out and its rules identified and displayed for what they were.

Morphology of the Folktale (see also Forrester) starts with a distinction between the "amount of material" and "methods of investigation," with Propp pointing out that the latter does not exist yet and then setting the goal of his book to define them (4). First, we assume that methodology of analysis, or algorithm, takes precedence over data creation. This is because categories of data creation depend on the criterion of selection, with the major question being what can count as a folktale or can be included in the folktale database.

The insight dictates that the study unfolds in a parallel way on two tracks. On the one hand, one assembles the data of potential folktales, which may, at some point, include folk creations like myths and legends. On the other hand, the scholar is also working on the terms of interpretation, continually adjusting them as they figure out more and more essential traits that also serve them to define their database.

The first analytic moment has Propp shift from the usual approach and the stock question—what is this tale about?—to the events' characteristics. The choice and the move are specific to this semiotic approach and represent the Marxist theory they are based on, about which a bit more below. This is to say that the transformation is not simply from one to another equal element of a tale (transformation *from* what a tale is about *to* characteristics of events), but a categorical shift in the approach used to understand what a tale is, how it signifies, and how it should be analyzed; if it is through its object (whatness) or the characteristics of events. This, in short, is a work of epistemology and not only a shift from content to form.

The move, too, can be understood as a version of close reading that substitutes focus on the "about," zeroing in on attending structures that make up the story. A close reading of form, if you will.

The new analytic model is set up with Propp suggesting that one pattern—the distinct kinds like "tales with fantastic content, tales of everyday life, and animal tales" (Propp 5)—should be substituted for a pattern of fantastic elements of their events. And the quality of events is not just one specific characteristic but the trait belonging to the narrative voice that characterizes the whole genre of folktales. Folktales are not simply *about* fantastic events; they are also tales in which this fantastic quality is presented openly and self-consciously, adding a new—self-referential, metadiscursive—attribute to the way tales are told.

We must notice a paradox here. While looking for a set of tales' specificity, Propp discovers a common characteristic that applies to the most general category of fiction. In the two, the attribute works on different levels. For fiction in general, it provides the framework that distinguishes it from other writing genres like history or science. In folk tales, it is a characteristic of the narrative voice or telling of this story specific to this genre but not necessarily to other genres.

In folk tales, self-reflexivity also denotes a doubling in the narrative point of view, which function as a meta-instance—a point of view about the tale that acknowledges its fantastic or fictional qualities—with both being integral to the story and intertwined with one another. With that structure, folktales approximate the play of frameworks, the kind we noted throughout this study where metadiscourse and discourse function together and produced a meaning, developing the continuity (the story) through these interruptions and intermingling of the registrars.

The same characteristic can also be described as the overarching trait of fiction in general so far as fiction is commonly presented as such (fiction) and understood to be such by readers. We see here that Propp's research's goal and methodology coincide with the theory of ideology, of explaining where signification comes from and why it follows specific steps. The two also unfold through the same interpretative steps. The first is that content is no longer considered the sole defining characteristic of an entity. The second, that form can take the traditional characteristics attributed to content. The third that formal analysis leads to a limited number of basic elements out of which viewpoints and stories or ideologies are constructed. And the fourth, and most importantly, the analysis of data and analysis of the terms of analysis or epistemology are aspects of the same processes that give us a view of the whole.

We can say the same thing in terms of close reading. Close reading that focuses solely on content is a pre-structuralist kind. Moving it from content to metadiscourse and reading structure updates it and prepares it to do "distant" reading that is more precisely described as a morphology. This commentary adds another kind of close reading to our growing list, as a detailed identification of formal elements that enter into the construction of meaning.

Propp's theory has a major companion in V.N. Vološinov's *Marxism and the Philosophy of Language*, which, too, was written in the late 1920s. The premise of that work is that words are like commodities. They are not only an expression of ideology but, most notably for our purposes, have materiality and specific value or significance to them. That is, signs are things. The connection is far-reaching because it allows us to count signs as things and physical objects as signs. Importantly, physical objects are not only signs, and signs are not only physical objects. The relation lends itself to what has been the most fruitful discourses in the humanities since Louis Althusser's pioneering work (Ramadanovic, "No Place"), because it shows how a belief system connects to material effects and what kind of impact the human signifying system has on the humans themselves and the world around them. The same discourse (on commodification) also allows literary studies to bring together form, ideology, aesthetics, and pattern analysis, and to do each of these in terms of the others and identify the specific materiality of literature.

DH and reading

In DH, so far, much of the work was, as in Underwood, focused on visualization of poetic texts (Jänicke et al., 2015, 2017), even when they deal with sound (McCurdy et al.). As it is readily recognized, visualization has the unfortunate, reductive effect of flattening out the aural, intellectual, and aesthetic experience of literature and not engaging much of what we can call the material aspects of literature. Distancing, indeed, is the correct term for the approach, except that we should receive it not as a new form of reading but as naming the process that is the opposite of a personal engagement with fiction and poetry. In Propp's structural analysis, no such cutting off takes place. A reader is a necessary category in the definition of folktales so far as they have to be identified as fictitious.[12]

Underwood goes over the pleasure or reader problem but, once again, in terms that are lacking (Underwood, *Distant* 155 and 166). The issue with pleasure in literature is not ephemeral to what literature is. It helps us understand how we can approach literature as an object and how it can be counted in the present context. It also defines how a literary work is consumed and therefore the forms of its plurality. Literary works can be part of many sets and genres but only as unique instances that are not explained by the larger category. Structuralism has a term for the specificity of literature: the poetic quality of language (Jakobson)—Jacques Lacan's name for the same phenomenon is the imaginary. And so on. The poetic or unique quality calls for an appropriate way of counting (close reading, too), a plurality of individual instances—which itself should be of interest to AI scientists because it is a way to define uniqueness.

The poetic quality, too, calls for the reader and the focus on the process of reading that has been—because these cannot be standardized—left out of DH. Without a theory of reading, DH is not about literature in the contemporary sense of the term. Recent linguistics draw on semiotics and Propp's morphology. They treat issues like translation between natural languages and between natural and computer languages (Sun et al.; Strang.; Zhang et al.) and the generation of short poetic forms with formulaic quality, like jokes (Petrović and Matthews). The linguists operate with a more complex notion of language than DH, and their forms of visualization have a more holistic approach to it.

The poetic quality also reflects the uniqueness of the work, which is the equivalent of self-reflexivity in the sense that a poem points to itself as a unique and specific work and use of language. But this self-reflexivity does not imply that there is pure data or data that is a part of some closed system of meaning independent from another language. We can see why this is the case when we look at Thomas Piketty's *Capital in the Twenty-First Century*, which Da claims, is an example of the description "of the data alone" (Da, "Critical Response" 916). Piketty is spurred to look for the data following the framework he defined for his book. And the fact that "the value of the book, as many have pointed out, comes from the fact that Piketty collected historical data that no one else has been able to get" (Da, "Critical Response" 917) should not be taken as affirming the separateness of this collection but its connectedness to the chain of frameworks which Piketty was able to extend in a new direction following his new assumptions which entered into the construction of the set. In this case, data comes together with a new interpretative theory created by Piketty because the latter is also a new framework that can be applied to create other sets. In this case again, the interpretation is in the framework not in the unusual data Piketty gathered.

Based on what we said in this chapter, DH scholars should be doing the precise opposite of what they are currently. Instead of importing digital technology and analyzing datasets, they should be using the experience of literary studies with interpretation to develop hermeneutic models that mimic literary works. In so far as both computer models and literary works are autonomous, self-contained, and self-replicating worlds, we have a ready-made starting point for such hermeneutics.

Turing test

At the end of this chapter, we circle back to AI as a cognition issue we started with to show its historical origin. The key source of the switch from computation to intelligence is, arguably, Alan Turing's famous experiment published in 1950 (Turing), with Stanley Kubrick's 1968 movie, *2001: The Space Odyssey*, providing a visceral experience of artificial intelligence's independence. It, as *Wikipedia* puts it, tests the "machine's ability to exhibit intelligent behavior equivalent to, or indistinguishable from, that of a human." The setup asks a human to identify if they are communicating with a machine or with another human. The proof of the machine's ability to think is when a human being is fooled and identifies the machine as another human being.

The interpretation in the Turing experiment is based on two series of reductions. The first is the claim that the test verifies intelligence. It measures only characteristics of computational power that allow a machine to respond in a way that humans might, though this is not how we would assess human intelligence or approach its definition. The second reduction is that the test becomes the basis for a new model of what human intelligence is which is then used to assess that human intelligence. In the process, the brain becomes the hardware, and the mind the software. The practical result is that one particular facet of intelligence—the ability to answer specific kinds of questions—is taken to be the whole of intelligence and understood as machines having the same kind of cognitive capacity as humans.

As Vladimir Tasić put it in *Mathematics and the Roots of Postmodern Thought,*

> What was initially a convenient abstract model of the human capacity for computation—agreed to by mathematicians because they needed a formal model of finitary intuitive computations—would become something of which the human mind is a particular instance. It is not that the computer is modeled on the mind. It is the other way round: The mind is a model of the computer. (78)

This approach's further consequence is the one we encountered at the beginning of this chapter, where digital technology and humanities are assumed to share specific methodologies and interpretative frameworks just based on the assumed symbiosis. Strictly speaking, the inflection point is the moment in history after the Turing experiment when computing and intelligence merge into one notion.

Turing based his machines on a "painstaking analysis of how humans perform computations" (Tasić 77). And so, it is to be expected that later computers would advance the same quality as well. Computations, calculations, analogy, pattern identification, even an ability to adapt are mechanisms of thinking; they are not *whole* thinking or *the* human way of thinking.

Unfortunately, in the general climate where machines are deified, there are no incentives for precision. On the contrary, most inducements run the other way. Affording technology miraculous, divine powers and letting it permeate popular culture without any control system is the welcome norm, which is why we have the present imbalance and not just between engineering and humanities but between what we can expect from technology and what it can deliver. We should call it a form of "fake news" to signal how serious this misinformation is and how detrimental its impact can be for modern societies, especially those where digital technology is providing new tools for control and discipline (Noyes et al.).

Epistemology

The conclusion of this chapter is that that DH is not the interdisciplinary model we want to follow. As a literary method, it is not likely to garner student interest. As we saw, it uses data, not big data; its discourse is not critical enough to be relevant, and its results are not only limited but can be reached by other means. DH is unlikely to have staying power as a literary discourse—unless the administrators decide to replace literary studies with DH. It brings us back to generic terms; offers illustration, not evidence; leaves the reader and reading as a process out, and costs a lot.

At the same time, different models for interdisciplinary cooperation that include technology are readily available. Literary studies have a unique opportunity to help scientists develop a more profound understanding of interpretation, including the way reality is created through construction. Most of us cannot assist in writing more effective algorithms. But we are good at examining the terms of interpretation and the prejudices and biases that enter into human creations. And we can do this as a kind of close reading which shifts its focus from the poetic qualities of the content to what in the traditional vocabulary appears as form and can also be called a metadiscourse. Or we can do it also by analyzing how the social construction of reality has changed in the time of Reddit, 4chan, and so on—for instance, following the model established by Donghee Yvette Wohn and Brian J Bowe in their essay, "Crystallization: How Social Media Facilitates Social Construction of Reality."

This is to say that in addition to peer review, epistemology, too, provides ways in which disciplines can continue to maintain their separateness while also creating means through which they can cooperate. Digital technology presents above all else a shared topic of general concern that no one discipline can own. It requires the equivalent of the approach to cancer we mentioned in the introduction. A coordinated effort to figure out, first, how it permeates all aspects of social and economic life which is in times of pandemic holds together (through Zoom and other applications that compensate for lack of physical contact); how it influences our belief systems and sense of community; as well as how it can be used in research in ways that are consistent with the poststructuralist understanding of interpretation.

Lastly, we have to take issue with Propp's structuralism. It does not recognize the complexity of dynamics but only the complexity of elements. Changes are presented as resulting from unified and regular processes, not from abrupt upheavals popularly known as Black Swan events—that is to say, events that may not be identifiable, predictable, and maybe entirely lost to archeology that complies data sets. Its formalism is about the idealized cases, and conditions and Propp's morphology examines closed systems. What allows us to see "folktales" as a genre or the identifying traits of these tales also limits what we can say and do with "tales," the kind of interpretation we can develop, how literary studies can interact with *its* outsides and other disciplines.

Notes

1 Da acknowledges precursors of her critique, Timothy Brennan, "The Digital-Humanities Bust," in *The Chronicle of Higher Education*, and Danielle Allington, Sarah Brouillette, and David Golumbia, "Neoliberal Tools (and Archives): A Political History of Digital Humanities," in *The Los Angeles Review of Books*, as well as Maurizio Ascari, "The Dangers of Distant Reading: Reassessing Moretti's Approach to Literary Genres," *Genre* 41 (Spring 2014): 1–19, and Archer, Jodie, and Matthew L. Jockers. *The Bestseller Code: Anatomy of the Blockbuster Novel*. And Daisy Hildyard, "Writing is Heavy Bombing," *Times Literary Supplement*. We can also add Alan Liu's "Where Is the Cultural Criticism in Digital Humanities?"
2 See also Humanities Lab at New York University ("Bennett-Polonsky Humanities Labs") and the Institute for Digital Research in the Humanities at the University of Kansas ("Institute for Digital Research").

3 I am citing here an anonymous reviewer to break what is a kind of third wall of scholarship we usually pretend does not exist. I wish I could acknowledge them by name.
4 Exceptions include Da's reference to Fish's article, and in this claim by Underwood, "we also need to ask how genre concepts change from one reader or social context to another" (Underwood, "Critical Response" 910). When Katherine Bode attempts to compare distant and close reading, her assessment goes back to terms of literary studies before culture wars, when we fought over objects of study (Bode, "Equivalence"). It, too, does not discus reading. As we explained in the first chapter of this book, the object of study in our discipline is and has always been interpretation, an approach to the text. The setup has only been obscured by the New Critical idealization of the poetic text, itself motivated, as we showed in the second chapter, by the institutional needs of literary studies. In her more recent "Why You Can't Model Away Bias," Bode moves in the right direction when she suggests that DH "conceptualizes the relationship between critical and scholarly practices, the epistemological standing and implications of computer models and algorithms, and the relative importance of aesthetic and political arguments" (96). But even that effort falls far short of where DH should be today since she preserves the statistical model without explaining what it has to do with hermeneutics.
5 Recent collection *Disrupting the Digital Humanities* has focused on the institutional aspects of the new field and its narratives but has stopped short of raising any of the fundamental questions about interpretation that in other literary studies contexts—since at least *The Signifying Monkey*—go with a discourse on race (Gates).
6 Compare to (Da, "Computational" 627).
7 For the survey of the field, see Velasquez-Manoff.
8 See Bostrom, Lanham, Russell, Tegmark.
9 See Da for a detailed critique of several examples of DH studies.
10 See Percy G. Adams's discussion of evolution in *Travel Literature and the Evolution of the Novel*.
11 See the "Digital Humanities," program at UCLA.
12 Work on Propp and digital humanities, to the best of my knowledge, has yet to include literary scholars based in the United States. See Fisseni et al.; Ledvai et al., Elliott.

5
CONVERGENCE
An interdisciplinary theory of interdisciplinarity

Introduction: from here to there

We do not expect that the entrenched views about the difference between scientific and humanistic approaches will disappear easily or quickly. If that were the case, there would be no need for this book. Instead, the change will be the result of step-by-step alterations. We propose the following: first, to rearticulate humanities and, specifically, literary studies and make it into an interdisciplinary discipline capable of serving as a metadiscourse to help with the convergences and integration of other disciplines, even philosophy. Second, to find issues of common concern, like peer review, and start using them as common practices to create a robust alternative interdisciplinary regime of truth, routines, and habits. Third, to create a similar alternative for interdisciplinary cooperation which, too, should be understood as a specific area of general interest and scholarly specialization in its own right. Fourth, to formulate a philosophically and politically compelling vision of universal knowledge and to explain why it is in the interest of researchers/teachers to support it. The last two are the topic of this final chapter.

Unlike other chapters, this one will begin with an exposition of our theory of interdisciplinarity. This because during our discussions in previous chapters, we have already assumed one and are now using the opportunity to explicate it. Only then we will do our customary reviews to show how extant works do not live up to their interdisciplinary goals.

Convergence

We will anchor this chapter by borrowing from *The International Journal of Management Reviews* under the assumption that defines the position of this chapter, which is that a theory about interdisciplinarity must itself be interdisciplinary. This because convergence—we borrow this term from the National Research Council study "Convergence: Facilitating Transdisciplinary Integration of Life Sciences, Physical Sciences, Engineering, and Beyond"—requires that disciplines transgress their methodologies and particularities not only when doing inter- or transdisciplinary work but, more importantly, when they are defining forms of interdisciplinarity and reviewing their own work. Disciplines, in other words, should not continue on the present track which takes interdisciplinarity to be an outgrowth of each discipline—as Peter Osborne put it, "[w]hich option [of interdisciplinary work] one finds most convincing will depend upon the formulation of the problem of disciplinarity, within the present, from which one sets out" ("Problematizing Disciplinarity" 4).[1]

The way we speak about epistemology, similarly, ought to be a new common language for communicating across fields, areas, and departments, to differently situated researchers. This goal will need us to work on attitude changes on the assumption that institutions, habits, and rituals are the first barriers as well as the first channels for cooperation. To that end, this chapter will review several scholarly interdisciplinary works to show how, when, and why disciplinary practice prevails over interdisciplinary. Our finding should not be surprising since the reason scholars comply with disciplinarity is that disciplines have institutional footholds and interdisciplinarity, by and large, does not. Disciplines like history of science and philosophy that do what is by definition interdisciplinary work are not an exception but rather the confirmation of the rules we just noted.

Our approach to the topic requires us to see the convergence not only in terms of interdisciplinary cooperation but also in terms of merging theory and practice of interdisciplinarity. In this respect, our goal will be to suggest that the practice of interdisciplinary interpretation must also be the theory and vice versa. This along the lines we already explained concerning interpretation, with the requirement that an interdisciplinary metadiscourse follows research. In a more traditional nomenclature, we are suggesting the bringing together of what appears as the most general and the most particular in the nested system: disciplines, interdisciplines, multidisciplines, transdisciplines, and metadisciplines, each of which is a broader category than the previous. Interdisciplinarity requires us to do scholarship with both, a new mindset and a new epistemology in mind. A mindset that puts cooperation before disciplinary and departmental demands and an epistemology developed as a metadiscourse through the teaching and scholarly practice of interdisciplinarity as well as the guide for the same. With this proposal we are adding one more genre (interdisciplinary scholarship on interdisciplinarity) to peer review whose goal is to serve as a connection between disciplines. From such perspective, it should be readily understandable why popular solutions like anti- and postdisciplinarity, or situationism cannot offer viable convergence. Because neither is in the position to develop an epistemology that can endure the institutional pressures on convergence and cooperation. They also cannot withstand the pressure of disciplines, exerted if not through methodology, then through the review system and other institutional formations and limitations.

For similar reasons, we disagree with another poststructuralist take on the topic, the above mentioned Peter Osborne's "Problematizing Disciplinarity, Transdisciplinary Problematics" and the special edition of the journal *Theory, Culture & Society* devoted to transdisciplinarity (Osborne 2015), with which our approach has much in common. From our point of view, Osborne and the collection cede too much ground to disciplinary knowledge and conceive of interdisciplinarity in dialectical terms, as raising out of many tensions between discipline and knowledge production, with the tensions being created by the very existence of disciplines and departments. For instance, Osborne can notice that "the department is a highly effective self-reproducing institutional machine for training and hiring academics and providing the means of career advancement" (8). But then Osborne does not recognize how his own work, though openly critical of the regime, contributes to its continuation by affirming disciplinary starting points.

Unlike most sources, we will also assume that the discussion of interdisciplinarity is a process and that such process has clearly delimited historical stages, with the consequence that what worked in the 1970s and 1980s does not have the same effect today. To insist today on the same approach (overcoming or decentering) to disciplinarity that informed early poststructuralism is to misunderstand the role institutions and their arrangements play in defining the problematic. It is also to misunderstand this theory that aims to be pragmatic and context sensitive.

By interdisciplinarity we will mean not the surfeit or excess of disciplinarity, tensions or dialectics, in any sense of those terms, but, to repeat, a starting point—a convergence as a process of perpetual aligning between knowledge (what we produce) and discourse (what we think we are doing). Here again scholarly work needs to meet two demands at the same time: it is a work of epistemology and a research/teaching or practice in its own right. In lapidary formulation, it is not how we cross disciplinary and institutional boundaries (which is what most works on interdisciplinarity set out to do, including Osborne's), but how we can construe scholarship that both respects such boundaries and has a general purview. Convergence understood this way—as depending on mindset, routines, and new ideological horizon—should remind of "culture" as it figures in cultural studies, only with a proviso that we take the discourse *about* the culture to be object of study as well. There is no other culture to apply this to but the one that we are immersed in as we produce scholarship, teach, and work as professors and instructors.

All that goes for scholarly interdisciplinarity also goes for teaching. Interdisciplinary teaching begins with convergence between disciplines as its first goal. This in contrast to the current model which has disciplines approach the same issue from their divergent positions with interdisciplinarity being the experience or the effect of the many-sided discourses that is thus created. In case of trans- or metadisciplinarity, a new constellation is often a mere synthesis of knowledge production that does not respect ether local variations or the complexity of the process of creating knowledge. The additive principle comes short of an interdisciplinary methodology, convergence, and so on as it also offers a simplistic form of universalization, which is tantamount to being at the same place at the same time. Foregrounding cooperation, overlaps, and similarities between disciplines allows teaching to develop *as* knowledge converges and does so not around a complex topic but firstly around the demands for the openness of interpretation and transparency of the process of knowledge production. In hospital, it is a recent practice that caregivers describe to patients what they are doing while they are doing it. Something similar should take place in our interdisciplinary classrooms with instructors and students commenting on their practice, explaining their methodology, and how their work relates to convergence.

In organizing convergence we should pay special attention to the ever present tendency to keep separate natural and cultural approaches, nature and culture as objects of study. Here we assume, with Bruno Latour (*Facing Gaia*), that the culture/nature dichotomy though on its way out is still the principle of scholarship and our institutional setups. If transgression has a place in the creation of interdisciplinary knowledge, it is in relation to this principle. We can, however, also circumvent nature/culture division by not respecting its many frameworks and divisions and configuring a new setup and a new starting position that also focuses on the culture of doing science.

If the culture wars came up with the motto of teaching conflicting views, we are proposing that we do not organize our collaborations based on tensions. Productive as they might have been, they, too, focused our attention on the boundaries and regarded them as the source of tension, which in practice tended to make them only more so. Such approach may even make it appear that disciplines and issues consist only of boundaries and that there is no other way to position scholarly and teaching attention in the humanities. Instead, as we just said, there are many complex topics, common assumptions about production of knowledge, views about its institutional place and history, and so on, that can turn scholars to collaboration—to how to bring researchers, scholars, and teachers, nature and culture together. Identifying those similarities and foregrounding the goal of cooperation should make it possible for the points of tension between different regimes, routines, and personalities to be identified but then also incorporated or otherwise negotiated in practice.

Complex topics can be the usual climate change or cancer. They can be topics that historically had both cultural and scientific status like race, madness, family, crime, carceral systems, pandemic, and so on. They can be any of the many elements that enter into construction of research like setting up a laboratory, making a diagnosis (or thesis), and so on. They, too, can be about the basic issue of forming explanations that do not separate social or cultural aspects from biological, chemical, and physical. Life in poverty is not determined only by the lack of access and resources. It too is shaped by the chemical conditions like pollution, food and health care availability, level of daily stress, and so on. Technology is not just about speed but also about many social interfaces and access. And so on. That is to say, nature and culture are intertwined, and our approach has to reflect that characteristic of life.

In this chapter, we will finally explain how poststructuralist systems work, which forms the main part of our methodology and is the core idea behind *Interdiscipline*. We have left it up to this point in order to set in place one such system and present an explanation only after we have been practicing it for a while. On this occasion, we will both harken back to models we already mentioned as well as move to those that are new to this project like Andrew Pickering's understanding of cybernetics and, more importantly, Bruno Latour's explanation of life on Earth as a systematicity without a system. This while maintaining a dual framework that does not transgress or otherwise leave out the disciplinary regime or institutions since we do not think that antidisciplinarity is a viable possibility.

The reason our many disagreements with our sources are not merely repeating the conflict model includes the place that boundaries play in them. We see boundaries, once again, as shared practices that can be used most directly to develop a priori interdisciplinary scholarship. Our disagreements are also always partial. Even with DH we share interest in patterns, assumption of the importance of general (distant) scope, the goal of creating a new framework, use of technology, AI, and big data, and so on.

The second part of this chapter will be devoted to Susan Buck-Morss's *Hegel, Haiti, and Universal History* which we will present and examine as a model interdisciplinary work in the humanities. In this case, interdisciplinarity will include a new scale that is not usually mentioned, namely, universal history, which we think is at stake in the new approach and at this stage of development of poststructuralist and interdisciplinary theory. This we will offer to contend with the posthumanism and postdisciplinarity we find philosophically inadequate because they do not offer the general view. In short, our focus will not be on decentering (human centered universe, disciplines, and so on) or overcoming but on explaining a new kind of starting point and a new horizon of thinking and working: a systematicity that can function as an open system.

Contradiction

We entered this chapter claiming interdisciplinary positionality and convergence as our starting point. This might appear to contradict what we suggested in previous chapters where we implicitly affirmed disciplinary boundaries—by, for instance, focusing on methods specific to literary studies, by emphasizing its uniqueness, by approaching peer review as a reading, and so on. In each of these, we have also defined disciplinarity based on a specific theory of interpretation that applies to interdisciplinary phenomena. Doing this, we have used the discipline of literary studies to create an interdisciplinary tool, to affirm interdisciplinary practices, and started creating interdisciplinary epistemology. We have done it, again, by practicing interdisciplinarity in a disciplinary fashion. Due to the work we have done, we are also no longer where we were at the beginning of this book but are situated in changed context with new assumptions in place.

Now, after some work has been done, we can again affirm that there is no ontological distinction between disciplines. Such distinction is one that is established through history of iterations and their institutional life. When those iterations and attitudes change, the results are different too. But, on the flip side, because of their presence in routines and institutional setups, disciplines cannot be simply disregarded—or rather they can be disregarded only to the disadvantage of any interdisciplinary endeavor. So, we find way to use disciplinarity of knowledge in defining systematicity necessary for the development of knowledge, but practiced with a priority on convergence and compatibility or openness which itself creates a different regime that is interdisciplinary.

The rule we follow is that only when repurposed, rearticulated, and practiced differently, disciplines will no longer stand in the way of the process of inter-, trans-, or multidiscipline. So, we do not start with disciplines but start with disciplines in a specific way using them as a form of convergence to unify divergent practices and approaches.

I Part: different interdisciplinarities

Definition

According to a recent comprehensive study of interdisciplinary phenomena—Frank Siedlok and Paul Hibbert's "The Organization of Interdisciplinary Research: Modes, Drivers and Barriers"—the main driving force behind interdisciplinarity lies in the understanding that complex issues of the real world required complex disciplinary approaches. Summing previous research (Buanes and Jentoft; König et al.; Jeffrey, "Smoothing the Waters"; Lyall et al.; Szostak; Bruns; Zoubir; He et al.; see also Knight et al.), Siedlok and Hibbert put it this way, "complex and ambiguous nature of [socio-environmental and technological] problems increasingly means that expertise from multiple disciplines is need to address them" (3). The first obstacle for a successful interdisciplinarity is the meaning of the term "interdisciplinarity," which is used without consistency (Huutoniemi; Duncker), hence making it difficult to manage in scientific interdisciplinary work in practice (Buanes and Jentoft; CoFIR 2004, EURAB 2004, He et al., Sung et al.).

As a remedy, Siedlok and Hibbert offer definitions. Interdisciplinary research is "a mode of research that transgresses traditional disciplinary boundaries" (Siedlok and Hibbert 10). Where the "disciplinary organization of knowledge is comprised in the development of systems of beliefs and values shared by researchers" (Siedlok and Hibbert 10). They add also the following two caveats, that the "criteria of excellence in academia tend to be largely based on disciplinary standards and leading journals often favour disciplinary research" (Siedlok and Hibbert 11) and also that

"Aram (2004) concluded that claims of interdisciplinarity can be dependent upon the clarity and distinctiveness of particular disciplinary boundaries. Thus disciplinary specialization and interdisciplinary development are complementary processes in the development of knowledge. (Siedlok and Hibbert 11)

Based on the first definition, Siedlok and Hibbert define multidisciplinary research as involving two or more divergent disciplines. They approach a research problem from within their own framings and by using their own established methods, at a level which requires cooperation rather than integrative collaboration. This based on the assumption that phenomena they are investigating are complex and require a complex, interdisciplinary approach. And so "[m]ulti-disciplinary approaches are essentially concerned with aligned but separate goals, often defined under the umbrella of a common field" (Siedlok and Hibbert 12).

In this constellation, "[t]ransdisciplinarity can be defined as the development of increasing coherence, unity and simplicity of knowledge in which disciplinary boundaries become irrelevant or are radically reshaped" (Siedlok and Hibbert 13).

Inter-, multi-, and trans- are all, then, forms of relations—cooperation and/or convergence—between disciplines. The first one relies on the traditional institutional frameworks and the other two are derived from it. The second, multidisciplinarity, is a form of cooperation between established disciplines on a shared problem with each discipline maintaining relative autonomy. And the third, transdisciplinary model, requires a building up of a new approach, based on a specific issue, object, or, most often, shared problem.

But another somewhat different, significant lesson can be derived from the end of Siedlok and Hibbert's article, where the authors address what we can call contextual or situational aspects of scholarly work. Disciplinary cooperation can be improved, Siedlok and Hibbert say, "if individuals have the opportunity for repeated interaction and the development of trust in the people and principles of different disciplines" (30). The conclusion is heartening as it is banal since it brings clarity to what is usually presented as conflicting and complex constellation of issues. According to this observation, scholarly work depends on interpersonal relations of involved researchers, them becoming familiar with each other, and finding a way to work together as individuals and researchers. The insight puts the above definitions in perspective as it also gives them a new ever-changing framework that goes beyond specific institutional setups and depends directly on subjectivities involved in the process of knowledge production.

At this point, we see the sociologist approach and definitions give way to a situationist concern which might tell us more about cooperation, institutional life of scholarship, as well as disciplines than just about anything else we can say using methods of our disciplines. Our scholarship is framed by attitudes and expectations of the so-called everyday people. Add to that their professional selves—that disciplines are "systems of beliefs and values shared by researchers" (Siedlok and

Hibbert 10)—and we have an understanding that disciplines are not regimes of truth with shared methodologies but that such views on disciplines is maintained by a given interpersonal practices—or cultures—based on interests and what we can call micro beliefs. The two together suggest malleability of disciplinary forms and present inter-, multi-, and transdisciplinary models as dependent on institutional/personal frameworks, even in case of a problem-based setup since it, too, being an unstable or temporary creation, is limited by context.

This recognition of ad hoc nature of cooperation should not, however, lead us to conclude that all scholarship then must be anti- or postdisciplinary or simply situationist as many scholars have. Another options is to understand interdisciplinarity as unfolding on two different tracks at the same time—which is consistent with how we treated mere reading and peer review. On the one hand, we should recognize that chance and context play a defining role in cooperative work, while, on the other hand, we also recognize that we can guide and organize such work around the very terms of cooperation and do so to define their starting position as collaboration.

The argument for metadiscursive scholarship we are making is typical for philosophy and poststructuralism but unusual in sciences—well, until the new trend commonly called reproducibility studies which has ushered a new epoch of metadiscursivity. The same, too, provides a way to unify nature and culture research, which current interdisciplinary trends can easily bypass and maintain multi- or metadisciplinary configuration even when there are no humanities involved if in no other way then by foregrounding the culture of research.

To understand the significance of this proposal, we can compare it to a recent article, "Research *In-between*: The Constitutive Role of Cultural Differences in Transdisciplinarity," by Ulli Vilsmaier et al. who argue for what seems a poststructuralist approach to transdisciplinarity based on differences. They do it under the assumptions that respecting differences leads to more effective cooperation. From our perspective, whether we start from differences or identity and uniformity, we can reach transdisciplinarity only in a limited sense. This because someone has to define the differences, which itself only confronts us with the same framing issue of collaboration we started with. Vilsmaier et al. believe that they are sensitive to power relations and hegemony and that a focus on the differences offers the more democratic way of arranging cooperation. It is time to say clearly: it does not. It offers fragmentation and particularization. We do not know who is there to judge if we have done a good job affirming the difference, even if we have engaged it at all. Such issues concerning the definition of difference only return us again and again to the traditional quandary and how we do interdisciplinary work in a disciplinary world.

We, instead, suggest the double strategy that recognizes diverging disciplinary demands on the institutional level and acknowledges the chaos of interpersonal relations (with their sexism and racism) that envelop all scholarship. The two have to be identified and become integral to research or participants are inevitably going to go to their individual and disciplinary fallback positions—to, this is to say, their differences. "Research *In-between*" rests on a poorly understood poststructuralism that is, unfortunately, common. The goal of this theory is not to affirm a difference by focusing on it. At least when scholarship is our topic, there is no epistemology that can do that. Instead, we are supposed to recognize how difference already characterizes our scholarly setup and that disciplines are open for interdisciplinarization because of that trait. We, then, should be prepared to set new common rules as interdisciplinary research proceeds because all identity characteristics are contingent on context. In our case, poststructuralism is more an attitude—a way to think about the *we*—than a set of precepts other than the simple recognition that disciplines are not, to repeat, ontological wholes.

Coming from the same place, I would like to encourage universities to look for an alternative to integration as defined in the reported by the National Academies of Sciences, Engineering, and Medicine titled *The Integration of the Humanities and Arts with Sciences, Engineering, and Medicine in Higher Education: Branches from the Same Tree* (Skorton and Bear). Metaphor of a tree does not lend itself easily to reform as it suggests an integrated finished state and a form of organic unity if not outright perfection.[2] Integration of the humanities and sciences requires work independent from either—an intermediation for which we propose a discourse that comes out of literary interpretation and can become equipped to negotiate divergent methodologies, individual idiosyncrasies, histories, as well as institutional limitations, all of which have been debated in literary scholarship. Integration is not disciplinarity done differently, but a wholly new kind of knowledge creation and dissemination that centers on convergence and forms of intermediation.

In what follows, we are going to build our argument by engaging different theories of interdisciplinarity, borrowing from them insights as well as showing why and how they fail to live up to the interdisciplinary promise.

Too much knowledge

It is a common assumption that the general economic well-being in the developed countries combined with the trend of specialization and with digital technology have made knowledge proliferation a new issue of concern. There, put simply, is just too much knowledge. The author of *Philosophical Analysis in the Twentieth Century*, Scott Soames, has summed up the condition this way:

> In earlier eras, when it was not obvious that the scope of human knowledge far exceeded what could be encompassed by a single mind, the challenge of explaining how everything hung together was not so clearly unmanageable. Today, it is, and the solution is not to do badly what cannot be done, but to do well what can be: to construct a series of limited, but accurate and overlapping syntheses that together illuminate reality as we know it. (Soames, Letter to Editor)

This too is a common assumption today, that the sheer quantity of new information makes it hard and harder to talk sensibly about superstructures. Our umbrella categories were defined some time ago, in different circumstances, for different time and place (the turn of the twentieth century, [Chandler]). The same goes for literary studies, where no student studying today could have the mastery of the "whole" akin to Eric Auerbach or the recently deceased Harold Bloom.

We can paint the same picture just with numbers. As Peter Weingart reports in "A Short History of Knowledge Formations," which was published in the first edition of *The Oxford Handbook of Interdisciplinarity*,

> The study of the development of the humanities in Germany from 1954–85 showed that in the discipline of English Language and Literature in 1954, 24 professors published 12 books and a smaller number of articles, all of which could be easily read by the community including students in the course of a year. In 1985, 300 professors published 60 books and 600 articles, too many publications to be read by any one member of the community. (10)

A similar search (performed in October 2019) for the total number of publications in the MLA database leads to 4,865 in 1954 and to ten times that number or 43,336 in 1985. 1995 has 56,351; 66,296 in 2005; and 2015 has 57,812 hits. The number of publications registered in the MLA database for the period between 1954 and 2015 exceeds two million.

We do not agree with such a positioning of the problem, however. We also disagree with solutions like the one suggested by Richard Rorty. Rorty objected especially to Soames's conclusion that "what seems to be the fragmentation in philosophy found at the end of the 20th century may be due to more than the institutional imperatives of specialisation and professionalisation. It may be inherent in the subject itself" ("How Many Grains"). As his test case Rorty offered what was self-evidently an irrelevant theory—how many grains of sand make a heap—and countered Soames's warning about generalizations with an imperative for knowledge to be socially relevant which itself was supposed to be an alternative measure of grouping and a suitable common category we often find across interdisciplinary formations.[3] When Rorty proposed that "hyper-professionalism is a symptom of senescence rather than of robustness," he was not commenting on the quality specializations must possess because they are specializations. Rorty was rather addressing specific kinds of professionalization that are narrowly focused and have other knowledge as their main, if not exclusive, referents, which may well relate to whole disciplines as well as the specific areas.

Our objection to Soames concerns the basis for unification which we want to identify as common methodology and epistemology, not as overlaps as he suggests. For us, the question is not if there is a way to connect all specializations into one vast network through links between already convergent specializations, but if there is a way to make all specializations open to and ready for collaboration and convergence. In that case the amount of knowledge and the plurality of it are no longer obstacles to universalization. The foregrounding of convergence can be done because epistemology is not a set of precepts that all of the researchers have to follow. It is the way we organize our research, scholarship, and teaching in respect to other research, scholarship, and teaching. If epistemology is concerned only with specialization and defined around it, a common framework is not going to be possible. Again, a good alternative starting point is peer review since it would help us align specializations, starting with the terms of evaluation, which can be repurposed for reconciliation. To Rorty we can respond that in order for knowledge to be socially relevant, it, first, has to take stock of its own sociality, which is to say its epistemology, without which it cannot develop toward other views.

We hence understand that neither economic well-being nor specialization nor technology creates new epistemic conditions no more than they would create a new ontology. Researchers, teachers, and scholars do. There has always been too much knowledge and figures like Bloom or Auerbach singled out in the above fashion follow from a misunderstanding. Too much knowledge is a symptom of an absence of the narrative that can bring it together in some way. It has nothing to do with quantity.

Extra-academic knowledge

Above we quoted from Peter Weingart who goes on to make a point about knowledge production that is somewhat different than Soames. We will follow it here because it includes a reference to non-academic sites as new centers of research with different priorities.[4] Understanding Weingart will give us also an opportunity to briefly review the historical background against which specialization and institutional diversification take place.

Weingart writes,

> the university has lost its monopoly as the institution of knowledge production since many other organizations are also performing that function. Transitory networks and contexts are formed which replace traditional disciplines. Knowledge production outside disciplines is no longer the search for basic laws (fundamental research) but takes place in contexts of application (Funtowicz and Ravetz 1993, p. 121; Gibbons *et al.* 1994, p. 4). Disciplines are no longer the crucial frames of orientation for the delineation of subject matters and the formulation of research problems. Research is, instead, characterized by transdisciplinarity: solutions to problems appear in contexts of application and research results are no longer communicated in journals. The criteria of quality are no longer determined by disciplines alone but additional criteria, social, political, and economical,

are applied to determine quality (Funtowicz and Ravetz 1993, p. 90; Gibbons *et al.* 1994, p. 8). (Weingart, "Short History" 12)

Weingart then also provides solutions and represents what is today the common view on inter- and transdisciplinarity compatible to Siedlok and Hibbert's. Weingart suggests,

> First, with the continuously growing number of specialties (i.e. research fields below the level of disciplines) the probability increases that, due to the proximity of such fields, new recombinations will occur which will result in new 'interdisciplinary' research fields. The organizational status of these fields, however, still follows the mode of 'internal' specialization. After a period of emergence they form into another specialized field. Second, inter- and transdisciplinary research fields are promoted by funding agencies in the interest of directing research to politically desired goals. This process is conditioned by the fact that the 'externally' defined subject matters, research problems, and values or interests can trigger sustained research. Examples for the first reason are physical chemistry and molecular biology, examples for the second are climate research and gender studies. The latter are combinations of disciplines or subdisciplines that are joined in research centers, journals, and funding programs but that remain intellectually independent and continue to develop individually. (Weingart, "Short History" 12–13)

Specialization in the form of links indicated by both Soames and Weingart put in question the system that has supported Western way of knowing since its modern standard was defined in Linnaeus's Classification System. The notion of knowledge as a system is breathed in new life with Charles Darwin's *The Origin of Species*, where species is a product of evolutionary adoptions over a long period of time. The addition is philosophically important because it displaces content-based classification of the Linnaean model and replaces it with the one where qualities that define entities are based on inter- and intra-species relations and processes—which is a structuralist solution. *The Origin of Species* also defines a new notion of the system that is not run by any external principle but be the inner principle of adaptation, which brings together an organism, its environment, and other organisms of the same and different kind.

The model results in an institutional setting in the first half of the twentieth century in the establishment of departments, colleges, and schools at modern universities. The setup suggests unity of knowledge on the general scale. It also suggests division according to the differences in methodologies and objects of study that bring various groups together and separates them from the rest. In this system that descends from Linnaeus, knowledge is a way to categorize information and organize research about it. "Such classifications," as Weingart puts it, "of which modern academic discipline are but one example, both reflect and, in turn, structure the production as well as the distribution of knowledge, i.e. research and teaching. Beyond that, they also shape the application of knowledge" (Weingart, "Short History").[5]

The term, "specialization" comes out of this history. Literally so in that it is related to the term "species" which comes from Latin *species*, denoting "a particular sort, kind, or type." *Species* originally stood for, "a sight, look, view, appearance." As *Online Etymology Dictionary* has it, *species* derives from "to look at, to see, behold." The implication is that the *look at* allows the observer to see common characteristics or what makes distinct parts of an entity fit together to form a higher category. Both species and specialization refer to knowledge as a coherent classificatory system, organized based on the principle of what was originally a visual whole.

Specialization can be seen even in technology assisted research. It may tend toward class-less in the new sense that digital pattern analysis makes it possible for data to belong to many classes at the same time. Still, species/specialization is a systemic and organizing principle even when we think of links and overlaps, or knowledge as a network.

On this account, specialization is not contrary to but compatible with Linnaeus's Classification System. It is a logical extension of it in the sense confirmed indirectly when scholars, who insist on the lack of a general view, still support the possibility of links and networks between the elements. The assumption that there is a network can be easily adjusted to accommodate external forces like the dictates of government funding or the demands of "real world" with this adaptation being a new branch, helping the tree metaphor along. The same way of thinking, too, can readily (but for institutional concerns) accommodate research done outside universities even when it has different priorities and orientation toward practical solutions. This because extra-academic research is, by definition, specialized.

The unfortunate effect of this setup is that culture/nature binary remains the organizing principle of both the institution and research since specializations due to their focused character cannot contest it. The same allows for limited forms of interdisciplinarity which support the division and, in our view, cannot include divergent disciplines and approaches or convergence of the kind we are arguing for here. What such approach lacks is a framework that would, as we already suggested, foreground convergence as a new priority of all specialization. The advantage of such turn is that it respects specializations and adds a bird's eye view, a general or universal scheme of things. We thus displace integration from the object of study and methodology to integration understood as a characteristic of a setup and a cultural expectation.

Antidiscipline/cybernetics/complex systems

Based on the current state of disciplines, antidisciplinarity should appear as a most logical response to the epistemic crisis. This especially because many obstacles

to convergence concern aspects of scholarly and institutional disciplinarity but are not inherent to knowledge. Here we will examine Andrew Pickering's "Ontology and Antidisciplinarity," because of its poststructuralist orientation and the specificity of the proposal that relies on the new discourse of cybernetics we have not yet mentioned though it is close to our own approach in some ways. For Pickering, cybernetics is scholarly free-form that allows us to make unusual connections and improvise, while studying communication and automatic control systems.

Pickering starts by defining two types of knowledge, one which focuses on predictable and one about unpredictable phenomena. The two approaches are distinct as two kinds of interpretative setups or frameworks. One is based on the assumption that it can fully comprehend or encircle its object. The other is open, "a science of adaptation" that continually transforms itself to keep up with what it studies. Its object is in flux, characterized by "performative interaction ... with the unpredictable becoming of the others" or what Pickering calls "dance of agency" (210). The latter, however, suffers from at least one inadequacy. It, Pickering says, cannot solve the problems of disciplines and does not contribute directly to their development or transformation. So, why does cybernetics have to offer to disciplinarity? Pickering finds a response in the characteristics of "complex systems" that are "refractory to 'command and control'" (216). The implication is that disciplines are not set up to be adaptive and, for that reason, cannot deal with complex problems since they must reduce the complexity to understand it. The implication is also that disciplines cannot accommodate interdisciplinarity or integration because each is a complex process.

Hence, Pickering presents antidiscipline in terms of control and as a form of politics. He says that the "domination through knowledge" should be replaced with "open-ended and performative engagement with an ultimately unknowable other" ("Ontology" 216). This solution is similar to how Silvio Waisbord speaks of postdiscipline in his *Communication: A Post-discipline*. The author is sociologist like Pickering and is a former editor in chief of the *Journal of Communication* and the *International Journal of Press/Politics*. In the book he speaks from his experience with the two journals, offering a commentary on the field he had witnessed from that position. He contends that institutional structure is the only factor that holds communication together. When that is the case, Waisbord argues, communication should be recognized as an heterogenous scholarly production without an "ontological center" (9). And the incoherence should be celebrated as a characteristic of a lively field. A postdiscipline, then, in Waisbord's view, is much like it was in Mario Biagioli's "Postdisciplinary Liaisons," a situationist production of knowledge that can only be called a discipline provisionally and therefore deserves the new typology of postdiscipline or antidiscipline.

Interestingly enough, in Pickering's essay, situationism gets one more attribute, that of mystical thinking, which, he says, traditionally characterizes cybernetics.

> The idea that the world is ultimately unknowable tends directly towards the sort of hylozoist awe at the performativity of matter expressed in Beer's poetry and Ashby's time worship. The idea that we are ourselves exceedingly complex systems points to an endlessly open horizon of possibilities, in which the spirits of the dead (and ESP, nirvana and yogic feats) might find a place. And the idea that we are adaptive systems, always mangled in a world of becoming, points to sort of decentering of the self that resonates strongly with Eastern philosophy and spirituality. ("Ontology" 214)

Pickering's article is important for our purposes because it brings complex systems and the adaptive character of knowledge production into our conversation as the defining aspects of knowledge production. If we can develop scholarship that sees itself as adaptive to other scholarship, if participants have in mind the general understanding of how complex systems operate, and if we expect these from all scholarship, there is a good chance that we will never need the binary setup Pickering starts with. The inadequacy of his model in our eyes is that it depends on the binary discipline-antidiscipline that itself needs to be rearticulated as knowledge production is reframed in terms that are both disciplinary because of history and institutional limitations *and* interdisciplinary because, again, knowledge does not respect boundaries. Otherwise, both disciplines and postdisciplines are obstacles to convergence. One because it is too limited, the other because it is not organized enough; and both because they do not offer institutionally viable channels for cooperation. Or, put another way, both are limited by context (and institutional setup) and context or frame or starting point is what an interdisciplinary epistemology needs to change.

Pre-discipline

A variant of antidisciplinarity is pre-disciplinarity. We encounter it in two essays published in Peter Osborne's edited issue of the journal *Theory, Culture & Society*. In "Logics of Generalization: Derrida, Grammatology and Transdisciplinarity" by David Cunningham which focuses on writing and in Nina Power's "Reading Transdisciplinarily: Sartre and Althusser" that focuses on reading. Both take text "*as* a transdisciplinary object" (Power 111) and both also examine philosophy as the traditional discourse of transdisciplinarity. We will see these two essays and their takes as intertwined but will start with a look at Cunningham's because his essay has an unusual angle, comparable to what *Interdiscipline* supposes. Cunningham's understanding that poststructuralism—and Jacques Derrida's early work in particular—is a critique of disciplinary knowledge will help explain in more detail what we mean by it.

Cunningham's understanding of discipline depends on the kind of radical revolution poststructuralism is trying to accomplish and is both the expression of and means for it. In, for instance, *Of Grammatology*, Derrida does not give up on generalization but investigates the possibilities for it. The traditional humanities, like linguistics and anthropology, is replaced by a "new thematic network" and a new object exemplified by writing. Writing is especially suitable for this role because,

> of those traditionally negative qualities associated with its empirical or narrow sense (mediation, representation, finitude, abstraction, exteriorization), while, at the same time, what it names at such a quasi-transcendental level must be utterly 'exorbitant', by definition, with regard to any such empirical sense itself. (Cunningham 91)

Writing, too, allows Derrida to include empirical relation, defying Kant's demand that "that 'absolutely no concepts must enter into it that contain anything empirical, or that the a priori cognition be entirely pure'" (Cunningham 92; Kant 134.). Writing constitutes a new, quasi-transcendental object, a supplement or trace, that gets its identity from that which it defines. The characteristic that it (as inscription) comes *before* what it relates to (mainly speech) makes writing also quasi-transcendental in respect to disciplinary division of knowledge. Cunningham calls it "reciprocally mediated transdisciplinary concept," explaining that

> [t]o the extent that the quasi-transcendental 'itself' can never consequently be mastered by philosophy (or indeed any other hegemonic discipline [like cybernetics, for instance]), it requires, practically, a certain transdisciplinary movement as a condition of its very articulations. (93)

The quasi-transcendental aligns with transdisciplinary status as "interlocking (but not identical) logics of generalization" (Cunningham 95).

Interlocking is a variant of the overlap or links we identified above. It gets this final note that is especially useful for our purposes since it brings science into conversation through Karen Barad's understanding and under Derrida's term *interscience* (Derrida, *Eyes* 197)

> the forms of pragmatics, relationality and historicity necessarily built into the construction of any such conceptual generality – the necessity of what Karen Barad calls, in her own account of the essential entanglement of 'matter and meaning', the 'cut' through which agential interventions are co-constituted with 'the determinate boundaries and properties' of that 'object of investigation' which, via such a cut, they produce (Barad, 2007: 148). (Cunningham 99)

We understand Cunningham to mean that institutional and philosophical demands have to be met at the same time. They form a reciprocal relation in the sense that my discipline can be in constant tension with my research only to the detriment of both. Therefore, scholars must introduce practices that interrupt the functioning of their system of knowledge production and devote special attention to those that like writing cut across divisions and serve as connections.

Cunningham also assumes that transcendental objects are defined as such by history. The two sides of the argument—that writing is not a category but a quasi-category *and* that historicity implies a respect for specific framework—are here made to be co-constitutive. Philosophy cannot simply revolutionize knowledge by starting with, say, *interscience,* but must organize a practice of *interscience* through resistance to the hegemony of other and of one's own discourse.

Our proposal is similar to Cunningham in that we, too, see the practice of *interscience* or *interdiscipline* as defining the theory. We, however, disagree that almost 50 years after Derrida's initial critique of disciplinarity we should assume the same historical context (and discipline in the same sense with philosophy holding the place of metadiscourse) that presents writing as the quasi-transcendental or pre-disciplinary category. If writing was the supplement Derrida pointed to, today there are many other quasi-transcendental concepts floating around. As we saw in the previous section, Pickering and Waisbord talk about discipline in these terms. When "discipline" is an empty category, as Waisbord claims, the whole humanistic universe it defines is up in the air, having nothing to ground it but the sense that it is a situationist/institutional arrangement. In that context, both "the humanities" and "discipline" are the substitutes, and our philosophical choices are no longer those that Derrida had.

Systematicity is a specific form of generalization that can accommodate a quasi-concept.[6] With this in mind, we can go back to works like *Of Grammatology* to notice what is not usually, namely that in-between figures come not alone but together with a general field or structure. In it, writing is the quasi-concept and grammatology is the system it puts in play. In "Plato's Pharmacy," similarly, writing is a "pharmakon" and system is identified with the name of "pharmacy." In "Structure, Sign, and Play," structuralism has the latter role, sign the former. In each of these cases, the supplement and the systematicity are but two ways to talk about the same issue of framing of knowledge production in a new, poststructuralist sense. Once there is no systematicity that a supplement can organize, or, once system itself behaves like a supplement, what it means to *do* poststructuralism must itself change. Put another way, the reason postdiscipline is not a poststructuralist notion is that there is only a supplement without a system that is informed by it. When that system has become dysfunctional, what is there is just an institution.

I take that there is actual evidence that another, new kind of systematicity is and has been at work for a while in the sciences, which have been adopting poststructuralism with some vigor and enthusiasm just as it became a pat position in the humanities. The trend, from our point of view, directly contradicts Cunningham's reading of Derrida since the sciences are on the brink of no longer serving the traditional role of referential point or master discourse that needs to be decentered by writing. The new work in the sciences, shows, too, that the nature/culture principle is no longer organizing knowledge production. We see the trend represented in attempts to explain the importance of meta-research (Ioannidis, "Meta-research;" Ioannidis, "All Science"). It is also in the recognition that certain aspects of scientific production are culturally constructed, like the recognition that women and minorities in the sciences are treated differently than men. In the recent Rebecca Jordan-Young and Katrina Karkazis's *Testosterone: An Unauthorized Biography*, social, historical, and biochemical aspects of the phenomenon are offered as an intersection that unites social and biochemical life (1). But, then, as a "great storyteller," *Testosterone* does not just describe the hormone but use it like a stone in the soup to tell a general story about larger issues in human behavior, relations, norms, and myths we create.

Nicola Mößner (*Visual Representations in Science: Concept and Epistemology*), though not a poststructuralist, has shown this discrepancy between philosophical work and scientific readership while defining the epistemology of visual representation. Her book is among few of its kind devoted to the epistemology of science, with other relevant representatives of the trend also written by European scholars, including Stephen Grimm, R. Christoph Baumberger, and Sabine Ammon's edited collection *Explaining Understanding: New Perspectives from Epistemology and Philosophy of Science* and Shahid Rahman, John Symons, Dov M. Gabbay, and Jean Paul van Bendegem's collection *Logic, Epistemology, and the Unity of Science*. The same works might be taken also as indicative of an interdisciplinary trend showing a nearing between the traditionally divided disciplines of analytic and continental philosophy, more on which below.

As sociologist Michèle Lamont reports, contemporary philosophy is among the most insular disciplines, believing not only in its transdisciplinary status but also in its distinctness not to say superiority (Lemont 65). While philosophy can claim to be the metadiscourse for all research, it cannot actually be that unless it also finds a way to communicate to other disciplines.

Poststructuralist philosophy, too, has a way to go to become a theory of interdisciplinarity. It is uniquely suited for the purpose because it can readily take into account all new characteristics of knowledge we identified above; those brought about by the technological advances, including simulation of truth, fragmentation of the universal, acceleration of distribution, and decentralization. But it, too, needs to adapt to the general institutional role. Among other things, the abstruse style that has become acceptable and even expected, should be seen as a framing device that runs contrary to epistemological and pragmatic goals and ontological understanding that make this theory.

Then there is the all too predictable investigation of the condition of possibility and other Kantian transcendentals as in, among many other works, Judith Butler's "Critique, Dissent, Disciplinarity." When Butler asks, "If a certain sort of critical inquiry is to be defended, how do we begin to go about understanding what that critical inquiry might be?" (Butler 774), the question is not a genuine one since she has been at it already, engaged in a "sort of critical inquiry." When she complicates the position of philosophy, the procedure seems routine, and she does not seem to want to consider that her questions have closed off the possibility of communication with other disciplines. In the article, the practice of scholarship is not what it was, for instance, at the opening of *Bodies that*

Matter, which directly addressed the institutional discourse of philosophy. In that groundbreaking book, Butler's departure from what she was expected to do as a student, a philosopher, and a lesbian *was* the work of interpretation and a way to introduce the body. The institution was the first, and in so many ways the main, reason bodies matter and not just to philosophy.

It is in the best interests of philosophy and theory to change so that they are able to participate in interdisciplinary integration. To be also in position to exert some control over the versions of poststructuralism that are coming from other disciplines, especially other humanities, like political science. From the present position we can say that, arguably, during the science wars, it is our, poststructuralist side that did not understand the terms of conversation, not just Sokal and Bricmont's.

If above we saw David Cunningham's "Logics of Generalization" define institutional/scholarly practice as determining one another, institution still figures in his work in the abstract sense of the division between philosophy and other disciplines. It is not (also) that institution consisting of scholars across campus with whom he might want or, given the stress philosophy is under, need to communicate. Cunningham and his editors do not seem to have in mind the category that would make his essay into an actual go-around. What exactly is the institution if it is not also *this* institution? What is writing if it is not also *this* writing?

As a discourse, science tends to be practical and this, among other things, has been the condition that poststructuralist theory has not been willing to meet as a part of its investigation of interdisciplinary formations—although, as we showed with the example of de Man, practical engagements and interventions were a mainstay of the early poststructuralism. A theory cannot *be* interdisciplinary if it does not start with addressing how we *do* scholarship, which, again, informed *Bodies that Matter* and many other early works but is not present in the current version of poststructuralism.

Interdisciplinarity as reading

In Nina Power's "Reading Transdisciplinarily: Sartre and Althusser," practice and theory seems to be reconciled as she treats transdisciplinarity from the standpoint "of reading and readers" (109). The point of view is extra-disciplinary and is defined by (and as) a practice of reading through which readers become readers. The essay also insists that a theory of transdisciplinarity must include a theory of reading and recognizes that fundamental poststructuralist works are transdisciplinary—in Power's words, "irreverent in the sense of crossing boundaries between disciplines and between languages" (Power 110). Power also explains that the beyond of disciplines is not a borderless area, but another form of coherence as she asks this pointed question: "what stance can operate as a marker of an explicitly transdisciplinary approach without engaging in the repetitive erection of new metadisciplines or falling into a black hole of boundarylessness?"

(Power 111). Power even warns about the new universal and that it may serve to reassert or "perversely reinforce the need for disciplines" (111). Power also seeks the solution to the conundrum of thinking about disciplinarity in the existence of texts, which she distinguishes from "schools, authors, methods" to separate them from all kinds of discursivity we can associate with the existing institutions (111). She hence wants "to defend a model of reading that is postdisciplinary but that also comes before the separation into disciplines, of the categorization of texts and their corresponding readers" (111).

The suggestion does much to prevent the kind of chaotic postdisciplinarity of Waisbord's model. It is defined by reading and as reading or interpretative practices that themselves organize the situationist environment. Calling it pre-disciplinary obligates reading to fit not one but more than one model. With this move, the interdisciplinary theory of reading has that much greater responsibility since reading practice has to fit in many different frameworks. Power also makes an unusual call for a universality—creation of "universal ownership" of knowledge that transcends disciplines (110).

But when Power has to choose the context in which she wants to find her reading, it is not an actual collaboration, site, place, forum, or any other example of current scholarship or teaching. It is instead Sartre's and Althusser's work and a proposition that describes potential solution for the division of labor, which imagines "for me to do one thing today and another tomorrow, to hunt in the morning, fish in the afternoon, rear cattle in the evening, criticise after dinner, just as I have a mind, without ever becoming hunter, fisherman, herdsman, or critic (Marx and Engels, 1970: 54)" (Power 113). This leads her to propose,

> A model of reading that is not related to a particular discipline *in advance* but breaks down the spheres of action (or, perhaps, in the speculative attempt at hand here, at least the spheres of thought) would be a notion of social reading, of reading as a collective practice – as practically absurd as this may sound, used as we are to conceiving reading as a wholly serial, atomized, even bourgeois activity, though it is interesting to note the perennial existence of book clubs at all levels of society. (Power 113)

As we saw above, such positioning neglects actual relation and the fact that disciplines are shored up by institutional, not ontological, forces. What Power refers to as social reading is just another abstraction. Absent from Power's account is the ability to cut across individual/collective university/real world relation and reconfigure reading as a practice that brings different entities together and does this in the context in which they are currently situated without asserting any transcendental objects.

Once again, disciplinarity is a process, not a thing or object of knowledge. When we study it, we study it as a process. We will return to philosophy after a look at practical solutions and the possibility that they offer a more suitable model for convergence.

Transdisciplinarity in environmental science

From the above theoretical solutions, we move to a constellation with practical goals based in scholarship-world relation to see what happens with interdisciplinarity starting from that end. This because disciplinarity is defined in practice and also because of the standing demand that contemporary knowledge production must be, as it is put in different discourses, either socially relevant, or produce measurable outcomes, be problem based, be practice oriented, and so on.

A recent call for papers for a special issue of *Environmental Science & Policy* journal, titled "Transdisciplinary Sustainability Research," focuses on the relation between scholarship and its results. Its authors are Martina Schäfer (the Center for Technology and Society, Berlin Institute of Technology), Alexandra Lux and Matthias Bergmann (Institute for Social-Ecological Research in Frankfurt). They introduce their call explaining,

> With the rise of transdisciplinary research programs (e.g. in the fields of climate change, sustainability, land use, urban development) funding organizations, universities and collaborating partners from business and government get more interested in evidence for the effectiveness of such research (Wiek et al. 2014). Many authors agree that evaluation of the quality of this research type has to be based on criteria beyond standard academic metrics (such as bibliometrics) and include relevance and societal effects (Walter et al. 2007, Bornmann 2013, Wiek et al. 2014). There is an emerging body of literature on evaluation in TDR with different strands, which – so far – are only partially connected to each other. (Defila & Di Giulio 1999, Bergmann et al. 2005, Klein 2006, Jahn & Keil 2015)

Despite the many good works, "until now there have been only few attempts to generate evidence for *links between the quality of the research process and generated outcomes and societal effects.*"

This is because, as most authors agree,

> there is no clear causal relationship between research results and effects, but that effects are the result of complex and non-linear communication processes, which are influenced by further actors (as e.g. knowledge brokers or intermediaries) and situational factors (Weiss 1980, Litfin 1995, Meyer 2010, Walter et al. 2007, Kaufmann-Hayoz et al. 2016, Krainer & Winiwarter 2016, Maag et al. 2018). There is an ongoing debate about *appropriate methods,* which allow capturing these complex interactions (Meagher et al. 2008; Boaz et al. 2009; Wiek et al. 2014; Hansson & Polk 2018). At the same time TD settings, where science and policy are entangled in processes of co-production are reflected critically, when it comes to evaluate the usefulness of the gained knowledge (Lövbrand 2011). (Schäfer et al.)

Thus, we see how a pragmatic positioning and real-world oriented research is hobbled by the lack of theoretical understanding and absence of a continuous efforts to define epistemology.

The lack leads Schäfer, Lux, and Bergmann identify the following questions for their volume,

> How does the choice of methods and procedures specific for TDR (e.g. joint problem formulation, stakeholder participation, knowledge integration, assuring transferability of results and experiences) influence the effects of transdisciplinary research processes and the quality of their results? Which methodological elements can be included in transdisciplinary research processes to strengthen their potential for (societal) effects? (Schäfer et al.)

From our perspective, the questions are going in the right direction of focusing on the epistemic issues but not far enough since the editors leave the basics out of consideration. What is the "research processes"? How do we distinguish between "research processes" and "outcomes"? What are the "societal effects"?

We do not want to give the impression that Schäfer, Lux, and Bergmann should solve these problems or answer these questions before they can create the kind of scholarship they think needed at this point in time. Instead, these are the questions that should be defined in each and every scholarly work while it is performed. The utility that stands in the way of efficacy might just as well be theoretical problem as a practical one. Take communication for instance. Does it falter because two researchers cannot comprehend each other or because there is no framework in which effective communication can take place? The answer is both, of course. It falters because there is no systematicity in place that would ask the participants to continually align various regimens, allegiances, exigencies, and goals. What goes on with integration between disciplines and among specializations is also the issue repeated in the relation between research and its results since both have to broach and bring together two radically different frameworks. Both, in other words, are issues of divergence.

Communication falters also possibly because journals that focus on transdisciplinary problems still rely on disciplinary standards to evaluate transdisciplinarity. As Schäfer admitted to me in an e-mail, "[i]n my view this [special collection] is not a transdisciplinary review but a normal scientific review on articles that deal with methods of transdisciplinarity. The normal criteria of coherent structure, sound description of methods and results etc. were applied."[7]

Design thinking

This is a good place to mention design thinking that took liberal arts and business schools by storm in recent years (Cross; Curedale; Lockwood; Mootee). It, too, is a form of transdisciplinary practical approach that centers on the process of research or decision making.

In our view, design thinking was popular because it afforded the ersatz epistemology many scholars felt missing. Being a process—divided into stages that allow for repeated reframing, calling for improvisation, inclusive of all participants, as well as goal oriented—design thinking presented a way not only to organize research and teaching but also to continually correct and reinvent our methodology, the process itself, and come up with manifold of potential solutions.

It—not actually offering an epistemology—is also often a ploy, open to manipulation by the organizer. This is most obvious when design thinking is used in classroom as a form of pedagogy. Speaking from experience, students often feel impowered by it as their inputs are given prominent place, but they, in the classes I participated in, learned little about research (from the process itself) and could not answer such simple questions as, why design thinking is what it is?; what advantages it offers?; how exactly it offers these?; and why?; and so on. As participants, students did not as much as realize that they were herded around from this stage to the next with the bird's eye view on the process and its meaning available only to the instructor. The instructor was also the only participant equipped to evaluate choices, make decisions about outcomes, and understand the results. What learning value it had for students was in their enthusiasm and willingness to participate.

The hodge-podge is summed up well in this advertisement for a design thinking teaching manual directed to future teachers,

> Educational design research blends scientific investigation with the systematic development and implementation of solutions to educational challenges. Empirical inquiry is conducted in real learning settings – not laboratories – to craft effective solutions to the complex challenges facing educational practitioners. At the same time, the research is carefully structured to produce theoretical understanding that can serve the work of others. (McKenney and Reeves)

In other words, in place of science, design thinking offers a "blend" of science and implementation. The instruction is whatever you want it to be, "real" as well as "carefully" staged. It treats problems as "challenges" which it solves by moving from one stage to the next. Pointing to the challenges and the outcomes, then, figures as a "theoretical understanding" of the process.

In balanced groups with smaller power differentials, design thinking can function in a more egalitarian and effective fashion. But even in that setting, the process cannot substitute for an epistemology. It also cannot give us insights into the problems with research and output and their relations as an epistemology could. It, too, cannot be science without being science, which is why interdisciplinarity needs to be based in actual disciplines. Saying this, we do not mean to affirm disciplinary boundaries or to return us to the scholarly universe defined by disciplines now that we need actual skills. We mean disciplines (and specializations) as routines that have resulted in establishment of reliable methodologies and systems of control. These methods are tools. They can be employed just as well in an interdisciplinary framework if they are adapted with an understanding of context and with the goal of convergence. And skills are always outcomes of a practice.

Design thinking aims to change habits and ways we do things but does that without situating itself in any one science or established interdisciplinary practice. In this, it resembles other postdisciplinary forms where the prominent position of the business schools is the main form of coherence that design thinking has. The issue with entropic models, as physicists know well, is that they tend to more and more chaos and cannot just like that return to previous states.

History of science as an interdiscipline

History of science has a built-in model of interdisciplinarity that consists of history and the sciences. It will be our next example because of that relative simplicity of its structure that rests on two criteria at the same time, one centered in a discipline and unified, and one that takes the discipline outside itself and toward another discipline. The model will help us explain how interdiscipline can be both, a discipline and a transdiscipline. This analysis, too, will add historical dimension to our analysis to show how disciplines have been transdisciplines.

A recent instance, Mitchell Ash's "Interdisciplinarity in Historical Perspective," offers "that the modern array of scientific and humanistic disciplines and interdisciplinarity emerged together" (619). The thesis is available to Ash because he sees "the history of science" he is intent on documenting as an "interdiscipline" (620). And Ash's own approach to this object of study is itself functioning as an interdiscipline.

The significance of this order and logic (interdiscipline is not subsequent to but contemporaneous with discipline) can be seen if we compare it with the usual nomenclature. Siedlok and Hibbert, to repeat, say that interdisciplinary research is "a mode of research that transgresses traditional disciplinary boundaries" (10) and the second edition of *The Oxford Book of Interdisciplinarity* suggests that interdisciplinarity is a "response to disciplines" and "to the specific forms of the organization of disciplines in the modern research university" (Turner 9). If, however, the same problem is seen from the point of view of an interdiscipline like history of science, disciplinarity and interdisciplinarity appear not to be sequential formations, the heterogenous following homogenous, a norm and a response. The two are, rather, contemporaneous, complementary, and coincidental. That is, interdisciplinarity and disciplinarity appear to be forms of one other, existing in an overlapping relation, within the same institutional spaces, and simultaneously.

The advantage of this understanding is that it shows how (through continuity, over time) disciplines get created out of scholarship that is interdisciplinary.

The claim also captures the historicity of the always changing meaning of the two terms, with the interdiscipline being an aspect of a discipline established as such in institutional terms. This is not exactly the dialectic we identified in Peter Osborne's work that focuses on the tension between discipline and interdiscipline since it allows that the same set of practices appears differently from different points of view. The dialectical model proved insufficient when Ash encountered the history of general knowledge,

> no longer limited either to the natural and medical sciences or to the history of disciplines, but [one that] also addresses the historical development of what might be called knowledge areas in the broadest sense, with the result that the history of science and the general history of knowledge are no longer entirely distinct activities. (see Alder 2013; Daston 2017)

And Ash's goal is, "to describe and analyze transformations both in knowledge and in the institutions in which it has been produced and distributed over time (for a programmatic statement see Ash 1999)" (Ash 620).

But then this interpretation breaks down at the moment when Ash has to explain what his own approach is. At that point, the interdisciplinary narrative melts away and Ash says that his work is "monodisciplinary" in methodological sense (620). When he has to substantiate what he has in mind, Ash adds that the precepts he follows are,

> keeping with Lorraine Daston's assessment of the current state of the field: "in large part because of the mandate to embed science in context, historians of science have become self-consciously disciplined, and the discipline to which they have submitted themselves is history" (Daston 2009, p. 808). (Ash 620)

Or, in somewhat different terms, "that institutionalized practices of ID [interdisciplinarity] cannot be taken as given, but also need to be historicized" (Ash 622). From our perspective, it is entirely possible that Ash is ironic but that he does not want to point to that irony in unequivocal terms.

We believe that Ash's findings are conclusively showing that interdiscipline's history overlaps with that of discipline. The significant claims include that "an increase in the number, variety, and kinds of disciplines inevitably leads to an even greater increase in the potential number and variety of ID [interdisciplinary] activities" (622); that the "specialization within and the fragmentation of disciplines that resulted from all this [establishment of norms for science and scholarship] was widely lamented from the beginning, yet it was also understood to be an inevitable result of the growth of knowledge" (626); that "[c]ontrary to widespread essentialistic mystifications of the 'two cultures' kind, the activities involved in the establishment of the humanities and social sciences, seen as institutionalized practices, differed surprisingly little from the ones involved in the establishment of natural, medical, or technical sciences" (626); and that "[i]t's not about connecting two or more boxes, but thinking outside the box" (623).

And, at the end of the article, "The emergence and increasing predominance of MD [multidisciplinary] and TD [transdisciplinary] program research has altered both ID [interdisciplinary] and disciplinarity alike in ways not foreseen by its advocates" (Ash 635), by which Ash means that the new trends have returned the interdisciplinarity (of non-additive kind) to center stage where, this time, it should be harder to ignore.

From our point of view, there is nothing about Ash's methodology that is specific to history up until the point that Ash designates it as such. Discipline of history is enshrined at that moment and through that gesture while Ash could have just as well argued that the same methodology can be used to meet the double logic of science *and* history. The understanding that meaning is context based does not belong to historiography but is, or can be, shared across scholarly discourses.

Paradoxically, when he reaches the point of the general history of knowledge, it seems that Ash has actually found another theory to explain meaning production. There is a view that resembles the one we argued for in Chapter 2, where we suggested that there is another framework that frames context-based understanding. That framework is not science of history as such but a specific view or theory about meaning. For Ash, that theory becomes visible when the general knowledge is recognized to be a concept, not a given. A construct is not defined by a context but by the theory and framework that inform it. A discipline of history, as Ash refers to it, must defend itself against such insight.

Othering and interdisciplinarity

From history of science, we turn back to our main readily identifiable interdisciplinary discipline, namely, philosophy, as it is presented in Jack Reynolds's "Philosophy's Shame: Reflections on an Ambivalent/Ambiviolent Relationship with Science." We will also review briefly how two main branches of philosophy, analytic and continental, understand science and therefore interdisciplinarity.

Reynolds's essay promises an account of the relation between science and humanities, to uncover its psychological motivation (othering), and resolve it by suggesting a new configuration of interdisciplinarity. Compared to Ash's essay above, Reynolds's offers a new model that accounts for the dialectic nature/culture in terms of a concept (othering), enhancing our understanding of the relation between disciplines and interdiscipline as well.

Reynolds begins by acknowledging the chief division of knowledge but argues that humanities are informed not simply by a distinction from sciences, but by a psychologically more complex *othering* of science. Humanities are, as we generally assume, operating based on the notion of truth as revelation and sciences on truth as *adaequatio* or equivalence. Reynolds borrows his strategy from Ann Murphy's *Violence and the Philosophical Imaginary* which itself is inspired by certain version of Derrida's work (*Rogues*). His argument is "that philosophy's identity and relation to itself depends on an intimate relationship with that which is designated as not itself (e.g. other academic disciplines and nonphilosophy in general)" (Reynolds 56). And his solution is that philosophy needs to move beyond the othering stage and transcend its boundaries to "become post-analytic and meta-continental" (Reynolds 56).

Reynolds argues the above by showing how unstable boundaries are—the external boundaries that make the discipline of philosophy, those that separate sciences from humanities, and those that separate academic from non-academic knowledge. In the next step, Reynolds identifies three modalities of relation between science and philosophy which also identify three types of borders. These are cannibalist incorporatism, scientific naturalism, and methodological separatism—or philosophy as unifying theory for all knowledge; philosophy that is self-consciously like science; and a version of C.P. Snow's two cultures where each discourse has its own, separate "methods and domains of inquiry" (Reynolds 59). Reynolds focuses first on the analytic tradition and its attempts to "align" with and be like science by adopting inductive method, limiting itself to empiricism, logical positivism, and small interpretative steps that are also in continuity with sciences (Reynolds 60). Significantly for our purposes, the tradition rejects epistemology, which Reynolds notes citing Ted Sider's *Four Dimensionalism*, "It would be foolish to require generally that epistemological foundations be established before substantive inquiry can begin. Mathematics did not proceed foundation first. Nor did physics. Nor has ethics, traditionally" (Sider 2001, xiv, qtd. Reynolds 60).

We disagree with Reynolds on principle regarding the approach that should be employed to understand interdisciplinarity at this point in the evolution of this topic. In the quotation, for instance, Sider rejects only one, traditional kind, not all epistemology. As it is evident from the opening pages of Sider's *Four Dimensionalism*, epistemology is "difficult" to argue for (xxiv) when it stands for a system of rules regulating "general truths about existence" (and conceptual analysis). That philosophers are abandoning traditional epistemology and opening a possibility for a new kind is, in fact, one of the tropes of contemporary philosophy in both of its discourses, continental as well as analytic. As Arun Iyer observes concerning Heidegger, at stake are new frameworks that "allow us to ... broaden our conception of knowledge and the knowing subject ... that goes beyond conceptual thinking" (Iyer 1) with going beyond the traditional form of conceptual thinking being among the shared goals.

Given the traits, we can choose to start by aligning analytic philosophy with science and the maintain that continental is other to it. Or, we can say that both traditions are engaged in formulating new epistemologies and start our analysis from that point of convergence or "overlap" (Leiter and Rosen 2). Reynolds comes to a similar conclusion concerning crossovers and impurity in discourses (Gutting). When he does that, his claim rests on disciplinarity as the principle of knowledge creation and disciplinary division is his starting point. What is impure or crossing over is that in relation to a model of discipline that is pure and self-same. Perhaps, it is time to recognize that this deconstructive methodology functions as a normalizing force in that it takes specific contexts and treats them as givens, which then leads to postdisciplinarity as the way out of the limiting framework.

Reynolds develops a new synthetic approach he christens "*post*-continental" philosophy (65), referring to Catherine Malabou's *What Should We Do With Our Brain?* which is an engagement between science and philosophy that takes place "in terms of a more fundamental and pre-given agenda that is socio-political" (Reynolds 67) or as "bastard phenomenology" (Reynolds 69). The same strategy is present in Tilottama Rajan's recent essay that tries to resurrect the positive, poststructuralist sense of institution and its critique. It, too, ends up arresting the conversation by returning to what she calls *an-arche* or pre-discursive, anarchic origin (Rajan 424), just as David Cunningham and Nina Power turned to pre-postdiscipline in their essays we considered above. If interdisciplinary institutions are to be built, they are to be constructed out of already existing practices, in already defined spaces, which are—as we do with narratives—given new prominence in our different framework just as Mitchell Ash did it in assembling his history of interdiscipline.

Now, one could argue that the mentioned theorists mean exactly what we are saying here. On this, they are not saying that pre- (in logical sense) is the condition that comes before an action can be constituted, or that pre- (in temporal sense) is a history of scholarship which then determines institution for what it is. With these terms, they rather designate events that erupt and force scholars to reconfigure disciplinarity again and again. But if these interruptions are not counted *as* disciplinary practices, but assigned the status of an event (origin, pre-discursive, and so on), what is a discipline? If we agree to such cutting off, there isn't much that is left. Or, put another way, what are the bases (but some notion of discipline) to distinguish what is other from what is the same, pre-discursive as opposed to discursive?

We take discipline to be a set of routines that overtime form evaluative methods which in turn constitute disciplines as distinct entities within schools and universities. The disarticulations are their constitutive events, as are the articulations, each confirmed by the effect it has on the development of frameworks that make a discipline, itself confirmed (or not) in the subsequent iterations. In short, disciplines *are* processes of articulation taking place on different levels at the same time, institutional, theoretical, individual, and social. They are neither centered nor decentered, chaotic or unified. We can positively identify what they are only after we have a systematicity in place to do that. Up until that point, we are forced to either fall back or use some notion of discipline as our referential point which betrays the very interdisciplinary project it is meant to support. Both Reynolds and Rajan as well as other theorists we discussed above do articulate such strategy. And they do it in the face of the other choice that is always available: namely, to reject the usual starting point (that ghost of a discipline) and foreground a sense of wholeness and discipline that fits with an interdisciplinary or open knowledge production and call it what it is, not pre- or post- but just discipline.

The institution of discipline is a linking of practices so that they hang together in some fashion, forming a whole when given a title (book or course), the name of the author (teacher), and finalized with publication, readings, and readings of those readings. Interdiscipline is the same just with practices oriented toward convergence, general scope, theory that is practice. One could say that the difference between the two is in complexity of the processes or problems they are about. But interdiscipline could always be about the complex issues of knowledge production and disciplinarity, which is our preferred model. They can be defined based on the complexity of the approach, not based on the complex problem they tackle.

II Part: Hegel, Haiti, and universal history

Philosophy, political science, and history together

Here is, then, an examination of an interdisciplinary work that compares favorably to all of the above examples. The main distinction between Susan Buck-Morss study, *Hegel, Haiti, and Universal History*, and the essays we just criticized—for our purposes—is their starting point.

Instead of cybernetics, pre- or postdiscipline, definitions, supposition of interdisciplinarity of all knowledge we saw above, Susan Buck-Morss begins by, simply, putting in question the framework within which she is supposed to operate as a historian, philosophers, and political theorist. Mimicking Hegel's *The Phenomenology of Mind*—where the Preface is a book in its own right on the limits of scientific cognition—*Hegel, Haiti, and Universal History* is structured through addressing various frameworks that define her analysis and research. We focus on this structure since even a visualization of its contents affords an insight into how disciplinary inquiry takes place. It looks like this:

Preface
Part One: Hegel and Haiti
Introduction to Part One
Hegel and Haiti
Part Two: Universal History
Introduction to Part Two
Universal History

Note, first, the symmetry that each of the two main parts has, consisting of an introduction and chapter. Note then also the other kind of symmetry that requires the whole to have its introduction, too. This framing speaks of the way we understand and construct scholarship as formal or visual wholes, responding to an unacknowledged sense of equilibrium. The gestalt is there as the additional proof, if one is needed, for the kind of whole and uniformity the author (publisher, reviewers) feels they need to create.

Preface

Buck-Morss's "Preface" offers steps that link the central essay, "Hegel and Haiti," to the disciplinary perspective that the essay's argument violated. The essay was originally published in *Critical Inquiry* and has caused some controversy. This not only after its publication but also before it as we can deduce from its length (over 40 journal pages), the number and character of end notes (127). In this, it is an unusual case that, to repeat, discloses the entire process of scholarly production that consists of several cycles of research, peer review, and publication. We hence take the book as both an example of scholarship in its own right as well as a document on how humanities institutions function to produce a piece of knowledge.

The essay, the "Preface" explains, was an "intellectual event" because of the "unconventional topologies of time and space that it mapped out" (ix). Notably, it did not please "the academic critics of Eurocentrism" (ix), because it tried to salvage "modernity's universal intent, rather than calling for a plurality of alternative modernities" (ix). The book "appeared tantamount to collusion with Western imperialism—or perhaps more precisely, American imperialism" (ix). To respond to these critics, the "Preface" suggests, *Hegel, Haiti, and Universal History* also includes a second essay, titled "Universal History," that offers an additional explanation of the universal the author is arguing for and why she does it.

The warnings and realignments of the "Preface" prepares us for the next framing sections, titled "Introduction to Part One," whose task is to explain step-by-step why and how the author deviated from the expected path of multiple modernities and got to liking Hegel and Haiti. She describes her essays in terms like "event" (ix) and "accident" (3) that testify to the character of the discovery which, too, emphasize the siloed nature of contemporary political historiography. To bring Hegel and Haiti into alignment and make the connection palatable for her readers, Buck-Morss writes,

> Conceptually, the revolutionary struggle of slaves, who overthrow their own servitude and establish a constitutional state, provides the theoretical hinge that takes Hegel's analysis out of the limitlessly expanding colonial economy and onto the plane of world history, which he defines as the realization of freedom—a theoretical solution that was taking place in practice in Haiti at that very moment. (Buck-Morss 11–12).

Only after the event and the topic, theory and practice have been synchronized with the usual disciplinary view are we ready for the "Hegel and Haiti."

Hegel and Haiti

The essay—that is, the book's first chapter—starts with its own discussion of frames. These pertain to most immediate context of Buck-Morss's historical and philosophical research. The first paragraph situates the Enlightenment metaphor of freedom in respect to the contemporary practice of slavery (21). The second paragraph notes the "glaring discrepancy between thought [of freedom] and practice" of slavery (22). But then the fourth paragraph offers a parallel between the historical context in which Hegel worked and the one in which Buck-Morss works today:

> If this paradox [the fact that slave economy functioned at the time that proclaimed freedoms] did not seem to trouble the logical consciousness of contemporaries, it is perhaps more surprising that present-day writers, while fully cognizant of the facts, are still capable of constructing Western Histories as coherent narratives of human freedom. (22)

Buck-Morss identifies the source of ignorance in the very conditions of the disciplinary knowledge production, saying,

> The greater the specialization of knowledge, the more advanced the level of research, the longer and more venerable the scholarly tradition, the easier it is to ignore discordant facts. It should be noted that specialization and isolation are also a danger for those new disciplines such as African American studies, or new fields such as diaspora studies, that were established precisely to remedy the situation. Disciplinary boundaries allow counterevidence to belong to someone else's story. After all, a scholar cannot be an expert in everything. Reasonable enough. But such arguments are a way of avoiding the awkward truth that if certain constellations of facts are able to enter scholarly consciousness deeply enough, they threaten not only the venerable narratives, but also the entrenched academic disciplines that (re)produce them. For example, there is no place in the university in which the particular research constellation "Hegel and Haiti" would have a home. (22–23)

Which is to say that the nested structure of the books is there not only to supply the expected knowledge constellation but also to comment on the overall organization of knowledge which privileges specific positions. At this point, Buck-Morss's argument is no longer about the past but about the present and the way we set up our work. What this scholarly move allows us to see is what is missing when the world of knowledge is divided among specialization and there are only links between them without a view of the whole. Lost are those things—facts, events, connections, points of view—that fall between specializations as well as those attitudes that contradict the spirit and principles of specialization.

Buck-Morss's inquiry manages then to be new, interdisciplinary, disciplinary, and to address the general viewpoint as a historical, political, and a philosophical entity as well as contemporary scholarly practice. *Hegel, Haiti, and Universal History* is interesting for us also because it is an attempt that cannot be explained as either generalist or specialist, but one that cuts across fields and by its very existence criticizes the extant divisions both vertical and horizontal. In this respect, a small island in the Atlantic Ocean becomes one of the two centers for an inquiry into the idea of universality, its legacy, as well as their impacts 200 years later while it is paired with classical German philosophy and a contemporary academic universe divided into specializations. A specialist knowledge of the island and Hegel are a funnel for the universal which emerges on the other end transformed into a new term as it intervenes in the contemporary postdisciplinary academic setting. This, again, is to say that the work is important for our purposes because of how it treats contemporary academic context, and only then because of what it says about Haiti and Hegel.

Across the humanities, it should be harder and harder to justify the long publications like monographs and collections of essays that are not positioned in way similar to Buck-Morss's, interrogating a set of frameworks while also making specific contributions to several existing area of specialization like the political history of Atlantic slavery, Hegel's philosophy, Enlightenment politics, historicity, political science, and philosophy. This work is, strictly speaking, both specialist and generalist, as well as undermining and transcending such boundaries. Specialist because it focuses on relatively limited number of questions, processes, and geographic locations. And generalist, because it is devoted to explaining the very moment in history of philosophy and politics when the general, that is to say the universal, became the framework for self-understanding. And transformational because it is not defined by the existing lines of demarcation—disciplinary but also political—and suggests new constellations.

For these reasons, we find accusation of centrism missing the point. The one center that the project has is the disciplinary framework that Buck-Morss obviously works to redefine in interdisciplinary terms. Otherwise, this book is neither centering nor decentering. It is devoted to opening new, intersectional academic space in which Haiti and Hegel are not an unusual paring but related subjects. The use of Enlightenment may appear to center the project in European history, but such identification seems knee-jerk since Buck-Morss's discussion takes place on two different tracks, with the second involving the very terms of scholarship that can be shared by differently situated subjects working today.

For the same reasons, we find that the complaints that Buck-Morss is not a good reader of Hegel are missing the point. The point missed is at the same time Hegel's and Buck-Morss's, concerning the possibility of universal history. I do agree that some of Buck-Morss's references to Hegel's philosophy's relation to Haiti revolution are stretched. For instance, Buck-Morss renders lordship and bondage with some regularity as "master and slave" or as "master-slave dialectic." She, too, splits her references between *The Phenomenology of Mind* and Hegel as an historical figure and author. When she does reference Hegel's work, she is often documenting context in which he learned about Haiti, not actually commenting on his philosophy. And when she does offer a specialist reading of Hegel, it is not precise or nuanced but one that repeats general points (e.g., Buck-Morss, "Hegel and Haiti" 846–849). Extensive endnotes accompanying these pages seem to be there to show her expertise—this perhaps because it was contested by *Critical Inquiry* reviewers. But even that display of expertise is more concerned with the history of the manuscripts and influence than with details Hegel's philosophy about which Buck-Morss does not have much to say. Thus, if the analysis of Hegel appears stretched, this is from the point of view of a specialist who, while they read Hegel, do not keep in mind the general perspective but are focusing their attention narrowly on specific elements of his *The Phenomenology of Mind*. Adding a perspective is a legitimate kind of close reading that challenges text and its reception. It happens to be a Hegelian move, too.

In place of a new expert close reading, the reader could find what may be at this point in time a more valuable contribution and that is the way to connect such reading and make it relevant for creating a shared or universal perspective that includes Haiti. By these means, both Hegel and Haiti or Atlantic studies can be enriched by a different sense of close reading as well as a different sense of expertise. Both are constructed no longer around text, period, and author, but around the way to approach these and rearticulate scholarly concerns for the future context we are engaged in creating. These other readings—from our point of view and at this point in time—are more faithful to one, universal aspect of Hegel and Haiti than the expert close readings. They, too, can help make Hegel and Haiti relevant for the creation of the new universal that transcends both subjects and is not called either pre- or post-discipline.

III Part: systematicity

Intersectionality

To explain the significance of this proposal we will take a quick look at intersectional theory as defined by Kimberle Crenshaw in "Mapping the Margins: Intersectionality, Identity Politics, and Violence Against Women of Color." Briefly, Buck-Morss's book is much like Crenshaw's essay, interested in reframing traditional boundaries between issues and disciplines, with intersectionality defined as "a provisional concept linking contemporary politics with postmodern [or poststructuralist, in our terms] theory" (Crenshaw "Mapping" 1244). The goals are similar, too, in that Crenshaw wants "to suggest a methodology that will ultimately disrupt the tendencies to see race and gender as exclusive or separable" (1244). In part one, Crenshaw presents "structural" intersectionality, or "[w]here systems of race, gender, and class domination converge" (Crenshaw 1246). Part two addresses political and part three is devoted to representational intersectionality. The key similarity between projects, however, lies in what can be done with the analysis provided by intersectional theory and Buck-Morss's book. While it might seem that Crenshaw's goal is to particularize oppression and define it in detail, the experiences of poor black women also define a universal platform, countering "tendencies to see race and gender as exclusive or separable" (Crenshaw 1244). Dubbed black political economy by Patricia Hill Collins, it is not only a theory that can tell that poor black women are oppressed by their gender *and* race *and* class. With the three categories in place, it, too, is a tool to integrate knowledge of oppression in general and to get scholars in position to define an inclusive political economy—as we add indigenous and immigrant subjects as well.

If analysis should be sensitive to specifics and contexts of marginalization, this is so only for so long as there are new intersections of race, class, gender, sex, or status under the law to be accounted for. After the setup is formulated (and the list of position is a short one), its analytic tool becomes the opposite, and can serve the purpose of gathering. In this, the categories of race, gender, class, and sex are not fragmenting but intersecting as well as organizing vehicles. Seen thus, intersectional theory is an example of systematicity without a system, or a systematicity that creates and continually recreates the system. Unfortunately, this universalizing potential of intersectional theory is often overlooked as we focus on the key elements—poor, black, woman—as if they were defining only one category. The most specific and particular identity, due to its position, is also the most general term that defines the given economy. It, too, brings together the usually divided and fragmented analyses of the system and offers a way toward their mutual rearticulation. Multimodality, at some point in the process, begins to define a universal or an inclusive platform and is inseparable from it.

This, in the simplest of terms, means that whatever helps poor black women also helps everyone else. It also a universalizing tool because with the intersecting categories of race, sex, and class, it can be used to identify other marginalized subjects like undocumented immigrants or poor sexual minorities.

At this last chapter we are, finally, treating interdisciplinarity as intersectional systematicity, which is our last topic, with the emphasis on the synthetic aspect of this theory. Buck-Morss's work is our choice here because it is devoted to convergence and is doing that, as we already saw, by focusing on institutional frameworks that stand in the way. In contrast, black political economy is dedicated to social institutions and general economy and has not been applied—to the best of my knowledge—to understanding scholarship and its institutional aspects of knowledge production. It, too, is too often used to particularize identity and, unfortunately, prevent coalition building for the fear of erasure.

If the thematic of the above mentioned intersectional works appears different, their methodology, due to common interest in structure and structuralism, is compatible with ours. It can be applied to afford new generalization, to explain knowledge production, and to create new forms of cooperation. This by foregrounding intersections over other identity markers. Using intersectional theory, we can name several avenues, starting with understanding how differently situated researchers, teachers, and scholars, who seemingly have little or nothing in common, can find shared interests by treating their differences—gender, race, class, field, area of specialization, approach, but also micro distinctions—as potential sources of at least temporary commonality. It can help us by approaching first the complex problems (like poverty) and allowing those to dictate intersections of research and approaches and expecting disciplinarity to be adjusted to the general scale. Or by showing how intra- and inter-group dynamics intersect. And these are just some of the ways in which intersectional theory can be used to create systematicity.

Universal argument

Buck-Morss's book is relevant for our purposes also because it puts together an epistemology by combining it with overarching issue concerning the legacy of Enlightenment and its concept of the universal. *Hegel, Haiti, and Universal History* allows us to lay the claim on the connection between the general issue of interdisciplinarity and the notion of the universal which are, in our view, inseparable, one being the means for the other. As for Buck-Morss, for us the assumption is that the two go together, with interdisciplinarity as the way toward the universal and the universal providing the new intersectional framework for the inquiry into interdisciplinarity. For postdisciplinary models, the opposite appears to be the case. They are postdiscipline in precisely this sense that they do not envision another form of systematicity or unity of knowledge production on a large scale but harken back to the notion of discipline, some classical sense of institution and knowledge formation, and then define themselves negatively or in terms of overcoming.

For our purposes, it is paramount that the author arrives to her argument about the universal history by treating institutional aspects, the frameworks we saw addressed above. These allow her to treat knowledge not only as a thing, text, or set of positions and frameworks but also as a kind of production. The approach, in turn, helps us identify systematicity not as a principle that particular knowledge follows or extends but as characteristic of its making. The construction stretches from education to research to habilitation to education again. In this sense, universal is a condition and process (of opening toward convergence), not, strictly speaking, a category or quality.

In the central part of her second chapter, entitled "Universal History," the institution figures through an acrimonious scholarly debate between Peter Linebaugh and Marcus Rediker, authors of *The Many-Headed Hydra: Sailors, Slaves, Commoners, and The Hidden History of The Revolutionary Atlantic*, and, on the other side David Brion Davis, the author of *The Problem of Slavery in The Age of Revolution, 1770–1823* and *Inhuman Bondage: The Rise and Fall of Slavery in the New World*. The details of the exchange are not important for Buck-Morss's argument and so we will identify only the line of their separation. For Linebaugh and Rediker, Davis does not recognize "blinding effects of concepts of race, class, and nation that have guided most accounts of the past" (Rediker and Linebaugh, "Exchange" 2001). For Davis, according to Buck-Morss, Linebaugh and Rediker's "scholarship as full of factual errors and misleading interpretations, which he [Davis] attributes to their 'Marxist' message" (*Hegel, Haiti* 107).

Buck-Morss does not side with either though she is more inspired by the Linebaugh and Rediker's position, and offers an argument that transcends both. Thus, instead of mediating in the debate, Buck-Morss goes on to change the context for it. She poses the fundamental question of her entire project and what she believes should be the central question of historiography today, "how are we to make sense out of the temporal unfolding of collective, human life?" (109). And she responds with a unifying concern of her book, identifying it as, "[t]he need to rethink this question today in a global context, that is, as *universal* history, has not been felt so strongly for centuries—perhaps not since Hegel, Haiti, and the Age of Revolution" (109). That is to say that she is choosing the collective fight for freedom as the basis and model for universalization.

She presents it also in terms of a universal recognition of vulnerability that informs the first step in the slave's independence from the master:

> Universality is in the moment of the slaves' self-awareness that the situation was not humanly tolerable, that it marked the betrayal of civilization and the limits of cultural understanding, the nonrational, and nonrationalizable course of human history that outstrips in its *in*humanity anything that a cultural outlaw could devise. (133–134)

The recognition is supposed to resonate with other similar universal revelations about trauma. With, for instance, Frederick Douglass's "a smile or a tear has no nationality. Joy and sorrow speak alike in all nations, and they above all the confusion of tongues proclaim the brotherhood of man" (Douglass 300). And the same is supposed to speak to us today and serve as a gathering point with the recognition of humanity without condition.

The affirmation of vulnerability is followed by a discussion of international movements like Freemasons and Vodou. Freemasons enter conversation after the stary sky that Immanuel Kant, Heinrich Heine and Hegel, sailors and slaves are gazing at (119). These are referenced as common system of signs or vehicles that transcend languages and cultures (120). The three point to realms of nature (informed by commerce with technology and politics connoted); society and social practices; and religious and cultural norms. As such, they cover overlapping domains of signs that define human world.

The unity embodied in these figures is opposed to the solutions and paradigms common to historiography today, which insists of fragmentations and different temporalities captured by terms like "multiple modernities," "diversity," and "multiversality" (Buck-Morss, *Hegel* 138–139). With Buck-Morss diagnosing that "[c]ritical theoretical practice today is caught within the prisonhouse of its own academic debates" *(Hegel* 2009 139). That is, if the world is fragmented, prone to particularized points of view, contemporary scholarship has played a major role in making it that. We have organized our critical practice around showing differences without much regard for the synthetic possibilities. And here we understand that the time is ripe for a universal discourse not because of the political events like the end of the Cold War or the resurgence of nationalism and totalitarianism, police brutality or refugee crises or the status of native reservations. Instead, in our view, fragmentation of knowledge itself has opened up the analytic space for realization of multiple points of contact that can turn "multiple modernities," "diversality," and "multiversality" into new forms of universality. Which is to say that we are not calling for the return to the old modern universal but are construing one for our time out of the debris the current scholarly practices have produced. And, of course, based on the same, enduring recognition of human vulnerability and finitude. Think of it as repurposing Hegel and Haiti and rearticulating colonial discourse.

Buck-Morss ends her second chapter distinguishing between syncretic and synthetic knowledge. She says,

> There is no end to this project [of making universal history], only an infinity of connecting links. And if these are to be connected without domination, then the links will be lateral, additive, syncretic rather than synthetic. The project of universal history does not come to an end. It begins again, somewhere else. (151)

To answer that question how we can get from syncretism and fragmentation to universal history, we now return to what Bruno Latour means by systematicity in the work we mentioned at the end of Chapter 1.

Latour

We have left Latour's *Facing Gaia: Eight Lectures on the New Climatic Regime* after our first reading. Here is our second as a way to round up all of our conversations with a new, poststructuralist notion of systematicity.

The notion presents a departure for Latour, too, when compared for instance with the 1991's *We Have Never Been Modern,* where the existing approaches were criticized for segmentation onto nature, politics, and discourse. That line of thinking culminates in "Why Has Critique Run Out of Steam? From Matters of Fact to Matters of Concern," in this alarmed critique of poststructuralism. The

> entire Ph.D. programs are still running to make sure that good American kids are learning the hard way that facts are made up, that there is no such thing as natural, unmediated, unbiased access to truth, that we are always prisoners of language, that we always speak from a particular standpoint, and so on, while dangerous extremists are using the very same argument of social construction to destroy hard-won evidence that could save our lives.
> 227

In *Facing Gaia,* systematicity is based on a specific notion that is supposed to motivate general and collective action. The way to get to the universal participation is by offering a new narrative of the system (the Earth) that is not a whole or sum of coordinated parts, does not have a center, an inside and outside. It, instead, is a notion that brings macro and micro scale into relation. It relies on both the sciences and humanities to do that. And, in order to foreground action, it replaces terms like "Modern" and "modernity" with "Anthropocene" (Latour, *Facing* 106). The last, in contrasts to much current posthumanism, has Latour argue that in the age of Anthropocene, the question is not how to displace the human from the supposed center or dismantle the unity of the subject, but the opposite. How we can learn to "situate human action" and "to participate" in common geohistory of the planet which itself offers the context and the horizon for the both the understanding and action (Latour, *Facing* 107).

In what is for our purpose the most important of the eight lectures, "Gaia, A (Finally Secular) Figure for Nature," Latour starts with James Lovelock's "Gaia hypothesis" because it presents a unique understanding of the whole of life. It is a theory about the most general self-sustaining system that the Earth is as a biosphere. As Latour emphasizes, the Earth has such a system not because it has reached the point of balance like Mars, but because it is in a "chemical disequilibrium" (78). The understanding is the principle behind Lovelock's theory that allows him to see systematicity in a new way (on a new scale both spatial and temporal), including relations among particular organisms and the role they play in functioning of the whole. The system is approached as an entity that has endured over a long period, at a phase when micro-organisms are playing vital roles like helping absorb carbon dioxide into the ground or transforming nitrogen into building blocks of life to create proteins and DNA used by other organisms.

Latour comments,

> What is moving in Lovelock's prose ... is that every element that we ignorant readers would have seen as part of the *background* of the majestic cycles of nature, against which human history had always stood out, becomes active and mobile thanks to the introduction of new invisible characters capable of reversing the order and the hierarchy of the agents.... The humblest accessories henceforth play a role, as if there were no more distinctions between the main characters and the extras. Everything that was a simple intermediary serving to transport a slim concatenation of causes and consequences becomes a mediator adding its own grain of salt to the story.
>
> 93

Second, Latour explains why the Earth is not to be regarded as a living organism or a superorganism and why Lovelock's theory is not one that sees Earth as a totality, but offers a new kind of systematicity. This system functions *as* a whole without forming one in the sense of a self-enclosed or self-balancing entity (97). The functioning is unlike the one normally understood as "organism"—a result of successful coordination of parts that form a higher unit. For Lovelock, the objects that make life possible are *"neither parts nor a whole"* (Latour, *Facing* 95).

As Latour explains, only "in technological systems, in fact, can we distinguish between parts and a whole" (95).

Lovelock's model shows "how to obtain effects of *connection* among agencies without relying on an untenable conception of *the whole*" (Latour, *Facing* 97) and do so in synchrony with scientific explanations of particular bio-chemical process. If there is only one Earth, Earth is not one. It is "creating a composition that encompassed ... all living entities within the limits of the fragile envelope;" living entities acting "'as' a superorganism but their unity cannot be attributed to any Governor figure." And, most importantly, this connection or commonality is given new expression by "abandoning the idea of parts,"

> For Lovelock, organisms, taken as the point of departure for a biochemical reaction, do not develop "in" an environment; rather, each one bends the environment around itself, as it were, the better to develop. In this sense, every organism intentionally manipulates what surrounds it "in its own interest." (Latour 2017 98).

By interest, Latour means that all forms of life no matter how small have an agency, in the sense that they act to define the environment around them according to their needs. They are not *in* an environment because they create that environment. This description may appear anthropomorphic but intentionality is attributed to all life and does not include a human sense of resolve or conscious determination and will. It, instead, consists of what we can call mere actions that support a life cycle of a specific family of organisms. The system can then be described as functioning by being "*interrupted* at each point by the interposition of the just as robust intentions and interests of the *other organisms*" (Latour, *Facing* 99). Each organism acting as an agent neutralizes the possibility of a central principle and allows for a view of an *intersectional* dynamic or "waves of action." Latour paints the picture,

> a neighbor ... is actively manipulating his neighbors and all the others who are manipulating the first one defines what could be called *waves of action*, which respect no borders and, even more importantly, never respect any fixed scale. (Latour, *Facing* 101)

The reason that this systemic explanation is not like the neoliberal economics or like the "selfish gene" theory is that it does not rest on the notion of "individual" or "self" which serve to ground those views. Lovelock's system, instead, is run by incalculable chaos of life-sustaining-actions; it is without borders or fixed scale in the sense that a byproduct of one life form becomes the source for another at the same or, more often, different scale and size, and so on. The state, too, is a result of extreme duration.

In considering the Earth, Lovelock thus manages to unite the opposites, parts and whole, small and large, particular and universal. His explanation, too, gets rid of the inside/outside distinction. What is left is a systematicity without a system or a coherence of a process established through interruptions. The condition of coherence is that the impetus for agent's action is beyond their control but such that it sustains their life and defines their place in respect to other organisms as well as the whole. If we can capture the same constellation in terms of a network which is Latour's most popular term widely used across disciplines, this one privileges the entity that functions together *as* a whole. The new explanation isolates such an entity (the Earth), undoing, as Latour insists, certain aspects of the Copernican revolution and, we can add, much other science and philosophy at least at their most general. The Earth appears as the center of life—a specific center or a Gaia.

In a just published collection of essays on Latour, Anders Blok and Casper Bruun Jensen comment that in the Lovelock lecture Latour is not calling for "unification of the scientific and the mythical" which they call "unlikely" (143). In our reading, Latour is doing just that since no other mode of storytelling and no science but myth can have the mobilizing power needed to combat climate change at this late date. The myth, on this occasion, is informed by science and also appears as a part of secular religion.

We mention foundational myth here not because of any content or ideological underpinnings we endorse but to define the scope at which the new narrative about Gaia needs to be offered.

By the end of the lecture, Latour identifies "a desperate need for ... forms of homodiversity." But such that they follow a new "universal standard of behavior"—not based on globalization, individualism, or usual forms of "management" and "governance" but based on the ecological concerns (108). Lacking today are pre-modern forms that would readily recognize the force of Gaia which predates the appearance of the Greek pantheon. In that framework, nature and culture, freedom and necessity were not separated. He is critical toward "*mono*naturalism" and "*multi*culturalism" (108) alike, as he also notes that the general tendency to particularize has led to a divided view of the world. For instance, caution over biological reductionism (108) has resulted in separating neurons, neurotransmitters, hormones, brain structure from social explanations of behavior, with the bifurcation reasserting the nature/culture division. Even scholars seem to have hard time explicating the unity of the Earth and many forms of connectedness that makes up life. While disciplines are necessary to understand discrete elements of life and its history, they too are limited by their separate perspectives and would benefit from the convergence that the new model calls for.

Latour even speaks of the necessity of "anthropo*morphism*,"

> Not in the old sense in which it would "project human values onto an inert world of mute objects," but, on the contrary, in the sense that it "gives humans a shape," or, as one can say in English, that it is beginning to morph humans into a more realistic image. (Latour, *Facing* 109)

Latour's lecture ends with this inscription of the human place in the most general context of life on Earth or what he calls geohistory and geostory with the rest of *Facing Gaia,* devoted to explaining the Anthropocene.

The systematicity without a system has also opened new possibilities for the terms that poststructuralists have a habit of rejecting. Terms like whole, totality, parts, unity, balance, coherence, universal, and particular are there for new redefinitions that fit the Lovelock's model. These terms are free to enter into new relations not limited by the traditional framework in which they were mutually defined—whole and parts, universal and particular; where balance is the opposite of disequilibrium; where scale separates and unity de-singularizes. Or, put another way, we are free to see them in new way as we define new terms of conversation, new coalitions, and the new universal.

The framework, as we will see when we get to Karen Barad, comes together with an experimental invalidation of the Newtonian metaphysical setup and validation of the comparable to Gaia explanation of the incompleteness model of physics (Barad 292).

Postcolonial condition

Calling for the scientific universal response to climate change is one of the ways in which Latour answers frequent criticism that he does not address postcolonial concerns. As Dipesh Chakrabarty put it in *Provincializing Europe,* concept like "the state," "public sphere," "subject" and so on are inseparable from Europe and "political modernity" (4). The point at which Latour aligns with Chakrabarty's critique, however, is not a new notion of modernity or its pluralization. The point is rather if discussion of terms of conversation allows for a general convergence. For Chakrabarty, the universal depends on provincializing Europe, realizing particularity of its history, and assigning its countries the same status that, for instance, India has. But West is the category that is defined by history, not necessarily the category that has to define our future, too. The current generation is free to negotiate its terms of convergence which Chakrabarty can easily do from his position at the University of Chicago, which is one of the most formidable academic institutions in the world.

I think Latour's strategy more effective than Chakrabarty's in so far as it starts its universal thinking with the opposite assumption, that there are no parts. Latour does not simply break with the past as he orients the systematicity toward what *could* be created. The consequence is that each of the entities in the complex system *could* be autonomous and therefore not definable as a part of either a political or historical whole. There are also political reasons why we may not want to provincialize Europe and the Western world yet—because of the growing influence of China and its current stance that democracy, rule of law, and transparency are not in the interest of the world.

The hard part is how to construct the political reality for the new universal and do so with some urgency to counteract the radical right, the cult-like regimens, for instance, Modi's in India and Trump's in America. The question is if politicians in the middle and on the left, in coalition with secularists, scientists, postcolonial and poststructuralist theorists, Pope Francis, artists, public figures, civil rights and BLM activists, and many others, can find stories and ways to mobilize "the Earthbound" for a different set of values.

Geographic information system

Lovelock's model might be compatible with the geographic information system (GIS), if the software is not used in the common way to produce local maps or as a spatial tool, but used as a tool for three-dimensional layering. GIS has already been employed in the humanities, for instance, to create comprehensive account about undesirable effects of urban renewal in Richmond, Virginia, titled "Renewing Inequality" (Digital Scholarship Lab) or to document religious oppression, "Mapping Islamophobia." As Jen Jack Gieseking reports,

> The production of maps and other data visualizations related to history, literature, and the arts is an important contribution in and of itself. However, the most significant impact of the digital humanities is that step farther: the critical analysis of the data visualizations and archives that come from its research. (646)

In our view, to be useful for the Lovelock's model, GIS has to move beyond documentation to become also an interpretative tool—beyond, that is, the pre-set choices—to realize new connections and create new analytic options. We disagree with Gieseking's reasoning along the lines we used already in the previous chapter, concerning the place of the analytic discourse in new technology like GIS. In case of humanities projects, like the two mentioned above, mapping is a *result* of analysis. In this sense, its narratives, even if there are a few of them, can be seen as closed because they document, illustrate, represent, or explain its topic like the injustice. In such a case, the map tells a simple story.

To be useful for theory, the tool has to be an open data set, allow for nonhierarchical wholes consisting of independently functioning parts; simultaneous and sequential level connections; blurring of background/foreground, inside/outside; narratives other than those its authors want to tell; and so on. That is to say, GIS models should function like our most complex novels, allowing for new interpretative narratives that are put together by the reader. Otherwise, GIS is just a more vivid map.

Posthuman

In this discussion of Latour, we see one of the key poststructuralist theorists explicitly call for figuring out a new general, systematic approach, and for defining a role for the human in this new narrative. The theory goes in the direction contrary to the atomism proposed by much of posthumanism. We can show this quickly by reviewing how Rosi Braidotti employs "convergence" in her recent *Posthuman Knowledge*. For her, convergence takes place between a "critique of Humanism" and "complex challenge of anthropocentrism." She says, for instance,

> The point about the convergence of posthumanism and post-anthropocentrism needs to be stressed, because in current debates the two are often either hastily assimilated in a sweeping deconstructive merger, or violently re-segregated and pitched against each other. While insisting that the posthuman convergence is decidedly not a statement of inhumane indifference, it is important to emphasize the mutually enriching effect of the intersection between these two lines of enquiry. At the same time, it is crucial to resist all tendencies to reduce posthumanism and post-anthropocentrism to a relation of equivalence, and to stress instead both their singularity and the transformative effects of their convergence. Unless a critique of Humanism is brought to bear on the displacement of anthropocentrism and vice-versa, we run the risk of setting up new hierarchies and new exclusions. (8–9)

By posthumanism, Braidotti means theory that "focuses on the critique of the Humanist ideal of 'Man' as the ... universal measure of all things." And by postanthropocentrism, she means theory that "criticizes species hierarchy and anthropocentric exceptionalism" (2). Combined, the two offer "zoe/geo/techno-mediated perspectives" (Braidotti, *Posthuman*) and they do this by deconstructing what they regard as the "Humanities." We see here the scale at which Braidotti wants posthumanism to operate, one that is mapped by humanism, itself assumed to be unitary and in need of recentering onto other centers such as animals, the planet, digital technology, and so on. Hence, for her, "the posthuman convergence points to ... a multi-directional opening that allows for multiple possibilities and calls for experimental forms of mobilization, discussion and at times even resistance" (Braidotti, *Posthuman*). While we sympathize with the goal, we don't see theory or practice getting there by further atomization, deconstruction of the humanities, or further emphasis on multiplicity. We also disagree that we should start with "the Humanities." And further: A "*zoe*-centered justice" runs the risk of being yet another example of a particular justice that further fragments the attention to systematicity. The same can be said about Braidotti's understanding of the evolution which she celebrates as a proto-posthumanist theory (Braidotti, *Posthuman*) precisely because it acknowledges granulation. For Latour, in contrast, Darwinism is still a burdened by the "final cause" (Latour, *Facing* 99, 100), based in "self-interest" (101), and rests on a "vestige of Providence" (102). According to Latour, "life is more chaotic than the economists and the Darwinians had imagined" (103). And we can add that life is more chaotic than posthumanists had imagined, too.

Our next and last step in this exegesis concerning poststructuralist theory is an understanding of another fundamental connection, life on Earth in general and human culture in particular as a form of matter. Our source is Karen Barad's attempt, which, as we will present it, introduces the notion of a measuring apparatus that connects the meaning and matter.

Meaning and matter

Karen Barad sees their work as posthumanist and in presenting it as poststructuralist and oriented by systematicity we are somewhat departing from their self-understanding. By posthumanism, Barad means principally that humans are not the measure of the world. This, however, is a spurious point since the measuring devices made by humans provide the link between scholarship and the world on which their argument turns. We will see the organization as, once again, neither centered nor decentered, but resulting from an attempt to bring the universe together and provide one framework and one kind of systematicity for convergence. We think that the question of humanism is no longer the referential point and are replacing it—following Barad who follows Foucault on this point—with the question concerning the apparatus. Apparatuses, we understand in an expansive way, not only as concrete measuring instruments, but, by extension, also including all kinds of measure, interpretation, and knowledge organization. We, too, can count in the referential system as used in trauma theory (Ramadanovic, "Time").

This is to say that if apparatus was in poststructuralist theory initially linked to oppression and represented as its means, we can rearticulate the same interpretation by focusing on convergences and transformations that are accomplished through it. Common to the two approaches is that apparatuses are forms of articulation that align what is, in classical vocabulary, the interpreter and the interpreted, the oppressor and the oppressed, allowing for mutual definition. In our take, device has a similar role. It produces the environment that it measures, is itself a product, and serves to define the interpretative or scientific approach. A kind of alternating current-like dialectical device.

The starting point of Barad's analysis is Niels Bohr quantum physics model defined by a double task, "understanding both the nature of nature and the nature of science" (247). Barad, too, sees their own work as engaged "*in the practice of science while addressing entangled question about the nature of scientific practice*" (248). The main question is the one discovered by quantum physics, where inquiry takes place in "the absence of a coherent interpretative framework" (Barad 250). Barad distinguishes between Heisenberg and Bohr's versions and interpretations. The principle of uncertainty "favors the notion that measurements disturb existing values, thereby placing a limit on our knowledge of the situation." Indeterminacy, on the other hand, suggests "that properties are only determinate given the existence of particular material arrangements that give definition to the corresponding concept in question" (Barad 261). The key point of Barad's explanation is Bohr's understanding that in the absence of appropriate device, "the value of the corresponding property will not be determinate" (263). In this case, we say that the property "is the result of the *inter-action* of the particle with the device" and we assign to *phenomenon* the meaning of action of measuring, no longer using it to identify "some preexisting measurement-independent object" (Barad 264).

This does not imply that "human observers determine the results" but "rather that the specific nature of the material arrangement of the apparatus is responsible" for the outcome (Barad 264). Indeed, such experiments have "definite, consistent, and reproducible" results regardless of who runs them (Barad 265). A corollary is a definition of reality as state determined through or recorded by a device. That is, the experimental setup allows us to again speak of "physical reality." Not as "an observation-independent object" but as property "'attached' to the notion of a phenomena that includes the ... experimental arrangement" (Barad 274–275). Real is an adjective and that which has been designed and defined by an experiment as such.

The switch from the Newtonian metaphysical setup to the incompleteness theory is no longer just a thought project. Since a 1964 paper, "On the Einstein Podolsky Rosen Paradox," by John Bell, there is an experiment confirming it. As Barad says, the boundary between physical and metaphysical worlds has moved to new position where physics can experimentally prove that reality is not independent from our devices (289), itself illustrating one of the main poststructuralist suppositions that interpretation plays a constitutive part in reality.

Bell's paper shows that the EPR (Einstein-Podolsky-Rosen paradox) rests on the assumption that there is no intervention whereas the setup of their thought experiment is already such intrusion. According to Barad, Bell's paper offers, "*empirical evidence for the existence of a different metaphysics than the one underlying Newtonian mechanics*" (291–292). And this goes not just for the quantum scale of infinitely small particles but for the universe, which fits quantum, not Newtonian, principles.

On this thinking, properties of "position" or "momentum" are not givens but "idealizations or abstractions" and do not have "determinate meanings" (Barad 296). Such values are supplied through interaction with a measuring device. The approach allows for an explanation of convergence for phenomena like particle and wave that are defined as contradictory in other frameworks including not just Newton's physics but also Heisenberg's uncertainty for which Bohr's indeterminacy is a corrective (Barad 301–302).

The central metaphor for the Bohr theory is an *entanglement* between "the object of observation" and the "agencies of observation" (Barad 308). The same metaphor offers new explanation for the complementarity principle which characterizes much of quantum physics and analysis by humanities scholars like Arkady Plotnitsky. Complementarity is usually understood in terms of independent properties of matter, like spin along different axes, position and momentum, wave or particle properties, entanglement or coherence, which cannot be determined at the same time because they are mutually exclusive. Barad shows, however, that such understanding rests on the ontological "inseparability of objects and agencies of observation" (Barad 308), which itself defines a convergence between the observer and the observed that this theory of indeterminacy provides. Physicist do not yet agree on this point, even though there is some experimental evidence for it. We think agreement is a matter of time, however, since it appears incoherent from our position that "reality" can have an independent status which the complementarity model presumes.

The contrary of incompleteness theory would depend on a wholly different theoretical setup which would have to prove the independence of reality from devices. As far as I can understand, the difficulty in accepting Barad's account on Bohr's indeterminacy theory is not scientific, but rather cultural, since what is at stake is the view of the world that supposes representational, not agential nature of science. Secular science requires us to be consequential which at this state of its development means providing explanations for the relation between knowledge production and material construction of reality in terms of agency. With Barad's theory, we are saying that reality is participatory, a result of practice and interactions between human beings, their apparatuses, and the world.

Once again, such theory does not say that reality is a projection that specific authors make. It suggests that phenomena we measure and the scholar are co-constituted in the process of observation. The old quandary whether the tree makes a noise when it falls in the woods has a simple answer in this setup: this is not the question to ask when the goal is to understand the nature of reality. Instead, we say that the tree, the fall, the noise, and the philosopher who can ask such a question are co-constituted. The terms used are all abstractions that in the process of coming together get concretized by that very action of asking a question and bringing the named entities or states into relations.

Put another way, we don't know what "tree," "noise," "woods," and so on mean until they become elements of the question, when "hearing" is presented as the criterion of presence and existence. In this case, the changing optics that allow us to notice the question as a device (noise as a property, philosopher as a part of the setup, and so on) is this new theory.

Put yet another way, the usual form of the question presumes a framework of philosophy and questioning that it does not account for in what it asks. Once we add that framework, we also rearticulate what "reality" is and see it then as *neither* a given nor the Kantian "for us." It is instead the setup that is put together through the thought experiment. In it, facts are what the measuring apparatus measures, and the outcome it proposes—the tree and noise/no-noise are again abstract options that get actualized in the inquiry.

The theory allows us to see essential convergence between humanities and scientific models of the world, which meet in this understanding of an interactive construction. Now, to repeat, this is no longer the social construction of reality. It, instead, is material, chemical, biological, and physical construction, a consequence of an interaction between the observed, the observer, and the apparatus that connects them.

Most importantly, with the new insights we can do away with the perspectival understanding according to which specific insights are characteristics of theories, not of reality they interpret. In the new setup, the approaches are all framed together through another viewpoint that sees reality as a material construct accomplished through particularly situated agents and their observations/actions.

The setup should be familiar to any scholar in literary studies. This because our reading has played the role of the apparatus for at least a generation. But there is also a crucial difference in so far as the attitude is no longer one of identifying particular position but constructing a new and different framework around the fragmented landscape by actively creating commonalities and gathering.

Notes

1 The approach is our alternative to, for instance, what Julian Williams et al. tried to do in *Interdisciplinary Mathematics Education*, by surveying historical disciplinarity, defining disciplinary knowledge, and then describing categories that are between interdisciplinarity and metadisciplinarity. From our position, the issue of interdisciplinarity is not one of generality but one of practice, goals, and adjustments.
2 The actual quote by Albert Einstein from which the phrase is borrowed also includes religion. He said, "All religions, arts and sciences are branches of the same tree" (Einstein 9).
3 *From Mathematics to Philosophy* by Hao Wang makes a similar point about "empty artificial structures" of analytic philosophy but in relation to content and facts (Wang 3).
4 Inkeri Koskinen and Uskali Mäki suggest that scholars are only beginning to systematize the divide and account for the impact of "extra-academic parties in academic knowledge production" (Koskinen and Mäki 419).
5 See also Stehr, Nico, and Peter Weingart, eds. *Practising Interdisciplinarity*.
6 Cunningham speaks of generalization but not of systematicity though he recognizes—in passing in an endnote—that system, like structure, is a "transdisciplinary concept" (Cunningham 104).
7 The email exchange took place on 10/24/2019.

CONCLUSION

Interdisciplinary curricular organization and the glue that holds it together

The argument of this book has moved toward the general point reached in the last chapter. Here, in lieu of a conclusion, I will sum up the steps for a curricular reform consistent with the approach defined in this book. I am presenting these steps, again, not as a specialist but as they follow from *Interdiscipline*.

I am well aware of the irony that education has seen continuous, failed attempts at reform. Proposing yet another makes little sense unless we try to change it all. Only an aspiration for a thoroughgoing reform that starts with pre-K could make a difference.

So, first, education reform should be a part of wider economic and political reforms whose goal is to lessen feudal differences in wealth and reaffirm the Enlightenment ideals of equality, liberty, and unity, of pursuit of truth in education and public life, and pursuit of happiness for everyone in their private lives. These reforms would follow the models of Reconstruction, the New Deal, and the GI Bill, and would also include indigenous people following the narrative of decolonization consistent with Roxanne Dunbar-Ortiz's *An Indigenous Peoples' History of the United States*.

Second, there should be one general framework for primary and secondary education.

Third, primary education should consist of integrated stories that include elements of biology, chemistry, physics, as well as history, philosophy, and psychology even in preschool—all a part of one great narrative that includes everyone and everything.

As the grades progress, the same framework would gain more and more detail.

The learning of writing should focus on learning the student's own language. Words like "atom," "cell," "molecule," and "force" can be learned in the first and second grades together with their rudimentary definitions. The silly fascination

DOI: 10.4324/9781003119616-7

with dinosaurs offered without context, for instance, could be replaced with the equally fascinating, context-specific micro life of prokaryotes and eukaryotes and other hard to pronounce mighty microorganisms and the role they play in the life on Earth. The story would continue through other basic processes of matter-transformation that sustain life, like photosynthesis, digestion, and breathing. Blood, red cells, white cells, T-cells, and organs, too, have their individual roles—all a part of a bigger picture that involves subjects like history, philosophy, psychology, and social studies.

In the current model, subjects, even when linked, tend to be presented without their relation to the general framework. This leads to shards of understanding. It also supports the belief that knowledge consists of fragments alone, that viewpoints cannot be reconciled, and that specializations are their own goal.

The reading materials for the lower elementary grades in my children's school were all poor-quality fiction. No science, history, or philosophical stories were told or read. Fiction is great only if children can distinguish the freedom and pleasure it affords from the demands of history and science. If there is no balance, the benefits from literature and the arts are bound to be limited, too.

Telling stories and reading is one of the most powerful tools we have. Children can begin to comprehend the fascinating Earth and the human story from an early age and the earliest times: the road from Africa, out of Africa again, around the Mediterranean, meeting Neanderthals and Denisovans, to Asia, to Australia, to the Americas, accompanied by the climate changes, skills and tools acquisition, art production, and settlements that changed it all. Students would thus create one overarching framework and bring together what are today still separate narratives of geography, history, and climate. Such a scaffolding supports easier processing of new information.

The story would be told again and again with another level of detail added with each iteration. The advantage of the approach is that students would be familiar with the framework while gradually learning new details and elements. They, too, would define their own place in respect to larger perspectives.

Math can be a part of the same framework. It too can be taught as a form of engagement, and from the big picture toward the particulars.

The principle is this: load students with great stories, with great connected details, by means of complex, comprehensive narratives with general reach, while explaining how students' own lives fit into the bigger pictures. In every task, combine abstract with particular, dwell on the meaning of words, and detail organization from sentence to paragraph to essay and beyond, to gadget to environment. Teach specifics and ask students to link them in writing again and again. A hands-on experience can acquire quite a different meaning when conceived through a narrative framework.

Today's education takes place in the context of lives led in front of screens, offering networks, games, movies, series, and other fictional accounts people tell, which have all but replaced students' social lives. In the process, the imagination is fed until one's sense of common reality bursts. Not having another structure that would help us understand the world makes the impact all that more devastating.

The proposal may sound like a secular religion and it is, in the sense that it offers one fascinating, overarching narrative about the miracle and fragility of the Earth, of which all other multiverses, including one's own, are intersecting parts.

One life. One planet. One story. One great puzzle.

This as a means to challenge other myths to which we cling in the absence of a common one.

Literary studies/the glue

Literary studies, due to its flexibility, can provide an overarching narrative for all education and scholarship by focusing on language, composition, and storytelling. It can also serve as the glue that brings the parts together and holds them there for a while. But this, again, if we are willing to revise what we are doing now and rearticulate literary studies as a theory and practice of interpretation, reading, and writing. Literature—novels, poems, dramas but also all other forms of fiction and text—can remain the privileged object of study due to its unique qualities. But this on condition that literature, too, is seen as a form among others; that narratives are approached for their connective and inclusive qualities, and that the understanding of interpretation includes scientific perspectives.

Interdiscipline has covered cognitive science, ecology, quantum physics, and digital technology. The explanations I have offered are not based on expertise in these fields, but on my shallow general knowledge and on the skills I developed as a reader that allowed me to learn quickly and make new information and ways of thinking a part of my interpretation. I am noting this to explain further the role that interpretation, this glue, plays in creating this whole, the links between distant entities, but also how far—with the aid of Google Book and Google Scholar search—one can get in understanding sciences without specialist knowledge, if only there is a general scaffolding (and a reading skill) as a reference system to accept the new information.

Such is the role of literary studies because it instructs us in reading, writing, and interpretation, providing a way to construct a whole in which parts keep their autonomy, maintain their agency, and are still ready for convergence with even divergent elements. Again, the reason to single out literary studies in this fashion is its closeness to language, as well as its privileged access to representation and storytelling or interpretation, which play key roles in integration of disparate and diverging elements and, hence, in this reform.

Curriculum organization can take a variety of shapes that combine skill development with content expertise. I am, however, going to refrain from defining an actual setup. The reader can see, for instance, what Eric Hayot has offered recently—a skill and theme four-course module based system, which is not unlike Brown University's curricular organization (Hayot, "Humanities as We Know Them").[1] Among the more important realizations of *Interdiscipline* is that we don't know how to do interdisciplinarity and often revert to disciplinary habits, behaviors, and ways of thinking. The most important change that needs to happen is not organizational but concerns the attitude with which we enter knowledge production. Creating that attitude shift and what we can call organic convergences will take time, effort, and a lot of good will.

The reason to preserve the integrity of disciplines is to provide continuity between old and new models and to benefit from what disciplines do well, namely, monitor boundaries, define methodologies, and defend the integrity of scholarship (even to its detriment). Self-protection can be reoriented from infighting, science and culture war-type battles to the political arena to help universities and education in general defend themselves against neoliberal and totalitarian attacks by writing op-eds, organizing marches and boycotts, and getting otherwise politically engaged. What should not be preserved, however, is the assumption that a discipline provides for the coherence of knowledge or even that it makes an adequate methodology available or that the discipline cannot be done differently.

The process of interdisciplinarization can start in the humanities by redesigning existing courses to include other disciplinary perspectives (following the principle of convergence, not an additive structure). I teach a lower-level course on race in the United States that offers literary, philosophical, historical, economic, cognitive, political, legal, and genetic understandings, each of which is meant to contribute to explaining what it means that race is a constructed category. Literature provides a world defined not just by race but, more importantly, by othering. Philosophy explains what race is, how it is related to literary representation, and nation building. History shows the means (science, journalism, fiction, politics) through which race in the United States got defined following the Civil War. Economics shows how the creation of generational wealth depends on race and class, what role government plays, and how the gap can be remedied. Cognitive science adds insight concerning implicit bias and how it can be altered. Political science allows us to see the tools we can use to alter constructions of race. Legal studies explains how and why police unions can resist change. Genetic understandings explain differences between groups on a genetic level, and how and why race is not a scientific category, and then also how individuals' development might depend on the chemical environment they live in. Having one instructor in this class makes it easier to receive the different insights as a part of the same complex narrative. A sense of unity is also provided through our routines and methodology. Our interpretations are based on close readings, during which we try to draw connections, and strive to identify elements of one composite picture. The same structure can be shared by several instructors willing to be led by convergence and to devote time to the complex work of integration. It is already shared by students who come from all over the campus and help me with their skills and expertise as we move through their areas of specialization.

Convergence can be grounded in the complex term "construction," which, at this time, provides the most immediate but also perhaps the only clear, significant, and common term of interdisciplinary knowledge production. This same organization is the most basic blueprint for other courses in literary studies that offer intersectional, synthetic accounts of complex problems by focusing first on the terms of construction and convergence.

Literature is about issues of general significance and part of what I am suggesting is already common practice in literary studies. However, currently, we ground our problem-based courses in our current notion of interdisciplinarity, which is additive and therefore inadequate, because it keeps the scientific and humanistic methodologies and interpretation separate. The goal is to replace that structure and the logic of centering classes around the objects of disciplines. We can do interdisciplinarity instead by focusing on creating common methodologies and epistemology through the practice of interpretation.

The Western system of periodization, the dominant model of literary studies even after the culture wars, is not generalizable. It therefore cannot serve to present a universal form or framework. This does not imply, however, that the literary studies that grew up as a Western or Anglo-American discipline must be West-centric. The discipline is open, and not because every culture has a narrative form of some kind. It is open based on the mindset with which we enter creation of a new universal framework. The model can grow from literary studies to other humanistic disciplines and then to other schools and colleges, respecting the need for the development of basic skills appropriate for each disciplinary methodology.

If the reader disagrees with the model proposed here, they can reject it only in whole. Any partial acceptance would mean the election of a categorically different setup, theory, and practice. In such a case, there is no possibility of another universal structure, but only a continuation of one or another form of fragmentation or a reversal to a one-size-fits-all model propagated by the original Enlightenment. Barring a catastrophe, however, we don't think that such a reversal is possible while continuing the drift in the current balkanized or postdisciplinary state is detrimental to literary studies, the humanities, and education in general.

The main advantage of this proposal is that it builds on existing university divisions, which it would reorganize from within by creating channels and centers—say, one per college or school—for interdisciplinary scholarship and education. These centers would split course organization with departments and offer an institutional stepping-stone for the transition. They would also become new homes for scholarly careers, redefining tenure and promotion requirements in the process. The more interdisciplinary engagements we want professors to have, the fewer publications they will be able to produce—because at this point in its development convergence is tantamount to another scholarly specialization. Implementing the practice of convergence at a university is equivalent to teaching. Universities also need to provide time and space for the work of integration to unfold, for faculty to become comfortable collaborating in changing configurations, and for new priorities to emerge.

The interdisciplinary centers would first teach general education courses, then gradually reorganize parts of the major curricula to make them as interdisciplinary as possible. Getting to this future from where we are requires faculty to change their attitudes and start thinking beyond their specializations, departments, and colleges; to cut out much waste that happens during the semester; to not teach courses that are easy A's; to believe that new content is exciting and necessary; and so on. We would not have to sacrifice teaching disciplinary methodology, but we would need to organize it differently and more efficiently, as a part of the development of cross-cutting skills.

The motivation to recognize the importance of convergence and a shared future should be spurred by necessity, of course, and today that necessity is perhaps clearer than it has been in a long while, since the modern, secular worldview is under threat and it and the state of the Earth are closely intertwined. Scientific, technical, and business schools and corporations are already well aware of the stakes. There is also an increasing number of attempts to bridge the divide nature/culture in scholarship and start creating a scientific worldview by humanist means.

Time wise, even though universities are like huge ships, because there is already a widespread interest in interdisciplinarity, significant changes can be seen within a decade.

A restricted version of the model would have humanities scholars teaching the majority of interdisciplinary courses and serving as convergence arbiters. This would be the case if public funds continue to diminish, and neoliberalism continues to win over American voters, or another tyrant is in office. In this case, faculty, students, and all allies would need to engage in civil disobedience. Elite universities would have to take on a new role—not only advocating for the general good but taking forceful political actions directed at the moneyed and political elites who disproportionally benefit from them.

An unrestricted version would have humanists increasingly join science, technology, and business projects. Initially, their role would be like that of the NGOs in the public sphere: to advocate for the parties or causes that could be impacted by research, including interdisciplinarity and convergences; as well as to help with the setup of research by carefully examining all those aspects of teaching and scholarship that could be considered cultural or constructed. A new relation between cultural and natural research would emerge out of such collaborations, as would new roles for humanists, new methodologies that bridge the nature/culture divide, and new understandings of how we can measure outcomes.

There is also a specific kind of danger that could be created, for instance, by a sudden influx of federal funds or by other limited financial improvements. Dominated by older faculty who benefit from the current arrangement, departments (literary studies first) might continue to refuse change in hopes that the effects of the crises would be finally reversed. Since the cycle of reproduction of both knowledge and professional positions in the humanities and especially literature departments has already been interrupted to a significant degree, the diminishment of the place we occupy in general knowledge production would only continue, regardless of the funds we receive.

To my mind, it is not just difficult but also liberating when you have no choice. Now is such a time and not only for the humanities but for post-Enlightenment society in general. Since many of the changes we define here are already underway, the additional steps we have proposed—systematizing the trends through common epistemology (bringing disparate, divergent efforts together by fostering reading skills) and orienting institutional reform toward fighting climate change, preserving the integrity of science, and lessening economic inequality—add up to a new and exciting scholarly agenda. If each generation has its specific task, creation of the new universal is ours.

Note

1 Hayot's *Humanist Reason: A History. An Argument. A Plan* has come to my attention only at the point of writing this conclusion. I am happy that *Interdiscipline* shares key ideas with his book, including a focus on epistemology, metadiscourse, truth, interdisciplinarity with the sciences, and the need for clarity, basic definitions, and order—though our approach, detail, and the processes we suggest could not be more different.

BIBLIOGRAPHY

Abbott, Andrew. *Chaos of Disciplines*, Chicago University Press, 2001.
Adams, Percy G. *Travel Literature and the Evolution of the Novel*, University Press of Kentucky, 2014.
Adorno, Theodor. *Negative Dialectics*. 1966. Translated by E.B. Ashton, Routledge, 1973.
Ahmed, Sara. *The Promise of Happiness*, Duke University Press, 2010.
Alaimo, Stacy. "Introduction: Science Studies and the Blue Humanities." *Configurations*, vol. 27, no. 4, 2019, pp. 429–432.
———. guest editor. *Science Studies and the Blue Humanities*. Special Issue of *Configurations*, vol. 27, no. 4, 2019, pp. 429–573.
———. *Exposed: Environmental Politics and Pleasures in Posthuman Times*, University of Minnesota Press, 2016.
———. "Sustainable This, Sustainable That: New Materialisms, Posthumanism, and Unknown Futures." *PMLA*, vol. 127, no. 3, 2012, pp. 558–564.
Alcoff, Linda Martín. "Comparative Epistemology." *Philosophy East and West*, vol. 69, no. 3, 2019, pp. 849–856.
———. "Mignolo's Epistemology of Coloniality." *CR: The New Centennial Review*, vol. 7, no. 3, Singularities of Latin American Philosophy, winter 2007, pp. 79–101.
———. *Real Knowing: New Versions of the Coherence Theory*, Cornell University Press, 1996.
Alder, Ken. "History of Science as Oxymoron: From Scientific Exceptionalism to Episcience." *Isis*, vol. 104, no. 1, 2013, pp. 88–101.
Allen, Amy. "Foucault and Enlightenment: A Critical Reappraisal." *Constellations*, vol. 10, no.2, 2002, pp. 180–198.
Alliez, Éric. "Rhizome (With no Return): From Structure to Rhizome: Transdisciplinarity in French Thought (2)." *Radical Philosophy*, vol. 167, no.1, 2011, pp. 36–42.
Allison, Sarah, et al. "Quantitative Formalism: An Experiment." *Stanford Literary Lab*, 15 January 2011, litlab.stanford.edu/LiteraryLabPamphlet1.pdf.
Althusser, Louis. "Ideology and Ideological State Apparatus." *Lenin and Philosophy and Other Essays*. Translated by Ben Brewster, New Left Books, 1971, pp. 85–126.
Altieri, Charles. "Appreciating Appreciation." *Criticism after Critique*, edited by Jeffrey Di Leo, Palgrave Macmillan, 2014, pp. 45–65.

Alvarez, Travis A. and Julie A. Fiez. "Current Perspectives on the Cerebellum and Reading Development." *Neuroscience & Biobehavioral Reviews*, vol. 92, 2018, pp. 55–66.

Ambroży, Paulina. *(Un)concealing the Hedgehog: Modernist and Postmodernist American Poetry and Contemporary Critical Theories*, Adam Mickiewicz University, 2012.

Anderson, Chris. "The End of Theory: The Data Deluge Makes the Scientific Method Obsolete." *Wired Magazine*, 23 June 2008, http://www.uvm.edu/pdodds/files/papers/others/2008/anderson2008a.pdf.

Anker, Elizabeth S. and Rita Felski, editors. *Critique and Postcritique*, Duke University Press, 2017.

Antonijević, Smiljana. *Amongst Digital Humanists: An Ethnographic Study of Digital Knowledge Production*, Springer, 2016.

Anzaldúa, Gloria. *Borderlands/La Frontera*, Aunt Lute Books, 1987.

Applebaum, Anne. "History Will Judge the Complicit." *The Atlantic*, July/August 2020, https://www.theatlantic.com/magazine/archive/2020/07/trumps-collaborators/612250/.

———. "A Warning From Europe: The Worst Is Yet to Come." *The Atlantic*, October 2018, https://www.theatlantic.com/magazine/archive/2018/10/poland-polarization/568324/.

———. *Red Famine: Stalin's War on Ukraine*, Signal, 2017.

Aram, John D. "Concepts of Interdisciplinarity: Configurations of Knowledge and Action." *Human Relations*, vol. 57, 2004, pp. 379–412.

The Arc of Narrative. "The Arc of Narrative." Accessed 21 March 2021. https://www.arcofnarrative.com.

Arendt, Hannah. *The Origins of Totalitarianism*, Houghton Mifflin Harcourt, 1973.

Armstrong, Isobel. *The Radical Aesthetic*, Wiley-Blackwell, 2000.

Aronowitz, Stanley. "The Last Good Job in America." *Social Text*, vol. 51, no. 2, 1997, pp. 93–108.

Ash, Mitchell G. "Interdisciplinarity in Historical Perspective." *Perspectives on Science*, vol. 27, no. 4, 2019, pp. 619–642.

———. "Die Wissenschaften in der Geschichte der Moderne." (The Sciences in the History of Modernity). *Österreichische Zeitschrift für Geschichtswissenschaften*, vol. 10, 1999, pp. 105–129. English abstract p. 131.

Atkin, Emily. "Scott Pruitt Has Laid Bare the Growing Environmental Schism Within Christianity." *Mother Jones*, 4 March 2018, https://www.motherjones.com/environment/2018/03/scott-pruitt-has-laid-bare-the-growing-environmental-schism-within-christianity/.

Attridge, Derek. "The Department of English and the Experience of Literature." *English Studies: The State of the Discipline, Past, Present, and Future*, edited by Niall Gildea et al., Springer, 2014, pp. 42–47.

Badiou, Alain. *I Know There Are So Many of You*. Translated by Susan Spitzer. John Wiley & Sons, 2018.

Bal, Mieke. *Travelling Concepts in the Humanities: A Rough Guide*, University of Toronto Press, 2002.

Baldick, Chris. *Criticism and Literary Theory 1890 to the Present*, Longman, 1996.

———. *The Social Mission of English Criticism, 1848–1932*, Clarendon, 1983.

Balsiger, Philip W. "Supradisciplinary Research Practices: History, Objectives and Rationale." *Futures*, vol. 36, no. 4, 2004, pp. 407–421.

Banac, Ivo, Jean Bethke Elshtain, and Robert Weisbuch. *The Humanities and Its Publics*. No. 61, American Council of Learned Societies, 2006.

Banta, Martha. "Editor's Column: Mental Work, Metal Work." *PMLA*, vol. 113, no. 2, 1998, pp. 199–211.
Barad, Karen. *Meeting the Universe Halfway: Quantum Physics and the Entanglement of Matter and Meaning*, Duke University Press, 2007.
Barker, Chris. *Cultural Studies: Theory and Practice*, Sage, 2003.
Barnett, Ronald. *Understanding the University: Institution, Idea, Possibilities*, Routledge, 2015.
———. *Imagining the University*, Routledge, 2013.
———. *Being a University*, Routledge, 2010.
Barrett, Lisa Feldman. *How Emotions Are Made: The Secret Life of the Brain*, Houghton Mifflin Harcourt, 2017.
———. "The Theory of Constructed Emotion: An Active Inference Account of Interoception and Categorization." *Social Cognitive and Affective Neuroscience*, vol. 12, no.1, 2017, pp. 1–23.
Barrow, Clyde W. *Universities and the Capitalist State: Corporate Liberalism and the Reconstruction of American Higher Education, 1894–1928*, University of Wisconsin Press, 1990.
Barry, Andrew and Georgina Born, editors. *Interdisciplinarity: Reconfigurations of the Social and Natural Sciences*, Routledge, 2013.
Barry, Andrew, Georgina Born, and Gisa Wezkalnys. "Logics of Interdisciplinarity." *Economy and Society*, vol. 37, 2008, pp. 20–49.
Barthes, Roland. "The Death of the Author." *Contributions in Philosophy*, vol. 83, 2001, pp. 3–8.
Belfield, Chris et al. "The Relative Labour Market Returns to Different Degrees." Department for Education (UK). Digital Education Resource Archive (DERA), https://dera.ioe.ac.uk/33025/1/The_relative_labour_market-returns_to_different_degrees.pdf.
Belfiore, Eleonora and Anna Upchurch. *Humanities in the Twenty-First Century: Beyond Utility and Markets*, Springer, 2013.
Belsey, Catherine. "Constructing the Subject: Deconstructing the Text." *Feminist Criticism and Social Change*, vol. 53, 1985, pp. 45–64.
Benjamin, Walter. *The Work of Art in the Age of Mechanical Reproduction*. Translated by J.A. Underwood, Penguin UK, 2008.
———. "On Surrealism." *Reflections*. Translated by Edmund Jephcott. Edited by Peter Demetz, Schocken Books, 1986.
Bennett, Andrew. "The Values of Literary Studies: Critical Institutions, Scholarly Agendas." *Textual Practice*, vol. 30, no. 6, 2016, pp. 1135–1137.
Bennett, Katherine Egan, Reshma Jagsi, and Anthony Zietman. "Radiation Oncology Authors and Reviewers Prefer Double-Blind Peer Review." *Proceedings of the National Academy of Sciences of the United States of America*, vol. 115, no. 9, 2018, p. E1940.
Benneworth, Paul. "Tracing How Arts and Humanities Research Translates, Circulates and Consolidates in Society." *Arts and Humanities in Higher Education*, vol. 14, no. 1, 2015, pp. 45–60.
Bergmann, Matthias et al. *Quality Criteria of Transdisciplinary Research. A Guide for the Formative Evaluation of Research Projects*. ISOE-Studientexte, 13. Frankfurt am Main: ISOE – Institute for Social-Ecological Research, 2005.
Bertolaso, Marta. "Epistemology in Life Sciences. An Integrative Approach to a Complex System Like Cancer." *Ludus Vitalis*, vol. 19, no. 36, 2016, pp. 245–249.
———. *Philosophy of Cancer*, Springer, 2016.
Bérubé, Michael. "The Way We Review Now." *PMLA*, vol. 133, no. 1, 2018, pp. 132–138.

———. "The Humanities, Declining? Not According to the Numbers." *The Chronicle of Higher Education*, 1 July 2013, https://www.chronicle.com/article/the-humanities-declining-not-according-to-the-numbers.

———. *The Employment of English: Theory, Jobs, and the Future of Literary Studies*, New York University Press, 1998.

Best, Stephen and Sharon Marcus. "Surface Reading: An Introduction." *Representations*, vol. 108, no.1, 2009, pp. 1–21.

Biagioli, Mario. "Postdisciplinary Liaisons: Science Studies and the Humanities." *Critical Inquiry*, Special issue, "The Fate of Disciplines" edited by James Chandler and Arnold I. Davidson, vol. 35, no. 4, 2009, pp. 816–833.

———. "From Book Censorship to Academic Peer Review." *Emergences*, vol. 12, no. 1, 2002, pp. 11–45.

Binder, Amy J. and Kate Wood. *Becoming Right: How Campuses Shape Young Conservatives*, Princeton University Press, 2014.

Blok, Anders and Casper Bruun Jensen. "Redistributing Critique." *Latour and the Humanities*, edited by Rita Felski and Stephen Muecke, Johns Hopkins University Press, 2020, pp. 132–157.

Bloom, Harold. *The Western Canon*, Houghton Mifflin Harcourt, 2014.

Boaz, Annette, Siobhan Fitzpatrick, and Ben Shaw. "Assessing the Impact of Research on Policy: A Literature Review." *Science and Public Policy*, vol. 36, no. 4, pp. 255–270.

Bode, Katherine. "Why You Can't Model Away Bias." *Modern Language Quarterly*, vol. 81, no. 1, 2020, pp. 95–124.

———. "The Equivalence of 'Close' and 'Distant' Reading; Or, Toward a New Object for Data-rich Literary History." *Modern Language Quarterly*, vol. 78, no. 1, 2017, pp. 77–106.

Bollinger, Laurel. "'I Shall Be Telling This with a Sigh': Choice Blindness and Cognitive Processing in Frost's 'The Road Not Taken'." *Teaching American Literature*, vol. 8, no. 1, 2015, pp. 1–10.

Bono, James, Tim Dean, and Ewa Plonowska Ziarek. *A Time for the Humanities: Futurity and the Limits of Autonomy*, Fordham University Press, 2009.

Booth, Alison. "Mid-range Reading: Not a Manifesto." *PMLA*, vol. 132, no. 3, 2017, pp. 620–627.

Booth, Alison and Miriam Posner. "Introduction: The Materials at Hand." *Special Topic: Varieties of Digital Humanities*. PMLA, vol. 135, no. 1, 2020, pp. 9–22.

Booth, Stephen. *An Essay on Shakespeare's Sonnets*, Yale University Press, 1969.

Booth, Wayne C. *The Rhetoric of Fiction*, University of Chicago Press, 2010.

Borgman, Christine L. *Scholarship in the Digital Age: Information, Infrastructure, and the Internet*, MIT University Press, 2010.

Bornmann, Lutz and Hans-Dieter Daniel "Reliability of Reviewers' Ratings When Using Public Peer Review: A Case Study." *Learned Publishing*, vol. 23, no. 2, 2010, pp. 124–131.

Bostrom, Nick. *Superintelligence: Paths, Dangers, Strategies*, Oxford University Press, 2014.

Boucaud-Victoire, Kévin. "How Michel Foucault Got Neoliberalism So Wrong—Interview with Daniel Zamora." Trans. Seth Ackerman. Jacobin. 09/06/2019. https://jacobinmag.com/2019/09/michel-foucault-neoliberalism-friedrich-hayek-milton-friedman-gary-becker-minoritarian-governments

Bourdieu, Pierre. *The Logic of Practice*. Translated by Richard Nice, Stanford University Press, 1980.

Bové, Paul A. *Mastering Discourse: The Politics of Intellectual Culture*, Duke University Press, 1992.

boyd, danah and Kate Crawford. "Critical Questions for Big Data." *Information, Communication & Society*, vol. 15, no. 5, 2012, pp. 662–679.

Boyd, Ryan L., Kate G. Blackburn, and James W. Pennebaker. "The Narrative Arc: Revealing Core Narrative Structures through Text Analysis." *Science Advances*, vol. 6, no. 32, 2020, https://advances.sciencemag.org/content/6/32/eaba2196/tab-pdf.

Boyington, Briana and Emma Kerr. "Years of Tuition Growth at National Universities." *US News*, 21 September 2020, https://www.usnews.com/education/best-colleges/paying-for-college/articles/2017-09-20/see-20-years-of-tuition-growth-at-national-universities#:~:text=But%20data%20from%20the%20past, out%2Dof%2Dstate%20students.&text=The%20average%20tuition%20and%20fees, National%20Universities%20have%20jumped%20144%25.

Boym, Svetlana. *The Future of Nostalgia*, Basic Books, 2008.

Bozovic, Marijeta. "Whose Forms? Missing Russians in Caroline Levine's Forms." *PMLA*, vol. 132, no. 5, 2017, pp. 1181–1186.

Braidotti, Rosi. *Posthuman Knowledge*, John Wiley & Sons, 2019.

———. "A Theoretical Framework for the Critical Posthumanities." *Theory, Culture & Society*, vol. 36, no. 6, 2018, pp. 31–61.

Breithaupt, Fritz. "Designing a Lab in the Humanities." *The Chronicle of Higher Education*, 6 February 2017, https://www.chronicle.com/article/designing-a-lab-in-the-humanities.

Breu, Christopher. Review of *The Humanities "Crisis" and the Future of Literary Studies*, by Paul Jay. *College Literature*, vol. 42, no. 2, 2015, pp. 348–351.

Brint, Steven. *In an Age of Experts: The Changing Role of Professionals in Politics and Public Life*, Princeton University Press, 1996.

Britton, Austin Dennis and Kimberly Ann Coles. "Spenser and Race: An Introduction." *Spenser Studies*, vol. 35, 2021, pp. 1–19.

Brooks, Cleanth and Robert Penn Warren. *Understanding Poetry*, Holt Rinehart and Winston, 1960.

Brown, Angus Connell. "Cultural Studies and Close Reading." *PMLA*, vol. 132, no. 5, 2017, pp. 1187–1193.

Brown, Jeffrey R. and Caroline M. Hoxby, editors. *How the Financial Crisis and Great Recession Affected Higher Education*, University of Chicago Press, 2014.

Brown, Wendy. *Undoing the Demos: Neoliberalism's Stealth Revolution*, MIT Press, 2015.

Brown University. "Africana Studies." https://africana.brown.edu/

Brown University. "Departments, Centers, Programs and Institutes." https://bulletin.brown.edu/departments-centers-programs-institutes/

Brubaker, Rogers. "Populism and Nationalism." *Nations and Nationalism*, vol. 26, no. 1, 2020, pp. 44–66.

Bruce, Rachel et al. "Impact of Interventions to Improve the Quality of Peer Review of Biomedical Journals: A Systematic Review and Meta-analysis." *BMC Medicine*, vol. 14, 2016, https://bmcmedicine.biomedcentral.com/articles/10.1186/s12916-016-0631-5.

Brukner, Časlav. "A No-go Theorem for Observer-Independent Facts." *Entropy*, vol. 20, no.350, 2018.

Brummett, Barry. *Techniques of Close Reading*, Sage Publications, 2018.

Bruns, Gerald L. "Literary Study without Aims and Methods." *ADE Bulletin*, vol. 81, 1985, pp. 26–31.

Bruns, Hille. "Working Alone Together: Coordination in Collaboration across Domains of Expertise." *Academy of Management Journal*, vol. 56, no. 1, 2013, pp. 62–83.

Buanes, Arild and Svein Jentoft. "Building Bridges: Institutional Perspectives on Interdisciplinarity." *Futures*, vol. 41, no. 7, 2009, pp. 446–454.

Buchanan, Ian and Celina Jeffery. "Towards A Blue Humanity." Symplokē, vol. 27, no. 1–2, 2019, pp. 11–14.
Buck-Morss, Susan. *Hegel, Haiti, and Universal History*. University of Pittsburgh Press, 2009.
——. "Hegel and Haiti." *Critical Inquiry*, vol. 26, no. 4, 2000, pp. 821–865.
Budd, Graham E. et al. "History Is Written by the Victors: The Effect of the Push of the Past on the Fossil Record." *Evolution*, vol. 72, no. 11, 2018, pp. 2276–2291.
Burdick, Anne et al. eds. *Digital Humanities*, MIT Press, 2012.
Burnham, John C. "The Evolution of Editorial Peer Review." *JAMA*, vol. 263, no. 10, 1990, pp. 1323–1329.
Butler, Judith. "Critique, Dissent, Disciplinarity." *Critical Inquiry*. Special issue, "The Fate of Disciplines" edited by James Chandler and Arnold I. Davidson, vol. 35, no. 4, 2009, pp. 773–795.
——. *Bodies that Matter: On the Discursive Limits of Sex*. Routledge, 2011.
Byrne, Kathryn. *The Give and Take of Peer Review: Utilizing Modeling and Imitation*. 2016. Kent State University, PhD Dissertation.
Cabral, Angelica. "The Renaissance of the Humble Radio Drama." *Slate*, 20 July 2017, https://slate.com/technology/2017/07/radio-dramas-still-have-an-important-place-in-the-entertainment-world.html.
Calude, Cristian S. and Giuseppe Longo. "The Deluge of Spurious Correlations in Big Data." *Foundations of Science*, vol. 22, 2017, pp. 595–612.
Camera, Lauren. "Across the Board, Scores Drop in Math and Reading for U.S. Students." *US News*, 30 October 2019, https://www.usnews.com/news/education-news/articles/2019-10-30/across-the-board-scores-drop-in-math-and-reading-for-us-students.
Caputi, Mary and Vincent J. Del Casino Jr, editors. *Derrida and the Future of the Liberal Arts: Professions of Faith*, A&C Black, 2013.
Caracciolo, Marco. "Flocking Together: Collective Animal Minds in Contemporary Fiction." *PMLA*, vol. 135, no. 2, 2020, pp. 239–253.
Cartwright, Kent. "The Health of the English Major." *Inside Higher Ed*. 3, January 2019, https://www.insidehighered.com/views/2019/01/03/examination-strengths-and-weaknesses-english-major-opinion.
Caruth, Cathy, editor. *Trauma: Explorations in Memory*, Johns Hopkins University Press, 1995.
Casadevall, Arturo and Ferric C. Fang, "Specialized Science." *Infection and Immunity*, vol. 82, no. 4, 2014, pp. 1355–1360.
Cassuto, Leonard and Robert Weisbuch. *The New PhD: How to Build a Better Graduate Education*, Johns Hopkins University Press, 2021.
Chakrabarty, Dipesh. *Provincializing Europe: Postcolonial Thought and Historical Difference*, Princeton University Press, 2008.
Chandler, James. "Introduction: Doctrines, Disciplines, Discourses, Departments." *Critical Inquiry*. Special issue, "The Fate of Disciplines" edited by James Chandler and Arnold I. Davidson, vol. 35, no. 4, 2009, pp. 729–746.
Charan, Mona. *Sex Matters: How Modern Feminism Lost Touch with Science, Love, and Common Sense*, New York: Penguin, 2018.
Chase, James and Jack Reynolds. *Analytic Versus Continental: Arguments on the Methods and Value of Philosophy*, Routledge, 2014.
Chenoweth, Erica and Maria J. Stephan. *Why Civil Resistance Works: The Strategic Logic of Nonviolent Conflict*, Columbia University Press, 2011.

Choi, Bernard CK and Anita W. P. Pak. "Multidisciplinarity, Interdisciplinarity and Transdisciplinarity in Health Research, Services, Education and Policy: 1. Definitions, Objectives, and Evidence of Effectiveness." *Clinical and Investigative Medicine*, vol. 29, no. 6, pp. 351–364.

Christian, Brian. *The Alignment Problem: Machine Learning and Human Values*, Norton, 2020.

Citton, Yves. "Fictional Attachment and Literary Weavings in the Antropocene." *Latour and the Humanities*, edited by Rita Felski and Stephen Muecke, Johns Hopkins University Press, 2020 pp. 200–224.

Clabaugh, Gary K. "The Educational Legacy of Ronald Reagan." *Educational Horizons*, vol. 82, no. 4, 2004, pp. 256–259.

Clement, Tanya and Gretch Gueguen. "Annotated Overview of Selected Electronic Resources." *Companion to Digital Literary Studies*, edited by Susan Schreibman and Ray Siemens, Blackwell, 2008, http://www.digitalhumanities.org/companion/view?docId=blackwell/9781405148641/9781405148641.xml&chunk.id=ss1-6-13&toc.depth=1&toc.id=ss1-6-13&brand=9781405148641_brand.

Clune, Michael W. "Formalism as the Fear of Ideas." *PMLA*, vol. 132, no. 5, 2017, pp. 1194–1199.

Coates, Ta-Nehisi. "The Case for Reparations." *The Atlantic*, vol. 313, no. 5, 2014, pp. 54–71.

Cohen, Tom. "Toxic Assets: de Man's Remains and the Eco-catastrophic Imaginary (An American Fable)." *Theory and the Disappearing Future: On de Man, on Benjamin*, edited by Tom Cohen, Claire Colebrook, and J. Hillis Miller, Routledge, 2012, pp. 89–129.

Colebrook, Claire. *New Literary Histories: New Historicism and Contemporary Criticism*, Manchester University Press, 1997.

Collini, Stefan. *Speaking of Universities*, Verso Books, 2017.

———. "Seeing a Specialist: The Humanities as Disciplines." *Past and Present*, vol. 229, no. 1, 2015, pp. 271–281.

———. *What Are Universities For?* Penguin UK, 2012.

———. "Postscript: Disciplines, Canons, and Publics. The History of the History of Political Thought in Comparative Perspective." *The History of Political Thought in National Context*, edited by Dario Castiglione and Iain Hampsher-Mark, Cambridge University Press, 2001, pp. 280–302.

Collins, Patricia Hill and Sirma Bilge. *Intersectionality*, John Wiley & Sons, 2016.

———. *Black Feminist Thought: Knowledge, Consciousness, and the Politics of Empowerment*, Routledge, 2002.

———. "Gender, Black Feminism, and Black Political Economy." *The Annals of the American Academy of Political and Social Science*, vol. 568, no. 1, 2000, pp. 41–53.

Committee on Facilitating Interdisciplinary Research. *Facilitating Interdisciplinary Research*. National Academies, 2005, https://www.nap.edu/read/11153/chapter/1.

Committee on Reproducibility and Replicability in Science. "Reproducibility and Replicability in Science." National Academies of Sciences, Engineering, and Medicine, National Academies Press, 2019, https://www.nationalacademies.org/our-work/reproducibility-and-replicability-in-science.

Comparative Literary Studies, "Comparative Literary Studies Journal," https://complit.la.psu.edu/journals/comparative-literature-studies, Accessed 20 March 2021.

Coward, Harold and Toby Foshay, editors. *Derrida and Negative Theology*, SUNY Press, 1992.

Crane, Ronald Salmon. "History versus Criticism in the University Study of Literature." *The English Journal*, vol. 24, 1935, pp. 645–667.

Crenshaw, Kimberlé. "Mapping the Margins: Intersectionality, Identity Politics, and Violence against Women of Color." *Stanford Law Review*, vol. 43, no. 6, 1991, pp. 1241–1299.

———. "Demarginalizing the Intersection of Race and Sex: A Black Feminist Critique of Antidiscrimination Doctrine, Feminist Theory and Antiracist Politics." *University of Chicago Legal Forum*, vol. 1, no. 8, 1989, pp. 139–167.

Crews, Frederick. *Freud: The Making of an Illusion*, Profile Books, 2017.

Cross, Nigel. *Design Thinking: Understanding How Designers Think and Work*, Berg, 2011.

Culler, Jonathan. "The Closeness of Close Reading." *ADE Bulletin*, vol. 149, 2010, pp. 20–25.

———. *Framing the Sign: Criticism and its Institutions*, University of Oklahoma Press, 1988.

Cullum, Angela et al. "Cerebellar Activation During Reading Tasks: Exploring the Dichotomy Between Motor vs. Language Functions in Adults of Varying Reading Proficiency." *The Cerebellum*, vol. 18, no. 4, 2019, pp. 688–704.

Cunningham, David. "Logics of Generalization: Derrida, Grammatology and Transdisciplinarity." *Theory, Culture & Society*, vol. 32, no. 5–6, 2015, pp. 79–107.

Curedale, Robert. *Design Thinking: Process and Methods Manual*, Design Community College, 2013.

Da, Nan Z. "Critical Response III. On EDA, Complexity, and Redundancy: A Response to Underwood and Weatherby." *Critical Inquiry*, vol. 46, no. 4, 2020, pp. 913–924.

———. "The Computational Case against Computational Literary Studies." *Critical inquiry*, vol. 45, no. 3, 2019, pp. 601–639.

Damasio, Antonio R. *Self Comes to Mind: Constructing the Conscious Brain*, Vintage, 2012.

Darling, E. S. "Use of Double-blind Peer Review to Increase Author Diversity." *Conservation Biology*, vol. 29, no. 1, 2015, pp. 297–299.

Daston, Lorraine. "History of Science and History of Knowledge." *Know: A Journal on the Formation of Knowledge*, vol. 1, no. 1, 2017, pp. 131–154.

———. "Science Studies and the History of Science." *Critical Inquiry*, Special issue, "The Fate of Disciplines" edited by James Chandler and Arnold I. Davidson, vol. 35, 2009, pp. 798–813.

Davidson, N. Cathy. "Humanities 2.0: Promise, Perils, Predictions." *PMLA*, vol. 123, no. 3, 2008, pp. 707–717.

Davidson, Cathy N and Valerie Strauss, "The Surprising Thing Google Learned about Its Employees–and What It Means for Today's Students." *Washington Post*, 20 December 2017, https://www.washingtonpost.com/news/answer-sheet/wp/2017/12/20/the-surprising-thing-google-learned-about-its-employees-and-what-it-means-for-todays-students/.

Davis, Colin. *After Poststructuralism: Reading, Stories and Theory*, Routledge, 2004.

Dawkins, Richard. *The Selfish Gene*, Oxford University Press, 1976.

Deacon, Terrence. *Incomplete Nature: How Mind Emerged from Matter*, Norton, 2012.

Defila, Rico and Antonietta Di Giulio. "Evaluating Transdisciplinary Research," *PANORAMA (Newsletter of the Swiss Priority Program Environment, Swiss National Science Foundation)*, 1999, http://www.ikaoe.unibe.ch/forschung/ip/Specialissue.Pano.1.99.pdf, accessed 25 May 2018.

Delbanco, Andrew. "A New Day for Intellectuals." *Chronicle of Higher Education*, 13 February 2009, http://chronicle.com/article/A-New-Day-for-Intellectuals/21359.

Deleuze, Gilles. *Empiricism and Subjectivity: An Essay on Hume's Theory of Human Nature*. Translated by Constantin V. Boundas, Columbia University Press, 1989.

Deleuze, Gilles and Félix Guattari. *A Thousand Plateaus: Capitalism and Schizophrenia*. Translated by Brian Massumi, Continuum, 2004.

de Man, Paul. "The Return to Philology." *The Resistance to Theory*, University of Minnesota Press, 1986, pp. 21–26.

———. "Criticism and Crisis." *Blindness and Insight: Essays in the Rhetoric of Contemporary Criticism*, vol. 197, no. 1, 1983, pp. 3–19.

———. "Literary History and Literary Modernity" *Daedalus*, Vol. 99, no. 2, Theory in Humanistic Studies (Spring, 1970), pp. 384–404.

Denson, Shane. "Open Peer-Review as Multimodal Scholarship." *Cinema Journal*, vol. 56, no. 4, 2017, pp. 141–143.

Derrida, Jacques. *Dissemination*. Translated by Barbara Johnson, Continuum, 2004.

———. *Eyes of the University: Right to Philosophy 2*. Translated by Jan Plug, et al., Stanford University Press, 2004.

———. *Rogues: Two Essays on Reasons*, Stanford University Press, 2004.

———. "Che cos' è la poesia?" *Angelus Novus*, 2003.

———. "The University without Condition." *Without Alibi*. Translated by Peggy Kamuf, Stanford University Press, 2002, pp. 202–237.

———. *Archive Fever: A Freudian Impression*. Translated by Eric Prenowitz, University of Chicago Press, 1998.

———. *Monolingualism of the Other, or, the Prosthesis of Origin*. Translated by Patrick Mensah, Stanford University Press, 1998.

———. *On the Name*. Translated by David Wood, et al., Stanford University Press, 1995.

———. *Specters of Marx: The State of the Debt, the Work of Mourning, and the New International*. Translated by Peggy Kamuf, Routledge, 1994.

———. "The Purveyor of Truth." Translated by Alan Bass. *The Purloined Poe*, edited by John P. Muller and William J. Richardson, Johns Hopkins University Press, 1988, pp. 173–212.

———. *The Post Card: From Socrates to Freud and Beyond*, University of Chicago Press, 1987.

———. "Geschlecht II: Heidegger's Hand." *Deconstruction and Philosophy: The Texts of Jacques Derrida*, edited by John Sallis. Translated by John P. Leavey, Jr., University of Chicago Press, 1987, pp. 161–196.

———. *Positions*. Translated by Alan Bass, University of Chicago Press, 1981.

———. "Structure, Sign, and Play in the Discourse of the Human Sciences." *Writing and Difference*. University of Chicago Press, 1978, pp. 278–294.

———. "Limited Inc. a b c ..." Translated by Samuel Weber. *Glyph*, no. 2, 1977.

———. *Of Grammatology*. Translated by Gayatri Chakravorty Spivak, Johns Hopkins University Press, 1976.

———. "The Purveyor of Truth." Translated by Willis Domingo, James Hulbert, Moshe Ron, M.-R. L. *Yale French Studies*, No. 52, 1975, pp. 31–113.

Devezer, Berna, Nardin Luis G. et al. "Scientific Discovery in a Model-centric Framework: Reproducibility, Innovation, and Epistemic Diversity." *PLoS ONE*, vol. 14, no. 5, 2019, e0216125, https://doi.org/10.1371/journal.pone.0216125

de Vrieze, Jop. "Bruno Latour, a Veteran of the 'Science Wars,' Has a New Mission." *Science Magazine*, 10 October 2017, https://www.sciencemag.org/news/2017/10/bruno-latour-veteran-science-wars-has-new-mission.

Di Leo, Jeffrey R. "Editor's Note." *symplokē*, vol. 27, no. 1–2, Blue Humanities, 2019, pp. 7–10.

———. *Corporate Humanities in Higher Education: Moving Beyond the Neoliberal Academy*, Springer, 2013.

Diamond, Jared. *Guns, Germs and Steel: A Short History of Everybody for the Last 13,000 Years*, Random House, 2013.

Digital Humanities. UCLA. Accessed 21 March 2021, https://dh.ucla.edu/

Digital Scholarship Lab, University of Richmond, "Renewing Inequality: Urban Renewal, Family Displacement, and Race, 1955–1966," Renewing Inequality, 2017, dsl.richmond.edu/panorama/renewal/.

Dillenbourg, Pierre. "What do You Mean by Collaborative Learning?" *Collaborative-learning: Cognitive and Computational Approaches*, edited by Pierre Dillenbourg, Elsevier, 1999, pp. 1–19.

Dobson, James E. *Critical Digital Humanities: The Search for a Methodology*, University of Illinois Press, 2019.

Donoghue, Frank. *The Last Professors: The Corporate University and the Fate of the Humanities*, Fordham University Press, 2018.

Douglass, Frederick. "One Composite Nationality." *The Speeches of Frederick Douglass: A Critical Edition*, edited by John R. McKivigan, Julie Husband, and Heather L. Kaufman. Yale University Press, 2018, pp. 278–303.

Dovey, Jon. "Context and Debates." *Journal of Media Practice*, vol. 8, no. 1, 2007, pp. 63–70.

Doyle, Bob. "How the Mind Uses Natural Constraints to Further Its Goals." *BioScience*, vol. 62, no. 3, 2012, pp. 311–313.

Drucker, Johanna. "Why Distant Reading Isn't." *PMLA*, vol. 132, no. 3, 2017, pp. 628–635.

Dunbar-Ortiz, Roxanne. *An Indigenous Peoples' History of the United States*, Beacon Press, 2014.

Duncker, Elke. "Symbolic Communication in Multidisciplinary Cooperations." *Science, Technology & Human Values*, vol. 26, 2001, pp. 349–386.

Du Bois, William Edward Burghardt. *The Conservation of Races*, Good Press, 2020.

———. *The Souls of Black Folk*, Oxford University Press, 2008.

Eaglestone, Robert. *Doing English: A Guide for Literature Students*, Routledge, 2017.

———. "The Future of English and Institutional Consciousness: Threats and Disengagement." *English Studies: The State of the Discipline, Past, Present, and Future*, edited by Niall Gildea, et al., 2014, pp. 100–113.

———. "Framing Theory." *English: The Condition of the Subject*, edited by Philip W. Martin, Palgrave Macmillan, 2006, pp. 161–167.

Eagleton, Terry. *After Theory*, Penguin UK, 2004.

———. *The Ideology of the Aesthetic*, Blackwell, 1990.

Earlie, Paul. "Derrida's *Archive Fever*: From Debt to Inheritance." *Paragraph*, vol. 38, no. 3, 2015, pp. 312–328.

Edington, Mark. "Losing Our Modesty: The Content and Communication of Peer Review." *Journal of Scholarly Publishing*, vol. 49, no. 3, 2018, pp. 287–319.

Edmundson, Mark. *Why Teach? In Defense of a Real Education*, Bloomsbury, 2014.

Einstein, Albert. *Out of My Later Years: The Scientist, Philosopher, and Man Portrayed Through His Own Words*, Citadel Press, 1956.

Eliot, Thomas Stearns. *The Sacred Wood: Essays on Poetry and Criticism*, Methuen, 1920.

Elliott, Jack. "Unsupervised Learning of Plot Structure: A Study in Category Romance." *DH*, 2013, pp. 172–173.

Ellrich, Robert J. "De Man's Purloined Meaning." *MLN*, vol. 106, no. 5, 1991, pp. 1048–1051.

Empson, William. *Seven Types of Ambiguity*, New Directions, 1947.

European Union Research Advisory Board. *Interdisciplinarity in Research*, 2004, http://europa.eu.int/comm/research/eurab/pdf/.

Eve, Martin Paul. *Close Reading with Computers: Textual Scholarship, Computational Formalism, and David Mitchell's Cloud Atlas*, Stanford University Press, 2019.

Fabiato, Alexandre. "Autonomy of Reviewers." *Cardiovascular Research*, vol. 28, 1994, pp. 1134–1139.
Farias, Victor. *Heidegger and Nazism*, Temple University Press, 1989.
Farina, Gabriella. "Some Reflections on the Phenomenological Method." *Dialogues in Philosophy, Mental and Neuro Sciences*, vol. 7, no. 2, 2014, pp. 50–62.
Favareau, Donald. *Essential Readings in Biosemiotics: Anthology and Commentary*, Springer Science & Business Media, 2010.
Faye, Emmanuel. *Heidegger, the Introduction of Nazism into Philosophy in Light of the Unpublished Seminars of 1933–1935*, Yale University Press, 2009.
Federico, Annette. *Engagements with Close Reading*, Taylor and Francis, 2015.
Felman, Shoshana and Dori Laub. *Testimony: Crises of Witnessing in Literature, Psychoanalysis, and History*, Taylor & Francis, 1992.
Felski, Rita. *The Limits of Critique*, University of Chicago Press, 2015.
———. *Uses of Literature*, John Wiley & Sons, 2011.
Ferguson, Frances. "Planetary Literary History: The Place of the Text." *New Literary History*, vol. 39, no. 3, 2008, pp. 657–684.
Ferris, Darcia J. "Elon Musk to Unveil Neuralink Progress with Real-Time Neuron Demonstration This Week." *Teslarati*, 23 August 2020, https://www.teslarati.com/elon-musk-neuralink-neuron-demonstration-event.
Feyerabend, Paul. *Against Method*, Verso, 1993.
Fish, Stanley. "Being Interdisciplinary Is So Very Hard to Do." *Profession*, 1989, pp. 15–22.
———. "No Bias, No Merit: The Case against Blind Submission." *PMLA*, vol. 103, no. 5, 1988, pp. 739–745.
———. "How to Recognize a Poem When You See One." *Is There a Text in This Class? The Authority of Interpretive Communities*, Harvard University Press, 1980, pp. 322–337.
———. *Is There a Text in This Class? The Authority of Interpretive Communities*, Harvard University Press, 1980.
Fisseni, Bernhard, Aadil Kurji, and Benedikt Löwe, "Annotating With Propp's *Morphology of the Folktale*: Reproducibility and Trainability." *Literary and Linguistic Computing*, vol. 29, no. 4, 2014, pp. 488–510.
Fitzpatrick, Kathleen. *Generous Thinking: A Radical Approach to Saving the University*, Johns Hopkins University Press, 2019.
———. *Planned Obsolescence: Publishing, Technology, and the Future of the Academy*, New York University Press, 2011.
Flynn, Elizabeth A. and Patrocinio P. Schweickart. *Gender and Reading Essays on Readers, Texts, and Contexts*, Johns Hopkins University Press, 1986.
Forrester, Sibelan, editor. *The Russian Folktale by Vladimit Yakovlevic Propp*. Translated by Sibelan Forrester, Wayne State University Press, 2012.
Foster, Ian et al., editors. *Big Data and Social Science: A Practical Guide to Methods and Tools*, Taylor and Francis Group, 2019.
Foucault, Michel. *Archaeology of Knowledge*, Routledge, 2013.
———. "The Art of Telling the Truth." *Critique and Power: Recasting the Foucault/Habermas Debate*, edited by Michael Kelly, MIT Press, 1994, pp. 139–148.
———. "What Is Enlightenment?" *The Foucault Reader*, edited by Paul Rabinow, Pantheon, 1984, pp. 32–50.
———. *Power/ Knowledge: Selected Interviews and Other Writings 1972–1977*, edited by Colin Gordon. Translated by Colin Gordon, Leo Marshall, John Mepham, and Kate Soper, Pantheon, 1980.

France, Anatole. "The Adventures of the Soul." *The Book of Modern Criticism*. Translated and edited by L. Lewisohn, New York, 1919, pp. 1–3.
Frauchiger, Daniela and Renato Renner. "Quantum Theory Cannot Consistently Describe the Use of Itself." *Nature Communications*, vol. 9, no. 1, 2018, pp. 1–10.
Freud, Sigmund. *Civilization and its Discontents*, Broadview, 2015.
———. "Project for a Scientific Psychology (1950 [1895])." *The Standard Edition of the Complete Psychological Works of Sigmund Freud, Volume I (1886–1899): Pre-Psycho-Analytic Publications and Unpublished Drafts*, Penguin, 1966, pp.281–391.
Friedman, Susan Stanford. "Both/And: Critique and Discovery in the Humanities." *PMLA*, vol. 132, no. 2, 2017, pp. 344–351.
Frodeman, Robert, Julie Thompson Klein, and Roberto Carlos Dos Santos Pacheco, editors. *The Oxford Handbook of Interdisciplinarity*, Oxford University Press, 2017.
Frodeman, Robert, Julie Thompson Klein, and Carl Mitcham. *The Oxford Handbook of Interdisciplinarity*, Oxford University Press, 2010.
Frost, Robert. "The Road Not Taken." https://www.poetryfoundation.org/poems/44272/the-road-not-taken
Gadamer, Hans-Georg. *Truth and Method*. Translated by Joel Weinsheimer and Donald G. Marshall, Continuum, 1975.
Galison, Peter. "Ten Problems in History and Philosophy of Science." *Isis*, vol. 99, no. 1, 2008, pp. 111–124.
Gallese, Vittorio and Corrado Sinigaglia. "Embodied Resonance." *The Oxford Handbook of 4E Cognition*, Oxford, 2018, pp. 417–432.
Gallop, Jane. "Close Reading in 2009." *ADE Bulletin*, vol. 149, 2010, pp. 15–19.
———. "The Historicization of Literary Studies and the Fate of Close Reading." *Profession*, vol. 1, 2007, pp. 181–186.
Garber, Marjorie. *A Manifesto for Literary Studies*, University of Washington Press, 2003.
Gardiner, Judith Kegan, "In the Name of the Mother: Feminism, Psychoanalysis, Methodology." *LIT: Literature Interpretation Theory*, vol. 1, no. 4, 1990, pp. 239–252.
Gates, Henry Louis. *The Signifying Monkey: A Theory of African American Literary Criticism*, Oxford University Press, 2014.
Gates, Henry Louis and Nellie Y. McKay. "Talking Books." *The Norton Anthology of African American Literature*, edited by Gates and McKay, Norton, 1997, pp. xxvii–xli.
Geiger, Roger L. *To Advance Knowledge: The Growth of American Research Universities, 1900–1940*, Routledge, 2017.
Geoghegan, Bernard Dionysius. "From Information Theory to French Theory: Jakobson, Levi-Strauss, and the Cybernetic Apparatus." *Critical Inquiry*, vol. 38, no. 1, 2011, pp. 96–126.
Gere, Anne Ruggles. *Writing groups: History, Theory, and Implications*, Southern Illinois University Press, 1987.
Gibbons, Michael, Camille Limoges, Helga Novotny, Simon Schwartzman, Peter Scott, and Martin Trow. *The New Production of Knowledge. The Dynamics of Science and Research in Contemporary Societies*, Sage, 1994.
Giedd, Jay N. "The Digital Revolution and Adolescent Brain Evolution." *Journal of Adolescent Health*, vol. 51, no, 2, 2012, pp. 101–105.
Gieseking, Jen Jack. "Where Are We? The Method of Mapping with GIS in Digital Humanities." *American Quarterly*, vol. 70, no. 3, 2018, pp. 641–648.
Gildea, Niall et al., eds. *English Studies: The State of the Discipline, Past, Present, and Future*, Springer, 2014.
Gilroy, Paul. *The Black Atlantic: Modernity and Double Consciousness*, Verso, 1993.

Godway, Eleanor and Geraldine Finn, editors. *Who is this "We:" Absence of Community*, Black Rose Books, 1994.
Graff, Gerald. *Professing Literature: An Institutional History*, University of Chicago Press, 2008.
———. *Beyond the Culture Wars: How Teaching the Conflicts Can Revitalize American Education*. Norton, 1993.
Graff, Harvey J. *Undisciplining Knowledge: Interdisciplinarity in the Twentieth Century*, Johns Hopkins University Press, 2015.
Graham, S. Scott. *The Politics of Pain Medicine: A Rhetorical-Ontological Inquiry*, University of Chicago Press, 2015.
Grant, Sean. "Peer Review Process Completion Rates and Subsequent Student Perceptions within Completely Online versus Blended Modes of Study." *System: An International Journal of Educational Technology and Applied Linguistics*, vol. 62, 2016, pp. 93–101.
Greenblatt, Stephen. "What is the History of Literature?" *Critical Inquiry*, vol. 23, no. 3, 1997, pp. 460–481.
Grimm, Stephen R., Christoph Baumberger, and Sabine Ammon, editors. *Explaining Understanding: New Perspectives from Epistemology and Philosophy of Science*, Taylor & Francis, 2016.
Guillory, John and Jeffrey J. Williams. "Toward a Sociology of Literature: An Interview with John Guillory." *Minnesota Review*, vol. 61, no. 1, 2004, pp. 95–109.
Gutting, Gary, "Introduction: What Is Continental Philosophy of Science?" *Continental Philosophy of Science*, edited by Gary Gutting, John Wiley & Sons, 2008, pp. 1–16.
Habermas, Jurgen. "Martin Heidegger: On the Publication of the Lectures of 1935." Translated by William S. Lewis. *The Heidegger Controversy: A Critical Reader*, edited by Richard Wolin, MIT Press, 1991, pp. 186–197.
Hacking, Ian. *The Social Construction of What?* Harvard University Press, 1999.
Haider, Jutta and Fredrik Åström. "Dimensions of Trust in Scholarly Communication: Problematizing Peer Review in the Aftermath of John Bohannon's 'Sting' in Science." *Journal of the Association for Information Science and Technology*, vol. 68, no. 2, 2017, pp. 450–467.
Halacy, Daniel Stephen. *Cyborg: Evolution of the Superman*, Harper and Row, 1965.
Hanson, Victor Davis. "The Liberal Arts Weren't Murdered—They Committed Suicide." *National Review*, 18 December 2018, nationalreview.com/2018/12/liberal-arts-education-politicized-humanities/.
Hansson, Stina and Merritt Polk. "Assessing the Impact of Transdisciplinary Research: The Usefulness of Relevance, Credibility, and Legitimacy for Understanding the Link Between Process and Impact." *Research Evaluation*, vol. 27, no. 2, 2018, pp. 132–144.
Haraway, Donna. "A Manifesto for Cyborgs: Science, Technology, and Socialist Feminism in the 1980s." *The Postmodern Turn: New Perspectives on Social Theory*, edited by Steven Seidman, Cambridge University Press, 1994, pp. 82–115.
Hardt, Michael and Antonio Negri. *Empire*, Harvard University Press, 2000.
Harford, Tim. *The Data Detective: Ten Easy Rules to Make Sense of Statistics*, Penguin, 2021.
Harpham, Geoffrey Galt, Jeffrey Skoblow, James Holstun, Sieglinde Lug, Grace Tiffany, Roger Seamon, Lawrence W. Hyman, and Stanley Fish. "Fish on Blind Submission." *PMLA*, vol. 104, no. 2, 1989, pp. 215–221.
Hartocollis, Anemona. "Colleges Face Rising Revolt by Professors." *The New York Times*, 3 July 2020, https://www.nytimes.com/2020/07/03/us/coronavirus-college-professors.html.

Hayles, N. Katherine. "Can Computers Create Meanings? A Cyber/Bio/Semiotic Perspective." *Critical Inquiry*, vol. 46, no. 1, 2019, pp. 32–55.

———. *Unthought: The Power of the Cognitive Nonconscious*, University of Chicago Press, 2017.

———. *How We Think: Digital Media and Contemporary Technogenesis*. University of Chicago Press, 2012.

———. "How We Read: Close, Hyper, Machine." *ADE Bulletin*, vol. 150, 2010, pp. 62–79.

———. *How We Became Posthuman: Virtual Bodies in Cybernetics, Literature, and Informatics*, University of Chicago Press, 2008.

———. "Print Is Flat, Code Is Deep: The Importance of Media-specific Analysis." *Poetics Today*, vol. 25, no. 1, 2004, pp. 67–90.

———. "Deeper into the Machine: Learning to Speak Digital." *Computers and Composition*, vol. 19, no. 4, 2002, pp. 371–386.

———. "The Transformation of Narrative and the Materiality of Hypertext." *Narrative*, vol. 9, no. 1, 2001, pp. 21–39.

Hayot, Eric. *Humanist Reason: A History. An Argument. A Plan*, Columbia University Press, 2021.

———. "The Humanities as We Know Them Are Doomed. Now What?" *The Chronicle of Higher Education*, 1 July 2018, https://www.chronicle.com/article/the-humanities-as-we-know-them-are-doomed-now-what.

Hays, Priya Venkatesan. *Molecular Biology in Narrative Form: A Study of the Experimental Trajectory of Science*, Peter Lang, 2006.

Heidegger, Martin. *Being and Time.* Translated by John Macquarrie, and Edward Robinson, Harper and Row, 1962.

Hinrichs, Peter L. "Trends in Employment at US Colleges and Universities, 1987–2013." *Economic Commentary, Federal Reserve Bank of Cleveland*, 2016, https://www.clevelandfed.org/en/newsroom-and-events/publications/economic-commentary/2016-economic-commentaries/ec-201605-trends-in-employment-at-us-colleges-and-universities.aspx.

He, Zi-Lin, Xue-Song Geng, and Colin Campbell-Hunt. "Research Collaboration and Research Output: A Longitudinal Study of 65 Biomedical Scientists in a New Zealand University." *Research Policy*, vol. 38, no. 2, 2009, pp. 306–317.

Healey, Robert A. "Quantum Theory and the Limits of Objectivity." *Foundations of Physics*, vol. 48, 2018, pp. 1568–1589.

Hegel, Georg Wilhelm Friedrich. *The Phenomenology of Spirit.* Translated by Terry Pinkard, Cambridge University Press, 2018.

———. *The philosophy of Right.* Translated by Alan White, Hackett Publishing, 2015.

Hirsch Jr, Eric D., Joseph F. Kett, and James S. Trefil. *Cultural Literacy: What Every American Needs to Know*, Vintage, 1988.

Hirsch, Marianne. "Editor's Column: What Can a Journal Essay Do?" *PMLA*, vol. 121, no. 3, 2006, pp. 617–626.

———. "Editor's Column." *PMLA*, vol. 120, no. 3, 2005, pp. 713–714.

Hoemann Katie, Fei Xu and Lisa Feldman Barrett. "Emotion Words, Emotion Concepts, and Emotional Development in Children: A Constructionist Hypothesis." *Developmental Psychology*, vol. 55, no. 9, 2019, https://www.ncbi.nlm.nih.gov/pmc/articles/PMC6716622/.

Hoffmeyer, Jesper. *Biosemiotics: An Examination into the Signs of Life and the Life of Signs*, University of Scranton Press, 2008.

———. *Signs of Meaning in the Universe*. Translated by Barbara J. Haveland, University of Indian Press, 1996.

Hofstadter, Richard. *The Paranoid Style in American Politics*, Vintage, 2012.

———. *Anti-intellectualism in American Life*, Vintage, 1963.

Hogan, Patrick Colm. "Affect Studies and Literary Criticism." *Oxford Research Encyclopedia of Literature*, 2016, https://oxfordre.com/literature/view/10.1093/acrefore/9780190201098.001.0001/acrefore-9780190201098-e-105.

Holbrook, J. Britt. "Peer Review." *The Oxford Handbook of Interdisciplinarity*, edited by Robert Frodeman et al., Oxford University Press, 2010, pp. 321–332.

How it Works. "The Arc of Narrative." Accessed 21 March 2021. https://www.arcofnarrative.com/howitworks.

Howard, Jean E. "The New Historicism in Renaissance Studies." *English Literary Renaissance*, vol. 16, no. 1, 1986, pp. 13–43.

Howes, Andrew, Dimitrina Kaneva, David Swanson, and Julian Williams. "Re-envisioning STEM Education: Curriculum, Assessment and Integrated, Interdisciplinary Studies." *Vision for C&A Royal Society Report*, The University of Manchester, 2013, https://royalsociety.org/~/media/education/policy/vision/reports/ev-2-vision-research-report-20140624.pdf.

Hussar, Bill et al. "Employment Outcomes of Bachelor's Degree Holders," *The Condition of Education 2020*, National Center for Education Statistics, 2020, https://nces.ed.gov/programs/coe/pdf/coe_sbc.pdf.

Husserl, Edmund. *The Crisis of European Sciences and Transcendental Phenomenology: An Introduction to Phenomenological Philosophy*, Northwestern University Press, 1970.

Hutner, Gordon and Feisal G. Mohamed, editors. *A New Deal for the Humanities: Liberal Arts and the Future of Public Higher Education*, Rutgers University Press, 2015.

Huutoniemi, Katri. "Communicating and Compromising on Disciplinary Expertise in the Peer Review of Research Proposals." *Social Studies of Science*, vol. 42, no. 6, 2012, pp. 897–921.

Ioannidis, JPA. "All Science Should Inform Policy and Regulation." *PLoS Med*, vol. 15, no. 5, 2018, e1002576. https://doi.org/10.1371/journal.pmed.1002576

———. "Meta-research: Why Research on Research Matters." *PLoS Biology*, vol. 16, no. 3, 2018, e2005468. https://doi.org/10.1371/journal.pbio.2005468.

Iyer, Arun. *Towards an Epistemology of Ruptures: The Case of Heidegger and Foucault*, Bloomsbury, 2015.

Jacobs, Jerry A. and Scott Frickel. "Interdisciplinarity: A Critical Assessment." *Annual Review of Sociology*, vol. 35, pp. 43–65.

Jagadish, Hosagrahar Visvesva. "Big Data and Science: Myths and Reality." *Big Data Research*, vol. 2, no. 2, 2015, pp. 49–52.

Jahn, Thomas and Florian Keil. "An Actor-specific Guideline for Quality Assurance in Transdisciplinary Research." *Futures*, vol. 65, 2015, pp. 195–208.

Jakobson, Roman. *Language in Literature*. Edited by Krystina Pomorska and Stephen Rudy, Harvard University Press, 1987.

Jänicke, Stefan et al. "Visual Text Analysis in Digital Humanities." *Computer Graphics Forum*, vol. 36, no. 6, 2017, pp. 226–250.

———. "On Close and Distant Reading in Digital Humanities: A Survey and Future Challenges." *EuroVis*, 2015.

Jay, Martin. "'The Aesthetic Ideology' as Ideology; or, What Does It Mean to Aestheticize Politics?" *Cultural Critique*, vol. 21, 1992, pp. 41–61.

Jay, Paul. *The Humanities "Crisis" and the Future of Literary Studies*, Springer, 2014.

Jeffrey, Paul. "Smoothing the Waters: Observations on the Process of Cross-Disciplinary Research Collaboration." *Social Studies of Science*, vol. 33, 2003, pp. 539–562.

Jefferson, Thomas. "From Thomas Jefferson to James Madison, 30 January 1787." *The Writings of Thomas Jefferson*. Collected and edited by Paul Leicaster Ford, vol. IV, pp. 361–368.

Jefferson, Tom, Rudin Melanie, Brodney Folse S. et al. "Editorial Peer Review for Improving the Quality of Reports of Biomedical Studies." *Cochrane Database of Systematic Reviews*, vol. 2, 2007, https://pubmed.ncbi.nlm.nih.gov/17443635/.

Jenson, Deborah. "Hegel and Dessalines: Philosophy and the African Diaspora." *New West Indian Guide/Nieuwe West-Indische Gids*, vol. 84, no. 3–4, 2010, pp. 269–275.

Johnson, Barbara. "Teaching Deconstructively." *Writing and Reading Differently*, edited by G. Douglas Atkins and M. L. Johnson, University of Kansas Press, 1986, pp. 140–148.

———. "The Frame of Reference: Poe, Lacan, Derrida." *Yale French Studies*, vol. 55/56, 1977, pp. 457–505.

Jordan-Young, Rebecca M. and Katrina Karkazis. *Testosterone: An Unauthorized Biography*, Harvard University Press, 2019.

Joselow, Maxine. "Labs Are for the Humanities, Too." *Inside Higher Ed*, 12 July 2016, https://www.insidehighered.com/news/2016/07/12/conference-explores-humanities-labs.

Joseph, Celucien L. "On Intellectual Reparations: Hegel, Franklin Tavarès, Susan Buck-Morss, Revolutionary Haiti, and Caribbean Philosophical Association." *Africology: The Journal of Pan African Studies*, vol. 9, no. 7, 2016, pp. 167–175.

Kaji-O'Grady, Sandra, Chris L. Smith, and Russell Hughes. *Laboratory Lifestyles: The Construction of Scientific Fictions*, MIT Press, 2018.

Kant, Immanuel. *Critique of Power of Judgment*. Translated by Paul Guyer and Eric Matthews, Cambridge University Press, 2000.

———. *Critique of Pure Reason*. Translated by Paul Guyer and Allen W. Wood, Cambridge University Press, 1998.

Katopodis, Christina and Cathy N. Davidson. "Changing Our Classrooms to Prepare Students for a Challenging World." *Profession*, Fall 2019, https://profession.mla.org/changing-our-classrooms-to-prepare-students-for-a-challenging-world/?utm_source=mlaoutreach&utm_medium=email&utm_campaign=proffall19.

Kaufmann-Hayoz, Ruth, Rico Defila, Antonietta Di Giulio, and Markus Winkelmann. "Was man sich erhoffen darf – Zur gesellschaftlichen Wirkung transdisziplinärer Forschung." *Transdisziplinär forschen – Zwischen Ideal und gelebter Praxis*, edited by Rico Defila and Antonietta Di Giulio, Campus, 2016, pp. 289–327.

Keating, Benjamin. "'A Good Development Thing:' A Longitudinal Analysis of Peer Review and Authority in Undergraduate Writing." *Developing Writers in Higher Education: A Longitudinal Study*, edited by Anne Ruggles Gere, University of Michigan Press, 2019, pp. 56–80.

Kellermann, Paul L. "I Love Teaching at Penn State, But Going Back This Fall Is a Mistake. 1,000 of My Colleagues Agree." *Esquire*, 26 June 2020, https://www.esquire.com/news-politics/a32973676/penn-state-university-covid-19-petition-professors/.

Kerby, Lauren R. *Saving History: How White Evangelicals Tour the Nation's Capital and Redeem a Christian America*, University of North Carolina Press, 2020.

Kim, Dorothy and Jesse Stommel. *Disrupting the Digital Humanities*, Punctum, 2018.

Kitcher, Patricia. "Revisiting Kant's Epistemology: Skepticism, Apriority, and Psychologism." *Noûs*, vol. 29, no. 3, 1995, pp. 285–315.

Kitchin, Rob. "Big Data, New Epistemologies and Paradigm Shifts." *Big Data & Society*, vol. 1, no. 1, 2014, https://journals.sagepub.com/doi/10.1177/2053951714528481.

Klein, Julie Thompson. *Humanities, Culture, and Interdisciplinarity: The Changing American Academy*, SUNY Press, 2012.

———. "Afterword: The Emergent Literature on Interdisciplinary and Transdisciplinary Research Evaluation." *Research Evaluation*, vol. 15, no. 1, 2006, pp. 75–80.

———. *Crossing Boundaries: Knowledge, Disciplinarities, and Interdisciplinarities*, University Press of Virginia, 1996.

Klein, Lauren F. "Dimensions of Scale: Invisible Labor, Editorial Work, and the Future of Quantitative Literary Studies." *PMLA*, vol. 135, no. 1, 2020, pp. 23–39.

Knight, David B., Lisa R. Lattuca, Ezekiel W. Kimball, and Robert D. Reason. "Understanding Interdisciplinarity: Curricular and Organizational Features of Undergraduate Interdisciplinary Programs." *Innovative Higher Education*, vol. 38, 2013, pp. 143–158.

Koh, Adeline. "A Letter to the Humanities: DH Will Not Save You," *Hybrid Pedagogy*, 19 April 2015, https://hybridpedagogy.org/a-letter-to-the-humanities-dh-will-not-save-you, accessed 24 April 2021.

König, Bettina, Katharina Diehl, Karen Tscherning, and Katharina Helming. "A Framework for Structuring Interdisciplinary Research Management." *Research Policy*, vol. 42, 2013, pp. 261–272.

Koskinen, Inkeri and Uskali Mäki. "Extra-academic Transdisciplinarity and Scientific Pluralism: What Might They Learn From One Another?" *European Journal for Philosophy of Science*, vol. 6, no. 3, 2016, pp. 419–444.

Krainer, Larissa and Verena Winiwarter. "Die Universität als Akteurin der transformativen Wissenschaft. Konsequenzen für die Messung der Qualität transdisziplinärer Forschung." *GAIA*, vol. 25, no. 2, 2016, pp. 110–116.

Krebs, Paula et al. "About Profession." *Profession*. Accessed 15 March 2021, https://profession.mla.org/about-profession.

Kronick, David. *"Devant le deluge" and Other Essays on Early Modern Scientific Communication*, Scarecrow, 1990.

Kurzweil, Ray. *How to Create a Mind: The Secret of Human Thought Revealed*, Penguin, 2013.

La Berge, Leigh Claire. "A Market Correction in the Humanities — What Are You Going to Do with That?" *Los Angeles Times Review of Books*, 26 August 2019, https://lareviewofbooks.org/article/a-market-correction-in-the-humanities-what-are-you-going-to-do-with-that/

Lacan, Jacques. "Seminar on "The Purloined Letter." *The Purloined Poe*. Translated by Jeffrey Mehlman. Edited by John P. Muller and William J. Richardson, Johns Hopkins University Press, 1988, pp. 28–54.

———. *Seminar XII: Crucial Problems for Psychoanalysis: 1964–1965*. Translated by Cormac Gallagher, www.LacaninIreland.com/seminars.

LaCapra, Dominick. *History in Transit: Experience, Identity, Critical Theory*, Cornell University Press, 2004.

———. *History and Memory after Auschwitz*. Cornell University Press, 1998.

———. "The University in Ruins?" *Critical Inquiry*, vol. 25 no. 1, 1998, pp. 32–55.

———. *Representing the Holocaust: History, Theory, Trauma*, Ithaca: Cornell University Press, 1994.

Lakatos, Imre and Paul Feyerabend. *For and Against Method: Including Lakatos's Lectures on Scientific Method and the Lakatos-Feyerabend Correspondence*. Edited by Matteo Motterlini. University of Chicago Press, 1999.

Lakatos, Imre and Alan Musgrave, editors. *Criticism and the Growth of Knowledge*. Cambridge University Press, 1970.

Laland, Kevin N. *Darwin's Unfinished Symphony: How Culture Made the Human Mind.* Princeton University Press, 2018.
Lamb, Anne T. and Preeya P. Mbekeani. "Private School Choice in the Wake of the Great Recession." *Association for Education Finance and Policy*, 2017, https://aefpweb.org/sites/default/files/webform/42/Lamb%20&%20Mbekeani_AEFP.pdf
Lamb, Mary R. and Jennifer M. Parrott, editors. *Digital Reading and Writing in Composition Studies*, Routledge, 2019.
Lambert, Ben et al. "The Pace of Modern Culture." *Nature Human Behaviour*, vol. 4, 2020, pp. 352–360.
Lamont, Michèle. *How Professors Think: Inside the Curious World of Academic Judgment*, Harvard University Press, 2009.
Lane, Richard J. *The Big Humanities: Digital Humanities/Digital Laboratories*, Taylor & Francis, 2016.
Lanham, Richard A. *The Electronic Word: Democracy, Technology, and the Arts*, University of Chicago Press, 2010.
Larivière Vincent, Stefanie Haustein, and Philipe Mongeon. "The Oligopoly of Academic Publishers in the Digital Era." *PLoS One*, vol. 10, no. 6, 2015, https://journals.plos.org/plosone/article?id=10.1371/journal.pone.0127502.
Latour, Bruno. "The Puzzling Face of a Secular Gaia." https://footnotes2plato.com/2013/03/01/reflections-on-bruno-latours-3rd-gifford-lecture-the-puzzling-face-of-a-secular-gaia, accessed 4 April 2021.
———. *Facing Gaia: Eight Lectures on the New Climatic Regime.* Translated by Catherine Porter, Polity Press, 2017.
———. "Agency at the Time of the Anthropocene." *New Literary History*, vol. 45, no. 1, 2014, pp. 1–18.
———. *An Inquiry into Modes of Existence: An Anthropology of the Moderns.* Translated by Catherine Porter, Harvard University Press, 2013.
———. *Reassembling the Social: An Introduction to Actor-Network-Theory*, Oxford University Press, 2005.
———. *Politics of Nature: How to Bring the Sciences into Democracy.* Translated by Catherine Porter, Harvard University Press, 2004.
———. "Why Has Critique Run Out of Steam? From Matters of Fact to Matters of Concern." *Critical inquiry*, vol. 30, no. 2, 2004, pp. 225–248.
———. "The Enlightenment without the Critique: A Word on Michel Serres' Philosophy." *Contemporary French Philosophy*, edited by A. Phillips Griffiths, Cambridge University Press, 1987, pp. 83–97.
Latour, Bruno and Steve Woolgar. *Laboratory Life: The Construction of Scientific Facts*, Princeton University Press, 2013.
Lee, Carole J. et al. "Bias in Peer Review." *Journal of the American Society for Information Science and Technology*, vol. 64, no. 1, 2013, pp. 2–17.
Lee, James Jaehoon and Joshua Beckelhimer. "Anthropocene and Empire: Discourse Networks of the Human Record." *PMLA*, vol. 35, no. 1, 2020, pp. 110–129.
Leiter, Brian and Michael Rosen, editors. *The Oxford Handbook of Continental Philosophy*, Oxford University Press, 2007.
Lendvai, Piroska et al. "Propp Revisited: Integration of Linguistic Markup into Structured Content Descriptors of Tales." *DH*, 2010, http://www.divaportal.org/smash/get/diva2:887060/FULLTEXT01.pdf
Lennon, Brian. "The Essay, in Theory." *diacritics*, vol. 38, no. 3, Fall 2008, pp. 71–92.
Lentricchia, Frank and Andrew DuBois, editors. *Close Reading: The Reader*, Duke University Press, 2003.

Levine, Caroline. *Forms: Whole, Rhythm, Hierarchy, Network*, Princeton University Press, 2015.
———. "Rethinking Peer Review and the Fate of the Monograph." *Profession*, 2007, pp. 100–106.
Levine, Michael G. *A Weak Messianic Power: Figures of a Time to Come in Benjamin, Derrida, and Célan*, Fordham University Press, 2013.
Levinson, Marjorie. "What is New Formalism?" *PMLA*, vol. 122, no. 2, 2007, pp. 558–569.
Lévi-Strauss, Claude. *The Savage Mind*, University of Chicago Press, 1966.
Leys, Ruth. *Trauma: A Genealogy*, University of Chicago Press, 2000.
Linebaugh, Peter and Marcus Rediker. *The Many-headed Hydra: Sailors, Slaves, Commoners, and the Hidden History of the Revolutionary Atlantic*, Beacon, 2013.
Lipscombe, Trevor. "Burn This Article: An Inflammatory View of Peer Review." *Journal of Scholarly Publishing*, vol. 47, no. 3, 2016, pp. 284–298.
Litfin, Karen T. "Framing Science: Precautionary Discourse and the Ozone Treaties." *Millennium: Journal of International Studies*, vol. 24, 1995, pp. 251–277.
Liu, Alan. Y. "Where is Cultural Criticism in the Digital Humanities?" *Debates in Digital Humanities*, https://liu.english.ucsb.edu/where-is-cultural-criticism-in-the-digital-humanities, accessed 27 April 2021.
Lockwood, Thomas. *Design Thinking: Integrating Innovation, Customer Experience, and Brand Value*, Simon and Schuster, 2010.
Loesberg, Jonathan. *A Return to Aesthetics: Autonomy, Indifference, and Postmodernism*, Stanford University Press, 2005.
———. "Cultural Studies, Victorian Studies, and Formalism." *Victorian Literature and Culture*, vol. 27, no. 2, 1999, pp. 537–544.
Logan, Robert K. "Review and Précis of Terrence Deacon's Incomplete Nature: How Mind Emerged from Matter." *Information*, vol. 3, no. 3, 2012, pp. 290–306.
Looney, Dennis and Natalia Lusin. "Enrollments in Languages Other than English in United States Institutions of Higher Education, Summer 2016 and Fall 2016: Preliminary Report." *Modern Language Association*, 2018, https://www.mla.org/content/download/83540/2197676/2016-Enrollments-Short-Report.pdf.
Lorde, Audre. *Sister Outsider: Essays and Speeches*, Crossing Press, 2007.
Lövbrand, Eva. "Co-producing European Climate Science and Policy: A Cautionary Note on the Making of Useful Knowledge." *Science and Public Policy*, vol. 38, no. 3, 2011, pp. 225–236.
Lukianoff, Greg and Jonathan Haidt. *The Coddling of the American Mind: How Good Intentions and Bad Ideas Are Setting Up a Generation for Failure*, Penguin Books, 2019.
Lyall, Catherine, Ann Bruce, Joyce Tait, and Laura Meagher, editors. *Interdisciplinary Research Journeys: Practical Strategies for Capturing Creativity*, Bloomsbury, 2011.
Lyotard, Jean-François. "Note on the Meaning of 'Post.'" *Postmodernism: A Reader*, edited by Thomas Docherty, Routledge, 1993, pp. 47–50.
———. *The Differend: Phrases in Dispute*. Translated by Georges Van Den Abbeele, University of Minnesota Press, 1988.
Maag, Simon, Timothy J. Alexander., Robert Kase, and Sabine Hoffmann. "Indicators for Measuring the Contributions of Individual Knowledge Brokers." *Environmental Science & Policy*, vol. 89, no. 11, 2018, pp. 1–9.
Macksey, Richard A. and Eugenio Donato, editors. *The Structuralist Controversy: The Languages of Criticism and the Sciences of Man*, Johns Hopkins University Press, 2007.
Madsbjerg, Christian. *Sensemaking: The Power of the Humanities in the Age of the Algorithm*, Hachette, 2017.

Malabou, Catherine. *What Should We Do With our Brain?* Translated by Sebastian Rand, Fordham University Press, 2008.
Malcolm, X. *The Autobiography of Malcolm X*, Ballantine Books, 2015.
Maldonado-Torres, Nelson. "Post-continental Philosophy: Its Definition, Contours, and Fundamental Sources." *Review of Contemporary Philosophy*, vol. 9, 2010, pp. 40–86.
Mancosu, Moreno, Salvatore Vassallo, and Cristiano Vezzoni. "Believing in Conspiracy Theories: Evidence from an Exploratory Analysis of Italian Survey Data." *South European Society and Politics*, vol. 22, no. 3, 2017, pp. 327–344.
Mapping Islamophobia. Accessed 21 March 2021, https://mappingislamophobia.org/.
Markovits, Daniel. *The Meritocracy Trap: How America's Foundational Myth Feeds Inequality Feeds Inequality, Dismantles the Middle Class*, and *Devours the Elite*, New York: Penguin, 2019.
Marshall, David. "Introduction." *The Humanities and Its Publics*, edited Ivo Banac, Jean Bethke Elshtain, and Robert Weisbuch, American Council of Learned Societies, 2006.
Martin, Ben and Henry Etzkowitz. "The Origin and Evolution of the University Species." *Science and Technology Policy Research Unit* (SPRU), Electronic Working Paper Series, Sussex University, 2000.
Marx, Karl. *The 18th Brumaire of Louis Bonaparte*, Wildside, 2008.
———. *Capital: A Critique of Political Economy, Volume I.* Translated by Ben Fowkes, Penguin Books, 1990.
Marx, Karl and Friedrich Engels. *The German Ideology*, edited by Arthur C. London, Lawrence and Wishart, 1970.
McClanahan, Annie J. "Becoming Non-Economic: Human Capital Theory and Wendy Brown's Undoing the Demos." *Theory & Event*, vol. 20, no. 2, 2017, pp. 510–519.
McCurdy, Nina et al. "Poemage: Visualizing the Sonic Topology of a Poem." *IEEE Transactions on Visualization and Computer Graphics*, vol. 22, no. 1, 2015, pp. 439–448.
McDonald, Rónán. Ed. *The Value of Literary Studies: Critical Institutions, Scholarly Agendas*, Cambridge University Press, 2015.
McGann, Jerome. "Culture and Technology: The Way We Live Now, What Is to Be Done?" *New Literary History*, vol. 36, no. 1, 2005, pp. 71–82.
McGurn, William. "Is Majoring in English Worth It?" *Wall Street Journal*, 9 September 2019, https://www.wsj.com/articles/is-majoring-in-english-worth-it-11568068987.
McKenney, Susan and Thomas C. Reeves. *Conducting Educational Design Research*, Routledge, 2018.
Meagher, Laura, Catherine Lyall, Sandra Nutley. "Flows of Knowledge, Expertise and Influence: A Method for Assessing Policy and Practice Impacts from Social Science Research." *Research Evaluation*, vol. 17, no. 3, 2008, pp. 163–173.
Melas, Natalie. "Afterlives of Comparison: Literature, Equivalence, Value." *The Value of Literary Studies: Critical Institutions, Scholarly Agendas*, edited by Rónán McDonald, Cambridge University Press, 2015, pp. 172–187.
Mentz, Steven. "Toward a Blue Cultural Studies: The Sea, Maritime Culture, and Early Modern English Literature." *Literature Compass*, vol. 6, no. 5, 2009, pp. 997–1013.
Merleau-Ponty, Maurice. *Phenomenology of Perception*. Translated by Colin Smith, Routledge, 1982.
Meyer, Morgan. "The Rise of the Knowledge Broker." *Science Communication*, vol. 32, no. 1, 2010, pp. 118–127.
Mikics, David. *Slow Reading in a Hurried Age*, Harvard University Press, 2013.
Miller, J. Hillis. "The Ethics of Reading." *Style*, vol. 21, no. 2, 1987, pp. 181–191.

Minh-Ha, Trinh T. *Framer Framed: Film Scripts and Interviews*, Routledge, 1992.
Mitchell, Melanie. *Artificial Intelligence: A Guide for Thinking Humans*, Farrar, Straus and Giroux, 2019.
Mitchell, Michael, Michael Leachman, Kathleen Masterson, and Samantha Waxman. "Unkept Promises: State Cuts to Higher Education Threaten Access and Equity." Center on Budget and Policy Priorities, https://www.cbpp.org/research/state-budget-and-tax/unkept-promises-state-cuts-to-higher-education-threaten-access-and.
Mittell, Jason; "Opening Up [in]Transition's Open Peer-Review Process." *Cinema Journal*, vol. 56, no. 4, 2017, pp. 137–141.
MLA Teagle Foundation Working Group. "Report to the Teagle Foundation on the Undergraduate Major in Language and Literature." *Profession*, vol. 1, 2009, pp. 285–312.
Moati, Raoul. *Derrida/Searle: Deconstruction and Ordinary Language*. Translated by Timothy Attanucci and Maureen Chun, Columbia University Press, 2014.
Modern Language Association of America. "Evaluating Translations as Scholarship: Guidelines for Peer Review." *Profession*, vol. 1, 2011, pp. 264–267.
Modlin Jr, E. Arnold, Derek H. Alderman, and Glenn W. Gentry. "Tour Guides as Creators of Empathy: The Role of Affective Inequality in Marginalizing the Enslaved at Plantation House Museums." *Tourist Studies*, vol. 11, no. 1, 2011, pp. 3–19.
Mol, Annemarie. *The Body Multiple: Ontology in Medical Practice*, Duke University Press, 2002.
Mondal, Mayukh, Jaume Bertranpetit, and Oscar Lao. "Approximate Bayesian Computation with Deep Learning Supports a Third Archaic Introgression in Asia and Oceania." *Nature Communications*, vol. 10, no. 1, 2019, pp. 1–9.
Mootee, Idris. *Design Thinking for Strategic Innovation: What They Can't Teach You at Business or Design School*, John Wiley & Sons, 2013.
Moran, Joe. *Interdisciplinarity*. Second Edition, Routledge, 2010.
Moretti, Franco. "Simulating Dramatic Networks: Morphology, History, Literary Study." *Journal of World Literature*, vol. 6, no. 1, 2020, pp. 1–21.
———. "Franco Moretti: A Response." *PMLA*, vol. 132, no. 3, 2017, pp. 686–689.
———. *Distant Reading*, Verso, 2013.
———. *Graphs, Maps, Trees: Abstract Models for a Literary History*, Verso, 2005.
Morillo, Fernando, María Bordons, and Isabel Gómez. "Interdisciplinarity in Science: A Tentative Typology of Disciplines and Research Areas." *Journal of the American Society for Information Science and Technology*, vol. 54, 2003, pp. 1237–1249.
Morozov, Evgeny. "Digital Intermediation of Everything: At the Intersection of Politics, Technology and Finance." *4th Council of Europe Platform Exchange on Culture and Digitisation. Empowering Democracy through Culture–Digital Tools for Culturally Competent Citizens*, 2017, https://rm.coe.int/digital-intermediation-of-everything-at-the-intersection-of-politics-t/168075baba.
Morris, Rosalind, ed. *Can the Subaltern Speak? Reflections on the History of an Idea*, Columbia University Press, 2010.
Mößner, Nicola. *Visual Representations in Science: Concept and Epistemology*, Routledge, 2018.
Motschenbacher, Heiko. *Language, Gender and Sexual Identity: Poststructuralist Perspectives*, John Benjamins, 2010.
Mullarkey, John. *Post-continental Philosophy: An Outline*, Bloomsbury, 2006.
Munafò, Marcus R. Brian A. Nosek et al. "A Manifesto for Reproducible Science." *Nature Human Behaviour* 1, Article number: 0021, 2017.
Murphy, Ann V. *Violence and the Philosophical Imaginary*, SUNY Press, 2012.

"National Cancer Act of 1937." National Cancer Center Institute, https://www.cancer.gov/about-nci/legislative/history/national-cancer-act-1937. Accessed 11 March 2021.

National Research Council. *Convergence: Facilitating Transdisciplinary Integration of Life Sciences, Physical Sciences, Engineering, and Beyond*, National Academies Press, 2014.

National Science Foundation. "Convergence Research at NSF." National Science Foundation, https://www.nsf.gov/od/oia/convergence/index.jsp. Accessed 11 March 2021.

Nersessian, Anahid. "What Is the New Redistribution?" *PMLA*, vol. 132, no. 5, 2017, pp. 1220–1225.

Nesbitt, Nick. "Haiti, Hegel, and the Politics of Prescription." *Postcolonial Studies*, vol. 13, no. 4, 2010, pp. 489–494.

New Literary History: About NHL, New Literary History, http://newliteraryhistory.org/about_NLH.php, Accessed 20 March 2021.

Newfield, Christopher. *Unmaking the Public University: The Forty-year Assault on the Middle Class*, Harvard University Press, 2008.

———. *Ivy and Industry: Business and the Making of the American University, 1880–1980*, Duke University Press, 2004.

Newkirk, Thomas. *The art of Slow Reading: Six Time-honored Practices for Engagement*, Heinemann, 2012.

Newman, Daniel Aureliano. *Modernist Life Histories: Biological Theory and the Experimental Bildungsroman*, Edinburgh University Press, 2019.

———. "Narrative: Common Ground for Literature and Science?" *Configurations*, vol. 26, no. 3, 2018, pp. 277–282.

Ngai, Sianne. *Theory of the Gimmick*, Harvard University Press, 2020.

———. *Ugly Feelings*, Harvard University Press, 2005.

Norris, Christopher. *Derrida*, Harvard University Press, 1987.

North, Joseph. *Literary Criticism*, Harvard University Press, 2017.

Norvig, Peter and Stuart Russell. *Artificial Intelligence: A Modern Approach*, Prentice Hall, 2002.

Noyes, Eilidh and Rob Jenkins. "Camera-to-subject Distance Affects Face Configuration and Perceived Identity." *Cognition*, vol. 15, no. 12, 2017, pp. 97–104.

Obama, Barack. "Speech, Selma, Alabama." *Time Magazine*, 7 March 2015, https://time.com/3736357/barack-obama-selma-speech-transcript/

Ohmann, Richard. *Politics of Letters*, Wesleyan University Press, 1987.

Olkowski, Dorothea. *Postmodern Philosophy and the Scientific Turn*, Indiana University Press, 2012.

Orr, David. "The Most Misread Poem in America." *The Paris Review*, 11 September 2015, https://www.theparisreview.org/blog/2015/09/11/the-most-misread-poem-in-america.

Ortega, Élika. "Media and Cultural Hybridity in the Digital Humanities." *PMLA*, vol. 135, no. 1, 2020, pp. 159–164.

Osborne, Peter. "Problematizing Disciplinarity, Transdisciplinary Problematics." Transdisciplinary Problematics, special issue of *Theory, Culture & Society*, edited by Osborne, vol. 32, no. 5–6, 2015, pp. 3–35.

———. "Philosophy in Cultural Theory." *Philosophy in Cultural Theory*, Routledge, 2013, pp. 1–19.

Park, Sowon S. "The Dilemma of Cognitive Literary Studies." *English Studies: The State of the Discipline, Past, Present, and Future*, edited by Niall Gildea et al., Springer, 2014, pp. 67–82.

Paulson, William R. *Literary Culture in a World Transformed: A Future for the Humanities*, Cornell University Press, 2001.

Persily, Nathaniel. "The 2016 US Election: Can Democracy Survive the Internet?" *Journal of Democracy*, vol. 28, no. 2, 2017, pp. 63–76.

Peters, Douglas P. and Stephen J. Ceci. "The Peters & Ceci Study of Journal Publications." *The Winnower*, 6 May 2014, https://thewinnower.com/discussions/7-_the-_peters-_ceci-_study-_of-_journal-_publications.

———. "A Naturalistic Study of Psychology Journals: The Fate of Published Articles Resubmitted." *Behavioral and Brain Sciences*, vol. 5, 1982, pp. 187–252.

Petrović, Saša and David Matthews. "Unsupervised Joke Generation from Big Data." *Proceedings of the 51st Annual Meeting of the Association for Computational Linguistics (Volume 2: Short Papers)*, Association for Computational Linguistics, 2013.

Pettersson, Bo. "Narratology and Hermeneutics: Forging the Missing Link." *Narratology in the Age of Cross-disciplinary Narrative Research*, edited by Sandra Heinen and Roy Sommer, Walter de Gruyter, 2009, pp. 11–34.

Petts, Judith, Susan Owens, and Harriet Bulkeley. "Crossing Boundaries: Interdisciplinarity in the Context of Urban Environments." *Geoforum*, vol. 39, no. 2, 2008, pp. 593–601.

Pew Research Center. "Sharp Partisan Divisions in Views of National Institutions." Pew Research Center, 10 July 2017, https://www.pewresearch.org/politics/2017/07/10/sharp-partisan-divisions-in-views-of-national-institutions/.

Pickering, Andrew. "Ontology and Antidisciplinarity." *Interdisciplinarity: Reconfigurations of the Social and Natural Sciences*, edited by Andrew Barry and Georgina Born, Routledge, 2013, pp. 209–225.

———. *The Cybernetic Brain: Sketches of Another Future*, Chicago University Press, 2010.

———. "Antidisciplines or Narratives of Illusion." *Knowledges: Historical and Critical Studies in Disciplinarity*, edited by Ellen Messer-Davidow, David R. Shumway, and David J. Sylvan, University Press of Virginia, 1993, pp. 103–123.

Piketty, Thomas. *Capital and Ideology*, Harvard University Press, 2020.

Pinker, Steven. *Enlightenment Now: The Case for Reason, Science, Humanism, and Progress*, Penguin, 2018.

———. *How the Mind Works*, Norton, 1997.

Plotnitsky, Arkady. "Structure, Sign, and Play and the Discourse of the Natural Sciences: After the Hyppolite-Derrida Exchange." *MLN*, vol. 134, no. 5, 2019, pp. 953–966.

———. *The Knowable and the Unknowable: Modern Science, Nonclassical Thought, and the "Two Cultures"*, University of Michigan Press, 2002.

———. *Complementarity: Anti-epistemology after Bohr and Derrida*, Duke University Press, 1994.

Plume, Andrew and Daphne van Weijen. "Publish or Perish? The Rise of the Fractional Author." *Research Trends Issue*, vol. 38, no. 3, 2014, pp. 16–18.

Pollock, Sheldon. "Future Philology? The Fate of a Soft Science in a Hard World." *Critical Inquiry*, Special issue, "The Fate of Disciplines" edited by James Chandler and Arnold I. Davidson, vol. 35, 2009, pp. 931–961.

Pooley, Jefferson. "Review of *Communication: A Post-discipline*, by Silvio R. Waisbord." *Communications: The European Journal of Communication Research*, 2019.

Powell, Jeffrey, editor. *Heidegger and Language*, Indiana University Press, 2013.

Power, Nina. "Reading Transdisciplinarily: Sartre and Althusser." *Theory, Culture & Society*, vol. 32, no. 5–6, 2015, pp. 109–124.

Priaulx, Nicky and Martin Weinel. "Connective Knowledge: What We Need to Know about Other Fields to 'Envision' Cross-disciplinary Collaboration." *European Journal of Futures Research*, vol. 6, no. 1, 2018, pp. 1–18.

Proietti, Massimiliano et al. "Experimental Test of Local Observer Independence." *Science Advances*, vol. 5, no. 9, 2019, eaaw9832.

Propp, Vladimir. *Morphology of the Folktale*. Second edition, revised and edited by Louis A. Wagner. Translated by Laurence Scott, University of Texas Press, 1968.

Pym, Anthony. *Exploring Translation Theories*, Routledge, 2014.

Raaper, Rille. "Academic Perceptions of Higher Education Assessment Processes in Neoliberal Academia." *Critical Studies in Education*, vol. 57, no. 2, 2016, pp. 175–190.

Racimo, Fernando et al. "Evidence for Archaic Adaptive Introgression in Humans." *Nature Reviews Genetics*, vol. 16, no. 6, 2015, pp. 359–371.

Rafols, Ismael et al. "How Journal Rankings Can Suppress Interdisciplinary Research: A Comparison Between Innovation Studies and Business & Management." *Research Policy*, vol. 41, no. 7, 2012, pp. 1262–1282.

Rahman, Shahid et al., editors. *Logic, Epistemology, and the Unity of Science*, Springer, 2004.

Rajan, Tilottama. "Against Institution." *Symploke*, vol. 27, no. 1, 2019, pp. 419–425.

Ramadanovic, Petar. "Between Post-Structuralism and Science: Who Gets to Define Disciplines and their Boundaries?" *Cultural Critique*, vol. 107, 2020, pp. 1–28.

———. "Convergence and Overwriting: Toward an Interdisciplinary Study of Memory." *Memory Studies*, vol. 13, no. 6, 2020, pp. 1337–1351.

———. "Interruptions: Passage to the Act and the End of Interpretation." *The Undecidable Unconscious: A Journal of Deconstruction and Psychoanalysis*, vol. 5, 2018, pp. 107–136.

———. "No Place Like Ideology (On Slavoj Žižek): Is There a Difference Between the Theory of Ideology and the Theory of Interpretation?" *Cultural Critique*, vol. 86, Winter 2014, pp. 119–140.

———. "The time of Trauma: Rereading *Unclaimed Experience* and *Testimony*," *The Journal of Literature and Trauma Studies*, vol. 3, no. 2, Fall 2014, pp. 1–24.

———. "How to Talk About Nature When There Is No More Nature to Talk About: Toward a Sustainable Universal." *Sustaining Ecocriticism: Comparative Perspectives*, special issue of *Comparative Literature Studies*, edited by Hsinya Huang and John Beusterien, vol. 50, no. 1, 2013, pp. 7–24.

———. *Forgetting/Futures: On Memory, Trauma, and Identity*, Lexington Books, 2001.

———. "When 'To Die in Freedom' Is Written in English." *diacritics*, vol. 38, no. 4, 1998, pp. 54–67.

Rambsy, Howard. "African American Scholars and the Margins of DH." *PMLA*, vol. 135, no. 1, 2020, pp. 152–158.

Ransom, John Crowe. "Criticism, Inc." *Virginia Quarterly Review*, vol. 13, 1939, pp. 586–603.

Ravitch, Diane. *National Standards in American Education: A Citizen's Guide*, Brookings Institution Press, 2011.

———. "Education after the Culture Wars." *Daedalus*, vol. 131, no. 3, 2002, pp. 5–21.

Readings, Bill. *The University in Ruins*, Harvard University Press, 1996.

Rediker, Marcus and Peter Linebaugh. "'The Many-Headed Hydra': An Exchange." *New York Review of Books*, 20 September 2001, https://www.nybooks.com/articles/2001/09/20/the-many-headed-hydra-an-exchange.

Reisz, Matthew. "Google Leads Search for Humanities PhD Graduates." *Times Higher Education* 19 May 2011, www.timeshighereducation.com/news/google-leads-search-for-humanities-phd-graduates/416190.article#survey-answer.

Rennie, Drummond. "Let's Make Peer Review Scientific." *Nature*, vol. 535, no. 7610, 2016, pp. 31–33.

———. "Editorial Peer Review: Its Development and Rationale." *Peer Review in Health Sciences*, edited by Fiona Godlee and Tom Jefferson, BMJ Books, 2003, pp. 1–13.

Rennie, Drummond and Annette Flanagin. "Three Decades of Peer Review Congresses." *JAMA*, vol. 319, no. 4, 2018, pp. 350–353.

Resnyansky, Lucy. "Conceptual Frameworks for Social and Cultural Big Data Analytics: Answering the Epistemological Challenge." *Big Data & Society*, vol. 6, no. 1, 2019, pp. 1–12.

Reynolds, Jack. "Philosophy's Shame: Reflections on an Ambivalent/Ambiviolent Relationship with Science." *Sophia*, vol. 55, no. 1, 2016, pp. 55–70.

Richards, Ivor Armstrong. *Practical Criticism: A Study of Literary Judgment*, Kegan Paul, Trench, Trubner, 1929.

Richardson, Alan and Ellen Spolsky, editors. *The Work of Fiction: Cognition, Culture, and Complexity*, Routledge, 2017.

Richardson, Alan and Francis F. Steen. "Literature and the Cognitive Revolution: An Introduction." *Poetics Today*, vol. 23, no. 1, 2002, pp. 1–8.

Rifkin, Jeremy. *The End of Work: The Decline of the Global Labor Force and the Dawn of the Post-market Era*, GP Putnam's Sons, 1995.

Robbins, Bruce. *Secular Vocations: Intellectuals, Professionalism, Culture*, Verso, 1993.

Robinson, Brian et al. "Human Values and the Value of Humanities in Interdisciplinary Research." *Cogent Arts & Humanities*, vol. 3, no. 1, 2016, www.tandfonline.com/doi/pdf/10.1080/23311983.2015.1123080?needAccess=true

Rockwell, Geoffrey. "On the Evaluation of Digital Media as Scholarship." *Profession*, vol. 1, 2011, pp. 152–168.

Roller, Emma. "From Snobs to 'Pointy-Headed College Professors' to 'Eggheads.'" *The Chronicle of Higher Education*. 28 February 2012, https://www.chronicle.com/article/From-Snobs-to-Pointy-Headed/130960

Rorty, Richard. "How Many Grains Make a Heap?" *London Review of Books*, vol. 27, no. 2, 2005, https://www.lrb.co.uk/the-paper/v27/n02/richard-rorty/how-many-grains-make-a-heap

Ross, Andrew ed. *Science Wars*, Duke University Press, 1996.

Ross, Shawna. "In Praise of Overstating the Case: A Review of Franco Moretti, *Distant Reading*." *Digital Humanities Quarterly*, vol. 8, no. 1, 2014, www.digitalhumanities.org/dhq/vol/8/1/000171/000171.html.

Ross-Hellauer, Tony. "What is Open Peer Review? A Systematic Review." *F1000Research*, vol. 6, 2017, https://f1000research.com/articles/6-588.

Roth, Wolff-Michael. "Interdisciplinary Approaches in Mathematics Education." *Encyclopedia of Mathematics Education*, edited by Steve Lerman, Springer, 2020, pp. 415–419.

Russell, Stuart. *Human Compatible: Artificial Intelligence and the Problem of Control*, Penguin, 2019.

Sabaj Meruane, Omar, Carlos González Vergara, and Álvaro Pina-Stranger. "What We Still Don't Know About Peer Review." *Journal of Scholarly Publishing*, vol. 47, no. 2, 2016, pp. 180–212.

Saenpoch, Petcharat. *Peer Review in a Graduate Writing Class: Case Studies of First- and Second-Language Students*. University of Texas, El Paso, PhD Dissertation, 2016.

Salmon, Peter. *An Event, Perhaps: A Biography of Jacques Derrida*, Verso Books, 2020.

Sandel, Michael J. *What Money Can't Buy: The Moral Limits of Markets*, Macmillan, 2012.

Schäfer, Martina, Alexandra Lux, and Matthias Bergmann, "Call for Papers of Special Issue on Transdisciplinary Sustainability Research." *Environmental Science & Policy*, accessed 21 March 2021, https://www.journals.elsevier.com/environmental-science-and-policy/call-for-papers/linking-research-processes-and-outputs-to-societal-effects

Schaefer, William D. "Anonymous Review: A Report from the Executive Director." *MLA Newsletter*, vol. 10, no. 2, 1978, pp. 4–6.

Scholes, Robert. *Structuralism in Literature: An Introduction*, Yale University Press, 1974.

Scholes, Robert, James Phelan, and Robert Kellogg. *The Nature of Narrative: Revised and Expanded*, Oxford University Press, 2006.

Schooler, Jonathan, Nelson Leif, Jon Krosnick, and Brian Nosek. "The Prospective Replication Project." http://projectimplicit.net/nosek/fetzer.html

Schummer, Joachim. "Multidisciplinarity, Interdisciplinarity, and Patterns of Research Collaboration in Nanoscience and Nanotechnology." *Scientometrics*, vol. 59, 2004, pp. 425–465.

Sedgwick Kosofsky, Eve. *Epistemology of the Closet*, University of California Press, 1990.

Seeber, Marco and Alberto Bacchelli. "Does Single Blind Peer Review Hinder Newcomers?" *Scientometrics*, vol. 113, no. 1, 2017, pp. 567–585.

Segado-Boj, Francisco, Juan Martín-Quevedo, and Juan José Prieto-Gutiérrez. "Attitudes toward Open Access, Open Peer Review, and Altmetrics among Contributors to Spanish Scholarly Journals." *Journal of Scholarly Publishing*, vol. 50, no. 1, 2018, pp. 48–70.

Seth, Anil. "Your Brain Hallucinates Your Conscious Reality." https://www.ted.com/talks/anil_seth_how_your_brain_hallucinates_your_conscious_reality?language=en

Shatz, David. *Peer Review: A Critical Inquiry*, Rowman and Littlefield, 2004.

Showalter, Elaine. "Editor's Column." *PMLA*, vol. 99, 1984, pp. 851–853.

Sider, Ted. *Four Dimensionalism*, Oxford University Press, 2001

Siedlock, Frank and Paul Hibbert. "The Organization of Interdisciplinary Research: Modes, Drivers and Barriers." *International Journal of Management Reviews*, vol. 16, no. 2, 2013, pp. 194–210.

Singleton, Brian. "Peer Review." *Contemporary Theatre Review*, vol. 25, no. 1, 2015, pp. 26–29.

Skorton, David and Ashley Bear, editors. *The Integration of the Humanities and Arts with Sciences, Engineering, and Medicine in Higher Education: Branches from the Same Tree*. National Academies of Sciences, Engineering, and Medicine, 2018.

Sloterdijk, Peter. *What Happened in the 20th Century?* Translated by Christopher Turner, Polity Press, 2018.

———. *Not Saved: Essays After Heidegger*. Translated by Ian Alexander Moore and Christopher Turner, Polity Press, 2017.

Small, Helen. *The Value of the Humanities*, Oxford University Press, 2013.

Smith, Barbara Herrnstein. "What Was 'Close Reading'? A Century of Method in Literary Studies." *The Minnesota Review*, vol. 87, 2016, pp. 57–75.

Smith, Christian. *The Bible Made Impossible: Why Biblicism Is Not a Truly Evangelical Reading of Scripture*, Baker Books, 2012.

Smith, David Woodruff. "Phenomenology." *The Stanford Encyclopedia of Philosophy* (Summer 2018 Edition), edited by Edward N. Zalta, https://plato.stanford.edu/archives/sum2018/entries/phenomenology/.

Smith, Z. Louise. "Who Was That Masked Author? The Faces of Academic Editing." *Personal Effects: The Social Character of Scholarly Writing*, edited by Deborah H. Holdstein and David Bleich, Utah State University Press, 2001, pp. 145–164.

Snell-Hornby, Mary, Franz Pöchhacker, and Klaus Kaindl, editors. *Translation Studies: An Interdiscipline: Selected Papers from the Translation Studies Congress, Vienna, 1992.* Vol. 2. John Benjamins, 1994.

Snow, Charles Percy. *The Two Cultures,* Cambridge University Press, 2012.

Snyder, Thomas D., Cristobal De Brey, and Sally A. Dillow. "Digest of Education Statistics 2016, NCES 2017–094." *National Center for Education Statistics,* 2018, https://nces.ed.gov/pubs2017/2017094.pdf.

Soames, Scott. *Philosophical Analysis in the Twentieth Century,* Princeton University Press, 2009.

———. Letter to Editor *London Review of Books,* vol. 27, no. 5, 3 March 2005, http://www.lrb.co.uk/v27/n02/richard-rorty/how-many-grains-make-a-heap.

Spaaij, Ramón and Ansgar Thiel. "Big Data: Critical Questions for Sport and Society." *European Journal for Sport and Society,* vol. 14, no. 1, 2017, pp. 1–4.

Spier, Ray. "The History of the Peer-Review Process." *TRENDS in Biotechnology,* vol. 20, no. 8, 2002, pp. 357–358.

Spierling, Karen. "The Humanities Must Go on Offensive." *The Chronicle of Higher Education,* 8 December 2019.

Spivak, Gayatri. *Death of a Discipline,* Columbia University Press, 2003.

———. *The Post-Colonial Critic,* Routledge, 1990.

Stanton, Domna C. "Editor's Column: Parker Prize Winners Reflect on *PMLA.*" *PMLA,* vol. 110 no. 5, 1995, pp. 983–991.

Stanton, Domna C. et al. "Report of the MLA Task Force on Evaluating Scholarship for Tenure and Promotion." *Profession,* 2007, pp. 9–71.

Starkey, Ken and Paula Madan. "Bridging the Relevance Gap: Aligning Stakeholders in the Future of Management Research." *British Journal of Management,* vol. 12, no. 1, 2001, pp. S3–S26.

Steele, Meili. *Hiding from History: Politics and Public Imagination,* Cornell University Press, 2018.

Stehr, Nico and Peter Weingart, editors. *Practising Interdisciplinarity,* University of Toronto Press, 2000.

Stone, Deborah. *Counting: How We Use Numbers to Decide What Matters,* Liveright, 2020.

Strang, Lee J. "How Big Data Can Increase Originalism's Methodological Rigor: Using Corpus Linguistics to Reveal Original Language Conventions." *UC Davis Law Review,* vol. 50, 2016, pp. 1181–1241.

Strauss, Valerie. "The Surprising Thing Google Learned about Its Employees—And what it Means for Today's Students." *Washington Post,* 20 December 2017, https://www.washingtonpost.com/news/answer-sheet/wp/2017/12/20/the-surprising-thing-google-learned-about-its-employees-and-what-it-means-for-todays-students/.

Sullivan, Patrick, Howard B. Tinberg, and Sheridan D. Blau, editors. *Deep Reading: Teaching Reading in the Writing Classroom,* National Council of Teachers of English, 2017.

Sun, Maosong et al. *Chinese Computational Linguistics and Natural Language Processing Based on Naturally Annotated Big Data,* Springer International Publishing, 2015.

Sung, Nancy S. et al. "Educating Future Scientists." *Science,* vol. 301, no. 5639, p. 1485.

Suskind, Ron. "Faith, Certainty and the Presidency of George W. Bush." *The New York Times Magazine,* 17 October 2004, https://www.nytimes.com/2004/10/17/magazine/faith-certainty-and-the-presidency-of-george-w-bush.html

Szostak, Rick. "How and Why to Teach Interdisciplinary Research Practice." *Journal of Research Practice,* vol. 3, no. 2, 2007, https://files.eric.ed.gov/fulltext/EJ800362.pdf.

Tampio, Nicholas. *Common Core: National Education Standards and the Threat to Democracy*, John Hopkins University Press, 2018.

Tasić, Vladimir. *Mathematics and the Roots of Postmodern Thought*, Oxford University Press, 2001.

Tayeb, Haythum et al. "f-MRI Correlates of Single-Word Reading in Arabic Bilinguals (P4. 017)." *Neurology*, vol. 86, no. 16, supplement, 2016.

Tegmark, Max. *Life 3.0: Being Human in the Age of Artificial Intelligence*, Knopf, 2017.

Tennant, Jonathan P. et al. "A Multi-disciplinary Perspective on Emergent and Future Innovations in Peer Review." *F1000Research*, vol. 6, no. 1151. https://www.ncbi.nlm.nih.gov/pmc/articles/PMC5686505.2/

Terras, Melissa, Ernesto Priego, Alan Liu, Geoffrey Rockwell, Stéfan Sinclair, Christine Henseler, and Lindsay Thomas. *The Humanities Matter!* 4Humanities, 2014.

Tomkins, Andrew, Min Zhang, and William D. Heavlin. "Reviewer Bias in Single- versus double-blind Peer Review." *Proceedings of the National Academy of Sciences*, vol. 114, no. 48, 2017, pp. 12708–12713.

Tough, Paul. *The Years That Matter Most: How College Makes or Breaks Us*, Houghton Mifflin, 2019.

Townsend, Robert B. "Where Have All the Majors Gone?" *MLA Newsletter*, vol. 2, no. 2, Summer 2021, pp. 1 and 4.

Tress, Gunther, Bärbel Tress, and Gary Fry. "Clarifying Integrative Research Concepts in Landscape Ecology." *Landscape Ecology*, vol. 20, 2004, pp. 479–493.

Trexler, Adam and Adeline Johns-Putra. "Climate Change in Literature and Literary Criticism." *Wiley Interdisciplinary Reviews: Climate Change*, vol. 2, no. 2, 2011, pp. 185–200.

Turing, Alan M. "Computing Machinery and Intelligence (1950)." *The Essential Turing: The Ideas that Gave Birth to the Computer Age*, edited by B. Jack Copeland, Oxford University Press, 2004, pp. 433–464.

Tuvel, Rebecca. "In Defense of Transracialism." *Hypatia*, vol. 32, no, 2, 2017, pp. 263–278.

Underwood, Ted. "Critical Response II. The Theoretical Divide Driving Debates about Computation." *Critical Inquiry*, vol. 46, no. 4, 2020, pp. 900–912.

———. "Machine Learning and Human Perspectives." Special Topic: Varieties of Digital Humanities. Alison Booth and Miriam Posner, editors. *PMLA*, vol. 135, no. 1, 2020, pp. 92–109.

———. *Distant Horizons: Digital Evidence and Literary Change*, University of Chicago Press, 2019.

———. "Why Digital Humanities Isn't Actually 'The Next Thing in Literary Studies.'" *The Stone and the Shell*, 27 December 2011, https://tedunderwood.com/2011/12/27/why-we-dont-actually-want-to-be-the-next-thing-in-literary-studies/.

Van Dijk, Jan AGM and Kenneth L. Hacker. *Internet and Democracy in the Network Society: Theory and Practice Continued*, Routledge, 2018.

Van Dyke, Nella and Holly J. McCammon. *Strategic Alliances: Coalition Building and Social Movements*, University of Minnesota Press, 2010.

Veeser, Harold Aram, editor. *The New Historicism*, Routledge, 1989.

Velasquez-Manoff, Moises. "The Brain Implants That Could Change Humanity." *The New York Times*, 28 August 2020.

Vilsmaier, Ulli et al. "Research *In-Between*: The Constitutive Role of Cultural Differences in Transdisciplinarity." *Transdisciplinary Journal of Engineering & Science*, vol. 8, 2017, pp. 169–179.

Vinge, Vernor. "The Coming Technological Singularity: How to Survive in the Posthuman Era." *Science Fiction Criticism: An Anthology of Essential Writings*, edited by Rob Latham, Bloomsbury, 1993, pp. 352–363.
Vivian, Jesse C. "New FDA Strategy: Criminal Charges against Pharma Executives." *US Pharm*, vol. 36, no. 6, 2011, pp. 58–62.
Vološinov, Valentin Nikolaevich, and Michail M. Bachtin. *Marxism and the Philosophy of Language*. Translated by Ladislav Matejka and I.R. Titunik. Harvard University Press, 1986.
Waechter, Steven. "Why Liberal Arts Degrees Are Worthless." Blog post. 4 December 2016, https://www.linkedin.com/pulse/why-liberal-arts-degrees-worthless-steven-waechter
Waisbord, Silvio. *Communication: A Post-discipline*, John Wiley & Sons, 2019.
Walter, Alexander I. et al. "Measuring Societal Effects of Transdisciplinary Research Projects: Design and Application of an Evaluation Method." *Evaluation and Program Planning*, vol. 30, 2007, pp. 325–338.
Wang, Hao. *From Mathematics to Philosophy (Routledge Revivals)*, Routledge, 2016.
Washburn, Jennifer. *University, Inc.: The Corporate Corruption of Higher Education*, Basic Books, 2008.
Weatherby, Leif. "Critical Response I. Prolegomena to a Theory of Data: On the Most Recent Confrontation of Data and Literature." *Critical Inquiry*, vol. 46, no. 4, 2020, pp. 891–899.
Weber, Brian. "Honest Academic Job Postings." *McSweeneys*, 26 December 2019, https://www.mcsweeneys.net/articles/honest-academic-job-postings
Weingart, Peter. "A Short History of Knowledge Formations." *The Oxford Handbook of Interdisciplinarity*, edited by Robert Frodeman, Julie Thompson Klein, and Carl Mitcham, Oxford University Press, 2010, pp. 3–14.
———. "Interdisciplinarity: The Paradoxical Discourse." *Practising Interdisciplinarity*, edited by Weingart and Nico Stehr, University of Toronto Press, 2000, pp. 25–41.
Weiss, Carol H. "Knowledge Creep and Decision Accretion." *Knowledge*, vol. 1, 1980, pp. 381–404.
Wellek, Rene and Austin Warren. *Theory of Literature*, Harcourt, Brace & World, 1956.
Wellmon, Chad and Andrew Piper, "Publication, Power, and Patronage: On Inequality and Academic Publishing," *Critical Inquiry*, 2017, https://criticalinquiry.uchicago.edu/publication_power_and_patronage_on_inequality_and_academic_publishing/.
Wen, Haijun et al. "On the Low Reproducibility of Cancer Studies." *National Science Review*, vol. 5, no. 5, 2018, pp. 619–624.
West, Darrell M. *Digital Schools: How Technology Can Transform Education*, Brookings Institution Press, 2012.
Wheeler, Wendy. *Expecting the Earth: Life, Culture, Biosemiotics*, Lawrence & Wishart, 2016.
———. *The Whole Creature: Complexity, Biosemiotics and the Evolution of Culture*, Lawrence & Wishart, 2006.
Wiek, Arnim, Sonia Talwar, Meg O'Shea, and John Robinson (2014) "Toward a Methodological Scheme for Capturing Societal Effects of Participatory Sustainability Research." *Research Evaluation*, vol. 23, pp. 117–132.
Wiener, Anna. "Girl, Disrupted." *The New Yorker*, 30 September 2019, pp. 56–68.
Will, Madeline. "Enrollment Is Down at Teacher Colleges. So They're Trying to Change." *Education Week*. 9 August 2018, https://www.edweek.org/teaching-learning/enrollment-is-down-at-teacher-colleges-so-theyre-trying-to-change/2018/08.
Williams, James. *Understanding Poststructuralism*, Routledge, 2014.

Williams, Julian, Wolff-Michael Roth, David Swanson, Brian Doig, Susie Groves, Michael Omuvwie, Rita Borromeo Ferri, and Nicholas Mousoulides. *Interdisciplinary Mathematics Education*, Springer Nature, 2016.
Williams, Raymond. *Marxism and Literature*, Oxford University Press, 1977.
Wimsatt, William Kurtz and Monroe Beardley. "The Affective Fallacy." Wimsatt, *The Verbal Icon: Studies in the Meaning of Poetry*, University Press of Kentucky, 1954, pp. 21–40.
Winnubst, Shannon. "Why Tuvel's Article So Troubled Its Critics." *The Chronicle of Higher Education*, 8 May 2017, www.chronicle.com/article/Why-Tuvel-s-Article-So/240029.
World Health Organization, "Gender." https://www.who.int/genomics/gender/en/index1.html
Wood, Allen W. *Kant*, New York: Blackwell, 2005.
Wohn, Donghee Yvette and Brian J. Bowe. "Crystallization: How Social Media Facilitates Social Construction of Reality." *Proceedings of the Companion Publication of the 17th ACM Conference on Computer Supported Cooperative Work & Social Computing.* 2014.
Wright, Richard. *Native Son*, Random House, 2016.
Wu, Katherine J. "Between the (Gender) Lines: The Science of Transgender Identity." https://sitn.hms.harvard.edu/flash/2016/gender-lines-science-transgender-identity/, accessed 27 April 2021.
Yetisen, Ali K. "Biohacking." *Trends in Biotechnology*, vol. 36, no. 8, 2018, pp. 744–747.
Young, Robert J. C. "The Dislocations of Cultural Translation." *PMLA*, vol. 132, no. 1, 2017, pp. 186–197.
Zabalbeascoa, Patrick. "Humor and Translation—An Interdiscipline." *Humor*, vol. 18, no. 2, 2005, pp. 185–207.
Zemsky, Robert, Gregory R. Wegner, and William F. Massy. *Remaking the American University: Market-Smart and Mission-Centered*, Rutgers University Press, 2005.
Zhang, Ce et al. "Big Data Versus the Crowd: Looking for Relationships in All the Right Places." *Proceedings of the 50th Annual Meeting of the Association for Computational Linguistics: Long Papers-Volume 1*. Association for Computational Linguistics, 2012.
Zerofsky, Elisabeth. "Viktor Orbán's Far-Right Vision for Europe." *The New Yorker.* January 14, 2019.
Ziarek, Ewa. "At the Limits of Discourse: Heterogeneity, Alterity, and the Maternal Body in Kristeva's Thought." *Hypatia*, vol. 7, no. 2, 1992, pp. 91–108.
Zima, Peter V. *Deconstruction and Critical Theory*, A&C Black, 2002.
Zimmerman, Jeffrey. *Neuro-narrative Therapy: New Possibilities for Emotion-filled Conversations*, Norton, 2018.
Žižek, Slavoj. *In Defense of Lost Causes*, Verso, 2009.
———. "The Most Sublime of Hysterics: Hegel with Lacan." *Interrogating the Real*, Bloomsbury Publishing, 2006, pp. 19–38.
———. "Why Does a Letter Always Arrive at Its Destination?" *Enjoy your Symptom!* Routledge, 2001, pp. 1–34.
———. *Mapping Ideology*, Verso, 1994.
Zoubir, Abdelhak. "Interdisciplinary Research: A Catalyst for Innovation." *IEEE Signal Processing Magazine*, vol. 29, no. 3, 2012, pp. 2–4.
Zunshine, Lisa, editor. *The Oxford Handbook of Cognitive Literary Studies*, Oxford University Press, 2015.
———, editor. *Introduction to Cognitive Cultural Studies*, Johns Hopkins University Press, 2010.

INDEX

Note: Page numbers followed by "n" refer to notes.

activism 45, 53, 64, 98, 205
additive 5, 15, 56, 151, 153, 167, 189, 200, 214, 215
ADE Bulletin and *ADFL Bulletin* 65
aestheticism 56, 80, 85–7
aesthetics 3, 56, 61n23, 80, 87, 159
affect 16, 56, 86, 116
Alcoff, Linda 20n7, 113–4
Althusser, Louis 156
Anglo-American (analytic philosophy) 71–4, 79, 181, 189–91, 210n3, 215
Anzaldúa, Gloria 11
Applebaum, Anne 25–7, 60n6
area of expertise/specialization 7–8, 11, 19, 34, 43, 47, 68, 107, 122–3, 130, 132, 137, 164, 170, 172–6, 197, 214–5
Arendt, Hannah 25–7
Aronowitz, Stanley 1, 18
Arsić, Branka 1
artificial intelligence (AI) 10, 49, 138, 143, 145, 147, 159–60, 168
Ash, Mitchell 187–9, 191
Attridge, Derek 47

Badiou, Alain 66
Banta, Martha 38–9
Barad, Karen 5, 9, 11–3, 179, 204, 207–9
Barrett, Lisa Feldman 13, 16–7, 74, 78–9, 99, 138
Bell, John 208
Benjamin, Walter 144

Bennett, Andrew 53–4
Berlant, Lauren 71
Bertolaso, Marta 14
Bérubé, Michael 15, 28–9, 103, 107–8
Biagioli, Mario 1, 109, 113, 177
Blok, Anders and Casper Bruun Jensen 203
Bloom, Harold 3, 173, 174
Bode, Katherine 146, 163n4
Bohr, Niels 10, 207–9
Booth, Alison 135, 156, 182
Booth, Wayne 118, 150
border 10–1, 85, 190, 202
boundary 12, 16, 51, 86, 130, 146–7, 208
Bourdieu, Pierre 1, 122
Bozovic, Marijeta 68, 80
Braidotti, Rosi 4, 60n3, 67, 206
Brown University 8, 213
Brown, Wendy 25
Brummett, Barry 73
Buck-Morss, Susan ix, 18, 41, 96, 168, 192–200
Burnham, John C. 110–11

Caracciolo, Marco 57–9
Caruth, Cathy 56
Chakrabarty, Dipesh 204
close reading 3, 54, 60, 63–85, 88, 95, 97, 100n4, 104, 116, 135, 137, 150–1, 157–9, 162, 163n4, 196
Clune, Michael W. 68

coalition 25–6, 28, 36–7, 40, 50, 61n11, 118, 197, 204–5
Coates, Ta-Nehisi 40
cognitive science 16, 44, 58, 63–4, 78–9, 84, 90, 98, 140, 142, 145, 160, 213–4
cognitive studies of literature 15
Collins, Patricia Hill 11, 197
colonialism/colonial 11, 35, 53, 90, 114, 193, 200
comparative literature 1, 33, 43, 53, 64, 87, 105
Comparative Literature Studies viii, 105
Crenshaw, Kimberlé 11, 196–7
crisis of legitimation 63, 69
Critical Inquiry 136, 138, 140, 193, 196
Culler, Jonathan 20n6, 70, 73, 77, 81–3
cultural studies 1, 3, 17, 21n15, 43–4, 61n23
culture wars 2–4, 13, 20n6, 44, 54, 65–6, 73, 80, 85, 90, 96, 101, 115, 123, 150, 152, 163n4, 167, 215
Cunningham, David 178–82, 191, 210n6
cybernetics 168, 176–9, 192

Da, Nan Z. 136–9, 145, 160, 162n1, 163n6, 163n9
Darwin, Charles/Darwinism 9, 37, 141, 175, 206
Daston, Lorraine 188
Davidson, Cathy N. 41–2
Dawkins, Richard 140
Deacon, Terrence 140–1
decolonization 80, 211
Deleuze, Gilles 63
de Man, Paul 74–8, 80–3, 87–9
Derrida, Jacques 10, 15, 20n9, 36, 47–53, 72–3, 94–5, 141–2, 153, 178–80
de Saussure, Ferdinand 10
design thinking 185–7
diacritics 17, 105
Digital Humanities (DH) ix, 44, 65, 83, 135–163, 205
Dimock, Wai Chee 39, 61n13
discrimination 35, 90, 126–9, 147
Donoghue, Frank 2–3, 21n19, 60n3, 65
Drucker, Johanna 152, 156
Dunbar-Ortiz, Roxanne 11, 211

Eaglestone, Robert 2, 32, 110
environmental science 44, 167, 175, 184–5, 202–4, 212, 217
ethics of reading 66
Eve, Martin Paul 71, 81
evolution 90, 95, 139–42, 151–3, 163n10, 206

"fake news" 26, 83, 120, 161
Favareau, Donald 141
Federico, Annette 70, 75–6, 83
Felski, Rita 3, 24, 63–4
Ferguson, Frances 87–8
Feyerabend, Paul 118–9
Fish, Stanley 104, 116–28, 146–7, 183
Fitzpatrick, Kathleen 61n11, 108–10, 113, 133n5
Foucault, Michel 62–3, 79, 113–5, 153, 207
fragmentation 1, 3, 19, 90, 111, 113–5, 129, 131, 171, 173, 181, 188, 200, 215
Freud, Sigmund 10, 17, 79

Gadamer, Hans-Georg 93–4
Gallop, Jane 54, 70, 72, 77, 79, 81
Garber, Marjorie 55, 90
genre 3, 21m19, 70, 74, 84, 97–8, 100n2, 107, 117, 148, 150, 154, 157–8, 162, 163n4
geographic information system (GIS) 205
Gieseking, Jen Jack 205
Gildea, Niall 2, 23, 65
Gödel's theorem 10, 16
Graff, Gerald 20n6, 73
Graham, S. Scott 39, 56–7, 59
Greenblatt, Stephen 85–6
Greimas, Algirdas Julien 150
Guillory, John 65

Haraway, Donna 142
Hayles, N. Katherine 4, 54, 59, 139–41, 143, 145, 156
Hayot, Eric 213, 217n1
Hegel, Georg Wilhelm Friedrich 10, 18, 41, 88, 120, 191–6
Heidegger, Martin 49, 75, 80, 97, 142, 190
Heisenberg, Werner 207–8
hermeneutics 1, 3, 21n20, 62–100, 104, 122, 136, 138, 146, 160, 163n4
heteronomy 5, 177, 187
historicism 44, 69–70, 85–98, 110, 120, 151, 192–196, 198–200
history of science 20n9, 57, 61n17, 165, 187–9
Hoemann et al 16–7
Howard, Jean 89
Humanities Lab 8, 162n2
Hutner, Gordon and Faisal Mohamed 2, 24, 27

ideology 77, 79, 85, 87, 90, 142–3, 158–9
intermediation 140, 142, 172
interruption 74, 76–7, 79, 87, 90, 158, 191, 203

interscience 20n9, 179–80
intersectional theory 11, 196–8
Irigaray, Luce 7

Jakobson, Roman 100n7, 159
Jameson, Frederic 89
Jay, Martin 85
Jay, Paul 2–3, 18, 28–9, 42, 54–5, 59, 60n3, 65, 86–7, 96
Johnson, Barbara 81–2

Kant, Immanuel/Kantian 54, 56, 61n23, 62–3, 88, 120, 179, 181, 199, 209
Kitchin, Robert 13, 136, 155

La Berge, Leigh Claire 32–3
Lacan, Jacques 153
Lamont, Michèle 181
Latour, Bruno 11, 18, 23, 50, 58–9, 94, 167, 200–6
Levine, Caroline 3, 64–5, 68–70, 87, 90–5, 97
Levinson, Marjorie 86–7
Lévi-Strauss, Claude 86, 137, 141
Linebaugh, Peter and Marcus Rediker 198–9
Linnaeus, Carl 175–6
literalism 83–4
literary techniques 70, 74, 79
Loesberg, Jonathan 86
Lorde, Audre 99
Lukianoff, Greg and Jonathan Haidt 40

Malabou, Catherine 191
McDonald, Rónán 2, 23, 43–4, 65
Melas, Natalie 40, 45, 53
mere reading 63, 70–99, 116, 118, 120, 123, 171
methodology 3, 7, 17–8, 20n4, 57, 63–5, 71–2, 76–7, 80, 82, 84, 86, 93, 96, 101, 103–6, 115–121, 127, 144–6, 148–50, 157–8, 161, 166–8, 173, 186, 190–1, 196, 198, 214–6
Miller, J. Hillis 66
MLA 29–31, 38, 60n9, 69, 102–3, 106, 122, 128, 155, 173
Mößner, Nicola 181
Moretti, Franco 3, 64, 71, 82, 150–4
Motschenbacher, Heiko 7

Nagoshi, Julie L. 7
narrative 13, 39, 43, 56–9, 63, 89, 100n2, 136, 143–4, 151, 153, 157–8, 174, 188, 201, 203, 205, 211–5

nature/culture opposition 4, 13, 16–7, 28, 59, 74, 78, 140–1, 167, 176, 181, 189, 193, 203, 207, 216
Neiman, Susan 41
neoliberalism 1, 25–7, 33–7, 51, 55, 60n4, 162n1, 202, 214, 216
Nersessian, Anahid 68–9
neurology 13, 44, 84, 90–1, 98, 140
New Criticism/New Critical 44, 54, 60, 63, 70–1, 73–4, 80, 100n4, 104, 114–6, 123, 138, 163n4
New Literary History 105, 116
Newman, Daniel Aureliano 15
Ngai, Sianne 56, 71, 87
North, Joseph 3, 6, 20n6, 44, 61n23, 65, 80, 100n3
Nosek, Brian 13, 110, 133n9

Obama, Barack 27, 61n14
open peer review 103, 107, 126, 130–3, 133n14
Osborne, Peter 165–6, 178, 188
outcomes 110, 112, 184–6, 216

Paulson, William 3
peer review 2, 8, 12, 14, 18, 20n8, 44, 60, 68, 97, 101–34, 137, 162, 164–5, 168, 171, 174, 193
Peer Review Congress 104
Peters, Douglas and Stephen Ceci 104, 107, 121
Pickering, Andrew 168, 177–8, 180
Pinker, Steven 98–9, 143
Plotnitsky, Arkady 208
pluralization 1, 3–5, 7, 10, 14, 44, 58, 204
PMLA 20n8, 38–9, 44, 57, 64–5, 68–70, 97, 102–3, 107, 114, 121, 125, 128, 136, 146, 151–2, 154–5
porous 12, 84, 147
Posner, Miriam 135, 155–6
postcolonialism 53, 64, 115, 204–5
postcritique 4, 64
postdiscipline 4–5, 7, 80, 171, 177, 183, 187, 191–2, 195, 198, 215
post-poststructuralist 64, 191
posthumanism 1, 4, 12, 45, 168, 201, 206–7
Power, Nina 178, 182–3, 191
Propp, Vladimir 137, 154, 157–9, 163n9

race 41, 127, 134n15, 156, 163n5, 167, 196–8, 214
racism 35, 37, 40–1, 108, 171

Rajan, Tilottama 191–2
Ransom, John Crowe 71–3, 78, 100n4
Readings, Bill 1, 55
reconstruction 68, 89, 96–8
Rennie, Drummond 104, 127, 132, 133n4
Reynolds, Jack 189–91
Richards, I.A. 71, 74, 76
Rifkin, Jeremy 49–50
Rorty, Richard 173–4

Schaefer, William 102, 121, 133n13
Schäfer, Martina, Alexandra Lux and Matthias Bergmann 184–5
Scholes, Robert 153
science wars 2, 13, 133n8, 182
Shatz, David 107, 109–10, 124
Showalter, Elaine 102, 133n2
Sider, Ted 190
Siedlok, Frank and Paul Hibbert 169–71, 175, 187
situationism viii, 7–8, 14, 20n4, 57, 156, 165, 170–1, 177, 180, 183
Skorton, David and Ashley Bear 172
Sloterdijk, Peter 97
Small, Helen 23, 45–7, 52
Smith, Barbara Herrnstein 70–1, 8
Smith, Christian 83
Snow, C.P. 12, 16, 110, 190
Soames, Scott 172–5
social justice 15, 64, 66, 94, 129
Spaaij, Ramón and Ansgar Thiel 155
Stanton, Domna 65, 102–3, 128

structuralism 54, 80, 85, 92, 137, 139, 141, 143, 150–3, 156–9, 162, 175, 180, 197
sustainability 21n15, 150

Tasić, Vladimir 10, 161
"Theories and Methodologies" 64–6, 69, 99n1
Thinking Rooms 21n12
totalitarianism 25–8, 31, 33, 37, 41, 53, 84, 149, 200, 214
training 1, 15, 34–5, 40, 45, 54, 148, 166
trauma 56, 61n23, 100n6, 100n11, 199, 207
tree (metaphor) 137, 152–3, 172, 176
Trump, Donald/Trumpism 25–6, 35, 37, 60n6
Turing, Alan 160–1

Underwood, Ted 138, 146–50, 154–5, 157, 159, 163n4
University at Albany 22n21

Vilsmaier, Ulli et al 171
Vološinov, V. N. 158

Waisbord, Silvio 12, 177, 180, 183
Weatherby, Leif 136, 138
Weingart, Peter 173–176, 210n5
Wimsatt, William and Monroe Beardsley 116–7

Young, Robert J. C. 97–8

Žižek, Slavoj 15

For Product Safety Concerns and Information please contact our EU
representative GPSR@taylorandfrancis.com
Taylor & Francis Verlag GmbH, Kaufingerstraße 24, 80331 München, Germany

www.ingramcontent.com/pod-product-compliance
Lightning Source LLC
Chambersburg PA
CBHW061346300426
44116CB00011B/2006